ELEMENTS OF THE THEORY OF COMPUTATION

ELEMENTS OF THE THEORY OF COMPUTATION

Second Edition

Harry R. Lewis

Gordon McKay Professor of Computer Science
Harvard University
and Dean of Harvard College
Cambridge, Massachusetts

Christos H. Papadimitriou

C. Lester Hogan Professor of Electrical Engineering
and Computer Science
University of California
Berkeley, California

PRENTICE-HALL, Upper Saddle River, New Jersey 07458

Library of Congress Cataloging-in-Publication Data

Lewis, Harry R.
   Elements of the theory of computation / Harry R. Lewis and
   Christos H. Papadimitriou. — 2nd ed.
      p. cm.
   Includes bibliological references and index.
   ISBN: 0-13-262478-8
   1. Machine theory. 2. Formal languages. 3. Computational
complexity. 4. Logic, Symbolic and mathematical.
   I. Papadimitriou, Christos H.   II. Title.
QA267.L49   1998
511.3—dc21   97-13879
                                  CIP

Publisher: Alan Apt
Development Editor: Sondra Chavez
Editorial/Production Supervision: Barbara Kraemer
Managing Editor: Bayani Mendoza DeLeon
Editor-in-Chief: Marcia Horton
Assistant Vice President of Production and Manufacturing: David W. Riccardi
Art Director: Jayne Conte
Manufacturing Manager: Trudy Pisciotti
Manufacturing Buyer: Donna Sullivan
Editorial Assistant: Toni Holm

The author and publisher of this book have used their best efforts in preparing this book. These efforts
include the development, research, and testing of the theories and programs to determine their effectiveness.
The author and publisher make no warranty of any kind, expressed or implied, with regard to these programs
or the documentation contained in this book. The author and publisher shall not be liable in any event for
incidental or consequential damages in connection with, or arising out of, the furnishing, performance, or
use of these programs.

Printed in the United States of America

10 9 8 7 6 5 4 3 2 1

ISBN   0-13-262478-8

Prentice-Hall International (UK) Limited, London
Prentice-Hall of Australia Pty. Limited, Sydney
Prentice-Hall Canada Inc., Toronto
Prentice-Hall Hispanoamericana, S.A., Mexico
Prentice-Hall of India Private Limited, New Delhi
Prentice-Hall of Japan, Inc., Tokyo
Simon & Schuster Asia Pte. Ltd., Singapore
Editora Prentice-Hall do Brasil, Ltda., Rio de Janeiro

To our daughters

Contents

Preface to the First Edition

This book is an introduction, on the undergraduate level, to the classical and contemporary theory of computation. The topics covered are, in a few words, the theory of automata and formal languages, computability by Turing machines and recursive functions, uncomputability, computational complexity, and mathematical logic. The treatment is mathematical but the viewpoint is that of computer science; thus the chapter on context-free languages includes a discussion of parsing, and the chapters on logic establish the soundness and completeness of resolution theorem-proving.

In the undergraduate curriculum, exposure to this subject tends to come late, if at all, and collaterally with courses on the design and analysis of algorithms. It is our view that computer science students should be exposed to this material earlier —as sophomores or juniors— both because of the deeper insights it yields on specific topics in computer science, and because it serves to establish essential mathematical paradigms. But we have found teaching to a rigorous undergraduate course on the subject a difficult undertaking because of the mathematical maturity assumed by the more advanced textbooks. Our goal in writing this book has been to make the essentials of the subject accessible to a broad undergraduate audience in a way that is mathematically sound but presupposes no special mathematical experience.

The whole book represents about a year's worth of coursework. We have each taught a one-term course covering much of the material in Chapters 1 through 6, omitting on various occasions and in various combinations the sections of parsing, on recursive functions, and on particular unsolvable decision problems. Other selections are possible; for example, a course emphasizing computability and the foundations of mechanical logic might skip quickly over Chapters 1 through 3 and concentrate on Chapters 4, 6, 8, and 9. However, it is used, our fervent hope is that the book will contribute to the intellectual development of the next generation of computer scientists by introducing them at an early stage of their education to crisp and methodical thinking about computational problems.

We take this opportunity to thank all from whom we have learned, both teachers and students. Specific thanks go to Larry Denenberg and Aaron Temin for their proofreading of early drafts, and to Michael Kahl and Oded Shmueli for their assistance and advice as teaching assistants. In the spring of 1980 Albert Meyer taught a course at M.I.T. from a draft of this book, and we thank him warmly for his criticisms and corrections. Of course, the blame for any remaining errors rests with us alone. Renate D'Arcangelo typed and illustrated the manuscript with her characteristic but extraordinary perfectionism and rapidity.

Preface to the Second Edition

Much has changed in the fifteen years since the *Elements of the Theory of Computation* first appeared —and much has remained the same. Computer science is now a much more mature and established discipline, playing a rôle of ever increasing importance in a world of ubiquitous computing, globalized information, and galloping complexity —more reasons to keep in touch with its foundations. The authors of the *Elements* are now themselves much more mature and busy —that is why this second edition has been so long in coming. We undertook it because we felt that a few things could be said better, a few made simpler —some even omitted altogether. More importantly, we wanted the book to reflect how the theory of computation, and its students, have evolved during these years. Although the theory of computation is now taught more widely in absolute terms, its relative position within the computer science curriculum, for example *vis à vis* the subject of algorithms, has not been strengthened. In fact, the field of the design and analysis of algorithms is now so mature, that its elementary principles are arguably a part of a basic course on the theory of computation. Besides, undergraduates today, with their extensive and early computational experience, are much more aware of the applications of automata in compilers, for example, and more suspicious when simple models such as the Turing machine are presented as general computers. Evidently, the treatment of these subjects needs some updating.

Concretely, these are the major differences from the first edition:

○ Rudiments of the design and analysis of algorithms are introduced informally already in Chapter 1 (in connection with closures), and algorithmic questions are pursued throughout the book. There are sections on algorithmic problems in connection with finite automata and context-free grammars in Chapters 2 and 3 (including state minimization and context-free recognition), algorithms for easy variants of $\mathcal{NP}$-complete problems, and a section that reviews algorithmic techniques for "coping with $\mathcal{NP}$-completeness" (special case algorithms, approximation algorithms, backtracking and branch-and-bound, local improvement, and simulated annealing algorithms).

o The treatment of Turing machines in Chapter 4 is more informal, and the simulation arguments are simpler and more quantitative. A random access Turing machine is introduced, helping bridge the gap between the clumsiness of Turing machines and the power of computers and programming languages.

o We included in Chapter 5 on undecidability some recursive function theory (up to Rice's Theorem). Grammars and recursive numerical functions are introduced and proved equivalent to Turing machines earlier, and the proofs are simpler. The undecidability of problems related to context-free grammars is proved by a simple and direct argument, without recourse to the Post correspondence problem. We kept the tiling problem, which we revisit in the $\mathcal{NP}$-completeness chapter.

o Complexity is done in a rather novel way: In Chapter 6, we define no other time bounds besides the polynomial ones —thus $\mathcal{P}$ is the first complexity class and concept encountered. Diagonalization then shows that there are exponential problems not in $\mathcal{P}$. Real-life problems are introduced side-by-side with their language representations (a distinction that is deliberately blurred), and their algorithmic questions are examined extensively.

o There is a separate $\mathcal{NP}$-completeness chapter with a new, extensive, and, we think, pedagogically helpful suite of $\mathcal{NP}$-completeness reductions, culminating with the equivalence problem for regular expressions —closing a full circle to the first subject of the book. As mentioned above, the book ends with a section on algorithmic techniques for "coping with $\mathcal{NP}$-completeness."

o There are no logic chapters in the new edition. This was a difficult decision, made for two reasons: According to all evidence, these were the least read and taught chapters of the book; and there are now books that treat this subject better. However, there is extensive treatment of Boolean logic and its satisfiability problems in Chapter 6.

o Overall, proofs and exposition have been simplified and made more informal at some key points. In several occasions, as in the proof of the equivalence of context-free languages and pushdown automata, long technical proofs of inductive statements have become exercises. There are problems following each section.

As a result of these changes, there is now at least one more way of teaching out of the material of this book (besides the ones outlined in the first edition, and the ones that emerged from its use): A semester-length course aiming at the coverage of the basics of *both* the theory of computation and algorithms may be based on a selection of material from Chapters 2 through 7.

We want to express our sincere thanks to all of our students and colleagues who provided feedback, ideas, errors, and corrections during these fifteen years— it is impossible to come up with a complete list. Special thanks to Martha Sideri for her help with the revision of Chapter 3. Also, many thanks to our editor, Alan Apt, and the people at Prentice-Hall —Barbara Kraemer, Sondra Chavez, and Bayani de Leon— who have been so patient and helpful.

Finally, we would appreciate receiving error reports or other comments, preferably by electronic mail to the address elements@cs.berkeley.edu. Confirmed errors, corrections, and other information about the book can also be obtained by writing to this address.

ELEMENTS OF THE THEORY OF COMPUTATION

Introduction

Look around you. Computation happens everywhere, all the time, initiated by everybody, and affecting us all. Computation can happen because computer scientists over the past decades have discovered sophisticated methods for managing computer resources, enabling communication, translating programs, designing chips and databases, creating computers and programs that are faster, cheaper, easier to use, more secure.

As it is usually the case with all major disciplines, the practical successes of computer science build on its *elegant and solid foundations*. At the basis of physical sciences lie fundamental questions such as *what is the nature of matter?* and *what is the basis and origin of organic life?* Computer science has its own set of fundamental questions: *What is an algorithm? What can and what cannot be computed? When should an algorithm be considered practically feasible?* For more than sixty years (starting even before the advent of the eiectronic computer) computer scientists have been pondering these questions, *and coming up with ingenious answers that have deeply influenced computer science.*

The purpose of this book is to introduce you to these fundamental ideas, models, and results that permeate computer science, the *basic paradigms* of our field. They are worth studying, for many reasons. First, much of modern computer science is based more or less explicitly on them —and much of the rest should... Also, these ideas and models are powerful and beautiful, excellent examples of mathematical modeling that is elegant, productive, and of lasting value. Besides, they are so much a part of the history and the "collective subconscious" of our field, that it is hard to understand computer science without first being exposed to them.

It probably comes as no surprise that these ideas and models are *mathematical* in nature. Although a computer is undeniably a physical object, it is also

1

true that very little that is useful can be said of its physical aspects, such as its molecules and its shape; the most useful abstractions of a computer are clearly mathematical, and so the techniques needed to argue about them are necessarily likewise. Besides, practical computational tasks require the ironclad guarantees that only mathematics provides (we want our compilers to translate correctly, our application programs to eventually terminate, and so on). However, the mathematics employed in the theory of computation is rather different from the mathematics used in other applied disciplines. It is generally *discrete*, in that the emphasis is not on real numbers and continuous variables, but on finite sets and sequences. It is based on very few and elementary concepts, and draws its power and depth from the careful, patient, extensive, layer-by-layer manipulation of these concepts —just like the computer. In the first chapter you will be reminded of these elementary concepts and techniques (sets, relations, and induction, among others), and you will be introduced to the style in which they are used in the theory of computation.

The next two chapters, Chapters 2 and 3, describe certain restricted models of computation capable of performing very specialized string manipulation tasks, such as telling whether a given string, say the word *punk*, appears in a given text, such as the collective works of Shakespeare; or for testing whether a given string of parentheses is properly balanced —like () and (())(), but not)(). These restricted computational devices (called *finite-state automata* and *pushdown automata,* respectively) actually come up in practice as very useful and highly optimized components of more general systems such as circuits and compilers. Here they provide fine warm-up exercises in our quest for a formal, general definition of an algorithm. Furthermore, it is instructive to see how the power of these devices waxes and wanes (or, more often, is preserved) with the addition or removal of various features, most notably of *nondeterminism*, an intriguing aspect of computation which is as central as it is (quite paradoxically) unrealistic.

In Chapter 4 we study general models of algorithms, of which the most basic is the *Turing machine*,[†] a rather simple extension of the string-manipulating devices of Chapters 2 and 3 which turns out to be, surprisingly, a general frame-

---

[†] Named after Alan M. Turing (1912–1954), the brilliant English mathematician and philosopher whose seminal paper in 1936 marked the beginning of the theory of computation (and whose image, very appropriately, adorns the cover of this book). Turing also pioneered the fields of artificial intelligence and chess-playing by computer, as well as that of morphogenesis in biology, and was instrumental in breaking *Enigma*, the German naval code during World War II. For more on his fascinating life and times (and on his tragic end in the hands of official cruelty and bigotry) see the book *Alan Turing: The Enigma*, by Andrew Hodges, New York: Simon Schuster, 1983.

work for describing arbitrary algorithms. In order to argue this point, known as the *Church-Turing thesis*, we introduce more and more elaborate models of computation (more powerful variants of the Turing machine, even a *random access Turing machine* and *recursive definitions of numerical functions*), and show that they are all precisely equivalent in power to the basic Turing machine model.

The following chapter deals with *undecidability*, the surprising property of certain natural and well-defined computational tasks to lie *provably* beyond the reach of algorithmic solution. For example, suppose that you are asked whether we can use tiles from a given finite list of basic shapes to tile the whole plane. If the set of shapes contains a square, or even any triangle, then the answer is obviously "yes." But what if it consists of a few bizarre shapes, or if some of the shapes are mandatory, that is, they *must* be used at least once for the tiling to qualify? This is surely the kind of complicated question that you would like to have answered by a machine. In Chapter 5 we use the formalism of Turing machines to prove that this and many other problems *cannot be solved by computers at all.*

Even when a computational task is amenable to solution by *some* algorithm, it may be the case that there is no *reasonably fast, practically feasible* algorithm that solves it. In the last two chapters of this book we show how real-life computational problems can be categorized in terms of their *complexity:* Certain problems can be solved within reasonable, *polynomial* time bounds, whereas others seem to require amounts of time that grow astronomically, *exponentially.* In Chapter 7 we identify a class of common, practical, and notoriously difficult problems that are called $\mathcal{NP}$-*complete* (the traveling salesman problem is only one of them). We establish that all these problems are *equivalent* in that, if one of them has an efficient algorithm, then all of them do. It is widely believed that all $\mathcal{NP}$-complete problems are of inherently exponential complexity; whether this conjecture is actually true is the famous $\mathcal{P} \neq \mathcal{NP}$ problem, one of the most important and deep problems facing mathematicians and computer scientists today.

This book is very much about algorithms and their formal foundations. However, as you are perhaps aware, the subject of algorithms, their analysis and their design, is considered in today's computer science curriculum quite separate from that of the theory of computation. In the present edition of this book we have tried to restore some of the unity of the subject. As a result, this book also provides a decent, if somewhat specialized and unconventional, introduction to the subject of algorithms. Algorithms and their analysis are introduced informally in Chapter 1, and are picked up again and again in the context of the restricted models of computation studied in Chapters 2 and 3, and of the natural computational problems that they spawn. This way, when general models of algorithms are sought later, the reader is in a better position to appreciate the scope of the quest, and to judge its success. Algorithms play a major role in our exposition of complexity as well, because there is no better way to appreciate a complex problem than to contrast it with another, amenable to an efficient algorithm. The last chapter culminates in a section on *coping with $\mathcal{NP}$-completeness*, where we present an array of algorithmic techniques that have been successfully used in attacking $\mathcal{NP}$-complete problems (approximation algorithms, exhaustive algorithms, local search heuristics, and so on).

Computation is essential, powerful, beautiful, challenging, ever-expanding —and so is its theory. This book only tells the beginning of an exciting story. It is a modest introduction to a few basic and carefully selected topics from the treasure chest of the theory of computation. We hope that it will motivate its readers to seek out more; the references at the end of each chapter point to good places to start.

1 | Sets, Relations, and Languages

1.1 SETS

They say that mathematics is the language of science —it is certainly the language of the theory of computation, the scientific discipline we shall be studying in this book. And the language of mathematics deals with *sets*, and the complex ways in which they overlap, intersect, and in fact take part themselves in forming new sets.

A **set** is a collection of objects. For example, the collection of the four letters a, b, c, and d is a set, which we may name L; we write $L = \{a, b, c, d\}$. The objects comprising a set are called its **elements** or **members**. For example, b is an element of the set L; in symbols, $b \in L$. Sometimes we simply say that b is in L, or that L contains b. On the other hand, z is not an element of L, and we write $z \notin L$.

In a set we do not distinguish repetitions of the elements. Thus the set $\{\text{red}, \text{blue}, \text{red}\}$ is the same set as $\{\text{red}, \text{blue}\}$. Similarly, the order of the elements is immaterial; for example, $\{3, 1, 9\}$, $\{9, 3, 1\}$, and $\{1, 3, 9\}$ are the same set. To summarize: Two sets are equal (that is, the same) if and only if they have the same elements.

The elements of a set need not be related in any way (other than happening to be all members of the same set); for example, $\{3, \text{red}, \{d, \text{blue}\}\}$ is a set with three elements, one of which is itself a set. A set may have only one element; it is then called a **singleton**. For example, $\{1\}$ is the set with 1 as its only element; thus $\{1\}$ and 1 are quite different. There is also a set with no element at all. Naturally, there can be only one such set: it is called the **empty** set, and is denoted by $\emptyset$. Any set other than the empty set is said to be nonempty.

So far we have specified sets by simply listing all their elements, separated by commas and included in braces. Some sets cannot be written in this way, because they are infinite. For example, the set $\mathbf{N}$ of natural numbers is infinite; we may suggest its elements by writing $\mathbf{N} = \{0, 1, 2, \ldots\}$, using the three dots and your intuition in place of an infinitely long list. A set that is not infinite is finite.

Another way to specify a set is by referring to other sets and to properties that elements may or may not have. Thus if $I = \{1, 3, 9\}$ and $G = \{3, 9\}$, G may be described as the set of elements of I that are greater than 2. We write this fact as follows.

$$G = \{x : x \in I \text{ and } x \text{ is greater than } 2\}.$$

In general, if a set A has been defined and P is a property that elements of A may or may not have, then we can define a new set

$$B = \{x : x \in A \text{ and } x \text{ has property } P\}.$$

As another example, the set of odd natural numbers is

$$O = \{x : x \in \mathbf{N} \text{ and } x \text{ is not divisible by } 2\}.$$

A set A is a **subset** of a set B —in symbols, $A \subseteq B$— if each element of A is also an element of B. Thus $O \subseteq \mathbf{N}$, since each odd natural number is a natural number. Note that any set is a subset of itself. If A is a subset of B but A is not the same as B, we say that A is a **proper subset** of B and write $A \subset B$. Also note that the empty set is a subset of every set. For if B is any set, then $\emptyset \subseteq B$, since each element of $\emptyset$ (of which there are none) is also an element of B.

To prove that two sets A and B are equal, we may prove that $A \subseteq B$ and $B \subseteq A$. Every element of A must then be an element of B and vice versa, so that A and B have the same elements and $A = B$.

Two sets can be combined to form a third by various *set operations*, just as numbers are combined by arithmetic operations such as addition. One set operation is **union**: the union of two sets is that set having as elements the objects that are elements of at least one of the two given sets, and possibly of both. We use the symbol $\cup$ to denote union, so that

$$A \cup B = \{x : x \in A \text{ or } x \in B\}.$$

For example,

$$\{1, 3, 9\} \cup \{3, 5, 7\} = \{1, 3, 5, 7, 9\}.$$

The **intersection** of two sets is the collection of all elements the two sets have in common; that is,

$$A \cap B = \{x : x \in A \text{ and } x \in B\}.$$

For example,

$$\{1,3,9\} \cap \{3,5,7\} = \{3\},$$

and

$$\{1,3,9\} \cap \{a,b,c,d\} = \emptyset.$$

Finally, the **difference** of two sets A and B, denoted by $A - B$, is the set of all elements of A that are not elements of B.

$$A - B = \{x : x \in A \text{ and } x \notin B\}.$$

For example,

$$\{1,3,9\} - \{3,5,7\} = \{1,9\}.$$

Certain properties of the set operations follow easily from their definitions. For example, if A, B, and C are sets, the following laws hold.

Idempotency	$A \cup A = A$
	$A \cap A = A$
Commutativity	$A \cup B = B \cup A$
	$A \cap B = B \cap A$
Associativity	$(A \cup B) \cup C = A \cup (B \cup C)$
	$(A \cap B) \cap C = A \cap (B \cap C)$
Distributivity	$(A \cup B) \cap C = (A \cap C) \cup (B \cap C)$
	$(A \cap B) \cup C = (A \cup C) \cap (B \cup C)$
Absorption	$(A \cup B) \cap A = A$
	$(A \cap B) \cup A = A$
DeMorgan's laws	$A - (B \cup C) = (A - B) \cap (A - C)$
	$A - (B \cap C) = (A - B) \cup (A - C)$

Example 1.1.1: Let us prove the first of De Morgan's laws. Let

$$L = A - (B \cup C)$$

and

$$R = (A - B) \cap (A - C);$$

we are to show that $L = R$. We do this by showing (a) $L \subseteq R$ and (b) $R \subseteq L$.

(a) Let x be any element of L; then $x \in A$, but $x \notin B$ and $x \notin C$. Hence x is an element of both $A - B$ and $A - C$, and is thus an element of R. Therefore $L \subseteq R$.

(b) Let $x \in R$; then x is an element of both $A - B$ and $A - C$, and is therefore in A but in neither B nor C. Hence $x \in A$ but $x \notin B \cup C$, so $x \in L$.

Therefore $R \subseteq L$, and we have established that $L = R.\diamondsuit$

Two sets are **disjoint** if they have no element in common, that is, if their intersection is empty.

It is possible to form intersections and unions of more than two sets. If S is any collection of sets, we write $\bigcup S$ for the set whose elements are the elements of all the sets in S. For example, if $S = \{\{a,b\},\{b,c\},\{c,d\}\}$ then $\bigcup S = \{a,b,c,d\}$; and if $S = \{\{n\} : n \in \mathbf{N}\}$, that is, the collection of all the singleton sets with natural numbers as elements, then $\bigcup S = \mathbf{N}$. In general,

$$\bigcup S = \{x : x \in P \text{ for some set } P \in S\}.$$

Similarly,

$$\bigcap S = \{x : x \in P \text{ for each set } P \in S\}.$$

The collection of all subsets of a set A is itself a set, called the **power set** of A and denoted 2^A. For example, the subsets of $\{c,d\}$ are $\{c,d\}$ itself, the singletons $\{c\}$ and $\{d\}$ and the empty set $\emptyset$, so

$$2^{\{c,d\}} = \{\{c,d\},\{c\},\{d\},\emptyset\}.$$

A **partition** of a nonempty set A is a subset Π of 2^A such that $\emptyset$ is not an element of Π and such that each element of A is in one and only one set in Π. That is, Π is a partition of A if Π is a set of subsets of A such that

(1) each element of Π is nonempty;
(2) distinct members of Π are disjoint;
(3) $\bigcup \Pi = A$.

For example, $\{\{a,b\},\{c\},\{d\}\}$ is a partition of $\{a,b,c,d\}$, but $\{\{b,c\},\{c,d\}\}$ is not. The sets of even and odd natural numbers form a partition of $\mathbf{N}$.

Problems for Section 1.1

1.1.1. Determine whether each of the following is true or false.
  (a) $\emptyset \subseteq \emptyset$
  (b) $\emptyset \in \emptyset$
  (c) $\emptyset \in \{\emptyset\}$
  (d) $\emptyset \subseteq \{\emptyset\}$
  (e) $\{a,b\} \in \{a,b,c,\{a,b\}\}$
  (f) $\{a,b\} \subseteq \{a,b,\{a,b\}\}$
  (g) $\{a,b\} \subseteq 2^{\{a,b,\{a,b\}\}}$
  (h) $\{\{a,b\}\} \in 2^{\{a,b,\{a,b\}\}}$
  (i) $\{a,b,\{a,b\}\} - \{a,b\} = \{a,b\}$

1.1.2. What are these sets? Write them using braces, commas, and numerals only.
  (a) $(\{1,3,5\} \cup \{3,1\}) \cap \{3,5,7\}$
  (b) $\bigcup\{\{3\}, \{3,5\}, \bigcap\{\{5,7\}, \{7,9\}\}\}$
  (c) $(\{1,2,5\} - \{5,7,9\}) \cup (\{5,7,9\} - \{1,2,5\})$
  (d) $2^{\{7,8,9\}} - 2^{\{7,9\}}$
  (e) $2^{\emptyset}$

1.1.3. Prove each of the following.
  (a) $A \cup (B \cap C) = (A \cup B) \cap (A \cup C)$
  (b) $A \cap (B \cup C) = (A \cap B) \cup (A \cap C)$
  (c) $A \cap (A \cup B) = A$
  (d) $A \cup (A \cap B) = A$
  (e) $A - (B \cap C) = (A - B) \cup (A - C)$

1.1.4. Let $S = \{a, b, c, d\}$.
  (a) What partition of S has the fewest members? The most members?
  (b) List all partitions of S with exactly two members.

1.2 | RELATIONS AND FUNCTIONS

Mathematics deals with statements about objects and the relations between them. It is natural to say, for example, that "less than" is a relation between objects of a certain kind —namely, numbers— which holds between 4 and 7 but does not hold between 4 and 2, or between 4 and itself. But how can we express relations between objects in the only mathematical language we have available at this point —that is to say, the language of sets? We simply think of a relation as being itself a set. The objects that belong to the relation are, in essence, the combinations of individuals for which that relation holds in the intuitive sense. So the less-than relation is the set of all *pairs* of numbers such that the first number is less than the second.

But we have moved a bit quickly. In a pair that belongs to a relation, we need to be able to distinguish the two parts of the pair, and we have not explained how to do so. We cannot write these pairs as sets, since $\{4,7\}$ is the same thing as $\{7,4\}$. It is easiest to introduce a new device for grouping objects called an **ordered pair**.[†]

We write the ordered pair of two objects a and b as (a,b); a and b are called the **components** of the ordered pair (a,b). The ordered pair (a,b) is not the same as the set $\{a,b\}$. First, the order matters: (a,b) is different from (b,a),

---

[†] True fundamentalists would see the ordered pair (a,b) not as a new kind of object, but as identical to $\{a, \{a,b\}\}$.

whereas $\{a, b\} = \{b, a\}$. Second, the two components of an ordered pair need not be distinct; $(7, 7)$ is a valid ordered pair. Note that two ordered pairs (a, b) and (c, d) are equal only when $a = c$ and $b = d$.

The **Cartesian product** of two sets A and B, denoted by $A \times B$, is the set of all ordered pairs (a, b) with $a \in A$ and $b \in B$. For example,

$$\{1, 3, 9\} \times \{b, c, d\} = \{(1, b), (1, c), (1, d), (3, b), (3, c), (3, d), (9, b), (9, c), (9, d)\}.$$

A binary relation on two sets A and B is a subset of $A \times B$. For example, $\{(1, b), (1, c), (3, d), (9, d)\}$ is a binary relation on $\{1, 3, 9\}$ and $\{b, c, d\}$. And $\{(i, j) : i, j \in \mathbf{N} \text{ and } i < j\}$ is the less-than relation; it is a subset of $\mathbf{N} \times \mathbf{N}$ —often the two sets related by a binary relation are identical.

More generally, let n be any natural number. Then if $a_1, \ldots, a_n$ are any n objects, not necessarily distinct, $(a_1, \ldots, a_n)$ is an **ordered tuple**; for each $i = 1, \ldots, n$, a_i is the ith component of $(a_1, \ldots, a_n)$. An ordered m-tuple $(b_1, \ldots, b_m)$, where m is a natural number, is the same as $(a_1, \ldots, a_n)$ if and only if $m = n$ and $a_i = b_i$, for $i = 1, \ldots, n$. Thus $(4, 4)$, $(4, 4, 4)$, $((4, 4), 4)$, and $(4, (4, 4))$ are all distinct. Ordered 2-tuples are the same as the ordered pairs discussed above, and ordered 3-, 4-, 5-, and 6-tuples are called **ordered triples**, **quadruples**, **quintuples**, and **sextuples**, respectively. On the other hand, a **sequence** is an ordered n-tuple for some unspecified n (the **length** of the sequence). If $A_1, \ldots, A_n$ are any sets, then the n-**fold Cartesian product** $A_1 \times \cdots \times A_n$ is the set of all ordered n-tuples $(a_1, \ldots, a_n)$, with $a_i \in A_i$, for each $i = 1, \ldots, n$. In case all the A_i, are the same set A, the n-fold Cartesian product $A \times \cdots \times A$ of A with itself is also written A^n. For example, $\mathbf{N}^2$ is the set of ordered pairs of natural numbers. An n-**ary relation** on sets $A_1, \ldots, A_n$ is a subset of $A_1 \times \cdots \times A_n$; 1-, 2-, and 3-ary relations are called **unary**, **binary**, and **ternary relations**, respectively.

Another fundamental mathematical idea is that of a *function*. On the intuitive level, a function is an association of each object of one kind with a unique object of another kind: of persons with their ages, dogs with their owners, numbers with their successors, and so on. But by using the idea of a binary relation as a set of ordered pairs, we can replace this intuitive idea by a concrete definition. A **function** from a set A to a set B is a binary relation R on A and B with the following special property: for each element $a \in A$, there is *exactly one* ordered pair in R with first component a. To illustrate the definition, let C be the set of cities in the United States and let S be the set of states; and let

$$R_1 = \{(x, y) : x \in C, y \in S, \text{ and } x \text{ is a city in state } y\},$$

$$R_2 = \{(x, y) : x \in S, y \in C, \text{ and } y \text{ is a city in state } x\}.$$

Then R_1 is a function, since each city is in one and only one state, but R_2 is not a function, since some states have more than one city.[†]

In general, we use letters such as f, g, and h for functions and we write $f : A \mapsto B$ to indicate that f is a function from A to B. We call A the **domain** of f. If a is any element of A we write $f(a)$ for that element b of B such that $(a, b) \in f$; since f is a function, there is exactly one $b \in B$ with this property, so $f(a)$ denotes a unique object. The object $f(a)$ is called the **image** of a under f. To specify a function $f : A \mapsto B$, it suffices to specify $f(a)$ for each $a \in A$; for example, to specify the function R_1 above, it suffices to specify, for each city, the state in which it is located. If $f : A \mapsto B$ and A' is a subset of A, then we define $f[A'] = \{f(a) : a \in A'\}$ (that is, $\{b : b = f(a)$ for some $a \in A'\}$). We call $f[A']$ the **image** of A' under f. The **range** of f is the image of its domain.

Ordinarily, if the domain of a function is a Cartesian product, one set of parentheses is dropped. For example, if $f : \mathbf{N} \times \mathbf{N} \mapsto \mathbf{N}$ is defined so that the image under f of an ordered pair (m, n) is the sum of m and n, we would write $f(m, n) = m + n$ rather than $f((m, n)) = m + n$, simply as a matter of notational convenience.

If $f : A_1 \times A_2 \times \ldots \times A_n \mapsto B$ is a function, and $f(a_1, \ldots, a_n) = b$, where $a_i \in A_i$ for $i = 1, \ldots, n$ and $b \in B$, then we sometimes call $a_1, \ldots, a_n$ the **arguments** of f and b the corresponding **value** of f. Thus f may be specified by giving its value for each n-tuple of arguments.

Certain kinds of functions are of special interest. A function $f : A \mapsto B$ is **one-to-one** if for any two distinct elements $a, a' \in A$, $f(a) \neq f(a')$. For example, if C is the set of cities in the United States, S is the set of states, and $g : S \mapsto C$ is specified by

$$g(s) = \text{the capital of state } s$$

for each $s \in S$, then g is one-to-one since no two states have the same capital. A function $f : A \mapsto B$ is **onto** B if each element of B is the image under f of some element of A. The function g just specified is not onto C, but the function R_1 defined above is onto S since each state contains at least one city. Finally a mapping $f : A \mapsto B$ is a **bijection** between A and B if it is both one-to-one and onto B; for example, if C_0 is the set of capital cities, then the function $g : S \mapsto C_0$ specified, as before, by

$$g(s) = \text{the capital of state } s$$

is a bijection between S and C_0.

[†] We consider Cambridge, Massachusetts, and Cambridge, Maryland, not the same city, but different cities that happen to have the same name.

The **inverse** of a binary relation $R \subseteq A \times B$, denoted $R^{-1} \subseteq B \times A$, is simply the relation $\{(b, a) : (a, b) \in R\}$. For example, the relation R_2 defined above is the inverse of R_1. Thus, the inverse of a function need not be a function. In the case of R_1 its inverse fails to be a function since some states have more than one city; that is, there are distinct cities c_1 and c_2 such that $R_1(c_1) = R_1(c_2)$. A function $f : A \mapsto B$ may also fail to have an inverse if there is some element $b \in B$ such that $f(a) \neq b$ for all $a \in A$. If $f : A \mapsto B$ is a bijection, however, neither of these eventualities can occur, and f^{-1} is a function —indeed, a bijection between B and A. Moreover $f^{-1}(f(a)) = a$ for each $a \in A$, and $f(f^{-1}(b)) = b$ for each $b \in B$.

When a particularly simple bijection between two sets has been specified, it is sometimes possible to view an object in the domain and its image in the range as virtually indistinguishable: the one may be seen as a renaming or a way of rewriting the other. For example, singleton sets and ordered 1-tuples are, strictly speaking, different, but not much harm is done if we occasionally blur the distinction, because of the obvious bijection f such that $f(\{a\}) = (a)$ for any singleton $\{a\}$. Such a bijection is called a *natural isomorphism*; of course this is not a formal definition since what is "natural" and what distinctions can be blurred depend on the context. Some slightly more complex examples should make the point more clearly.

Example 1.2.1: For any three sets A, B, and C, there is a natural isomorphism of $A \times B \times C$ to $(A \times B) \times C$, namely

$$f(a, b, c) = ((a, b), c)$$

for any $a \in A$, $b \in B$, and $c \in C. \Diamond$

Example 1.2.2: For any sets A and B, there is a natural isomorphism ϕ from

$$2^{A \times B},$$

that is, the set of all binary relations on A and B, to the set

$$\{f : f \text{ is a function from } A \text{ to } 2^B\}.$$

Namely, for any relation $R \subseteq A \times B$, let $\phi(R)$ be that function $f : A \mapsto 2^B$ such that

$$f(a) = \{b : b \in B \text{ and } (a, b) \in R\}.$$

For example, if S is the set of states and $R \subseteq S \times S$ contains any ordered pair of states with a common border, then the naturally associated function $f : S \mapsto 2^S$ is specified by $f(s) = \{s' : s' \in S \text{ and } s' \text{ shares a border with } s\}. \Diamond$

Example 1.2.3: Sometimes we regard the inverse of a function $f : A \mapsto B$ as a function even when f is not a bijection. The idea is to regard $f^{-1} \subseteq B \times A$ as a function from B to 2^A, using the natural isomorphism described under Example 1.2.2. Thus $f^{-1}(b)$ is, for any $b \in B$, the set of all $a \in A$ such that $f(a) = b$. For example, if R_1 is as defined above —the function that assigns to each city the state in which it is located— then $R_1^{-1}(s)$, where s is a state, is the set of all cities in that state.

If Q and R are binary relations, then their composition $Q \circ R$, or simply QR, is the relation $\{(a, b) : \text{for some } c, (a, c) \in Q \text{ and } (c, b) \in R\}$. Note that the composition of two functions $f : A \mapsto B$ and $g : B \mapsto C$ is a function h from A to C such that $h(a) = g(f(a))$ for each $a \in A$. For example, if f is the function that assigns to each dog its owner and g assigns to each person his or her age, then $f \circ g$ assigns to each dog the age of its owner.$\Diamond$

Problems for Section 1.2

1.2.1. Write each of the following explicitly.
(a) $\{1\} \times \{1, 2\} \times \{1, 2, 3\}$
(b) $\emptyset \times \{1, 2\}$
(c) $2^{\{1,2\}} \times \{1, 2\}$

1.2.2. Let $R = \{(a, b), (a, c), (c, d), (a, a), (b, a)\}$. What is $R \circ R$, the composition of R with itself? What is R^{-1}, the inverse of R? Is R, $R \circ R$, or R^{-1} a function?

1.2.3. Let $f : A \mapsto B$ and $g : B \mapsto C$. Let $h : A \mapsto C$ be their composition. In each of the following cases state necessary and sufficient conditions on f and g for h to be as specified.
(a) Onto.
(b) One-to-one.
(c) A bijection.

1.2.4. If A and B are any sets, we write B^A for the set of all functions from A to B. Describe a natural isomorphism between $\{0, 1\}^A$ and 2^A.

1.3 | SPECIAL TYPES OF BINARY RELATIONS

Binary relations will be found over and over again in these pages; it will be helpful to have convenient ways of representing them and some terminology for discussing their properties. A completely "random" binary relation has no significant internal structure; but many relations we shall encounter arise out of specific contexts and therefore have important regularities. For example, the relation that holds between two cities if they belong to the same state has certain "symmetries" and other properties that are worth noting, discussing, and exploiting.

In this section we study relations that exhibit these and similar regularities. We shall deal only with binary relations on a set and itself. Thus, let A be a set, and $R \subseteq A \times A$ be a relation on A. The relation R can be represented by a **directed graph**. Each element of A is represented by a small circle —what we call a **node** of the directed graph— and an arrow is drawn from a to b if and only if $(a, b) \in R$. The arrows are the **edges** of the directed graph. For example, the relation $R = \{(a, b), (b, a), (a, d), (d, c), (c, c), (c, a)\}$ is represented by the graph in Figure 1-1. Note in particular the loop from c to itself, corresponding to the pair $(c, c) \in R$. From a node of a graph to another there is either no edge, or one edge —we do not allow "parallel arrows."

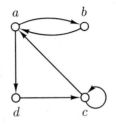

Figure 1-1

There is no formal distinction between binary relations on a set A and directed graphs with nodes from A. We use the term *directed graph* when we want to emphasize that the set on which the relation is defined is of no independent interest to us, outside the context of this particular relation. Directed graphs, as well as the *undirected graphs* soon to be introduced, are useful as models and abstractions of complex systems (traffic and communication networks, computational structures and processes, etc.). In Section 1.6, and in much more detail in Chapters 6 and 7, we shall discuss many interesting *computational problems* arising in connection with directed graphs.

For another example of a binary relation/directed graph, the less-than-or-equal-to relation $\leq$ defined on the natural numbers is illustrated in Figure 1-2. Of course, the entire directed graph cannot be drawn, since it would be infinite.

A relation $R \subseteq A \times A$ is **reflexive** if $(a, a) \in R$ for each $a \in A$. The directed graph representing a reflexive relation has a loop from each node to itself. For example, the directed graph of Figure 1-2 represents a reflexive relation, but that of Figure 1-1 does not.

A relation $R \subseteq A \times A$ is **symmetric** if $(b, a) \in R$ whenever $(a, b) \in R$.

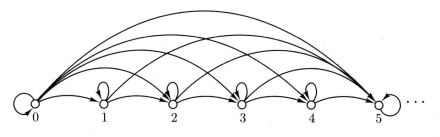

Figure 1-2

In the corresponding directed graph, whenever there is an arrow between two nodes, there are arrows between those nodes in both directions. For example, the directed graph of Figure 1-3 represents a symmetric relation. This directed graph might depict the relation of "friendship" among five people, since whenever x is a friend of y, y is also a friend of x. The relation of friendship is not reflexive, since we do not regard a person as his or her own friend. Of course, a relation could be both symmetric and reflexive; for example, $\{(a, b) : a$ and b are persons with the same father$\}$ is such a relation.

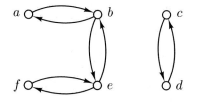

Figure 1-3

A symmetric relation *without pairs of the form* (a, a) is represented as an **undirected graph**, or simply a **graph**. Graphs are drawn without arrowheads, combining pairs of arrows going back and forth between the same nodes. For example, the relation shown in Figure 1-3 could also be represented by the graph in Figure 1-4.

A relation R is **antisymmetric** if whenever $(a, b) \in R$ and a and b are distinct, then $(b, a) \notin R$. For example, let P be the set of all persons. Then

$$\{(a, b) : a, b \in P \text{ and } a \text{ is the father of } b\}$$

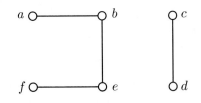

Figure 1-4

is antisymmetric. A relation may be neither symmetric nor antisymmetric; for example, the relation

$$\{(a, b) : a, b \in P \text{ and } a \text{ is the brother of } b\}$$

and the relation represented in Figure 1-1 are neither.

A binary relation R is **transitive** if whenever $(a, b) \in R$ and $(b, c) \in R$, then $(a, c) \in R$. The relation

$$\{(a, b) : a, b \in P \text{ and } a \text{ is an ancestor of } b\}$$

is transitive, since if a is an ancestor of b and b is an ancestor of c, then a is an ancestor of c. So is the less-than-or-equal relation. In terms of the directed graph representation, transitivity is equivalent to the requirement that whenever there is a sequence of arrows leading from an element a to an element z, there is an arrow directly from a to z. For example, the relation illustrated in Figure 1-5 is transitive.

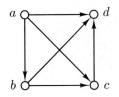

Figure 1-5

A relation that is reflexive, symmetric, and transitive is called an **equivalence relation**. The representation of an equivalence relation by an undirected graph consists of a number of *clusters*; within each cluster, each pair of nodes is connected by a line (see Figure 1-6). The "clusters" of an equivalence relation are called its **equivalence classes**. We normally write $[a]$ for the equivalence class containing an element a, provided the equivalence relation R is understood by the context. That is, $[a] = \{b : (a, b) \in R\}$, or, since R is symmetric, $[a] = \{b : (b, a) \in R\}$. For example, the equivalence relation in Figure 1-6 has three equivalence classes, one with four elements, one with three elements, and one with one element.

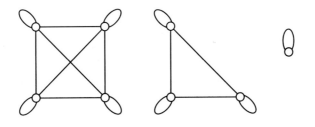

Figure 1-6

Theorem 1.3.1: *Let R be an equivalence relation on a nonempty set A. Then the equivalence classes of R constitute a partition of A.*

Proof: Let $\Pi = \{[a] : a \in A\}$. We must show that the sets in Π are nonempty, disjoint, and together exhaust A. All equivalence classes are nonempty, since $a \in [a]$ for all $a \in A$, by reflexivity. To show that they are disjoint, consider any two distinct equivalence classes $[a]$ and $[b]$, and suppose that $[a] \cap [b] \neq \emptyset$. Thus there is an element c such that $c \in [a]$ and $c \in [b]$. Hence $(a, c) \in R$ and $(c, b) \in R$; since R is transitive, $(a, b) \in R$; and since R is symmetric, $(b, a) \in R$. But now take any element $d \in [a]$; then $(d, a) \in R$ and, by transitivity, $(d, b) \in R$. Hence $d \in [b]$, so that $[a] \subseteq [b]$. Likewise $[b] \subseteq [a]$. Therefore $[a] = [b]$. But this contradicts the assumption that $[a]$ and $[b]$ are distinct.

To see that $\bigcup \Pi = A$, simply notice that each element a of A is in some set in Π —namely, $a \in [a]$, by reflexivity. ∎

Thus starting from an equivalence relation R, we can always construct a corresponding partition Π. For example, if

$$R = \{(a, b) : a \text{ and } b \text{ are persons and } a \text{ and } b \text{ have the same parents}\},$$

then the equivalence classes of R are all groups of siblings. Note that the construction of Theorem 1.3.1 can be reversed: from any partition, we can construct a corresponding equivalence relation. Namely, if Π is a partition of A, then

$$R = \{(a, b) : a \text{ and } b \text{ belong in the same set of } \Pi\}$$

is an equivalence relation. Thus there is a natural isomorphism between the set of equivalence relations on a set A and the set of partitions of A.

A relation that is reflexive, antisymmetric, and transitive is called a **partial order**. For example,

$$\{(a, b) : a, b \text{ are persons and } a \text{ is an ancestor of } b\}$$

is a partial order (provided we consider each person to be an ancestor of himself or herself). If $R \subseteq A \times A$ is a partial order, an element $a \in A$ is called **minimal** if the following is true: $(b, a) \in R$ only if $a = b$. For example, in the ancestor relation defined above, Adam and Eve are the only minimal elements. A finite partial order must have at least one minimal element, but an infinite partial order need not have one.

A partial order $R \subseteq A \times A$ is a **total order** if, for all $a, b \in A$, either $(a, b) \in R$ or $(b, a) \in R$. Thus the ancestor relation is not a total order since not any two people are ancestrally related (for example, siblings are not); but the less-than-or-equal-to relation on numbers is a total order. A total order cannot have two or more minimal elements.

A **path** in a binary relation R is a sequence $(a_1, \ldots, a_n)$ for some $n \geq 1$ such that $(a_i, a_{i+1}) \in R$ for $i = 1, \ldots, n - 1$; this path is said to be from a_1 to a_n. The **length** of a path $(a_1, \ldots, a_n)$ is n. The path $(a_1, \ldots, a_n)$ is a **cycle** if the a_i's are all distinct and also $(a_n, a_1) \in R$.

Problems for Section 1.3

1.3.1. Let $R = \{(a, c), (c, e), (e, e), (e, b), (d, b), (d, d)\}$. Draw directed graphs representing each of the following.
   (a) R
   (b) R^{-1}
   (c) $R \cup R^{-1}$
   (d) $R \cap R^{-1}$

1.3.2. Let R and S be the binary relations on $A = \{1, \ldots, 7\}$ with the graphical representations shown in the next page.
   (a) Indicate whether each of R and S is (i) symmetric, (ii) reflexive, and (iii) transitive.
   (b) Repeat (a) for the relation $R \cup S$.

1.3.3. Draw directed graphs representing relations of the following types.
   (a) Reflexive, transitive, and antisymmetric.
   (b) Reflexive, transitive, and neither symmetric nor antisymmetric.

1.3.4. Let A be a nonempty set and let $R \subseteq A \times A$ be the empty set. Which properties does R have?
   (a) Reflexivity.
   (b) Symmetry.
   (c) Antisymmetry.
   (d) Transitivity.

1.3.5. Let $f : A \mapsto B$. Show that the following relation R is an equivalence relation on A: $(a, b) \in R$ if and only if $f(a) = f(b)$.

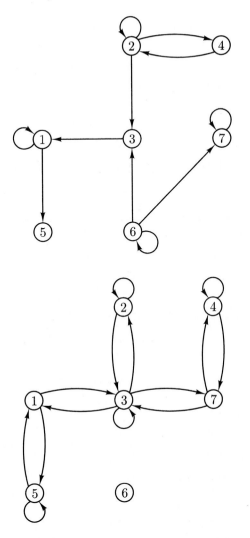

1.3.6. Let $R \subseteq A \times A$ be a binary relation as defined below. In which cases is R a partial order? a total order?

(a) $A =$ the positive integers; $(a, b) \in R$ if and only if b is divisible by a.

(b) $A = \mathbf{N} \times \mathbf{N}$; $((a, b)(c, d)) \in R$ if and only if $a \leq c$ or $b \leq d$.

(c) $A = \mathbf{N}$; $(a, b) \in R$ if and only if $b = a$ or $b = a + 1$.

(d) A is the set of all English words; $(a, b) \in R$ if and only if a is no longer than b.

(e) A is the set of all English words; $(a, b) \in R$ if and only if a is the same as b or occurs more frequently than b in the present book.

1.3.7. Let R_1 and R_2 be any two partial orders on the same set A. Show that $R_1 \cap R_2$ is a partial order.

1.3.8. (a) Prove that if S is any collection of sets, then $R_S = \{(A, B) : A, B \in S$ and $A \subseteq B\}$ is a partial order.
   (b) Let $S = 2^{\{1,2,3\}}$. Draw a directed graph representing the partial order R_S defined in (a). Which are the minimal elements of R_S?

1.3.9. Under what circumstances does a directed graph represent a function?

1.3.10. Show that any function from a finite set to itself contains a cycle.

1.3.11. Let S be any set, and let $\mathcal{P}$ be the set of all partitions of S. Let R be the binary relation on $\mathcal{P}$ such that $(\Pi_1, \Pi_2) \in R$ if and only if for every $S_1 \in \Pi_1$, there is an $S_2 \in \Pi_2$ such that $S_1 \subseteq S_2$; if $(\Pi_1, \Pi_2) \in R$ we say that Π_1 **refines** Π_2. Show that R is a partial order on $\mathcal{P}$. What elements of $\mathcal{P}$ are maximal and minimal? Suppose that $\mathcal{P}$ were an arbitrary collection of subsets of 2^S, which need not be partitions of S. Would R necessarily be a partial order?

1.4 | FINITE AND INFINITE SETS

A basic property of a finite set is its *size*, that is, the number of elements it contains. Some facts about the sizes of finite sets are so obvious they hardly need proof. For example, if $A \subseteq B$, then the size of A is less than or equal to that of B; the size of A is zero if and only if A is the empty set.

However, an extension of the notion of "size" to infinite sets leads to difficulties if we attempt to follow our intuition. Are there more multiples of 17 $(0, 17, 34, 51, 68, \ldots)$ than there are perfect squares $(0, 1, 4, 9, 16, \ldots)$? You are welcome to speculate on alternatives, but experience has shown that the only satisfactory convention is to regard these sets as having *the same size*.

We call two sets A and B **equinumerous** if there is a bijection $f : A \mapsto B$. Recall that if there is a bijection $f : A \mapsto B$, then there is a bijection $f^{-1} : B \mapsto A$; hence equinumerosity is a symmetric relation. In fact, as is easily shown, it is an equivalence relation. For example, $\{8, \text{red}, \{\emptyset, b\}\}$ and $\{1, 2, 3\}$ are equinumerous; let $f(8) = 1$, $f(\text{red}) = 2$, $f(\{\emptyset, b\}) = 3$. So are the multiples of 17 and the perfect squares; a bijection is given by $f(17n) = n^2$ for each $n \in \mathbf{N}$.

In general, we call a set **finite** if, intuitively, it is equinumerous with $\{1, 2, \ldots, n\}$ for some natural number n. (For $n = 0$, $\{1, \ldots, n\}$ is the empty set, so $\emptyset$ is finite, being equinumerous with itself.) If A and $\{1, \ldots, n\}$ are equinumerous, then we say that the cardinality of A (in symbols, $|A|$) is n. The cardinality of a finite set is thus the number of elements in it.

A set is **infinite** if it is not finite. For example, the set **N** of natural numbers is infinite; so are sets such as the set of integers, the set of reals, and the set of perfect squares. However, *not all infinite sets are equinumerous.*

A set is said to be **countably infinite** if it is equinumerous with **N**, and **countable** if it is finite or countably infinite. A set that is not countable is **uncountable**. To show that a set A is countably infinite we must exhibit a bijection f between A and **N**; equivalently, we need only suggest a way in which A can be enumerated as

$$A = \{a_0, a_1, a_2, \ldots\},$$

and so on, since such an enumeration immediately suggests a bijection —just take $f(0) = a_0, f(1) = a_1, \ldots$

For example, we can show that the union of any finite number of countably infinite sets is countably infinite. Let us only illustrate the proof for the case of three pairwise disjoint, countably infinite sets; a similar argument works in general. Call the sets A, B, and C. The sets can be listed as above: $A = \{a_0, a_1, \ldots\}$, $B = \{b_0, b_1, \ldots\}$, $C = \{c_0, c_1, \ldots\}$, Then their union can be listed as $A \cup B \cup C = \{a_0, b_0, c_0, a_1, b_1, c_1, a_2, \ldots\}$. This listing amounts to a way of "visiting" all the elements in $A \cup B \cup C$ by alternating between different sets, as illustrated in Figure 1-7. The technique of interweaving the enumeration of several sets is called "dovetailing" (for reasons that any carpenter can give after looking at Figure 1-7).

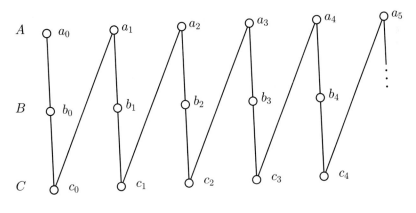

Figure 1-7

The same idea can be used to show that the union of a countably infinite collection of countably infinite sets is countably infinite. For example, let us show that $\mathbf{N} \times \mathbf{N}$ is countably infinite; note that $\mathbf{N} \times \mathbf{N}$ is the union of $\{0\} \times \mathbf{N}$, $\{1\} \times \mathbf{N}$, $\{2\} \times \mathbf{N}$, and so on, that is, the union of a countably infinite collection of countably infinite sets. Dovetailing must here be more subtle than in the example above: we cannot, as we did there, visit one element from each set before visiting the second element of the first set, because with infinitely many sets to visit we could never even finish the first round! Instead we proceed as follows (see Figure 1-8).

(1) In the first round, we visit one element from the first set: $(0,0)$.
(2) In the second round, we visit the next element from the first set, $(0,1)$, and also the first element from the second set, $(1,0)$.
(3) In the third round we visit the next unvisited elements of the first and second sets, $(0,2)$ and $(1,1)$, and also the first element of the third set, $(2,0)$.
(4) In general, in the nth round, we visit the nth element of the first set, the $(n-1)$st element of the second set, and the first element of the nth set.

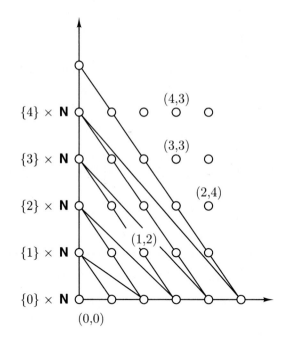

Figure 1-8

Another way of viewing this use of dovetailing is to observe that the pair (i,j) is visited mth, where $m = \frac{1}{2}[(i+j)^2 + 3i + j]$; that is to say, the function $f(i,j) = \frac{1}{2}[(i+j)^2 + 3i + j]$ is a *bijection* from $\mathbf{N} \times \mathbf{N}$ to $\mathbf{N}$ (see Problem 1.4.4).

At the end of the next section, we present a technique for showing that two infinite sets are *not* equinumerous.

Problems for Section 1.4

1.4.1. Prove that the following are countable.
- (a) The union of any three countable sets, not necessarily infinite or disjoint.
- (b) The set of all finite subsets of $\mathbf{N}$.

1.4.2. Explicitly give bijections between each of the following pairs.
- (a) $\mathbf{N}$ and the odd natural numbers.
- (b) $\mathbf{N}$ and the set of all integers.
- (c) $\mathbf{N}$ and $\mathbf{N} \times \mathbf{N} \times \mathbf{N}$.

(We are looking for formulas that are as simple as possible and involve only such operations as addition and multiplication.)

1.4.3. Let C be a set of sets defined as follows,
1. $\emptyset \in C$
2. If $S_1 \in C$ and $S_2 \in C$, then $\{S_1, S_2\} \in C$.
3. If $S_1 \in C$ and $S_2 \in C$, then $S_1 \times S_2 \in C$.
4. Nothing is in C except that which follows from (1), (2), and (3).
- (a) Explain carefully why it is a consequence of (1–4) that $\{\emptyset, \{\emptyset\}\} \in C$.
- (b) Give an example of a set S of ordered pairs such that $S \in C$, and $|S| > 1$.
- (c) Does C contain any infinite sets? Explain.
- (d) Is C countable or uncountable? Explain.

1.4.4. Show that the dovetailing method of Figure 1-8 visits the pair (i, j) mth, where

$$m = \frac{1}{2}[(i + j)^2 + 3i + j].$$

1.5	THREE FUNDAMENTAL PROOF TECHNIQUES

Every proof is different, since every proof is designed to establish a different result. But like games of chess or baseball, observation of many leads one to realize that there are patterns, rules of thumb, and tricks of the trade that can be found and exploited over and over again. The main purpose of this section is to introduce three fundamental principles that recur, under various disguises, in many proofs: *mathematical induction*, the *pigeonhole principle*, and *diagonalization*.

The Principle of Mathematical Induction: *Let A be a set of natural numbers such that*

(1) $0 \in A$, *and*

(2) for each natural number n, if $\{0, 1, \dots, n\} \subseteq A$, then $n + 1 \in A$.

Then $A = \mathbf{N}$.

In less formal terms, the principle of mathematical induction states that any set of natural numbers containing zero, and with the property that it contains $n + 1$ whenever it contains all the numbers up to and including n, must in fact be the set of all natural numbers.

The justification for this principle should be clear intuitively; every natural number must wind up in A since it can be "reached" from zero in a finite succession of steps by adding one each time. Another way to argue the same idea is by contradiction; suppose (1) and (2) hold but $A \neq \mathbf{N}$. Then some number is omitted from A. In particular, let n be the first number among $0, 1, 2, \dots$ that is omitted from $\mathbf{N}$.[†] Then n cannot be zero, since $0 \in A$ by (1); and since $0, 1, \dots, n - 1 \subseteq A$ by the choice of n, then $n \in A$ by (2), which is a contradiction.

In practice, induction is used to prove assertions of the following form: "For all natural numbers n, property P is true." The above principle is applied to the set $A = \{n : P \text{ is true of } n\}$ in the following way.

(1) In the *basis step* we show that $0 \in A$, that is, that P is true of 0.

(2) The *induction hypothesis* is the assumption that for some fixed but arbitrary $n \geq 0$, P holds for each natural number $0, 1, \dots, n$.

(3) In the *induction step* we show, using the induction hypothesis, that P is true of $n + 1$. By the induction principle, A is then equal to $\mathbf{N}$, that is, P holds for every natural number.

Example 1.5.1: Let us show that for any $n \geq 0$, $1 + 2 + \cdots + n = \frac{n^2 + n}{2}$.

Basis Step. Let $n = 0$. Then the sum on the left is zero, since there is nothing to add. The expression on the right is also zero.

Induction Hypothesis. Assume that, for some $n \geq 0$, $1 + 2 + \cdots + m = \frac{m^2 + m}{2}$ whenever $m \leq n$.

[†] This is a use of another principle, called the *least number principle*, that is actually equivalent to the principle of mathematical induction, so we are not really "proving" the principle of mathematical induction. The least number principle is: If $A \subseteq \mathbf{N}$ and $A \neq \mathbf{N}$, then there is a unique least number $n \in \mathbf{N} - A$; that is, a unique number n such that $n \notin A$ but $0, 1, \dots, n - 1 \in A$. A somewhat frivolous example of the least number principle is the fact that *there are no uninteresting numbers.* For suppose there were; then there would have to be a least such number, say n. But then n would have the remarkable property of being the least uninteresting number, which would surely make n interesting. . .

Induction Step.

$$1 + 2 + \cdots + n + (n+1) = (1 + 2 + \cdots + n) + (n+1)$$
$$= \frac{n^2 + n}{2} + (n+1) \quad \text{(by the induction hypothesis)}$$
$$= \frac{n^2 + n + 2n + 2}{2}$$
$$= \frac{(n+1)^2 + (n+1)}{2}$$

as was to be shown.$\Diamond$

Example 1.5.2: For any finite set A, $|2^A| = 2^{|A|}$; that is, the cardinality of the power set of A is 2 raised to a power equal to the cardinality of A. We shall prove this statement *by induction on the cardinality of A*.

Basis Step. Let A be a set of cardinality $n = 0$. Then $A = \emptyset$, and $2^{|A|} = 2^0 = 1$; on the other hand, $2^A = \{\emptyset\}$, and $|2^A| = |\{\emptyset\}| = 1$.

Induction Hypothesis. Let $n > 0$, and suppose that $|2^A| = 2^{|A|}$ provided that $|A| \le n$.

Induction Step. Let A be such that $|A| = n+1$. Since $n > 0$, A contains at least one element a. Let $B = A - \{a\}$; then $|B| = n$. By the induction hypothesis, $|2^B| = 2^{|B|} = 2^n$. Now the power set of A can be divided into two parts, those sets containing the element a and those sets not containing a. The latter part is just 2^B, and the former part is obtained by introducing a into each member of 2^B. Thus

$$2^A = 2^B \cup \{C \cup \{a\} : C \in 2^B\}.$$

This division in fact partitions 2^A into two disjoint equinumerous parts, so the cardinality of the whole is twice $2^{|B|}$, which, by the induction hypothesis, is $2 \cdot 2^n = 2^{n+1}$, as was to be shown.$\Diamond$

We next use induction to establish our second fundamental principle, the *pigeonhole principle*.

The Pigeonhole Principle: *If A and B are finite sets and $|A| > |B|$, then there is no one-to-one function from A to B.*

In other words, if we attempt to pair off the elements of A (the "pigeons") with elements of B (the "pigeonholes"), sooner or later we will have to put more than one pigeon in a pigeonhole.

Proof: *Basis Step.* Suppose $|B| = 0$, that is, $B = \emptyset$. Then there is *no function* $f : A \mapsto B$ *whatsoever*, let alone a one-to-one function.

Induction Hypothesis. Suppose that f is not one-to-one, provided that $f : A \mapsto B$, $|A| > |B|$, and $|B| \leq n$, where $n \geq 0$.

Induction Step. Suppose that $f : A \mapsto B$ and $|A| > |B| = n + 1$. Choose some $a \in A$ (since $|A| > |B| = n + 1 \geq 1$, A is nonempty, and therefore such a choice is possible). If there is another element of A, say a', such that $f(a) = f(a')$, then obviously f is not a one-to-one function, and we are done. So, suppose that a is the only element mapped by f to $f(a)$. Consider then the sets $A - \{a\}$, $B - \{f(a)\}$, and the function g from $A - \{a\}$ to $B - \{f(a)\}$ that agrees with f on all elements of $A - \{a\}$. Now the induction hypothesis applies, because $B - \{f(a)\}$ has n elements, and $|A - \{a\}| = |A| - 1 > |B| - 1 = |B - \{f(a)\}|$. Therefore, there are two distinct elements of $A - \{a\}$ that are mapped by g (and therefore by f) to the same element of $B - \{b\}$, and hence f is not one-to-one. ∎

This simple fact is of use in a surprisingly large variety of proofs. We present just one simple application here, but point out other cases as they arise in later chapters.

Theorem 1.5.1: *Let R be a binary relation on a finite set A, and let $a, b \in A$. If there is a path from a to b in R, then there is a path of length at most $|A|$.*

Proof: Suppose that $(a_1, a_2, \ldots, a_n)$ is the *shortest* path from $a_1 = a$ to $a_n = b$, that is, the path with the smallest length, and suppose that $n > |A|$. By the pigeonhole principle, there is an element of A that repeats on the path, say $a_i = a_j$ for some $1 \leq i < j \leq n$. But then $(a_1, a_2, \ldots, a_i, a_{j+1}, \ldots, a_n)$ is a shorter path from a to b, contradicting our assumption that $(a_1, a_2, \ldots, a_n)$ is the shortest path from a to b. ∎

Finally, we come to our third basic proof technique, the *diagonalization principle*. Although it is not as widely used in mathematics as the other two principles we have discussed, it seems particularly well-suited for proving certain important results in the theory of computation.

The Diagonalization Principle: *Let R be a binary relation on a set A, and let D, the diagonal set for R, be $\{a : a \in A$ and $(a, a) \notin R\}$. For each $a \in A$, let $R_a = \{b : b \in A$ and $(a, b) \in R\}$. Then D is distinct from each R_a.*

If A is a finite set, then R can be pictured as a square array; the rows and columns are labeled with the elements of A and there is a cross in the box with row labeled a and column labeled b just in case $(a, b) \in R$. The diagonal set D corresponds to the complement of the sequence of boxes along the main diagonal, boxes with crosses being replaced by boxes without crosses, and vice versa. The sets R_a correspond to the rows of the array. The diagonalization principle can then be rephrased: the complement of the diagonal is different from each row.

Example 1.5.3: Let us consider the relation $R = \{(a,b),(a,d),(b,b),(b,c),$
$(c,c),(d,b),(d,c),(d,e),(d,f),(e,e),(e,f),(f,a),(f,c),(f,d),(f,e)\}$; notice that
$R_a = \{b,d\}$, $R_b = \{b,c\}$, $R_c = \{c\}$, $R_d = \{b,c,e,f\}$, $R_e = \{a,e\}$, and $R_f = \{c,d,e\}$. All in all, R may be pictured like this:

	a	b	c	d	e	f
a		×		×		
b		×	×			
c			×			
d		×	×		×	×
e					×	×
f	×		×	×	×	

The sequence of boxes along the diagonal is

Its complement is

which corresponds to the diagonal set $D = \{a,d,f\}$. Indeed, D is different from
each row of the array; for D, because of the way it is constructed, differs from
the first row in the first position, from the second row in the second position,
and so on.◊

The diagonalization principle holds for infinite sets as well, for the same
reason: The diagonal set D always differs from the set R_a on the question of
whether a is an element, and hence cannot be the same as R_a for any a.

We illustrate the use of diagonalization by a classic theorem of Georg Cantor
(1845–1918).

Theorem 1.5.2: *The set $2^{\mathbf{N}}$ is uncountable.*

Proof: . Suppose that $2^{\mathbf{N}}$ is countably infinite. That is, we assume that that there is a way of enumerating all members of $2^{\mathbf{N}}$ as

$$2^{\mathbf{N}} = \{R_0, R_1, R_2, \ldots\}$$

(notice that these are the sets R_a in the statement of the diagonalization principle, once we consider the relation $R = \{(i, j) : j \in R_i\}$). Now consider the set

$$D = \{n \in \mathbf{N} : n \notin R_n\}$$

(this is the the diagonal set). D is a set of natural numbers, and therefore it should appear somewhere in the enumeration $\{R_0, R_1, R_2, \ldots\}$ But D cannot be R_0, because it differs from it with respect to containing 0 (it does if and only if R_0 does not); and it cannot be R_1 because it differs from it with respect to 1; and so on. We must conclude that D does not appear on the enumeration at all, and this is a contradiction.

To restate the argument a little more formally, suppose that $D = R_k$ for some $k \geq 0$ (since D is a set of natural numbers, and $\{R_0, R_1, R_2, \ldots\}$ was supposed to be a complete enumeration of all such sets, such a k must exist). We obtain a contradition by asking whether $k \in R_k$:

(a) Suppose the answer is yes, $k \in R_k$. Since $D = \{n \in \mathbf{N} : n \notin R_n\}$, it follows that $k \notin D$; but $D = R_k$, a contradiction.
(b) Suppose the answer is no, $k \notin R_k$; then $k \in D$. But D is R_k, so $k \in R_k$, another contradiction.

We arrived at this contradiction starting from the assumption that $2^{\mathbf{N}}$ is countably infinite, and continuing by otherwise impeccably rigorous mathematical reasoning; we must therefore conclude that this asumption was in error. Hence $2^{\mathbf{N}}$ is uncountable. ∎

For a different rendering of this proof, in terms of establishing that the set of real numbers in the interval $[0, 1]$ is uncountable, see Problem 1.5.11.

Problems for Section 1.5

1.5.1. Show by induction that

$$1 \cdot 2 \cdot 3 + 2 \cdot 3 \cdot 4 + \cdots + n \cdot (n+1) \cdot (n+2) = \frac{n \cdot (n+1) \cdot (n+2) \cdot (n+3)}{4}.$$

1.5.2. Show by induction that $n^4 - 4n^2$ is divisible by 3 for all $n \geq 0$.

1.5.3. What is wrong with the following purported proof that all horses are the same color?

Proof by induction on the number of horses:

Basis Step. There is only one horse. Then clearly all horses have the same color.

Induction Hypothesis. In any group of up to n horses, all horses have the same color.

Induction Step. Consider a group of $n+1$ horses. Discard one horse; by the induction hypothesis, all the remaining horses have the same color. Now put that horse back and discard another; again all the remaining horses have the same color. So all the horses have the same color as the ones that were not discarded either time, and so they all have the same color.

1.5.4. Show that, if A and B are any finite sets, then there are $|B|^{|A|}$ functions from A to B.

1.5.5. Prove by induction: Every partial order on a nonempty finite set has at least one minimal element. Need this statement be true if the requirement of finiteness is lifted?

1.5.6. Show that in any group of at least two people there are at least two persons that have the same number of acquaintances within the group. (Use the pigeonhole principle.)

1.5.7. Suppose we try to prove, by an argument exactly parallel to the proof of Theorem 1.5.2, that the set of all finite subsets of **N** is uncountable. What goes wrong?

1.5.8. Give examples to show that the intersection of two countably infinite sets can be either finite or countably infinite, and that the intersection of two uncountable sets can be finite, countably infinite, or uncountable.

1.5.9. Show that the difference of an uncountable set and a countable set is uncountable.

1.5.10. Show that if S is any set, then there is a one-to-one function from S to 2^S, but not vice versa.

1.5.11. Show that the set of all real numbers in the interval $[0, 1]$ is uncountable. (*Hint:* It is well known that each such number can be written in binary notation as an infinite sequence of 0s and 1s —such as .0110011100000... Assume that an enumeration of these sequences exists, and create a "diagonal" sequence by "flipping" the ith bit of the ith sequence.)

1.6 │ CLOSURES AND ALGORITHMS

Consider the two directed graphs R and R^* in Figure 1-9(a) and (b). R^* contains R; also, R^* is reflexive and transitive (whereas R is neither). In fact, it is easy to see that R^* is *the smallest possible directed graph* that has these properties —that is, contains R, is reflexive, and is transitive (by "smallest" we mean the one with the fewest edges). For this reason, R^* is called the *reflexive transitive closure of R*. We next define this useful concept formally:

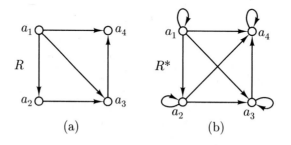

(a)   (b)

Figure 1-9

Definition 1.6.1: Let $R \subseteq A^2$ be a directed graph defined on a set A. The **reflexive transitive closure** of R is the relation

$$R^* = \{(a,b) : a, b \in A \text{ and there is a path from } a \text{ to } b \text{ in } R.\}$$

Notice the interesting contrast between the definition "from below" articulated in Definition 1.6.1 and the informal definition "from above" whereby we introduced the reflexive transitive closure (the smallest relation that contains R and is reflexive and transitive). It is perhaps intuitively clear that the two definitions are equivalent. Towards the end of this section we shall study more closely such "definitions from above," and the reason why they always correspond to an alternative definition "from below."

Algorithms

Definition 1.6.1 immediately suggests an *algorithm* for *computing* the reflexive transitive closure R^* of any given binary relation R over some finite set $A = \{a_1, a_2, \ldots, a_n\}$:

Initially $R^* := \emptyset$
for $i = 1, \ldots, n$ do
    for each i-tuple $(b_1, \ldots, b_i) \in A^i$ do
      if $(b_1, \ldots, b_i)$ is a path in R then add (b_1, b_i) to R^*.

The rigorous study of algorithms is in some sense what this book is all about; but to give a formal definition of an algorithm at this point would be to spoil the nice story we have to tell. Until a formal general model for algorithms is introduced, we shall be treating algorithms informally and somewhat nonrigorously, gradually increasing our insight and familiarity. It will then be clear that our definition of an algorithm, when its time comes, indeed captures correctly this important concept. Accordingly, this section only contains an intuitive treatment of algorithms and an informal introduction to their analysis.

Fortunately, it is easy to tell an algorithm when you see one. The procedure we describe above for computing R^* is a detailed and unambiguous sequence of instructions that produces a result —what we call R^*. It consists of elementary steps which we may reasonably assume are easy to carry out: Initializing R^* to $\emptyset$, adding new elements to R^*, testing whether $(b_j, b_{j+1}) \in R$ —this latter has to be done $i - 1$ times in the last line of the algorithm to test whether $(b_1, \ldots, b_i)$ is a path of R. We assume that somehow this algorithm operates on elements of A and R directly, so we need not specify how such sets and relations are *represented* for manipulation by the algorithm.

We shall next argue that the relation R^* computed by this algorithm is indeed the reflexive transitive closure of R (that is, the algorithm is *correct*). The reason is that our algorithm is just a straightforward *implementation* of Definition 1.6.1. It adds to R^*, initially empty, all pairs of elements of A that are connected by a path in R. Possible paths are checked one by one, in increasing length. We stop at sequences of length n because, by Theorem 1.5.1, if two nodes of A are connected by a path, then there is a path of length n or less that connects them.

It is thus clear that our algorithm will eventually terminate with the correct answer. One question that will prove most important and relevant to our concerns in this book is, *after how many steps will it terminate?* In the last part of the book we shall develop a whole theory of how the answer to such questions is calculated, and when the result is deemed satisfactory. But let us proceed informally for now.

What we need is an indication of how many elementary steps, how much "time," the algorithm requires when presented with a relation R as an input. As it is reasonable to expect that the algorithm will take more time on larger input relations, the answer will depend on how large the input relation is —more concretely, it will depend on the number n of elements in the set A. Thus, we are seeking a function $f : \mathbf{N} \mapsto \mathbf{N}$ such that, for each $n \geq 1$, if the algorithm is presented with a binary relation $R \subseteq A \times A$ with $|A| = n$, it will terminate after at most $f(n)$ steps. As is typical in the analysis of algorithms, we shall allow $f(n)$ to be a rough overestimate, as long as it has the correct *rate of growth*. Rates of growth are thus our next topic.

The Growth of Functions

Of these three functions from the set of natural numbers to itself, which is the largest?

$$f(n) = 1,000,000 \cdot n; \quad g(n) = 10 \cdot n^3; \quad h(n) = 2^n$$

Although for all values of n up to about a dozen we have $f(n) > g(n) > h(n)$, it should be intuitively clear that the correct ranking is the exact opposite; if we take n *large enough* we shall eventually have $f(n) < g(n) < h(n)$. In this subsection we shall develop the concepts necessary for ranking such functions according to their ultimate potential for producing large values.

Definition 1.6.2: Let $f : \mathbf{N} \mapsto \mathbf{N}$ be a function from the natural numbers to the natural numbers. The **order of** f, denoted $\mathcal{O}(f)$, is the set of all functions $g : \mathbf{N} \mapsto \mathbf{N}$ with the property that there are positive natural numbers $c > 0$ and $d > 0$ such that, for all $n \in \mathbf{N}$, $g(n) \leq c \cdot f(n) + d$. If in fact this inequality holds for all n, we say that $g(n) \in \mathcal{O}(f(n))$ **with constants** c **and** d.

If for two functions $f, g : \mathbf{N} \mapsto \mathbf{N}$ we have that $f \in \mathcal{O}(g)$ and $g \in \mathcal{O}(f)$, then we write $f \asymp g$. It is clear that the relation $\asymp$ defined on functions is an equivalence relation: It is reflexive (because always $f \in \mathcal{O}(f)$, with constants 1 and 0) and it is symmetric (because the roles of f and g are completely interchangeable in the definition of $\asymp$). Finally, it is transitive. Because suppose that $f \in \mathcal{O}(g)$ with constants c, d, and $g \in \mathcal{O}(h)$ with constants c', d'. Then for all n,

$$f(n) \leq c \cdot g(n) + d \leq c \cdot (c' \cdot h(n) + d') + d = (c \cdot c')h(n) + (d + c \cdot d').$$

Thus $f \in \mathcal{O}(h)$ with constants $c \cdot c'$ and $d + c \cdot d'$.

Thus, all functions from the set of natural numbers to itself are partitioned by $\asymp$ into equivalence classes. The equivalence class of f with respect to $\asymp$ is called the **rate of growth** of f.

Example 1.6.1: Consider the *polynomial* $f(n) = 31n^2 + 17n + 3$. We claim that $f(n) \in \mathcal{O}(n^2)$. To see this, notice that $n^2 \geq n$, and so $f(n) \leq 48n^2 + 3$, and thus $f(n) \in \mathcal{O}(n^2)$ with constants 48 and 3. Of course, also $n^2 \in \mathcal{O}(f(n))$ —with constants 1 and 0. Hence $n^2 \asymp 31n^2 + 17n + 3$, and the two functions have the same rate of growth.

Similarly, for any polynomial of degree d with nonnegative coefficients

$$f(n) = a_d n^d + a_{d-1} n^{d-1} + \cdots + a_1 n + a_0$$

where $a_i \geq 0$ for all i, and $a_d > 0$, it is easy to prove that $f(n) \in \mathcal{O}(n^d)$ —with constants $\sum_{i=1}^{d} a_i$ and a_0. *All polynomials of the same degree have the same rate of growth.*

Consider then two polynomials with different degrees; do they also have the same rate of growth? The answer here is negative. Since all polynomials with the same degree have the same rate of growth, it suffices to consider the two simplest representatives, namely two polynomials of the form n^i and n^j, with $0 < i < j$. Obviously, $n^i \in \mathcal{O}(n^j)$ with constants 1 and 0. We shall prove that $n^j \notin \mathcal{O}(n^i)$.

Suppose for the sake of contradiction that indeed $n^j \in \mathcal{O}(n^i)$ with constants c and d. That is, for all $n \in \mathbf{N}$ $n^j \leq cn^i + d$. But this is easily found to be absurd by trying $n = c + d$:

$$c(c+d)^i + d < (c+d)^{i+1} \leq (c+d)^j.$$

To summarize, for any two polynomials f and g, if they have the same degree then $f \asymp g$. Otherwise, if g has larger degree than f, then $f \in \mathcal{O}(g)$ but $g \notin \mathcal{O}(f)$; that is, *g has higher rate of growth* than f. $\diamondsuit$

Example 1.6.2: The previous example suggests that the rate of growth of a polynomial is captured by its degree. The larger the degree of f the higher the rate of growth. But there are functions with rate of growth higher than that of any polynomial. A simple example is the *exponential* function 2^n.

Let us first establish that, for all $n \in \mathbf{N}$, $n \leq 2^n$. We shall use induction on n. The result certainly holds when $n = 0$. So, suppose that it holds for all natural numbers up to and including n. Then we have

$$n + 1 \leq 2^n + 1 \leq 2^n + 2^n = 2^{n+1},$$

where in the first inequality we used the induction hypothesis, and in the second we used the fact that $1 \leq 2^n$ for all n.

We shall now extend this easy fact to all polynomials. We shall show that for any $i \geq 1$, $n^i \in \mathcal{O}(2^n)$; that is,

$$n^i \leq c2^n + d \tag{1}$$

for appropriate constants c and d. Take $c = (2i)^i$ and $d = (i^2)^i$. There are two cases: If $n \leq i^2$, then the inequality holds because $n^i \leq d$. If on the other hand $n \geq i^2$, then we shall show that the inequality (1) again holds because now $n^i \leq c2^n$. In proof, let m be the quotient of n divided by i —the unique integer such that $im \leq n < im + i$. Then we have

$$n^i \leq (im + i)^i \quad \text{by the definition of } m$$
$$= i^i(m + 1)^i$$
$$\leq i^i(2^{m+1})^i \quad \text{by the inequality } n \leq 2^n \text{ applied to } n = m + 1$$
$$\leq c2^{mi} \quad \text{by recalling that } c = (2i)^i$$
$$\leq c2^n \quad \text{again by the definition of } m.$$

Thus the rate of growth of any polynomial is no faster than that of 2^n. Can a polynomial have the same rate of growth as 2^n? If so, then any polynomial of larger degree would have the same rate of growth as well; and we saw in the previous example that polynomials of different degrees have different rates of growth. We conclude that 2^n *has a higher rate of growth than any polynomial.* Other exponential functions, such as 5^n, n^n, $n!$, 2^{n^2}, or, worse, 2^{2^n}, have even higher rates of growth.◊

Analysis of Algorithms

Polynomial and exponential rates of growth arise very naturally in the *analysis of algorithms*. For example, let us derive a rough estimate of the number of steps taken by the algorithm for the reflexive transitive closure introduced in the beginning of this section.

The algorithm examines each sequence $(b_1, \ldots, b_i)$ of length up to n to determine whether it is a path of R, and, if the answer is "yes," it adds (b_1, b_i) to R^*. Each such repetition can definitely be carried out in n or fewer "elementary operations" —testing whether $(a, b) \in R$, adding (a, b) to R^*. Thus, the total number of operations can be no more than

$$n \cdot (1 + n + n^2 + \cdots + n^n),$$

which is in $\mathcal{O}(n^{n+1})$. We have thus determined that the rate of growth of the *time requirements* of this algorithm is $\mathcal{O}(n^{n+1})$.

This outcome is rather disappointing because it is an *exponential* function, with an even higher rate of growth than 2^n. This algorithm is not efficient at all!

The question then arises, is there a faster algorithm for computing the reflexive transitive closure? Consider the following:

Initially $R^* := R \cup \{(a_i, a_i) : a_i \in A\}$
while there are three elements $a_i, a_j, a_k \in A$ such that
$(a_i, a_j), (a_j, a_k) \in R^*$ but $(a_i, a_k) \notin R^*$ do:
    add (a_i, a_k) to R^*.

This algorithm is perhaps even more natural and intuitive than the first one. It starts by adding to R^* all pairs in R and all pairs of the form (a_i, a_i) —thus guaranteeing that R^* contains R and is reflexive. It then repeatedly looks for violations of the transitivity property. Presumably this search for violations proceeds in some organized way not spelled out exactly in the algorithm, say by running through all values of a_i, for each of them through all values of a_j, and finally of a_k. If such a violation is discovered then it is corrected by adding an appropriate pair to R^*, and the search for a violation must start all over again. If at some point all triples are examined and no violation is found, the algorithm terminates.

When the algorithm terminates, R^* will certainly contain R, and it will be reflexive; besides, since no violation was found in the last iteration of the **while** loop, R^* must be transitive. Furthermore, R^* is the smallest relation that has all these properties (and it is thus the sought reflexive transitive closure of R). To see why, suppose that there is a proper subset of R^*, call it R_0, that contains R, and is reflexive and transitive. Consider then the first pair that does not belong to R_0, and still was added to R^* by the algorithm. It cannot be a pair in R, or a pair of the form (a_i, a_i), because all these pairs do belong to R_0. Thus, it must be a pair (a_i, a_k) such that both (a_i, a_j) and (a_j, a_k) belong to R^* at that point —and therefore also to R_0, since (a_i, a_k) was the first pair in which the two relations differ. But then R_0, by hypothesis a transitive relation, must also contain (a_i, a_k) —a contradiction. Therefore, the result will be the reflexive transitive closure of R and the algorithm is correct.

But when will the algorithm terminate? The answer is *after at most n^2 iterations of the while loop.* This is because after each successful iteration a pair (a_i, a_k) is added to R^* that was not there before, and there are at most n^2 pairs to be added. Hence the algorithm will terminate after at most n^2 iterations. And since each iteration can be carried out in $\mathcal{O}(n^3)$ time (all triples of elements of A need to be searched), the complexity of the new algorithm is $\mathcal{O}(n^2 \times n^3) = \mathcal{O}(n^5)$ —a *polynomial* rate of growth, and thus a spectacular improvement over our exponential first attempt.

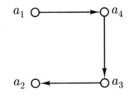

Figure 1-10

Example 1.6.3: Let us see how the new algorithm performs on the graph in Figure 1-10. We start in the first line with the graph plus all self-loops. Suppose that the search for triples (a_i, a_j, a_k) that violate transitivity is conducted in the "natural" order

$$(a_1, a_1, a_1), (a_1, a_1, a_2), \ldots, (a_1, a_1, a_4), (a_1, a_2, a_1), (a_1, a_2, a_2), \ldots, (a_4, a_4, a_4).$$

The first violation thus discovered is (a_1, a_4, a_3), so edge (a_1, a_3) is added. We next start checking all triples from the beginning —because the introduction of (a_1, a_3) may have caused a violation of transitivity in a triple that was examined in the previous iteration. Indeed, the next violation discovered is (a_1, a_3, a_2), and so (a_1, a_2) is added. We start once again from the beginning, this time to discover a violation for (a_4, a_3, a_2) —edge (a_4, a_2) is added. In the next iteration we go through all triples without discovering a violation, and hence we conclude that we have computed the reflexive transitive closure of the graph.$\Diamond$

This example illustrates the source of our algorithm's relative inefficiency, reflected in the steep n^5 growth of its complexity: A triple (a_i, a_j, a_k) must be tested again and again for possible violation of transitivity, since a newly inserted pair may create new violations *in triples that have been already checked.*

Can we do better? In particular, is there a way to order the triples so that newly added pairs never introduce transitivity violations in the already examined triples? Such an ordering would yield an $\mathcal{O}(n^3)$ algorithm, because each triple would then have to be examined once and only once.

As it turns out, such an ordering is possible: We order all triples (a_i, a_j, a_k) to be searched in *increasing j* —the middle index! We first look systematically for violations of transitivity of the form (a_i, a_1, a_k); those that are found are corrected by adding the appropriate pairs, and the search continues from the point it stopped. Once all triples of the form (a_i, a_1, a_k) have been examined, we look at all triples of the form (a_i, a_2, a_k), then (a_i, a_3, a_k), and so on. The precise order in which the triples within each group are examined is immaterial. Once we examine the last group, all triples of the form (a_i, a_n, a_k), then we stop, having computed the reflexive transitive closure. The full algorithm is this:

> Initially $R^* := R \cup \{(a_i, a_i) : a_i \in A\}$
> for each $j = 1, 2, \ldots, n$ do
>   for each $i = 1, 2, \ldots, n$ and $k = 1, 2, \ldots, n$ do
>   if $(a_i, a_j), (a_j, a_k) \in R^*$ but $(a_i, a_k) \notin R^*$ then add (a_i, a_k) to R^*.

Why does this idea work? Consider a path $(a_{i_0}, a_{i_1}, \ldots, a_{i_{k-1}}, a_{i_k})$ from a_{i_0} to a_{i_k}, where $1 \leq i_j \leq n$ for all j. Define the *rank* of the path to be the largest integer among $i_1, \ldots, i_{k-1}$; that is, the largest index appearing in any intermediate node. Trivial paths, such as edges and self-loops, have rank zero, as they have no intermediate nodes.

With this terminology we can argue about the correctness of our latest algorithm. In particular, we can prove the following statement: *For each $j =$*

$0, \ldots, n$, *immediately after the jth execution of the outer loop, R^* contains all pairs (a_i, a_k) such that there is a path of rank j or less from a_i to a_k in R.* Notice that, since all paths have rank at most n, this implies that in the end all pairs joined by any path will have been added in R^*.

The proof of this statement is by induction on j. The result is certainly true when $j = 0$ —no iterations yet, and accordingly R^* contains only pairs connected by trivial paths, of rank 0. For the induction hypothesis, suppose that the result holds for j up to some value, say $m < n$, and consider the $m + 1$st iteration. We must show that the $m + 1$st iteration adds to R^* precisely those pairs that are connected in R by paths of rank equal to $m + 1$, that is, in which the highest-indexed node is a_{m+1}. If two nodes a_i and a_k are connected by such a path, then they must be connected by such a path in which a_{m+1} appears exactly once —if a_{m+1} appears more than once, then omit the portion of the path between the first and the last appearance— while all other intermediate nodes are indexed m or less. And such a path would consist of a path of rank m or less from a_i to a_{m+1}, followed by a path of rank m or less from a_{m+1} to a_k. By the induction hypothesis, both pairs (a_i, a_{m+1}) and (a_{m+1}, a_k) must be in R^* at this point. Therefore, the algorithm will discover that $(a_i, a_{m+1}), (a_{m+1}, a_k) \in R^*$, but $(a_i, a_k) \notin R^*$, and will add the pair (a_i, a_k) to R^*. Conversely, the $m + 1$st iteration will add to R^* only pairs (a_i, a_j) that are connected by a path of rank exactly $m + 1$. The algorithm is correct.

Example 1.6.3 (continued): If we apply this algorithm to the graph in Figure 1-10, no edges are added when $j = 1$ and $j = 2$. Then when $j = 3$ the edge (a_4, a_2) is added, and when $j = 4$ the edges (a_1, a_3) and (a_1, a_4) are added.$\Diamond$

Closure Properties and Closures

The transitive closure of a relation is just one instance of an important style of defining larger sets (or relations) starting from smaller ones.

Definition 1.6.3: Let D be a set, let $n \geq 0$, and let $R \subseteq D^{n+1}$ be a $(n + 1)$-ary relation on D. Then a subset B of D is said to be **closed under** R if $b_{n+1} \in B$ whenever $b_1, \ldots, b_n \in B$ and $(b_1, \ldots, b_n, b_{n+1}) \in R$. Any property of the form "the set B is closed under relations $R_1, R_2, \ldots, R_m$" is called a **closure property** of B.

Example 1.6.4: The set of a person's ancestors is closed under the relation

$$\{(a, b) : a \text{ and } b \text{ are persons, and } b \text{ is a parent of } a\},$$

since the parent of an ancestor is also an ancestor.$\Diamond$

Example 1.6.5: Let A be a fixed set. We say that set S satisfies the *inclusion property associated with A* if $A \subseteq S$. Any inclusion property is a closure property, by taking the relation R to be the unary relation $\{(a) : a \in A\}$ (notice that we must take $n = 0$ in Definition 1.6.3).$\Diamond$

Example 1.6.6: We shall occasionally say that a set $A \subseteq D$ is closed under a *function $f : D^k \mapsto D$*. There should be no mystery as to what this means, since a function is a special kind of relation. For example, we may say that the natural numbers are *closed under addition*. We mean that for any $m, n \in \mathbf{N}$ we also have $m + n \in \mathbf{N}$ —since $(m, n, m + n)$ is a triple in the "addition relation" over the natural numbers. $\mathbf{N}$ is also closed under multiplication, but it is not closed under subtraction.$\Diamond$

Example 1.6.7: Since relations are sets, we can speak of one relation as being closed under one or more others. Let D be a set, let Q be the ternary relation on D^2 (that is, a subset of $(D \times D)^3$) such that

$$Q = \{((a, b), (b, c), (a, c)) : a, b, c \in D\}.$$

Then a relation $R \subseteq D \times D$ is closed under Q if and only if it is transitive. We conclude that transitivity is a closure property. On the other hand, reflexivity is a closure property, because it is the inclusion property of the set $\{(d, d) : d \in D\}$.$\Diamond$

A common type of mathematical construction is to pass from a set A to *the minimal set B that contains A and has property P*. By "minimal set B" we mean "a set B that does not properly include any other set B' that also contains A and has property P." Care must be taken, when a definition of this form is used, that the set B is well defined, that is, that there exists only one such minimal set. Since a set of sets can have many minimal elements or none at all, whether B is well defined depends on the nature of property P. For example, if P is the property "has either b or c as an element" and $A = \{a\}$, then B is not well defined since both $\{a, b\}$ and $\{a, c\}$ are minimal sets with A as a subset and with property P.

However, as the following result guarantees, if P is a closure property, then the set B is always well defined:

Theorem 1.6.1: *Let P be a closure property defined by relations on a set D, and let A be a subset of D. Then there is a unique minimal set B that contains A and has property P.*

Proof: Consider the set of all subsets of D that are closed under $R_1, \ldots, R_m$ and that have A as a subset. We call this set of sets $\mathcal{S}$. We need to show that $\mathcal{S}$

has a unique minimal element B. It is easy to see that $\mathcal{S}$ is nonempty, since it contains the "universe" D —itself trivially closed under each R_i, and certainly containing A.

Consider then the set B which is the intersection of all sets in $\mathcal{S}$,

$$B = \bigcap \mathcal{S}.$$

First, B is well defined, because it is the intersection of a non-empty collection of sets. Also, it is easy to see that it contains A —since all sets in $\mathcal{S}$ do. We next claim that B is closed under all R_i's. Suppose that $a_1, \ldots, a_{n_i-1} \in B$, and $(a_1, \ldots, a_{n_i-1}, a_{n_i}) \in R_i$. Since B is the intersection of all sets in $\mathcal{S}$, it follows that all sets in $\mathcal{S}$ contain $a_1, \ldots, a_{n_i-1}$. But since all sets in $\mathcal{S}$ are closed under R_i, they all also contain a_{n_i}. Therefore B must contain a_{n_i}, and hence B is closed under R_i. Finally B is minimal, because there can be no proper subset B' of B that has these properties (B' contains A and is closed under the R_i's). Because then B' would be a member of $\mathcal{S}$, and thus it would include B. ∎

We call B in Theorem 1.6.1 the **closure** of A under the relations $R_1, \ldots, R_m$.

Example 1.6.8: The set of all your ancestors (where we assume that each person is an ancestor of her- or himself) is the closure of the singleton set containing only yourself under the relation $\{(a, b) : a$ and b are persons, and b is a parent of $a\}$.◇

Example 1.6.9: The set of natural numbers $\mathbf{N}$ is the closure under addition of the set $\{0, 1\}$. $\mathbf{N}$ is closed under addition and multiplication, but not under subtraction. The set of integers (positive, negative, and zero) is the closure of $\mathbf{N}$ under subtraction.◇

Example 1.6.10: The reflexive, transitive closure of a binary relation R over some finite set A defined as

$$R^* = \{(a, b) : \text{there is a path in } R \text{ from } a \text{ to } b\}$$

(recall Definition 1.6.1) richly deserves its name: It turns out that it is the closure of R under transitivity and reflexivity —both closure properties.

First, R^* is reflexive and transitive; for there is a trivial path from a to a for any element a, and if there is a path from a to b, and a path from b to c, then there is a path from a to c. Also, clearly $R \subseteq R^*$, because there is a path from a to b whenever $(a, b) \in R$.

Finally, R^* is minimal. For let $(a, b) \in R^*$. Since $(a, b) \in R^*$, there is a path $(a = a_1, \ldots, a_k = b)$ from a to b. It follows by induction on k that (a, b) must belong to any relation that includes R and is transitive and reflexive.

The reflexive, transitive closure of a binary relation is only one of several possible closures. For example, the *transitive closure* of a relation R, denoted R^+, is the set of all (a, b) such that there is a *nontrivial* path from a to b in R —it need not be reflexive. And the *reflexive, symmetric, transitive closure* of any relation (there is no special symbol) is always an equivalence relation. As we shall show next, there are polynomial algorithms for computing all of these closures.◊

Any closure property over a finite set can be computed in polynomial time! Suppose that we are given relations $R_1 \subseteq D^{r_1}, \dots, R_k \subseteq D^{r_k}$ of various arities over the finite set D, and a set $A \subseteq D$; we are asked to compute the closure A^* of A under $R_1, \dots, R_k$. This can be carried out in polynomial time by a straightforward generalization of the $\mathcal{O}(n^5)$ algorithm we devised for the transitive closure problem in the last subsection:

> Initially $A^* := A$
> while there is an index i, $1 \leq i \leq k$, and r_i elements $a_{j_1}, \dots, a_{j_{r_i-1}} \in A^*$
>   and $a_{j_{r_i}} \in D - A^*$ such that $(a_{j_1}, \dots, a_{j_{r_i}}) \in R_i$ do:
>   add $a_{j_{r_i}}$ to A^*.

It is a straightforward extension of our argument for the transitive closure algorithm, which we leave as an exercise (Problem 1.6.9), to show that the above algorithm is correct, and that it terminates after $\mathcal{O}(n^{r+1})$ steps, where $n = |D|$ and r is the largest integer among $r_1, \dots, r_k$. It follows that the closure of any given finite set under any closure property defined in terms of given relations *of fixed arity* can be computed in polynomial time. As a matter of fact, in Chapter 7 we shall prove a very interesting *converse* statement: *Any* polynomial-time algorithm can be rendered as the computation of the closure of a set under some relations of fixed arity. In other words, the polynomial algorithm for closure shown above is *the mother of all polynomial algorithms*.

Problems for Section 1.6

1.6.1. Are the following sets closed under the following operations? If not, what are the respective closures?
  (a) The odd integers under multiplication.
  (b) The positive integers under division.
  (c) The negative integers under subtraction.
  (d) The negative integers under multiplication.
  (e) The odd integers under division.

1.6.2. What is the reflexive transitive closure R^* of the relation $R = \{(a, b), (a, c), (a, d), (d, c), (d, e)\}$? Draw a directed graph representing R^*.

$A = \{a, b, c, d, e\}$ R relat- of A^2

1.6.3. Is the transitive closure of the symmetric closure of a binary relation necessarily reflexive? Prove it or give a counterexample.

1.6.4. Let $R \subseteq A \times A$ be any binary relation.
   (a) Let $Q = \{(a,b) : a,b \in A$ and there are paths in R from a to b and from b to $a\}$. Show that Q is an equivalence relation on A.
   (b) Let Π be the partition of A corresponding to the equivalence relation Q. Let $\mathcal{R}$ be the relation $\{(S,T) : S,T \in \Pi$ and there is a path in R from some member of S to some member of $T\}$. Show that $\mathcal{R}$ is a partial order on Π.

1.6.5. Give an example of a binary relation that is not reflexive but has a transitive closure that is reflexive.

1.6.6. Recall the three functions in the beginning of the subsection on rates of growth:

$$f(n) = 1,000,000 \cdot n; \quad g(n) = 10 \cdot n^3; \quad h(n) = 2^n.$$

What are appropriate constants c and d for the inclusions $f(n) \in \mathcal{O}(g(n))$, $f(n) \in \mathcal{O}(h(n))$, and $g(n) \in \mathcal{O}(h(n))$? What is the smallest integer n such that the values $f(n) \leq g(n) \leq h(n)$?

1.6.7. Arrange these functions in order of increasing rate of growth. Identify any functions with the same rate of growth:

$$n^2, 2^n, n\lceil \log n \rceil, n!, 4^n, n^n, n^{\lceil \log n \rceil}, 2^{2^n}, 2^{2n}, 2^{2^{n+1}}.$$

1.6.8. You have five algorithms for a problem, with these running times:

$$10^6 n, \quad 10^4 n^2, \quad n^4, \quad 2^n, \quad n!$$

   (a) Your computer executes 10^8 steps per second. What is the largest size n you can solve by each algorithm in a second?
   (b) In a day? (Assume that a day is 10^5 seconds).
   (c) How would the numbers in (a) and (b) change if you bought a computer ten times faster?

1.6.9. Show that the algorithm given in the end of this section correctly computes the closure of a set $A \subseteq D$ under the relations $R_1 \subseteq D^{r_1}, \ldots, R_k \subseteq D^{r_k}$ in $\mathcal{O}(n^r)$ time, where $n = |D|$, and r is the maximum of the arities $r_1, \ldots, r_k$. (*Hint:* The argument is a straightforward generalization of the one for the $\mathcal{O}(n^5)$ transitive closure algorithm.)

1.7 | ALPHABETS AND LANGUAGES

The algorithms we studied informally in the last section have much that is left vague. For example, we have not specified exactly how the relations R and R^* that need to be accessed and modified are represented and stored. In computational practice, such *data* are encoded in the computer's memory as strings of bits or other symbols appropriate for manipulation by a computer. The mathematical study of the theory of computation must therefore begin by understanding *the mathematics of strings of symbols*.

We start with the notion of an **alphabet**: a finite set of **symbols**. An example is, naturally, the Roman alphabet $\{a, b, \ldots, z\}$. An alphabet particularly pertinent to the theory of computation is the **binary alphabet** $\{0, 1\}$. In fact, any object can be in an alphabet; from a formal point of view, an alphabet is simply a finite set of any sort. For simplicity, however, we use as symbols only letters, numerals, and other common characters such as $, or #.

A **string** over an alphabet is a finite sequence of symbols from the alphabet. Instead of writing strings with parentheses and commas, as we have written other sequences, we simply juxtapose the symbols. Thus *watermelon* is a string over the alphabet $\{a, b, \ldots, z\}$, and 0111011 is a string over $\{0, 1\}$. Also, using the natural isomorphism, we identify a string of only one symbol with the symbol itself; thus the symbol a is the same as the string a. A string may have no symbols at all; in this case it is called the **empty string** and is denoted by e. We generally use u, v, x, y, z, and Greek letters to denote strings; for example, we might use w as a name for the string abc. Of course, to avoid confusion it is a good practice to refrain from using as symbols letters we also use as names of strings. The set of all strings, including the empty string, over an alphabet Σ is denoted by Σ^*.

The **length** of a string is its length as a sequence; thus the length of the string $acrd$ is 4. We denote the length of a string w by $|w|$; thus $|101| = 3$ and $|e| = 0$. Alternatively (that is, via a natural isomorphism) a string $w \in \Sigma^*$ can be considered as a function $w : \{1, \ldots, |w|\} \mapsto \Sigma$; the value of $w(j)$, where $1 \leq j \leq |w|$, is the symbol in the jth position of w. For example, if $w = accordion$, then $w(3) = w(2) = c$, and $w(1) = a$. This alternative viewpoint brings out a possible point of confusion. Naturally, the symbol c in the third position is identical to that in the second. If, however, we need to distinguish identical symbols at different positions in a string, we shall refer to them as different **occurrences** of the symbol. That is, the symbol $\sigma \in \Sigma$ occurs in the jth position of the string $w \in \Sigma^*$ if $w(j) = \sigma$.

Two strings over the same alphabet can be combined to form a third by the operation of **concatenation**. The concatenation of strings x and y, written $x \circ y$ or simply xy, is the string x followed by the string y; formally, $w = x \circ y$ if and only if $|w| = |x| + |y|$, $w(j) = x(j)$ for $j = 1, \ldots, |x|$, and $w(|x| + j) = y(j)$ for $j = 1, \ldots, |y|$. For example, $01 \circ 001 = 01001$, and $beach \circ boy = beachboy$. Of course, $w \circ e = e \circ w = w$ for any string w. And concatenation is associative: $(wx)y = w(xy)$ for any strings w, x, and y. A string v is a **substring** of a string w if and only if there are strings x and y such that $w = xvy$. Both x and y could be e, so every string is a substring of itself; and taking $x = w$ and $v = y = e$, we see that e is a substring of every string. If $w = xv$ for some x, then v is a **suffix** of w; if $w = vy$ for some y, then v is a **prefix** of w. Thus $road$ is a prefix of $roadrunner$, a suffix of $abroad$, and a substring of both these and of $broader$. A string may have several occurrences of the same substring; for example, $ababab$ has three occurrences of ab and two of $abab$.

For each string w and each natural number i, the string w^i is defined as

$$w^0 = e, \quad \text{the empty string}$$
$$w^{i+1} = w^i \circ w \quad \text{for each } i \geq 0$$

Thus $w^1 = w$, and $do^2 = dodo$.

This definition is our first instance of a very common type: **definition by induction**. We have already seen *proofs* by induction, and the underlying idea is much the same. There is a basis case of the definition, here the definition of w^i for $i = 0$; then when that which is being defined has been specified for all $j \leq i$, it is defined for $j = i + 1$. In the example above, w^{i+1} is defined in terms of w^i. To see exactly how any case of the definition can be traced back to the basis case, consider the example of do^2. According to the definition (with $i = 1$), $(do)^2 = (do)^1 \circ do$. Again according to the definition (with $i = 0$) $(do)^1 = (do)^0 \circ do$. Now the basis case applies: $(do)^0 = e$. So $(do)^2 = (e \circ do) \circ do = dodo$.

The **reversal** of a string w, denoted by w^R, is the string "spelled backwards": for example, $reverse^R = esrever$. A formal definition can be given by induction on the length of a string:

(1) If w is a string of length 0, then $w^R = w = e$.
(2) If w is a string of length $n + 1 > 0$, then $w = ua$ for some $a \in \Sigma$, and $w^R = au^R$.

Let us use this definition to illustrate how a proof by induction can depend on a definition by induction. We shall show that for any strings w and x, $(wx)^R = x^R w^R$. For example, $(dogcat)^R = (cat)^R(dog)^R = tacgod$. We proceed by induction on the length of x.

Basis Step. $|x| = 0$. Then $x = e$, and $(wx)^R = (we)^R = w^R = ew^R = e^R w^R = x^R w^R$.

Induction Hypothesis. If $|x| \leq n$, then $(wx)^R = x^R w^R$.

Induction Step. Let $|x| = n + 1$. Then $x = ua$ for some $u \in \Sigma^*$ and $a \in \Sigma$ such that $|u| = n$.

$$
\begin{aligned}
(wx)^R &= (w(ua))^R \quad \text{since } x = ua \\
&= ((wu)a)^R \quad \text{since concatenation is associative} \\
&= a(wu)^R \quad \text{by the definition of the reversal of } (wu)a \\
&= au^R w^R \quad \text{by the induction hypothesis} \\
&= (ua)^R w^R \quad \text{by the definition of the reversal of } ua \\
&= x^R w^R \quad \text{since } x = ua
\end{aligned}
$$

Now we move from the study of individual strings to the study of finite and infinite *sets* of strings. The simple models of computing machines we shall soon be studying will be characterized in terms of regularities in the way they handle many different strings, so it is important first to understand general ways of describing and combining classes of strings.

Any set of strings over an alphabet Σ —that is, any subset of Σ^*— will be called a **language**. Thus Σ^*, $\emptyset$, and Σ are languages. Since a language is simply a special kind of set, we can specify a finite language by listing all its strings. For example, $\{aba, czr, d, f\}$ is a language over $\{a, b, \ldots, z\}$. However, most languages of interest are infinite, so that listing all the strings is not possible. Languages that might be considered are $\{0, 01, 011, 0111, \ldots\}$, $\{w \in \{0, 1\}^* : w \text{ has an equal number of 0's and 1's}\}$, and $\{w \in \Sigma^* : w = w^R\}$. Thus we shall specify infinite languages by the scheme

$$ L = \{w \in \Sigma^* : w \text{ has property } P\}, $$

following the general form we have used for specifying infinite sets.

If Σ is a finite alphabet, then Σ^* is certainly infinite; but is it a countably infinite set? It is not hard to see that this is indeed the case. To construct a bijection $f : \mathbf{N} \mapsto \Sigma^*$, first fix some ordering of the alphabet, say $\Sigma = \{a_1, \ldots, a_n\}$, where $a_1, \ldots, a_n$ are distinct. The members of Σ^* can then be enumerated in the following way.

(1) For each $k \geq 0$, all strings of length k are enumerated before all strings of length $k + 1$.
(2) The n^k strings of length exactly k are enumerated **lexicographically**, that is, $a_{i_1} \ldots a_{i_k}$ precedes $a_{j_1} \ldots a_{j_k}$, provided that, for some m, $0 \leq m \leq k - 1$, $i_\ell = j_\ell$ for $\ell = 1, \ldots, m$, and $i_{m+1} < j_{m+1}$.

For example, if $\Sigma = \{0, 1\}$, the order would be as follows:

$$ e, 0, 1, 00, 01, 10, 11, 000, 001, 010, 011, \ldots $$

If Σ is the Roman alphabet and the ordering of $\Sigma = \{a_1, \ldots, a_{26}\}$ is the usual one $\{a, \ldots, z\}$, then the lexicographic order for strings of equal length is the order used in dictionaries; however, the ordering described by (1) and (2) for all strings in Σ^* differs from the dictionary ordering by listing shorter strings before longer ones.

Since languages are sets, they can be combined by the set operations of union, intersection, and difference. When a particular alphabet Σ is understood from context, we shall write $\overline{A}$ —the **complement** of A— instead of the difference $\Sigma^* - A$.

In addition, certain operations are meaningful only for languages. The first of these is the **concatenation of languages**. If L_1 and L_2 are languages over Σ, their concatenation is $L = L_1 \circ L_2$, or simply $L = L_1 L_2$, where

$$L = \{w \in \Sigma^* : w = x \circ y \text{ for some } x \in L_1 \text{ and } y \in L_2\}.$$

For example, if $\Sigma = \{0, 1\}$, $L_1 = \{w \in \Sigma^* : w \text{ has an even number of 0's}\}$ and $L_2 = \{w : w \text{ starts with a 0 and the rest of the symbols are 1's}\}$, then $L_1 \circ L_2 = \{w : w \text{ has an odd number of 0's}\}$.

Another language operation is the **Kleene star** of a language L, denoted by L^*. L^* is the set of all strings obtained by concatenating zero or more strings from L. (The concatenation of zero strings is e, and the concatenation of one string is the string itself.) Thus,

$$L^* = \{w \in \Sigma^* : w = w_1 \circ \cdots \circ w_k \text{ for some } k \geq 0 \text{ and some } w_1, \ldots, w_k \in L\}.$$

For example, if $L = \{01, 1, 100\}$, then $110001110011 \in L^*$, since $110001110011 = 1 \circ 100 \circ 01 \circ 1 \circ 100 \circ 1 \circ 1$, and each of these strings is in L.

Note that the use of Σ^* to denote the set of all strings over Σ is consistent with the notation for the Kleene star of Σ, regarded as a finite language. That is, if we let $L = \Sigma$ and apply the definition above, then Σ^* is the set of all strings that can be written as $w_1 \circ \cdots \circ w_k$ for some $k \geq 0$ and some $w_1, \ldots, w_k \in \Sigma$. Since the w_i are then simply individual symbols in Σ, it follows that Σ^* is, as originally defined, the set of all finite strings whose symbols are in Σ.

For another extreme example, observe that $\emptyset^* = \{e\}$. For let $L = \emptyset$ in the above definition. The only possible concatenation $w_1 \circ w_2 \circ \cdots \circ w_k$ with $k \geq 0$ and $w_1, \ldots, w_k \in L$ is that with $k = 0$, that is, the concatenation of zero strings; so the sole member of L^* in this case is e!

As a final example, let us show that if L is the language $\{w \in \{0, 1\}^* : w \text{ has an unequal number of 0's and 1's}\}$, then $L^* = \{0, 1\}^*$. To see this, first note that for any languages L_1 and L_2, if $L_1 \subseteq L_2$, then $L_1^* \subseteq L_2^*$ as is evident from the definition of Kleene star. Second, $\{0, 1\} \subseteq L$, since each of 0 and 1, regarded as a string, has an unequal number of 0's and 1's. Hence $\{0, 1\}^* \subseteq L^*$; but $L^* \subseteq \{0, 1\}^*$ by definition, so $L^* = \{0, 1\}^*$.

We write L^+ for the language LL^*. Equivalently, L^+ is the language

$$\{w \in \Sigma^* : w = w_1 \circ w_2 \circ \cdots \circ w_k \text{ for some } k \geq 1 \text{ and some } w_1, \ldots, w_k \in L\}.$$

Notice that L^+ can be considered as the *closure* of L under the function of concatenation. That is, L^+ is the smallest language that includes L and all strings that are concatenations of strings in L.

Problems for Section 1.7

1.7.1. (a) Prove, using the definition of concatenation given in the text, that concatenation of strings is associative.
   (b) Give an inductive definition of the concatenation of strings.
   (c) Using the inductive definition from (b), prove that the concatenation of strings is associative.

1.7.2. Prove each of the following using the inductive definition of reversal given in the text.
   (a) $(w^R)^R = w$ for any string w.
   (b) If v is a substring of w, then v^R is a substring of w^R.
   (c) $(w^i)^R = (w^R)^i$ for any string w and $i \geq 0$.

1.7.3. Let $\Sigma = \{a_1, \ldots, a_{26}\}$ be the Roman alphabet. Carefully define the binary relation $<$ on Σ^* such that $x < y$ if and only if x would precede y in a standard dictionary.

1.7.4. Show each of the following.
   (a) $\{e\}^* = \{e\}$
   (b) For any alphabet Σ and any $L \subseteq \Sigma^*$, $(L^*)^* = L^*$.
   (c) If a and b are distinct symbols, then $\{a, b\}^* = \{a\}^*(\{b\}\{a\}^*)^*$.
   (d) If Σ is any alphabet, $e \in L_1 \subseteq \Sigma^*$ and $e \in L_2 \subseteq \Sigma^*$, then $(L_1 \Sigma^* L_2)^* = \Sigma^*$.
   (e) For any language L, $\emptyset L = L\emptyset = \emptyset$.

1.7.5. Give some examples of strings in, and not in, these sets, where $\Sigma = \{a, b\}$.
   (a) $\{w : \text{ for some } u \in \Sigma\Sigma, w = uu^R u\}$
   (b) $\{w : ww = www\}$
   (c) $\{w : \text{ for some } u, v \in \Sigma^*, uvw = wvu\}$
   (d) $\{w : \text{ for some } u \in \Sigma^*, www = uu\}$

1.7.6. Under what circumstances is $L^+ = L^* - \{e\}$?

1.7.7. The Kleene star of a language L is the closure of L under which relations?

1.8 | FINITE REPRESENTATIONS OF LANGUAGES

A central issue in the theory of computation is the representation of languages by finite specifications. Naturally, any finite language is amenable to finite representation by exhaustive enumeration of all the strings in the language. The issue becomes challenging only when infinite languages are considered.

Let us be somewhat more precise about the notion of "finite representation of a language." The first point to be made is that any such representation must itself be a string, a finite sequence of symbols over some alphabet Σ. Second, we certainly want different languages to have different representations, otherwise the term *representation* could hardly be considered appropriate. But these two requirements already imply that the possibilities for finite representation are severely limited. For the set Σ^* of strings over an alphabet Σ is countably infinite, so the number of possible representations of languages is countably infinite. (This would remain true even if we were not bound to use a particular alphabet Σ, so long as the total number of available symbols was countably infinite.) On the other hand, the set of all possible languages over a given alphabet Σ —that is, 2^{Σ^*}— is uncountably infinite, since $2^{\mathbf{N}}$, and hence the power set of any countably infinite set is not countably infinite. With only a countable number of representations and an uncountable number of things to represent, we are unable to represent all languages finitely. Thus, the most we can hope for is to find finite representations, of one sort or another, for at least some of the more interesting languages.

This is our first result in the theory of computation: No matter how powerful are the methods we use for representing languages, only countably many languages can be represented, so long as the representations themselves are finite. There being uncountably many languages in all, the vast majority of them will inevitably be missed under any finite representational scheme.

Of course, this is not the last thing we shall have to say along these lines. We shall describe several ways of describing and representing languages, each more powerful than the last in the sense that each is capable of describing languages the previous one cannot. This hierarchy does not contradict the fact that all these finite representational methods are inevitably limited in scope for the reasons just explained.

We shall also want to derive ways of exhibiting particular languages that cannot be represented by the various representational methods we study. We know that the world of languages is inhabited by vast numbers of such unrepresentable specimens, but, strangely perhaps, it can be exceedingly difficult to catch one, put it on display, and document it. Diagonalization arguments will eventually assist us here.

To begin our study of finite representations, we consider expressions —

strings of symbols— that describe how languages can be built up by using the
operations described in the previous section.

Example 1.8.1: Let $L = \{w \in \{0,1\}^* : w$ has two or three occurrences of 1,
the first and second of which are not consecutive}. This language can be described using only singleton sets and the symbols $\cup$, $\circ$, and * as

$$\{0\}^* \circ \{1\} \circ \{0\}^* \circ \{0\} \circ \{1\} \circ \{0\}^* \circ ((\{1\} \circ \{0\}^*) \cup \emptyset^*).$$

It is not hard to see that the language represented by the above expression is
precisely the language L defined above. The important thing to notice is that the
only symbols used in this representation are the braces { and }, the parentheses
(and), $\emptyset$, 0, 1, *, $\circ$, and $\cup$. In fact, we may dispense with the braces and $\circ$ and
write simply

$$L = 0^*10^*010^*(10^* \cup \emptyset^*).$$

$\Diamond$

Roughly speaking, an expression such as the one for L in Example 1.8.1 is
called a **regular expression**. That is, a regular expression describes a language
exclusively by means of single symbols and $\emptyset$, combined perhaps with the symbols
$\cup$ and *, possibly with the aid of parentheses. But in order to keep straight the
expressions about which we are talking and the "mathematical English" we are
using for discussing them, we must tread rather carefully. Instead of using $\cup$,
*, and $\emptyset$, which are the names in this book for certain operations and sets, we
introduce special symbols U, *, and $\oslash$, which should be regarded for the moment
as completely free of meaningful overtones, just like the symbols a, b, and 0 used
in earlier examples. In the same way, we introduce special symbols (and)
instead of the parentheses (and) we have been using for doing mathematics.
The regular expressions over an alphabet Σ^* are all strings over the alphabet
$\Sigma \cup \{(,), \oslash, \mathsf{U}, ^\star\}$ that can be obtained as follows.

(1) $\oslash$ and each member of Σ is a regular expression.
(2) If α and β are regular expressions, then so is $(\alpha\beta)$.
(3) If α and β are regular expressions, then so is $(\alpha\mathsf{U}\beta)$.
(4) If α is a regular expression, then so is $\alpha^\star$.
(5) Nothing is a regular expression unless it follows from (1) through (4).

Every regular expression represents a language, according to the interpreta-
tion of the symbols U and * as set union and Kleene star, and of juxtaposition of
expressions as concatenation. Formally, the relation between regular expressions
and the languages they represent is established by a function $\mathcal{L}$, such that if α
is any regular expression, then $\mathcal{L}(\alpha)$ is the language represented by α. That is,
$\mathcal{L}$ is a function from strings to languages. The function $\mathcal{L}$ is defined as follows.

(1) $\mathcal{L}(\oslash) = \emptyset$, and $\mathcal{L}(a) = \{a\}$ for each $a \in \Sigma$.

(2) If α and β are regular expressions, then $\mathcal{L}((\alpha\beta)) = \mathcal{L}(\alpha)\mathcal{L}(\beta)$.

(3) If α and β are regular expressions, then $\mathcal{L}((\alpha\cup\beta)) = \mathcal{L}(\alpha) \cup \mathcal{L}(\beta)$.

(4) If α is a regular expression, then $\mathcal{L}(\alpha^\star) = \mathcal{L}(\alpha)^*$.

Statement 1 defines $\mathcal{L}(\alpha)$ for each regular expression α that consists of a single symbol; if $n > 1$, then (2) through (4) define $\mathcal{L}(\alpha)$ for regular expressions of some length in terms of $\mathcal{L}(\alpha')$ for one or two regular expressions α' of smaller length. Thus every regular expression is associated in this way with some language.

Example 1.8.2: What is $\mathcal{L}(((a\cup b)^\star a))$? We have the following.

$$
\begin{aligned}
\mathcal{L}(((a\cup b)^\star a)) &= \mathcal{L}((a\cup b)^\star)\mathcal{L}(a) \text{ by}(2) \\
&= \mathcal{L}((a\cup b)^\star)\{a\} \text{ by } (1) \\
&= \mathcal{L}((a\cup b))^* \{a\} \text{ by } (4) \\
&= (\mathcal{L}(a) \cup \mathcal{L}(b))^* \{a\} \text{ by } (3) \\
&= (\{a\} \cup \{b\})^* \{a\} \text{ by } (1) \text{ twice} \\
&= \{a, b\}^* \{a\} \\
&= \{w \in \{a, b\}^* : w \text{ ends with an } a\}
\end{aligned}
$$

$\Diamond$

Example 1.8.3: What language is represented by $(c^\star(a\cup(bc^\star))^\star)$? This regular expression represents the set of all strings over $\{a, b, c\}$ that do not have the substring ac. Clearly no string in $\mathcal{L}((c^\star(a\cup(bc^\star))^\star))$ can contain the substring ac, since each occurrence of a in such a string is either at the end of the string, or is followed by another occurrence of a, or is followed by an occurrence of b. On the other hand, let w be a string with no substring ac. Then w begins with zero or more c's. If they are removed, the result is a string with no sub-string ac and not beginning with c. Any such string is in $\mathcal{L}((a\cup(bc^\star)))$; for it can be read, left to right, as a sequence of a's, b's, and c's, with any blocks of c's immediately following b's (not following a's, and not at the beginning of the string). Therefore $w \in \mathcal{L}((c^\star(a\cup(bc^\star))^\star))$.$\Diamond$

Example 1.8.4: $(0^\star\cup(((0^\star(1\cup(11)))((00^\star)(1\cup(11)))^\star)0^\star))$ represents the set of all strings over $\{0, 1\}$ that do not have the substring 111.$\Diamond$

Every language that can be represented by a regular expression can be represented by infinitely many of them. For example, α and $(\alpha\cup\emptyset)$ always represent the same language; so do $((\alpha\cup\beta)\cup\gamma)$ and $(\alpha\cup(\beta\cup\gamma))$. Since set union and concatenation are associative operations —that is, since $(L_1 \cup L_2) \cup L_3 = L_1 \cup (L_2 \cup L_3)$ for all L_1, L_2, L_3, and the same for concatenation— we normally omit the extra (and) symbols in regular expressions; for example, we treat $a\cup b\cup c$ as a regular expression even though "officially" it is not. For another example, the regular expression of Example 1.8.4 might be rewritten as $0^\star\cup 0^\star(1\cup 11)(00^\star(1\cup 11))^\star 0^\star$.

Moreover, now that we have shown that regular expressions and the languages they represent can be defined formally and unambiguously, we feel free, when no confusion can result, to blur the distinction between the regular expressions and the "mathematical English" we are using for talking about languages. Thus we may say at one point that a^*b^* is the set of all strings consisting of some number of a's followed by some number of b's —to be precise, we should have written $\{a\}^* \circ \{b\}^*$. At another point, we might say that a^*b^* is a regular expression representing that set; in this case, to be precise, we should have written $(a^\star b^\star)$.

The class of **regular languages** over an alphabet Σ is defined to consist of all languages L such that $L = \mathcal{L}(\alpha)$ for some regular expression α over Σ. That is, regular languages are all languages that can be described by regular expressions. Alternatively, regular languages can be thought of in terms of *closures*. The class of regular languages over Σ is precisely the closure of the set of languages

$$\{\{\sigma\} : \sigma \in \Sigma\} \cup \{\emptyset\}$$

with respect to the functions of union, concatenation, and Kleene star.

We have already seen that regular expressions do describe some nontrivial and interesting languages. Unfortunately, we cannot describe by regular expressions some languages that have very simple descriptions by other means. For example, $\{0^n1^n : n \geq 0\}$ will be shown in Chapter 2 *not* to be regular. Surely any theory of the finite representation of languages will have to accommodate at least such simple languages as this. Thus regular expressions are an inadequate specification method in general.

In search of a general method for finitely specifying languages, we might return to our general scheme

$$L = \{w \in \Sigma^* : w \text{ has property } P\}.$$

But which properties P should we entail? For example, what makes the preceding properties, "w consists of a number of 0's followed by an equal number of 1's" and "w has no occurrence of 111" such obvious candidates? The reader may ponder about the right answer; but let us for now allow *algorithmic properties*, and only these. That is, for a property P of strings to be admissible as a specification of a language, there must be an algorithm for deciding whether a given string belongs to the language. An algorithm that is specifically designed, for some language L, to answer questions of the form "Is string w a member of L?" will be called a **language recognition device**. For example, a device for recognizing the language

$$L = \{w \in \{0,1\}^* : w \text{ does not have } 111 \text{ as a substring}\}.$$

by reading strings, a symbol at a time, from left to right, might operate like this:

Keep a count, which starts at zero and is set back to zero every time a 0 is encountered in the input; add one every time a 1 is encountered in the input; stop with a No answer if the count ever reaches three, and stop with a Yes answer if the whole string is read without the count reaching three.

An alternative and somewhat orthogonal method for specifying a language is to describe how a generic specimen in the language is produced. For example, a regular expression such as $(e \cup b \cup bb)(a \cup ab \cup abb)^*$ may be viewed as a way of *generating* members of a language:

To produce a member of L, first write down either nothing, or b, or bb; then write down a or ab, or abb, and do this any number of times, including zero; all and only members of L can be produced in this way.

Such **language generators** are not algorithms, since they are not designed to answer questions and are not completely explicit about what to do (how are we to choose which of a, ab, or abb is to be written down?) But they are important and useful means of representing languages all the same. The relation between language recognition devices and language generators, both of which are types of finite language specifications, is another major subject of this book.

Problems for Section 1.8

1.8.1. What language is represented by the regular expression $(((a^*a)b)\cup b)$?

1.8.2. Rewrite each of these regular expressions as a simpler expression representing the same set.
(a) $\varnothing^* \cup a^* \cup b^* \cup (a \cup b)^*$
(b) $((a^*b^*)^*(b^*a^*)^*)^*$
(c) $(a^*b)^* \cup (b^*a)^*$
(d) $(a \cup b)^* a(a \cup b)^*$

1.8.3. Let $\Sigma = \{a, b\}$. Write regular expressions for the following sets:
(a) All strings in Σ^* with no more than three a's.
(b) All strings in Σ^* with a number of a's divisible by three.
(c) All strings in Σ^* with exactly one occurrence of the substring aaa.

1.8.4. Prove that if L is regular, then so is $L' = \{w : uw \in L \text{ for some string } u\}$. (Show how to construct a regular expression for L' from one for L.)

1.8.5. Which of the following are true? Explain.
   (a) $baa \in a^*b^*a^*b^*$
   (b) $b^*a^* \cap a^*b^* = a^* \cup b^*$
   (c) $a^*b^* \cap b^*c^* = \emptyset$
   (d) $abcd \in (a(cd)^*b)^*$

1.8.6. The **star height** $h(\alpha)$ of a regular expression α is defined by induction as follows.

$$h(\oslash) = 0$$
$$h(a) = 0 \text{ for each } a \in \Sigma$$
$$h(\alpha \cup \beta) = h(\alpha\beta) = \text{the maximum of } h(\alpha) \text{ and } h(\beta).$$
$$h(\alpha^\star) = h(\alpha) + 1$$

For example, if $\alpha = (((ab)^\star \cup b^\star)^\star \cup a^\star)$, then $h(\alpha) = 2$. Find, in each case, a regular expression which represents the same language and has star height as small as possible.
   (a) $((abc)^\star ab)^\star$
   (b) $(a(ab^\star c)^\star)^\star$
   (c) $(c(a^\star b)^\star)^\star$
   (d) $(a^\star \cup b^\star \cup ab)^\star$
   (e) $(abb^\star a)^\star$

1.8.7. A regular expression is in **disjunctive normal form** if it is of the form $(\alpha_1 \cup \alpha_2 \cup \cdots \cup \alpha_n)$ for some $n \geq 1$, where none of the α_i's contains an occurrence of $\cup$. Show that every regular language is represented by one in disjunctive normal form.

REFERENCES

An excellent source on informal set theory is the book

   ○ P. Halmos   *Naive Set Theory*, Princeton, N.J.: D. Van Nostrand, 1960.

A splendid book on mathematical induction is

   ○ G. Polya   *Induction and Analogy in Mathematics*, Princeton, N.J.: Princeton University Press, 1954.

A number of examples of applications of the pigeonhole principle appear in the first chapter of

   ○ C. L. Liu   *Topics in Combinatorial Mathematics*, Buffalo, N.Y.: Mathematical Association of America, 1972.

Cantor's original diagonalization argument can be found in

   ○ G. Cantor   *Contributions to the Foundations of the Theory of Transfinite Numbers* New York: Dover Publications, 1947.

The $\mathcal{O}$-notation and several variants were introduced in o D. E. Knuth "Big omicron and big omega and big theta," *ACM SIGACT News, 8* (2), pp. 18–23, 1976.

The $\mathcal{O}(n^3)$ algorithm for the reflexive-transitive closure is from

o S. Warshall "A theorem on Boolean matrices," *Journal of the ACM, 9,* 1, pp. 11-12, 1962.

Two books on algorithms and their analysis are

o T. H. Cormen, C. E. Leiserson, R. L. Rivest *Introduction to Algorithms,* Cambridge, Mass.: The MIT Press., 1990, and

o G. Brassard, P. Bratley *Fundamentals of Algorithms,* Englewood Cliffs, N.J.: Prentice Hall, 1996.

Two advanced books on language theory are

o A. Salomaa *Formal Languages* New York: Academic Press, 1973.

o M. A. Harrison *Introduction to Formal Language Theory,* Reading, Massach.: Addison-Wesley, 1978.

2 | Finite Automata

2.1 DETERMINISTIC FINITE AUTOMATA

This book is about mathematical models of computers and algorithms. In this and the next two chapters we shall define increasingly powerful models of computation, more and more sophisticated devices for accepting and generating languages. Seen in the light of the whole development of the book, this chapter will seem a rather humble beginning: Here we take up a severely restricted model of an actual computer called a **finite automaton,**[†] or **finite-state machine**. The finite automaton shares with a real computer the fact that it has a "central processing unit" of fixed, finite capacity. It receives its input as a string, delivered to it on an input tape. It delivers no output at all, except an indication of whether or not the input is considered acceptable. It is, in other words, a language recognition device, as described at the end of Chapter 1. What makes the finite automaton such a restricted model of real computers is the *complete absence of memory* outside its fixed central processor.

Such a simple computational model might at first be considered too trivial to merit serious study: of what use is a computer with no memory? But a finite automaton is not really without memory; it simply has a memory capacity that is fixed "at the factory" and cannot thereafter be expanded. It can be argued that the memory capacity of any computer is limited —by budget constraints, by physical limits, ultimately by the size of the universe. Whether the best mathematical model for a computer is one that has finite memory or one that has unbounded memory is an interesting philosophical question; we shall study both kinds of models, starting with the finite one and later dwelling much more

---

[†] An *automaton* (pronounced: o-**to**-ma-ton, plural: *automata*) is a machine designed to respond to encoded instructions; a robot.

on the unbounded one.

Even if one thinks, as we do, that the correct way to model computers and algorithms is in terms of an unbounded memory capacity, we should first be sure that the theory of finite automata is well understood. It turns out that their theory is rich and elegant, and when we understand it we shall be in a better position to appreciate exactly what the addition of auxiliary memory accomplishes in the way of added computational power.

A further reason for studying finite automata is their applicability to the design of several common types of computer algorithms and programs. For example, the *lexical analysis* phase of a compiler (in which program units such as 'begin' and '+' are identified) is often based on the simulation of a finite automaton. Also, the problem of finding an occurrence of a string within another —for example, whether any of the strings *air, water, earth,* and *fire* occur in the text of *Elements of the Theory of Computation*[†]— can also be solved efficiently by methods originating from the theory of finite automata.

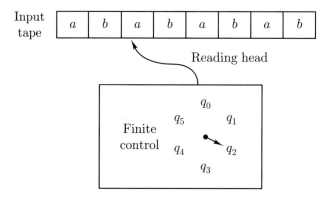

Figure 2-1

Let us now describe the operation of a finite automaton in more detail. Strings are fed into the device by means of an **input tape**, which is divided into squares, with one symbol inscribed in each tape square (see Figure 2-1). The main part of the machine itself is a "black box" with innards that can be, at any specified moment, in one of a finite number of distinct internal **states**. This black box —called the **finite control**— can sense what symbol is written at any position on the input tape by means of a movable **reading head**. Initially, the reading head is placed at the leftmost square of the tape and the finite control is set in a designated **initial state**. At regular intervals the automaton reads one symbol from the input tape and then enters a new state *that depends only on the*

[†] Three of them do.

current state and the symbol just read —this is why we shall call this device a *deterministic* finite automaton, to be contrasted to the *nondeterministic* version introduced in the next section. After reading an input symbol, the reading head moves one square to the right on the input tape so that on the next move it will read the symbol in the next tape square. This process is repeated again and again; a symbol is read, the reading head moves to the right, and the state of the finite control changes. Eventually the reading head reaches the end of the input string. The automaton then indicates its approval or disapproval of what it has read by the state it is in at the end: if it winds up in one of a set of **final states** the input string is considered to be **accepted**. The **language accepted** by the machine is the set of strings it accepts.

When this informal account is boiled down to its mathematical essentials, the following formal definition results.

Definition 2.1.1: A **deterministic finite automaton** is a quintuple $M = (K, \Sigma, \delta, s, F)$ where

> K is a finite set of **states**,
> Σ is an alphabet,
> $s \in K$ is the **initial state**,
> $F \subseteq K$ is the set of **final states**, and
> δ, the **transition function**, is a function from $K \times \Sigma$ to K.

The rules according to which the automaton M picks its next state are encoded into the transition function. Thus if M is in state $q \in K$ and the symbol read from the input tape is $a \in \Sigma$, then $\delta(q, a) \in K$ is the uniquely determined state to which K passes.

Having formalized the basic structure of a deterministic finite automaton, we must next render into mathematical terms the notion of a *computation* by an automaton on an input string. This will be, roughly speaking, a sequence of **configurations** that represent the status of the machine (the finite control, reading head, and input tape) at successive moments. But since a deterministic finite automaton is not allowed to move its reading head back into the part of the input string that has already been read, the portion of the string to the left of the reading head cannot influence the future operation of the machine. Thus a configuration is determined by the current state and the unread part of the string being processed. In other words, a **configuration of a deterministic finite automaton** $(K, \Sigma, \delta, s, F)$ is any element of $K \times \Sigma^*$. For example, the configuration illustrated in Figure 2-1 is $(q_2, ababab)$.

The binary relation $\vdash_M$ holds between two configurations of M if and only if the machine can pass from one to the other as a result of a single move. Thus if (q, w) and (q', w') are two configurations of M, then $(q, w) \vdash_M (q', w')$ if and only if $w = aw'$ for some symbol $a \in \Sigma$, and $\delta(q, a) = q'$. In this case we say that (q, w) **yields** (q', w') **in one step**. Note that in fact $\vdash_M$ is a function from $K \times \Sigma^+$ to $K \times \Sigma^*$, that is, for every configuration except those of the form (q, e) there is a uniquely determined next configuration. A configuration of the form (q, e) signifies that M has consumed all its input, and hence its operation ceases at this point.

We denote the reflexive, transitive closure of $\vdash_M$ by $\vdash_M^*$; $(q, w) \vdash_M^* (q', w')$ is read, (q, w) **yields** (q', w') (after some number, possibly zero, of steps). A string $w \in \Sigma^*$ is said to be **accepted** by M if and only if there is a state $q \in F$ such that $(s, w) \vdash_M^* (q, e)$. Finally, **the language accepted by** M, $L(M)$, is the set of all strings accepted by M.

Example 2.1.1: Let M be the deterministic finite automaton $(K, \Sigma, \delta, s, F)$, where

$$K = \{q_0, q_1\},$$
$$\Sigma = \{a, b\},$$
$$s = q_0,$$
$$F = \{q_0\},$$

and δ is the function tabulated below.

q	σ	$\delta(q, \sigma)$
q_0	a	q_0
q_0	b	q_1
q_1	a	q_1
q_1	b	q_0

It is then easy to see that $L(M)$ is the set of all strings in $\{a, b\}^*$ that have an even number of b's. For M passes from state q_0 to q_1 or from q_1 back to q_0 when a b is read, but M essentially ignores a's, always remaining in its current state when an a is read. Thus M counts b's modulo 2, and since q_0 (the initial state) is also the sole final state, M accepts a string if and only if the number of b's is even.

If M is given the input $aabba$, its initial configuration is $(q_0, aabba)$. Then

$$(q_0, aabba) \vdash_M (q_0, abba)$$
$$\vdash_M (q_0, bba)$$
$$\vdash_M (q_1, ba)$$
$$\vdash_M (q_0, a)$$
$$\vdash_M (q_0, e)$$

Therefore $(q_0, aabba) \vdash_M^* (q_0, e)$, and so $aabba$ is accepted by $M.\diamond$

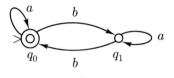

Figure 2-2

The tabular representation of the transition function used in this example is not the clearest description of a machine. We generally use a more convenient graphical representation called the **state diagram** (Figure 2-2). The state diagram is a directed graph, with certain additional information incorporated into the picture. States are represented by nodes, and there is an arrow labeled with a from node q to q' whenever $\delta(q, a) = q'$. Final states are indicated by double circles, and the initial state is shown by a $>$. Figure 2-2 shows the state diagram of the deterministic finite automaton of Example 2.1.1.

Example 2.1.2: Let us design a deterministic finite automaton M that accepts the language $L(M) = \{w \in \{a, b\}^* : w \text{ does not contain three consecutive } b\text{'s}\}$. We let $M = (K, \Sigma, \delta, s, F)$, where

$$K = \{q_0, q_1, q_2, q_3\},$$
$$\Sigma = \{a, b\},$$
$$s = q_0,$$
$$F = \{q_0, q_1, q_2\},$$

and δ is given by the following table.

q	σ	$\delta(q, \sigma)$
q_0	a	q_0
q_0	b	q_1
q_1	a	q_0
q_1	b	q_2
q_2	a	q_0
q_2	b	q_3
q_3	a	q_3
q_3	b	q_3

The state diagram is shown in Figure 2-3. To see that M does indeed accept the specified language, note that as long as three consecutive b's have not been read, M is in state q_i (where i is 0, 1, or 2) immediately after reading a run of i consecutive b's that either began the input string or was preceded by an a. In particular, whenever an a is read and M is in state q_0, q_1, or q_2, M returns to its initial state q_0. States q_0, q_1, and q_2 are all final, so any input string not containing three consecutive b's will be accepted. However, a run of three b's will drive M to state q_3, which is not final, and M will then remain in this state regardless of the symbols in the rest of the input string. State q_3 is said to be a *dead state*, and if M reaches state q_3 it is said to be *trapped*, since no further input can enable it to escape from this state.◇

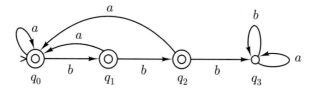

Figure 2-3

Problems for Section 2.1

2.1.1. Let M be a deterministic finite automaton. Under exactly what circumstances is $e \in L(M)$? Prove your answer.

2.1.2. Describe informally the languages accepted by the deterministic finite automata shown in the next page.

2.1.3. Construct deterministic finite automata accepting each of the following languages.
  (a) $\{w \in \{a, b\}^* : $ each a in w is immediately preceded by a $b\}$.
  (b) $\{w \in \{a, b\}^* : w$ has $abab$ as a substring$\}$.
  (c) $\{w \in \{a, b\}^* : w$ has neither aa nor bb as a substring$\}$.
  (d) $\{w \in \{a, b\}^* : w$ has an odd number of a's and an even number of b's$\}$.
  (e) $\{w \in \{a, b\}^* : w$ has both ab and ba as substrings$\}$.

2.1.4. A **deterministic finite-state transducer** is a device much like a deterministic finite automaton, except that its purpose is not to accept strings or languages but to transform input strings into output strings. Informally, it starts in a designated initial state and moves from state to state, depending on the input, just as a deterministic finite automaton does. On each step, however, it emits (or writes onto an output tape) a string of zero or one or more symbols, depending on the current state and the input symbol. The state diagram for a deterministic finite-state transducer looks like that for a deterministic finite automaton, except that the label on an arrow looks like

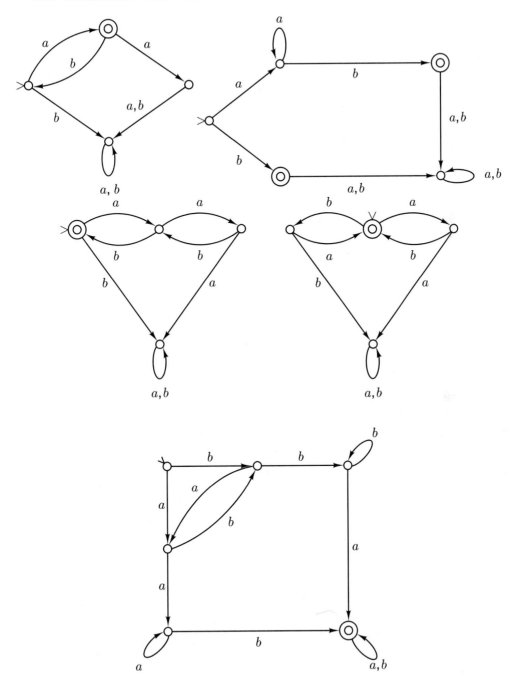

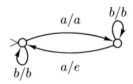

a/w, which means "if the input symbol is a, follow this arrow and emit output w". For example, the deterministic finite-state transducer over $\{a, b\}$ shown below transmits all b's in the input string but omits every other a.

(a) Draw state diagrams for deterministic finite-state transducers over $\{a, b\}$ that do the following.

  (i) On input w, produce output a^n, where n is the number of occurrences of the substring ab in w.

  (ii) On input w, produce output a^n, where n is the number of occurrences of the substring aba in w.

  (iii) On input w, produce a string of length w whose ith symbol is an a if $i = 1$, or if $i > 1$ and the ith and $(i-1)$st symbols of w are different; otherwise, the ith symbol of the output is a b. For example, on input $aabba$ the transducer should output $ababa$, and on input $aaaab$ it should output $abbba$.

(b) Formally define

  (i) a deterministic finite-state transducer;

  (ii) the notion of a configuration for such an automaton;

  (iii) the yields in one step relation $\vdash$ between configurations;

  (iv) the notion that such an automaton produces output u on input w;

  (v) the notion that such an automaton computes a function.

2.1.5. A deterministic 2-tape finite automaton is a device like a deterministic finite automaton for accepting pairs of strings. Each state is in one of two sets; depending on which set the state is in, the transition function refers to the first or second tape. For example, the automaton shown below accepts all pairs of strings $(w_1, w_2) \in \{a, b\}^* \times \{a, b\}^*$ such that $|w_2| = 2|w_1|$.

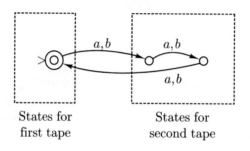

States for   States for
first tape   second tape

(a) Draw state diagrams for deterministic 2-tape finite automata that accept each of the following.

    (i) All pairs of strings (w_1, w_2) in $\{a, b\}^* \times \{a, b\}^*$ such that $|w_1| = |w_2|$, and $w_1(i) \neq w_2(i)$ for all i.

    (ii) All pairs of strings (w_1, w_2) in $\{a, b\}^* \times \{a, b\}^*$ such that the length of w_2 is twice the number of a's in w_1 plus three times the number of b's in w_1.

    (iii) $\{(a^n b, a^n b^m) : n, m \geq 0\}$.

    (iv) $\{(a^n b, a^m b^n) : n, m \geq 0\}$.

(b) Formally define

    (i) a deterministic 2-tape finite automaton;

    (ii) the notion of a configuration for such an automaton;

    (iii) the yields in one step relation $\vdash$ between configurations;

    (iv) the notion that such an automaton accepts an ordered pair of strings;

    (v) the notion that such an automaton accepts a set of ordered pairs of strings.

2.1.6. This problem refers to Problems 2.1.5 and 2.1.6. Show that if $f : \Sigma^* \mapsto \Sigma^*$ is a function that can be computed by a deterministic finite-state transducer, then $\{(w, f(w)) : w \in \Sigma^*\}$ is a set of pairs of strings accepted by some deterministic two-tape finite automaton.

2.1.7. We say that state q of a deterministic finite automaton $M = (K, \Sigma, \delta, q_0, F)$ is *reachable* if there exists $w \in \Sigma^*$ such that $(q_0, w) \vdash_M^* (q, e)$. Show that if we delete from M any nonreachable state, an automaton results that accepts the same language. Give an efficient algorithm for computing the set of all reachable states of a deterministic finite automaton.

2.2 | NONDETERMINISTIC FINITE AUTOMATA

In this section we add a powerful and intriguing feature to finite automata. This feature is called **nondeterminism**, and is essentially the ability to change states in a way that is only partially determined by the current state and input symbol. That is, we shall now permit several possible "next states" for a given combination of current state and input symbol. The automaton, as it reads the input string, may choose at each step to go into any one of these legal next states; the choice is not determined by anything in our model, and is therefore said to be *nondeterministic*. On the other hand, the choice is not wholly unlimited either; only those next states that are legal from a given state with a given input symbol can be chosen.

Such nondeterministic devices are not meant as realistic models of computers. They are simply a useful *notational generalization* of finite automata, as they can greatly simplify the description of these automata. Moreover, we shall see below that nondeterminism is an inessential feature of finite automata: every nondeterministic finite automaton is equivalent to a deterministic finite automaton. Thus we shall profit from the powerful notation of nondeterministic finite automata, always knowing that, if we must, we can always go back and redo everything in terms of the lower-level language of ordinary, down-to-earth deterministic automata.

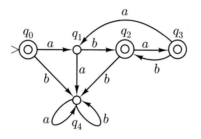

Figure 2-4

To see that a nondeterministic finite automaton can be a much more convenient device to design than a deterministic finite automaton, consider the language $L = (ab \cup aba)^*$, which is accepted by the deterministic finite automaton illustrated in Figure 2-4. Even with the diagram, it takes a few moments to ascertain that a deterministic finite automaton is shown; one must check that there are exactly two arrows leaving each node, one labeled a and one labeled b. And some thought is needed to convince oneself that the language accepted by this fairly complex device is the simple language $(ab \cup aba)^*$. One might hope to find a simpler deterministic finite automaton accepting L; unfortunately, it can be shown that no deterministic finite automaton with fewer than five states can accept this language (later in this chapter we develop methods for *minimizing* the number of states of deterministic finite automata).

However, L is accepted by the simple *nondeterministic* device shown in Figure 2-5. When this device is in state q_1 and the input symbol is b, there are two possible next states, q_0 and q_2. Thus Figure 2-5 does not represent a deterministic finite automaton. Nevertheless, there is a natural way to interpret the diagram as a device accepting L. A string is accepted if there is *some* way to get from the initial state (q_0) to a final state (in this case, q_0) while following arrows labeled with the symbols of the string. For example ab is accepted by going from q_0 to q_1, to q_0; aba is accepted by going from q_0 to q_1 to q_2, to q_0. Of course, the device might guess wrong and go from q_0 to q_1 to q_0 to q_1 on

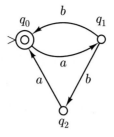

Figure 2-5

input *aba*, winding up in a nonfinal state; but this does not matter, since there is *some* way of getting from the initial to a final state with this input. On the other hand, the input *abb* is not accepted, since there is no way to get from q_0 back to q_0 while reading this string.

Indeed, you will notice that from q_0 there is no state to be entered when the input is *b*. This is another feature of nondeterministic finite automata: just as from some states with some inputs there may be several possible next states, so with other combinations of states and input symbols there may be no possible moves.

We also allow in the state diagram of a nondeterministic automaton arrows that are labeled by the empty string *e*. For example, the device of Figure 2-6 accepts the same language L. From q_2 this machine can return to q_0 either by reading an *a* or immediately, without consuming any input.

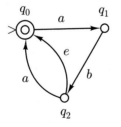

Figure 2-6

The devices illustrated in Figures 2-5 and 2-6 are instances of the following general type:

Definition 2.2.1: A **nondeterministic finite automaton** is a quintuple $M = (K, \Sigma, \Delta, s, F)$, where

K is a finite set of **states**,
Σ is an alphabet,

$s \in K$ is the **initial state**,

$F \subseteq K$ is the set of **final states**, and

Δ, the **transition relation**, is a subset of $K \times (\Sigma \cup \{e\}) \times K$.

Each triple $(q, u, p) \in \Delta$ is called a **transition** of M —the formal counterpart of an arrow labeled a from q to p in the state diagram of M. If M is in state q and the next input symbol is a, then M may next follow any transition of the form (q, a, p) or (q, e, p); if a transition (q, e, p) is followed, then no input symbol is read.

The formal definitions of computations by nondeterministic finite automata are very similar to those for deterministic finite automata. A **configuration** of M is, once again, an element of $K \times \Sigma^*$. The relation $\vdash_M$ between configurations (**yields in one step**) is defined as follows: $(q, w) \vdash_M (q', w')$ if and only if there is a $u \in \Sigma \cup \{e\}$ such that $w = uw'$ and $(q, u, q') \in \Delta$. Note that $\vdash_M$ need not be a function; for some configurations (q, w), there may be several pairs (q', w') —or none at all— such that $(q, w) \vdash_M (q', w')$. As before, $\vdash_M^*$ is the reflexive, transitive closure of $\vdash_M$ and a string $w \in \Sigma^*$ is **accepted** by M if and only if there is a state $q \in F$ such that $(s, w) \vdash_M^* (q, e)$. Finally $L(M)$, the language accepted by M, is the set of all strings accepted by M.

Example 2.2.1: Figure 2-7 shows one of several possible nondeterministic finite automata that accept the set of all strings containing an occurrence of the pattern bb or of the pattern bab (see Section 2.5 for a systematic study of automata for detecting patterns in the input string). Formally, this machine is $(K, \Sigma, \Delta, s, F)$, where

$$K = \{q_0, q_1, q_2, q_3, q_4\},$$
$$\Sigma = \{a, b\},$$
$$s = q_0,$$
$$F = \{q_4\},$$

and

$$\Delta = \{(q_0, a, q_0), (q_0, b, q_0), (q_0, b, q_1),$$
$$(q_1, b, q_2), (q_1, a, q_3), (q_2, e, q_4),$$
$$(q_3, b, q_4), (q_4, a, q_4), (q_4, b, q_4)\}.$$

When M is given the string $bababab$ as input, several different sequences of moves may ensue. For example, M may wind up in the nonfinal state q_0 in case

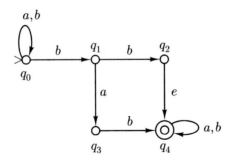

Figure 2-7

the only transitions used are (q_0, a, q_0) and (q_0, b, q_0):

$$(q_0, bababab) \vdash_M (q_0, ababab)$$
$$\vdash_M (q_0, babab)$$
$$\vdash_M (q_0, abab)$$

$$\vdots$$

$$\vdash_M (q_0, e)$$

The same input string may drive M from state q_0 to the final state q_4, and indeed may do so in three different ways. One of these ways is the following.

$$(q_0, bababab) \vdash_M (q_1, ababab)$$
$$\vdash_M (q_3, babab)$$
$$\vdash_M (q_4, abab)$$
$$\vdash_M (q_4, bab)$$
$$\vdash_M (q_4, ab)$$
$$\vdash_M (q_4, b)$$
$$\vdash_M (q_4, e)$$

Since a string is accepted by a nondeterministic finite automaton if and only if there is at least one sequence of moves leading to a final state, it follows that $bababab \in L(M)$.◇

Example 2.2.2: Let Σ be the alphabet $\Sigma = \{a_1, \ldots, a_n\}$, containing n symbols, where $n \geq 2$, and consider the following language:

$$L = \{w : \text{there is a symbol } a_i \in \Sigma \text{ not appearing in } w\}.$$

That is, L contains all those strings in Σ^* that fail to contain occurrences of all symbols in Σ. For example, if $n = 3$, then $e, a_1, a_2, a_1 a_1 a_3 a_1 \in L$, but $a_3 a_1 a_3 a_1 a_2 \notin L$.

It is relatively easy to design a nondeterministic finite automaton $M = (K, \Sigma, \Delta, s, F)$ that accepts this rather sophisticated language. Here K contains $n + 1$ states $K = \{s, q_1, q_2, \ldots, q_n\}$, all accepting ($F = K$). Δ has two kinds of transitions (see Figure 2-8 for an illustration of the case $n = 3$). The *initial transitions* are those of the form (s, e, q_i) for all i, $1 \leq i \leq n$, and the *main* transitions are all triples of the form (q_i, a_j, q_i), where $i \neq j$. This completes the list of transitions in Δ.

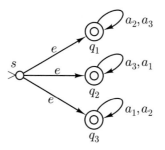

Figure 2-8

Intuitively, M starts its operation on an input by *guessing the symbol missing from the input*, and passing to the corresponding state. If the symbol selected is a_i, then state q_i is visited. At this state the automaton checks that indeed the symbol guessed does not occur in the string. If so, it ends up accepting. This automaton illustrates vividly the remarkable power of nondeterministic devices: they can *guess and always be right*, since one successful computation is all that is required for acceptance. As we shall see later in Section 2.5, any deterministic finite automaton that accepts the same language must be far more complicated.◊

A deterministic finite automaton is just a special type of a nondeterministic finite automaton: In a deterministic finite automaton, it so happens that the transition relation Δ is in fact a function from $K \times \Sigma$ to K. That is, a nondeterministic finite automaton $(K, \Sigma, \delta, s, F)$ is deterministic if and only if there are no transitions of the form (q, e, p) in Δ, and for each $q \in K$ and $a \in \Sigma$ there is exactly one $p \in K$ such that $(q, a, p) \in \Delta$. It is therefore evident that the class of languages accepted by deterministic automata is a *subset* of the class of languages accepted by nondeterministic automata. Rather surprisingly, these classes are in fact *equal*. Despite the apparent power and generality enjoyed by nondeterministic automata, they are no more powerful than the deterministic ones in terms of the languages they accept: A nondeterministic finite automaton can always be converted into an *equivalent* deterministic one.

Formally, we say that two finite automata M_1 and M_2 (deterministic or nondeterministic) are **equivalent** if and only if $L(M_1) = L(M_2)$. Thus two automata are considered to be equivalent if they accept the same language, even though they may "use different methods" to do so. For example, the three automata in Figures 2-4–2-6 are all equivalent.

Theorem 2.2.1: *For each nondeterministic finite automaton, there is an equivalent deterministic finite automaton.*

Proof: Let $M = (K, \Sigma, \Delta, s, F)$ be a nondeterministic finite automaton. We shall construct a deterministic finite automaton $M' = (K', \Sigma, \delta, s', F')$ equivalent to M. The key idea is to view a nondeterministic finite automaton as occupying, at any moment, not a single state but a *set* of states: namely, all the states that can be reached from the initial state by means of the input consumed thus far. Thus if M had five states $\{q_0, \ldots, q_4\}$ and, after reading a certain input string, it could be in state q_0, q_2, or q_3, but not q_1, or q_4, its state could be considered to be the *set* $\{q_0, q_2, q_3\}$, rather than an undetermined member of that set. And if the next input symbol could drive M from q_0 to either q_1 or q_2, from q_2 to q_0, and from q_3 to q_2, then the next state of M could be considered to be the set $\{q_0, q_1, q_2\}$.

The construction formalizes this idea. The set of states of M' will be $K' = 2^K$, the power set of the set of states of M. The set of final states of M' will consist of all those subsets of K that contain at least one final state of M. The definition of the transition function of M' will be slightly more complicated. The basic idea is that a move of M' on reading an input symbol $a \in \Sigma$ imitates a move of M on input symbol a, *possibly followed by any number of e-moves of* M. To formalize this idea we need a special definition.

For any state $q \in K$, let $E(q)$ be the set of all states of M that are reachable from state q without reading any input. That is,

$$E(q) = \{p \in K : (q, e) \vdash^*_M (p, e)\}.$$

To put it otherwise, $E(q)$ is the *closure* of the set $\{q\}$ under the relation

$$\{(p, r) : \text{there is a transition } (p, e, r) \in \Delta\}.$$

Thus, $E(q)$ can be *computed* by the following algorithm:

Initially set $E(q) := \{q\}$;
while there is a transition $(p, e, r) \in \Delta$ with $p \in E(q)$
and $r \notin E(q)$ do: $E(q) := E(q) \cup \{r\}$.

This algorithm is a specialization of our general algorithm for closure computations (recall the last algorithm in Section 1.6) to the situation in hand. It is guaranteed to terminate after at most $|K|$ iterations, because each execution of the while loop adds another state to $E(q)$, and there are at most $|K|$ states to be added. We shall see many instances of such closure algorithms later.

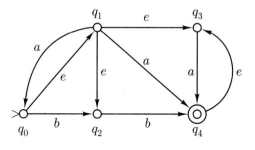

Figure 2-9

Example 2.2.3: In the automaton of Figure 2-9, we have $E(q_0) = \{q_0, q_1, q_2, q_3\}$, $E(q_1) = \{q_1, q_2, q_3\}$, and $E(q_2) = \{q_2\}.\Diamond$

We are now ready to define formally the deterministic automaton $M' = (K', \Sigma, \delta', s', F')$ that is equivalent to M. In particular,

$$K' = 2^K,$$
$$s' = E(s),$$
$$F = \{Q \subseteq K : Q \cap F \neq \emptyset\},$$

and for each $Q \subseteq K$ and each symbol $a \in \Sigma$, define

$$\delta'(Q, a) = \bigcup \{E(p) : p \in K \text{ and } (q, a, p) \in \Delta \text{ for some } q \in Q\}.$$

That is, $\delta'(Q, a)$ is taken to be the set of all states of M to which M can go by reading input a (and possibly following several e transitions). For example, if M is the automaton of Figure 2-9, then $s' = \{q_0, q_1\}$. Since the only transitions from q_1 on input a are (q_1, a, q_0) and (q_1, a, q_4), it follows that $\delta'(\{q_1\}, a) = E(q_0) \cup E(q_4) = \{q_0, q_1, q_2, q_3, q_4\}$.

It remains to show that M' is deterministic and equivalent to M. The demonstration that M' is deterministic is straightforward: we just notice that δ' is single-valued and well defined on all $Q \in K'$ and $a \in \Sigma$, by the way it was constructed. (That $\delta'(Q, a) = \emptyset$ for some $Q \in K'$ and $a \in \Sigma$ does not mean δ' is not well defined; $\emptyset$ is a member of K'.)

We now *claim* that for any string $w \in \Sigma^*$ and any states $p, q \in K'$,

$$(q, w) \vdash_M^* (p, e) \text{ if and only if } (E(q), w) \vdash_{M'}^* (P, e)$$

for some set P containing p. From this the theorem will follow easily: To show that M and M' are equivalent, consider any string $w \in \Sigma^*$. Then $w \in L(M)$ if and only if $(s, w) \vdash_M^* (f, e)$ for some $f \in F$ (by definition) if and only if $(E(s), w) \vdash_{M'}^* (Q, e)$ for some Q containing f (by the claim above); in other words, if and only if $(s', w) \vdash_{M'}^* (Q, e)$ for some $Q \in F'$. The last condition is the definition of $w \in L(M')$.

We prove the claim by induction on $|w|$.

Basis Step. For $|w| = 0$ —that is, for $w = e$— we must show that $(q, e) \vdash_M^* (p, e)$ if and only if $(E(q), e) \vdash_{M'}^* (P, e)$ for some set P containing p. The first statement is equivalent to saying that $p \in E(q)$. Since M' is deterministic, the second statement is equivalent to saying that $P = E(q)$ and P contains p; that is, $p \in E(q)$. This completes the proof of the basis step.

Induction Hypothesis. Suppose that the claim is true for all strings w of length k or less for some $k \geq 0$.

Induction Step. We prove the claim for any string w of length $k + 1$. Let $w = va$, where $a \in \Sigma$, and $v \in \Sigma^*$.

For the *only if* direction, suppose that $(q, w)) \vdash_M^* (p, e)$. Then there are states r_1 and r_2 such that

$$(q, w)) \vdash_M^* (r_1, a) \vdash_M (r_2, e) \vdash_M^* (p, e).$$

That is, M reaches state p from state q by some number of moves during which input v is read, followed by one move during which input a is read, followed by some number of moves during which no input is read. Now $(q, va) \vdash_M^* (r_1, a)$ is tantamount to $(q, v) \vdash_M^* (r_1, e)$, and since $|v| = k$, by the induction hypothesis $(E(q), v) \vdash_{M'}^* (R_1, e)$ for some set R_1 containing r_1. Since $(r_1, a) \vdash_M (r_2, e)$, there is a triple $(r_1, a, r_2) \in \Delta$, and hence by the construction of M', $E(r_2) \subseteq \delta'(R_1, a)$. But since $(r_2, e) \vdash_M^* (p, e)$, it follows that $p \in E(r_2)$, and therefore $p \in \delta'(R_1, a)$. Therefore $(R_1, a) \vdash_{M'} (P, e)$ for some P containing p, and thus $(E(q), va) \vdash_{M'}^* (R_1, a) \vdash_{M'} (P, e)$.

To prove the other direction, suppose that $(E(q), va) \vdash_{M'}^* (R_1, a) \vdash_{M'} (P, e)$ for some P containing p and some R_1 such that $\delta'(R_1, a) = P$. Now by the definition of δ', $\delta'(R_1, a)$ is the union of all sets $E(r_2)$, where, for some state $r_1 \in R_1$, (r_1, a, r_2) is a transition of M. Since $p \in P = \delta'(R_1, a)$, there is some particular r_2 such that $p \in E(r_2)$, and, for some $r_1 \in R_1$, (r_1, a, r_2) is a transition of M. Then $(r_2, e) \vdash_M^* (p, e)$ by the definition of $E(r_2)$. Also, by the induction hypothesis, $(q, v) \vdash_M^* (r_1, a)$ and therefore $(q, va) \vdash_M^* (r_1, a) \vdash_M (r_2, e) \vdash_M^* (p, e)$.

This completes the proof of the claim and the theorem. ∎

Example 2.2.4: The proof of Theorem 2.2.1 has the salutary property of being *constructive*, in that it provides an actual *algorithm* for constructing, starting from any nondeterministic finite automaton M, an equivalent deterministic M'.

Let us apply this algorithm then to the nondeterministic automaton in Figure 2-9. Since M has 5 states, M' will have $2^5 = 32$ states. However, only a few of these states will be relevant to the operation of M' —namely, those states that can be reached from state s' by reading some input string. Obviously, any state in K' that is not reachable from s' is irrelevant to the operation of M' and to the language accepted by it. We shall build this reachable part of M' by starting from s' and introducing a new state only when it is needed as the value of $\delta'(q, a)$ for some state $q \in K'$ already introduced and some $a \in \Sigma$.

We have already defined $E(q)$ for each state q of M. Since $s' = E(q_0) = \{q_0, q_1, q_2, q_3\}$,

$$(q_1, a, q_0), (q_1, a, q_4), \text{ and } (q_3, a, q_4)$$

are all the transitions (q, a, p) for some $q \in s'$. It follows that

$$\delta'(s', a) = E(q_0) \cup E(q_4) = \{q_0, q_1, q_2, q_3, q_4\}.$$

Similarly,

$$(q_0, b, q_2) \text{ and } (q_2, b, q_4)$$

are all the transitions of the form (q, b, p) for some $q \in s'$, so

$$\delta'(s', b) = E(q_2) \cup E(q_4) = \{q_2, q_3, q_4\}.$$

Repeating this calculation for the newly introduced states, we have the following.

$$\delta'(\{q_0, q_1, q_2, q_3, q_4\}, a) = \{q_0, q_1, q_2, q_3, q_4\},$$
$$\delta'(\{q_0, q_1, q_2, q_3, q_4\}, b) = \{q_2, q_3, q_4\},$$
$$\delta'(\{q_2, q_3, q_4\}, a) = E(q_4) = \{q_3, q_4\},$$
$$\delta'(\{q_2, q_3, q_4\}, b) = E(q_4) = \{q_3, q_4\}.$$

Next,

$$\delta'(\{q_3, q_4\}, a) = E(q_4) = \{q_3, q_4\},$$
$$\delta'(\{q_3, q_4\}, b) = \emptyset,$$

and finally

$$\delta'(\emptyset, a) = \delta'(\emptyset, b) = \emptyset.$$

The relevant part of M' is illustrated in Figure 2.10. F', the set of final states, contains each set of states of which q_4 is a member, since q_4 is the sole member

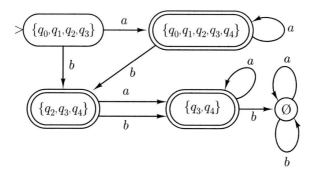

Figure 2-10

of F; so in the illustration, the three states $\{q_0, q_1, q_2, q_3, q_4\}$, $\{q_2, q_3, q_4\}$, and $\{q_3, q_4\}$ of M' are final.◊

Example 2.2.5: Recall the $n + 1$-state nondeterministic finite automaton in Example 2.2.2 with $\Sigma = \{a_1, \ldots, a_n\}$ for accepting the language $L = \{w \in \Sigma^* :$ there is a symbol $a_i \in \Sigma$ that does not occur in $w\}$. Intuitively, there is no way for a deterministic finite automaton to accept the same language with so few states.

Indeed, the construction is in this case exponential. The equivalent deterministic automaton M' has as initial state the set $s' = E(s) = \{s, q_1, q_2, \ldots, q_n\}$. Even in this case, M' has several irrelevant states —in fact, half of the states in 2^K are irrelevant. For example, state $\{s\}$ cannot be reached from s'; neither can any state that contains some q_i but not s. Alas, these are all the irrelevant states: as it turns out, all the remaining 2^n states of K' —that is to say, all states of the form $\{s\} \cup Q$ for some nonempty subset Q of $\{q_1, \ldots, q_n\}$— are reachable from s'.

One might hope, of course, that other kinds of optimizations may reduce the number of states in M'. Section 2.5 contains a systematic study of such optimizations. Unfortunately, it follows from that analysis that in the present case of automaton M', the exponential number of states in M' *is* the absolute minimum possible.◊

Problems for Section 2.2

2.2.1. (a) Which of the following strings are accepted by the nondeterministic finite automaton shown on the left below?

    (i) a

    (ii) aa

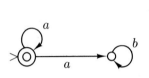 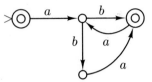

(iii) *aab*

(iv) *e*

(b) Repeat for the following strings and the nondeterministic finite automaton on the right above:

(i) *e*

(ii) *ab*

(iii) *abab*

(iv) *aba*

(v) *abaa*

2.2.2. Write regular expressions for the languages accepted by the nondeterministic finite automata of Problem 2.2.1.

2.2.3. Draw state diagrams for nondeterministic finite automata that accepts these languages.

(a) $(ab)^*(ba)^* \cup aa^*$

(b) $((ab \cup aab)^*a^*)^*$

(c) $((a^*b^*a^*)^*b)^*$

(d) $(ba \cup b)^* \cup (bb \cup a)*$

2.2.4. Some authors define a nondeterministic finite automaton to be a quintuple $(K, \Sigma, \Delta, S, F)$, where $K, \Sigma, \Delta,$, and F are as defined and S is a finite set of initial states, in the same way that F is a finite set of final states. The automaton may nondeterministically begin operating in any of these initial states.

(a) Show that the language $L \subseteq \{a_1, \ldots, a_n\}^*$ consisting of all strings that are missing at least one symbol (recall Example 2.2.2) would be accepted by such an automaton with n states $q_1, \ldots, q_n$, all of which are both final and initial, and the transition relation $\Delta = \{(q_i, a_j, q_i) : i \neq j\}$.

(b) Explain why this definition is not more general than ours in any significant way.

2.2.5. By what sequences of steps, other than the one presented in Example 2.2.1, can the nondeterministic finite automaton of Figure 2-7 accept the input *babababb*?

2.2.6. (a) Find a simple nondeterministic finite automaton accepting $(ab \cup aab \cup aba)^*$.

(b) Convert the nondeterministic finite automaton of Part (a) to a deterministic finite automaton by the method in Section 2.2.

(c) Try to understand how the machine constructed in Part (b) operates. Can you find an equivalent deterministic machine with fewer states?

2.2.7. Repeat Problem 2.2.6 for the language $(a \cup b)^* aabab$.

2.2.8. Repeat Problem 2.2.6 for the language $(a \cup b)^* a (a \cup b)(a \cup b)(a \cup b)$.

2.2.9. Construct deterministic finite automata equivalent to the nondeterministic automata shown below.

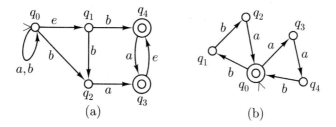

(a)   (b)

2.2.10. Describe exactly what happens when the construction of this section is applied to a finite automaton that is already deterministic.

2.3 | FINITE AUTOMATA AND REGULAR EXPRESSIONS

The main result of the last section was that the class of languages accepted by finite automata remains the same even if a new and seemingly powerful feature —nondeterminism— is allowed. This suggests that the class of languages accepted by finite automata has a sort of *stability*: Two different approaches, one apparently more powerful than the other, end up defining the same class. In this section we shall prove another important characterization of this class of languages, further evidence of how remarkably stable it is: The class of languages accepted by finite automata, deterministic or nondeterministic, is the same as the class of *regular languages* —those that can be described by regular expressions, recall the discussion in Section 1.8.

We have introduced the class of regular languages as the closure of certain finite languages under the language operations of union, concatenation, and Kleene star. We must therefore start by proving similar closure properties of the class of languages accepted by finite automata:

Theorem 2.3.1: *The class of languages accepted by finite automata is closed under*

(a) *union;*
(b) *concatenation;*
(c) *Kleene star;*
(d) *complementation;*
(e) *intersection.*

Proof: In each case we show how to construct an automaton M that accepts the appropriate language, given two automata M_1 and M_2 (only M_1 in the cases of Kleene star and complementation).

(a) *Union.* Let $M_1 = (K_1, \Sigma, \Delta_1, s_1, F_1)$ and $M_2 = (K_2, \Sigma, \Delta_2, s_2, F_2)$ be non-deterministic finite automata; we shall construct a nondeterministic finite automaton M such that $L(M) = L(M_1) \cup L(M_2)$. The construction of M is rather simple and intuitively clear, illustrated in Figure 2-11. Basically, M uses nondeterminism to *guess* whether the input is in $L(M_1)$ or in $L(M_2)$, and then processes the string exactly as the corresponding automaton would; it follows that $L(M) = L(M_1) \cup L(M_2)$. But let us give the formal details and proof for this case.

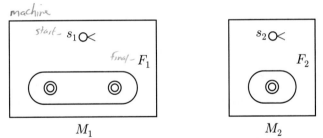

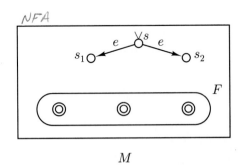

Figure 2-11

Without loss of generality, we may assume that K_1 and K_2 are disjoint sets. Then the finite automaton M that accepts $L(M_1) \cup L(M_2)$ is defined as follows (see Figure 2-11): $M = (K, \Sigma, \Delta, s, F)$, where s is a new state not in K_1 or K_2,

$$K = K_1 \cup K_2 \cup \{s\},$$
$$F = F_1 \cup F_2,$$
$$\Delta = \Delta_1 \cup \Delta_2 \cup \{(s, e, s_1), (s, e, s_2)\}.$$

That is, M begins any computation by nondeterministically choosing to enter either the initial state of M_1 or the initial state of M_2, and thereafter, M imitates either M_1 or M_2. Formally, if $w \in \Sigma^*$, then $(s, w) \vdash_M^* (q, e)$ for some $q \in F$ if and only if either $(s_1, w) \vdash_{M_1}^* (q, e)$ for some $q \in F_1$, or $(s2, w) \vdash_{M_2}^* (q, e)$ for some $q \in F_2$. Hence M accepts w if and only if M_1 accepts w or M_2 accepts w, and $L(M) = L(M_1) \cup L(M_2)$.

(b) *Concatenation*. Again, let M_1 and M_2 be nondeterministic finite automata; we construct a nondeterministic finite automaton M such that $L(M) = L(M_1) \circ L(M_2)$ The construction is shown schematically in Figure 2-12; M now operates by simulating M_1 for a while, and then "jumping" nondeterministically from a final state of M_1 to the initial state of M_2. Thereafter, M imitates M_2. We omit the formal definition and proof.

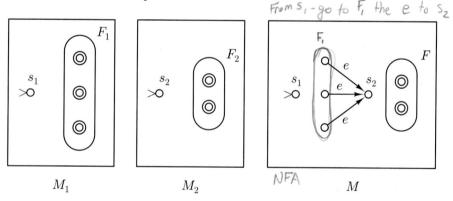

Figure 2-12

(c) *Kleene star*. Let M_1 be a nondeterministic finite automaton; we construct a nondeterministic finite automaton M such that $L(M) = L(M_1)^*$. The construction is similar to that for concatenation, and is illustrated in Figure 2-13. M consists of the states of M_1 and all the transitions of M_1; any final state of M_1 is a final state of M. In addition, M has a new initial state s. This new initial state is also final, so that e is accepted. From s there is an e-transition to the initial state s_1 of M_1, so that the operation of M_1 can be initiated after M has been started in state s. Finally, e-transitions are added from each final state of

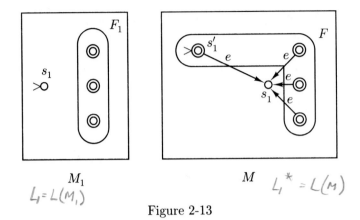

$$L_1 = L(M_1)$$

$$L_1^* = L(M)$$

Figure 2-13

M_1 back to s_1; this way, once a string in $L(M_1)$ has been read, computation can resume from the initial state of M_1.

(d) *Complementation.* Let $M = (K, \Sigma, \delta, s, F)$ be a *deterministic* finite automaton. Then the complementary language $\overline{L} = \Sigma^* - L(M)$ is accepted by the deterministic finite automaton $\overline{M} = (K, \Sigma, \delta, s, K - F)$. That is, $\overline{M}$ is identical to M except that final and nonfinal states are interchanged.

(e) *Intersection.* Just recall that

$$L_1 \cap L_2 = \Sigma^* - ((\Sigma^* - L_1) \cup (\Sigma^* - L_2)),$$

and so closedness under intersection follows from closedness under union and complementation ((a) and (d) above). ∎

We now come to the main result of this section, the identification of two important techniques for finitely specifying languages —in fact, of a language generator and a language acceptor:

Theorem 2.3.2: *A language is regular if and only if it is accepted by a finite automaton.*

Proof: *Only if.* Recall that the class of regular languages is the smallest class of languages containing the empty set $\emptyset$ and the singletons a, where a is a symbol, and closed under union, concatenation, and Kleene star. It is evident (see Figure 2-14) that the empty set and all singletons are indeed accepted by finite automata; and by Theorem 2.3.1 the finite automaton languages are closed under union, concatenation, and Kleene star. Hence every regular language is accepted by some finite automaton.

Example 2.3.1: Consider the regular expression $(ab \cup aab)^*$. A nondeterministic finite automaton accepting the language denoted by this regular expression can be built up using the methods in the proof of the various parts of Theorem 2.3.1, as illustrated in Figure 2-14.◊

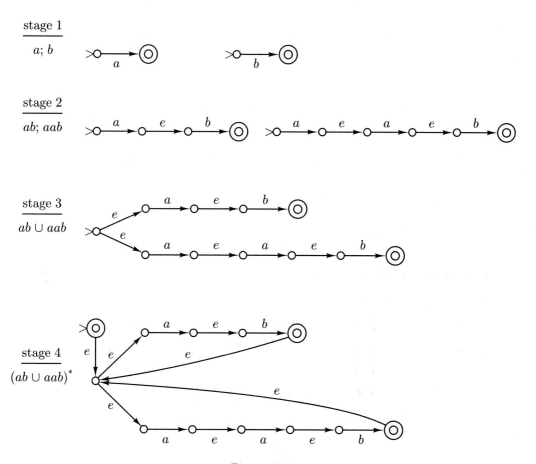

Figure 2-14

If. Let $M = (K, \Sigma, \Delta, s, F)$ be a finite automaton (not necessarily deterministic). We shall construct a regular expression R such that $L(R) = L(M)$. We shall represent $L(M)$ as the union of many (but a finite number of) simple languages. Let $K = \{q_1, \ldots, q_n\}$ and $s = q_1$. For $i, j = 1, \ldots, n$ and $k = 0, \ldots, n$, we define $R(i, j, k)$ as the set of all strings in Σ^* that may drive M from state q_i to state q_j without passing through any *intermediate* state numbered $k + 1$ or greater —the endpoints q_i and q_j are allowed to be numbered higher than k. That is, $R(i, j, k)$ is the set of strings spelled by all paths from q_i to q_j of *rank k* (recall the similar maneuver in the computation of the reflexive-transitive closure of a relation in Section 1.6, in which we again considered paths with progressively higher and higher-numbered intermediate nodes). When $k = n$, it follows that

$$R(i, j, n) = \{w \in \Sigma^* : (q_i, x) \vdash_M^* (q_j, e)\}.$$

Therefore

$$L(M) = \bigcup \{R(1, j, n) : q_j \in F\}.$$

The crucial point is that *all of these sets $R(i, j, k)$ are regular,* and hence so is $L(M)$.

The proof that each $R(i, j, k)$ is regular is by induction on k. For $k = 0$, $R(i, j, 0)$ is either $\{a \in \Sigma \cup \{e\} : (q_i, a, q_j) \in \Delta\}$ if $i \neq j$, or it is $\{e\} \cup \{a \in \Sigma \cup \{e\} : (q_i, a, q_j) \in \Delta\}$ if $i = j$. Each of these sets is finite and therefore regular.

For the induction step, suppose that $R(i, j, k-1)$ for all i, j have been defined as regular languages for all i, j. Then each set $R(i, j, k)$ can be defined combining previously defined regular languages by the regular operations of union, Kleene star, and concatenation, as follows:

$$R(i, j, k) = R(i, j, k - 1) \cup R(i, k, k - 1)R(k, k, k - 1)^* R(k, j, k - 1).$$

This equation states that to get from q_i to q_j without passing through a state numbered greater than k, M may either

(1) go from q_i to q_j without passing through a state numbered greater than $k - 1$; or
(2) go (a) from q_i to q_k; then (b) from q_k to q_k zero or more times; then (c) from q_k to q_j; in each case without passing through any intermediate states numbered greater than $k - 1$.

Therefore language $R(i, j, k)$ is regular for all i, j, k, thus completing the induction. ∎

Example 2.3.2: Let us construct a regular expression for the language accepted by the deterministic finite automaton of Figure 2-15. This automaton accepts the language

$$\{w \in \{a, b\}^* : w \text{ has } 3k + 1 \text{ } b\text{'s for some } k \in \mathbf{N}\}.$$

Carrying out explicitly the construction of the proof of the *if* part can be very tedious (in this simple case, thirty-six regular expressions would have to be constructed!). Things are simplified considerably if we assume that the nondeterministic automaton M has two simple properties:

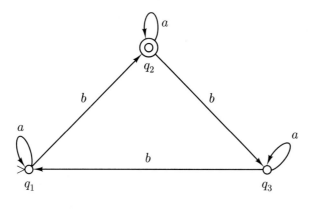

Figure 2-15

(a) It has a single final state, $F = \{f\}$.

(b) Furthermore, if $(q, u, p) \in \Delta$, then $q \neq f$ and $p \neq s$; that is, there are no transitions into the initial state, nor out of the final state.

This "special form" is not a loss of generality, because we can add to any automaton M a new initial state s and a new final state f, together with e-transitions from s to the initial state of M and from all final states of M to f (see Figure 2-16(a), where the automaton of Figure 2-15 is brought into this "special form"). Number now the states of the automaton $q_1, q_2, \ldots, q_n$, as required by the construction, so that $s = q_{n-1}$ and $f = q_n$. Obviously, the regular expression sought is $R(n-1, n, n)$.

We shall compute first the $R(i, j, 0)$'s, from them the $R(i, j, 1)$'s, and so on, as suggested by the proof. At each stage we depict each $R(i, j, k)$'s as a label on an arrow going from state q_i to state q_j. We omit arrows labeled by $\emptyset$, and self-loops labeled $\{e\}$. With this convention, the initial automaton depicts the correct values of the $R(i, j, 0)$'s —see Figure 2-16(a). (This is so because in our initial automaton it so happens that, for each pair of states (q_i, q_j) there is at most one transition of the form (q_i, u, q_j) in Δ. In another automaton we might have to combine by union all transitions from q_i to q_j, as suggested by the proof.)

Now we compute the $R(i, j, 1)$'s; they are shown in Figure 2-16(b). Notice immediately that state q_1 need not be considered in the rest of the construction; all strings that lead M to acceptance passing through state q_1 have been considered and taken into account in the $R(i, j, 1)$'s. We can say that state q_1 has been *eliminated*. In some sense, we have transformed the finite automaton of Figure 2-16(a) to an equivalent *generalized finite automaton*, with transitions that may be labeled not only by symbols in Σ or e, but by entire *regular expressions*. The resulting generalized finite automaton has one less state than the original one, since q_1 has been eliminated.

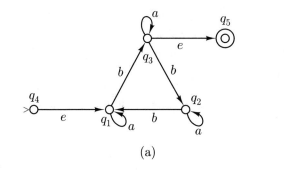

(a)

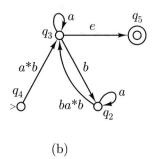

(b)

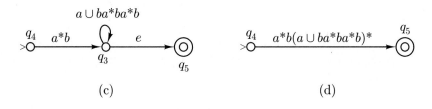

(c)   (d)

Figure 2-16

Let us examine carefully what is involved in general in eliminating a state q (see Figure 2-17). For each pair of states $q_i \neq q$ and $q_j \neq q$, such that there is an arrow labeled α from q_i to q and an arrow labeled β from q to q_j, we add an arrow from q_i to q_j labeled $\alpha\gamma^*\beta$, where γ is the label of the arrow from q to itself (if there is no such arrow, then $\gamma = \emptyset$, and thus $\gamma^* = \{e\}$, so the label becomes $\alpha\beta$). If there was already an arrow from q_i to q_j labeled δ, then the new arrow is labeled $\delta \cup \alpha\gamma^*\beta$.

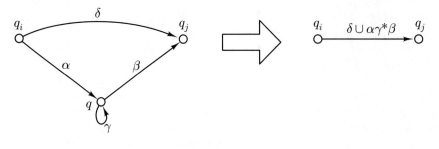

Figure 2-17

Continuing like this, we eliminate state q_2 to obtain the $R(i, j, 2)$'s in Figure 2-17(c), and finally we eliminate q_3. We have now deleted all states except the initial and final ones, and the generalized automaton has been reduced to a single transition from the initial state to the final state. We can now read the regular expression for M as the label of this transition:

$$R = R(4,5,5) = R(4,5,3) = a^*b(ba^*ba^*b \cup a)^*,$$

which is indeed $\{w \in \{a,b\}^* : w \text{ has } 3k+1 \text{ } b\text{'s for some } k \in \mathbf{N}\}.\Diamond$

Problems for Section 2.3

2.3.1. In part (d) of the proof of Theorem 2.3.1 why did we insist that M be deterministic? What happens if we interchange the final and nonfinal states of a nondeterministic finite automaton?

2.3.2. What goes wrong in the proof of Part (c) of Theorem 2.3.1 if we simply make s_1 final, and add arrows from all members of F_1 back to s_1 (without introducing a new starting state)?

2.3.3. Give a direct construction for the closure under intersection of the languages accepted by finite automata. (*Hint:* Consider an automaton whose set of states is the Cartesian product of the sets of states of the two original automata.) Which of the two constructions, the one given in the text or the one suggested in this problem, is more efficient when the two languages are given in terms of *nondeterministic* finite automata?

2.3.4. Using the construction in the proofs of Theorem 2.3.1, construct finite automata accepting these languages.
  (a) $a^*(ab \cup ba \cup e)b^*$
  (b) $((a \cup b)^*(e \cup c)^*)^*$
  (c) $((ab)^* \cup (bc)^*)ab$

2.3.5. Construct a simple nondeterministic finite automaton to accept the language $(ab \cup aba)^*a$. Then apply to it the construction of Part (c) of the proof of Theorem 2.3.1 to obtain a nondeterministic finite automaton accepting $((ab \cup aba)^*a)^*$.

2.3.6. Let $L, L' \subseteq \Sigma^*$. Define the following languages.
  1. $\text{Pref}(L) = \{w \in \Sigma^* : x = wy \text{ for some } x \in L, y \in \Sigma^*\}$ (the set of **prefixes** of L).
  1. $\text{Suf}(L) = \{w \in \Sigma^* : x = yw \text{ for some } x \in L, y \in \Sigma^*\}$ (the set of **suffixes** of L).
  3. $\text{Subseq}(L) = \{w_1w_2 \ldots w_k : k \in \mathbf{N}, w_i \in \Sigma^* \text{ for } i = 1, \ldots, k, \text{ and there is a string } x = x_0w_1x_1w_2x_2 \ldots w_kx_k \in L\}$ (the set of **subsequences** of L).

4. $L/L' = \{w \in \Sigma^* : wx \in L \text{ for some } x \in L'\}$ (the **right quotient** of L by L').

5. $\text{Max}(L) = \{w \in L : \text{if } x \neq e \text{ then } wx \notin L\}$.

6. $L^R = \{w^R : w \in L\}$.

Show that if L is accepted by some finite automaton, then so is each of the following.

(a) $\text{Pref}(L)$

(b) $\text{Suf}(L)$

(c) $\text{Subseq}(L)$

(d) L/L', where L' is accepted by some finite automaton.

(e) L/L', where L' is *any* language.

(f) $\text{Max}(L)$

(g) L^R

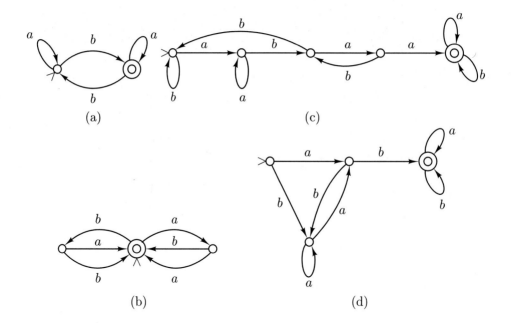

2.3.7. Apply the construction in Example 2.3.2 to obtain regular expressions corresponding to each of the finite automata above. Simplify the resulting regular expressions as much as you can.

2.3.8. For any natural number $n \geq 1$ define the nondeterministic finite automaton $M_n = (K_n, \Sigma_n, \Delta_n, s_n, F_n)$ with $K_n = \{q_1, q_2, \ldots, q_n\}$, $s_n = q_1$, $F_n = \{q_1\}$, $\Sigma_n = \{a_{ij} : i, j = 1, \ldots, n\}$, and $\Delta_n = \{(i, a_{ij}, j) : i, j = 1, \ldots, n\}$.

(a) Describe $L(M_n)$ in English.

(b) Write a regular expression for $L(M_3)$.

(c) Write a regular expression for $L(M_5)$.

It is conjectured that, for all polynomials p there is an n such that no regular expression for $L(M_n)$ has length smaller than $p(n)$ symbols.

2.3.9. (a) By analogy with Problem 2.1.5, define a **nondeterministic 2-tape finite automaton**, and the notion that such an automaton accepts a particular set of ordered pairs of strings.

(b) Show that $\{(a^m b, a^n b^p) : n, m, p \geq 0, \text{ and } n = m \text{ or } n = p\}$ is accepted by some nondeterministic 2-tape finite automaton.

(c) We shall see (Problem 2.4.9) that nondeterministic 2-tape finite automata cannot always be converted into deterministic ones. This being the case, which of the constructions used in the proof of Theorem 2.3.1 can be extended to demonstrate closure properties of the following?

(i) The sets of pairs of strings accepted by nondeterministic 2-tape finite automata.

(ii) The sets of pairs of strings accepted by deterministic 2-tape finite automata.

Explain your answers.

2.3.10. A language L is **definite** if there is some k such that, for any string w, whether $w \in L$ depends only on the last k symbols of w.

(a) Rewrite this definition more formally.

(b) Show that every definite language is accepted by a finite automaton.

(c) Show that the class of definite languages is closed under union and complementation.

(d) Give an example of a definite language L such that L^* is not definite.

(e) Give an example of definite languages L_1, L_2 such that $L_1 L_2$ is not definite.

2.3.11. Let Σ and Δ be alphabets. Consider a function h from Σ to Δ^*. Extend h to a function from Σ^* to Δ^* as follows.

$$h(e) = e.$$
$$h(w) = h(w)h(\sigma) \text{ for any } w \in \Sigma^*, \sigma \in \Sigma.$$

For example, if $\Sigma = \Delta = \{a, b\}$, $h(a) = ab$, and $h(b) = aab$, then

$$h(aab) = h(aa)h(b)$$
$$= h(a)h(a)h(b)$$
$$= ababaab.$$

Any function $h : \Sigma^* \mapsto \Delta^*$ defined in this way from a function $h : \Sigma \mapsto \Delta^*$ is called a **homomorphism**.

Let h be a homomorphism from Σ^* to Δ^*.

(a) Show that if $L \subseteq \Sigma^*$ is accepted by a finite automaton, then so is $h[L]$.

(b) Show that if L is accepted by a finite automaton, then so is $\{w \in \Sigma^* : h(w) \in L\}$. (*Hint:* Start from a deterministic finite automaton M accepting L, and construct one which, when it reads an input symbol a, tries to simulate what M would do on input $h(a)$.)

2.3.12. Deterministic finite-state transducers were introduced in Problem 2.1.4. Show that if L is accepted by a finite automaton, and f is computed by a deterministic finite-state transducer, then each of the following is true.

(a) $f[L]$ is accepted by a finite automaton.

(b) $f^{-1}[L]$ is accepted by a finite automaton.

2.4 | LANGUAGES THAT ARE AND ARE NOT REGULAR

The results of the last two sections establish that the regular languages are closed under a variety of operations and that regular languages may be specified either by regular expressions or by deterministic or nondeterministic finite automata. These facts, used singly or in combinations, provide a variety of techniques for showing languages to be regular.

Example 2.4.1: Let $\Sigma = \{0, 1, \dots, 9\}$ and let $L \subseteq \Sigma^*$ be the set of decimal representations for nonnegative integers (without redundant leading 0's) divisible by 2 or 3. For example, $0, 3, 6, 244 \in L$, but $1, 03, 00 \notin L$. Then L is regular. We break the proof into four parts.

Let L_1 be the set of decimal representations of nonnegative integers. Then it is easy to see that

$$L_1 = 0 \cup \{1, 2, \dots, 9\}\Sigma^*,$$

which is regular since it is denoted by a regular expression.

Let L_2 be the set of decimal representations of nonnegative integers divisible by 2. Then L_2 is just the set of members of L, ending in 0, 2, 4, 6, or 8; that is,

$$L_2 = L_1 \cap \Sigma^*\{0, 2, 4, 6, 8\},$$

which is regular by Theorem 2.3.1(e).

Let L_3 be the set of decimal representations of nonnegative integers divisible by 3. Recall that a number is divisible by 3 if and only if the sum of its digits is divisible by 3. We construct a finite automaton that keeps track in its finite control of the sum modulo 3 of a string of digits. L_3 will then be the intersection

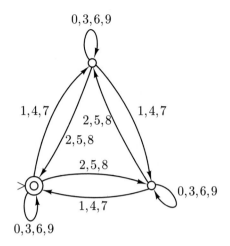

Figure 2-18

with L_1 of the language accepted by this finite automaton. The automaton is pictured in Figure 2-18.

Finally, $L = L_2 \cup L_3$, surely a regular language.◊

Although we now have a variety of powerful techniques for showing that languages are regular, as yet we have none for showing that languages are *not* regular. We know on fundamental principles that nonregular languages do exist, since the number of regular expressions (or the number of finite automata) is countable, whereas the number of languages is uncountable. But to demonstrate that any particular language is not regular requires special tools.

Two properties shared by all regular languages, but not by certain nonregular languages, may be phrased intuitively as follows:

(1) As a string is scanned left to right, the amount of memory that is required in order to determine at the end whether or not the string is in the language must be bounded, fixed in advance and dependent on the language, not the particular input string. For example, we would expect that $\{a^n b^n : n \geq 0\}$ is not regular, since it is difficult to imagine how a finite-state device could be constructed that would correctly remember, upon reaching the border between the a's and the b's, how many a's it had seen, so that the number could be compared against the number of b's.

(2) Regular languages with an infinite number of strings are represented by automata with cycles and regular expressions involving the Kleene star. Such languages must have infinite subsets with a certain simple repetitive structure that arises from the Kleene star in a corresponding regular expression or a cycle in the state diagram of a finite automaton. This would lead us to

expect, for example, that $\{a^n : n \geq 1$ is a prime$\}$ is not regular, since there is no simple periodicity in the set of prime numbers.

These intuitive ideas are accurate but not sufficiently precise to be used in formal proofs. We shall now prove a theorem that captures some of this intuition and yields the nonregularity of certain languages as an easy consequence.

Theorem 2.4.1: *Let L be a regular language. There is an integer $n \geq 1$ such that any string $w \in L$ with $|w| \geq n$ can be rewritten as $w = xyz$ such that $y \neq e$, $|xy| \leq n$, and $xy^i z \in L$ for each $i \geq 0$.*

Proof: Since L is regular, L is accepted by a deterministic finite automaton M. Suppose that n is the number of states of M, and let w be a string of length n or greater. Consider now the first n steps of the computation of M on w:

$$(q_0, w_1 w_2 \ldots w_n) \vdash_M (q_1, w_2 \ldots w_n) \vdash_M \ldots \vdash_M (q_n, e),$$

where q_0 is the initial state of M, and $w_1 \ldots w_n$ are the n first symbols of w. Since M has only n states, and there are $n + 1$ configurations $(q_i, w_{i+1} \ldots, w_n)$ appearing in the computation above, *by the pigeonhole principle* there exist i and j, $0 \leq i < j \leq n$, such that $q_i = q_j$. That is, the string $y = w_i w_{i+1} \ldots w_j$ drives M from state q_i back to state q_i, and this string is nonempty since $i < j$. But then this string could be removed from w, or repeated any number of times in w just after the jth symbol of w, and M would still accept this string. That is, M accepts $xy^i z \in L$ for each $i \geq 0$, where $x = w_1 \ldots w_i$, and $z = w_{j+1} \ldots w_m$. Notice finally that the length of xy, the number we called j above, is by definition at most n, as required. ∎

This theorem is one of a general class called *pumping theorems*, because they assert the existence of certain points in certain strings where a substring can be repeatedly inserted without affecting the acceptability of the string. In terms of its structure as a mathematical statement, the pumping theorem above is by far the most sophisticated theorem that we have seen in this book, because its assertion, however simple to prove and apply, involves *five alternating quantifiers*. Consider again what it says:

> *for each* regular language L,
> *there exists* an $n \geq 1$, such that
> *for each* string w in L longer than n,
> *there exist* strings x, y, z with $w = xyz$, $y \neq e$, and $|xy| \leq n$, such that
> *for each* $i \geq 0$ $xy^i z \in L$.

Applying the theorem correctly can be subtle. It is often useful to think of the application of this result as a *game* between yourself, the prover, who is striving to establish that the given language L is not regular, and an adversary who is insisting that L is regular. The theorem states that, once L has been fixed, the adversary must start by providing a number n; then you come up with a string w in the language that is longer than n; the adversary must now supply an appropriate decomposition of w into xyz; and, finally, you triumphantly point out i for which $xy^i z$ is not in the language. If you have a strategy that always wins, no matter how brilliantly the adversary plays, then you have established that L is not regular.

It follows from this theorem that each of the two languages mentioned earlier in this section is not regular.

Example 2.4.2: The language $L = \{a^i b^i : i \geq 0\}$ is not regular, for if it were regular, Theorem 2.4.1 would apply for some integer n. Consider then the string $w = a^n b^n \in L$. By the theorem, it can be rewritten as $w = xyz$ such that $|xy| \leq n$ and $y \neq e$ —that is, $y = a^i$ for some $i > 0$. But then $xz = a^{n-i} b^n \notin L$, contradicting the theorem.$\Diamond$

Example 2.4.3: The language $L = \{a^n : n \text{ is prime}\}$ is not regular. For suppose it were, and let x, y, and z be as specified in Theorem 2.4.1. Then $x = a^p$, $y = a^q$, and and $z = a^r$, where $p, r \geq 0$ and $q > 0$. By the theorem, $xy^n z \in L$ for each $n \geq 0$; that is, $p + nq + r$ is prime for each $n \geq 0$. But this is impossible; for let $n = p + 2q + r + 2$; then $p + nq + r = (q + 1) \cdot (p + 2q + r)$, which is a product of two natural numbers, each greater than 1.$\Diamond$

Example 2.4.4: Sometimes it pays to use closure properties to show that a language is not regular. Take for example

$$L = \{w \in \{a, b\}^* : w \text{ has an equal number of } a\text{'s and } b\text{'s}\}.$$

L is not regular, because if L were indeed regular, then so would be $L \cap a^* b^*$ —by closure under intersection; recall Theorem 2.3.1(e). However, this latter language is precisely $\{a^n b^n : n \geq 0\}$, which we just showed is not regular.$\Diamond$

In fact, Theorem 2.4.1 can be strengthened substantially in several ways (see Problem 2.4.11 for one of them).

Problems for Section 2.4

2.4.1. An **arithmetic progression** is the set $\{p + qn : n = 0, 1, 2, \ldots\}$ for some $p, q \in N$.
   (a) (Easy) Show that if $L \subseteq \{a\}^*$ and $\{n : a^n \in L\}$ is an arithmetic progression, then L is regular.
   (b) Show that if $L \subseteq \{a\}^*$ and $\{n : a^n \in L\}$ is a union of finitely many arithmetic progressions, then L is regular.

   (c) (Harder) Show that if $L \subseteq \{a\}^*$ is regular, then $\{n : a^n \in L\}$ is a union
       of finitely many arithmetic progressions. (This is the converse of Part
       (b).)
   (d) Show that if Σ is any alphabet and $L \subseteq \Sigma^*$ is regular, then $\{|w| : w \in L\}$ is a union of finitely many arithmetic progressions. (*Hint:* Use Part
       (c).)

2.4.2. Let $D = \{0, 1\}$ and let $T = D \times D \times D$. A correct addition of two numbers in
binary notation can be pictured as a string in T^* if we think of the symbols
in T as vertical columns. For example,

$$\begin{array}{r} 0\ 1\ 0\ 1 \\ +\ 0\ 1\ 1\ 0 \\ \hline 1\ 0\ 1\ 1 \end{array}$$

would be pictured as the following string of four symbols.

$$\begin{pmatrix} 0 \\ 0 \\ 1 \end{pmatrix} \begin{pmatrix} 1 \\ 1 \\ 0 \end{pmatrix} \begin{pmatrix} 0 \\ 1 \\ 1 \end{pmatrix} \begin{pmatrix} 1 \\ 0 \\ 1 \end{pmatrix}.$$

Show that the set of all strings in T^* that represent correct additions is a
regular language.

2.4.3. Show that each of the following is or is not a regular language. The decimal
notation for a number is the number written in the usual way, as a string
over the alphabet $\{0, 1, \ldots, 9\}$. For example, the decimal notation for 13 is
a string of length 2. In **unary notation**, only the symbol I is used; thus 5
would be represented as IIIII in unary notation.
   (a) $\{w : w$ is the unary notation for a number that is a multiple of 7$\}$.
   (b) $\{w : w$ is the decimal notation for a number that is a multiple of 7$\}$
   (c) $\{w : w$ is the unary notation for a number n such that there is a pair
       $p, p + 2$ of twin primes, both greater than $n\}$
   (d) $\{w : w$ is, for some $n \geq 1$, the unary notation for $10^n\}$
   (e) $\{w : w$ is, for some $n \geq 1$, the decimal notation for $10^n\}$
   (f) $\{w : w$ is a sequence of decimal digits that occurs in the infinite decimal
       expansion of $1/7\}$ (For example, 5714 is such a sequence, since $1/7 = 0.14285714285714\ldots$)

2.4.4. Prove that $\{a^n b a^m b a^{m+n} : n, m \geq 1\}$ is not regular.

2.4.5. Using the pumping theorem and closure under intersection, show that the
following are not regular.
   (a) $\{ww^R : w \in \{a, b\}^*\}$
   (b) $\{ww : w \in \{a, b\}^*\}$
   (c) $\{w\overline{w} : w \in \{a, b\}^*\}$, where $\overline{w}$ stands for w with each occurrence of a
       replaced by b, and vice versa.

2.4.6. Call a string x over the alphabet $\{(,)\}$ *balanced* if the following hold: (i) in any prefix of x the number of ('s is no smaller than the number of)'s; (ii) the number of ('s in x equals that of)'s. That is, x is balanced if it could be derived from a legal arithmetic expression by omitting all variables, numbers, and operations. (See the next chapter for a less awkward definition.) Show that the set of all balanced strings in $\{(,)\}^*$ is not regular.

2.4.7. Show that for any deterministic finite automaton $M = (K, \Sigma, \delta, s, F)$, M accepts an infinite language if and only if M accepts some string of length greater than or equal to $|K|$ and less than $2|K|$.

2.4.8. Are the following statements true or false? Explain your answer in each case. (In each case, a fixed alphabet Σ is assumed.)
(a) Every subset of a regular language is regular.
(b) Every regular language has a regular proper subset.
(c) If L is regular, then so is $\{xy : x \in L$ and $y \notin L\}$.
(d) $\{w : w = w^R\}$ is regular.
(e) If L is a regular language, then so is $\{w : w \in L$ and $w^R \in L\}$.
(f) If C is any set of regular languages, then $\bigcup C$ is a regular language.
(g) $\{xyx^R : x, y \in \Sigma^*\}$ is regular.

2.4.9. The notion of a deterministic 2-tape finite automaton was defined in Problem 2.1.5. Show that $\{(a^n b, a^m b^p) : n, m, p > 0, n = m$ or $n = p\}$ is not accepted by any deterministic 2-tape finite automaton. (*Hint:* Suppose this set were accepted by some deterministic 2-tape finite automaton M. Then M accepts $(a^n b, a^{n+1} b^n)$ for every n. Show by a pumping argument that it also accepts $(a^n b, a^{n+1} b^{n+q})$ for some $n \geq 0$ and $q > 0$, a contradiction.) By Problem 2.3.9, then, nondeterministic 2-tape finite automata cannot always be converted to deterministic ones, and by Problem 2.1.5, the sets accepted by deterministic 2-tape finite automata are not closed under union.

2.4.10. A **2-head finite automaton** is a finite automaton with two tape heads that may move independently, but from left to right only, on the input tape. As with a 2-tape finite automaton (Problem 2.1.5), the state set is divided into two parts; each part corresponds to reading and moving one tape head. A string is accepted if both heads wind up together at the end of the string with the finite control in a final state. 2-head finite automata may be either deterministic or nondeterministic. Using a state-diagram notation of your own design, show that the following languages are accepted by 2-head finite automata.
(a) $\{a^n b : n \geq 0\}$
(b) $\{wcw : w \in \{a, b\}^*\}$
(c) $\{a^1 b a^2 b a^3 b \dots b a^k b : k \geq 1\}$
In which cases can you make your machines deterministic?

2.4.11. This problem establishes a stronger version of the Pumping Theorem 2.4.1; the goal is to make the "pumped" part as long as possible. Let $M = (K, \Sigma, \delta, s, F)$ be a deterministic finite automaton, and let w be any string in $L(M)$ of length at least $|K|$. Show that there are strings x, y, and z such that $w = xyz$, $|y| \geq (|w| - |K| + 1)/|K|$, and $xy^n z \in L(M)$ for each $n \geq 0$.

2.4.12. Let $D = \{0, 1\}$ and let $T = D \times D \times D$. A correct *multiplication* of two numbers in binary notation can also be represented as a string in T^*. For example, the multiplication $10 \times 5 = 50$, or

$$
\begin{array}{r}
0\ 0\ 1\ 0\ 1\ 0 \\
\times\ 0\ 0\ 0\ 1\ 0\ 1 \\
\hline
1\ 1\ 0\ 0\ 1\ 0
\end{array}
$$

would be pictured as the following string of six symbols.

$$
\begin{pmatrix} 0 \\ 0 \\ 1 \end{pmatrix}
\begin{pmatrix} 0 \\ 0 \\ 1 \end{pmatrix}
\begin{pmatrix} 1 \\ 0 \\ 0 \end{pmatrix}
\begin{pmatrix} 0 \\ 1 \\ 0 \end{pmatrix}
\begin{pmatrix} 1 \\ 0 \\ 1 \end{pmatrix}
\begin{pmatrix} 0 \\ 1 \\ 0 \end{pmatrix} .
$$

Show that the set of all strings in T^* that represent correct multiplications is *not* a regular language. (*Hint:* Consider the multiplication $(2^n + 1) \times (2^n + 1)$.)

2.4.13. Let $L \subseteq \Sigma^*$ be a language, and define $L_n = \{x \in L : |x| \leq n\}$. The *density* of L is the function $d_L(n) = |L_n|$.
  (a) What is the density of $(a \cup b)^*$?
  (b) What is the density of $ab^* ab * ab^* a$?
  (c) What is the density of $(ab \cup aab)^*$?
  (d) Show that the density of any regular language is either bounded from above by a polynomial, or bounded from below by an exponential (a function of the form 2^{cn} for some n). In other words, densities of regular languages cannot be functions of intermediate rate of growth such as $n^{\log n}$. (*Hint:* Consider a deterministic finite automaton accepting L, and all cycles —closed paths without repetitions of nodes— in the state diagram of this automaton. What happens if no two cycles share a node? What happens if there are two cycles that share a node?)

2.5 | STATE MINIMIZATION

In the last section our suspicion that deterministic finite automata are poor models of computers was verified: Computation based on finite automata cannot

achieve such trivial computational tasks as comparing the number of a's and the
number of b's in a string. However, finite automata are useful as basic *parts*
of computers and algorithms. In this regard, it is important to be able to
minimize the number of states of a given deterministic finite automaton, that is,
to determine an equivalent deterministic finite automaton that has as few states
as possible. We shall next develop the necessary concepts and results that lead
to such a *state minimization algorithm*.

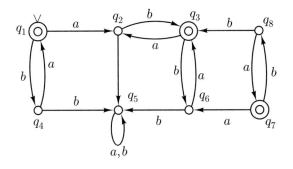

Figure 2-19

Given a deterministic finite automaton, there may be an easy way to get rid
of several states. Let us take, for example, the deterministic automaton in Figure
2-19, accepting the language $L = (ab \cup ba)^*$ (as it is not very hard to check).
Consider state q_7. It should be clear that this state is *unreachable*, because
there is no path from the start state to it in the state diagram of the automaton.
This is the simplest kind of optimization one can do on any deterministic finite
automaton: Remove all unreachable states and all transitions in and out of them.
In fact, this optimization was implicit in our conversion of a nondeterministic
finite automaton to its equivalent deterministic one (recall Example 2.2.4): We
omitted from consideration all states (sets of states of the original automaton)
that are not reachable from the start state of the resulting automaton.

Identifying the reachable states is easy to do in polynomial time, because
the set of reachable states can be defined as the closure of $\{s\}$ under the relation
$\{(p, q) : \delta(p, a) = q$ for some $a \in \Sigma\}$. Therefore, the set of all reachable states
can be computed by this simple algorithm:

$R := \{s\}$;
while there is a state $p \in R$ and $a \in \Sigma$ such that $\delta(p, a) \notin R$ do
    add $\delta(p, a)$ to R.

However, the remaining automaton after the deletion of unreachable states
(Figure 2-20) still has more states than are really needed, this time for subtler
reasons. For example, states q_4 and q_6 are *equivalent*, and therefore they *can be*

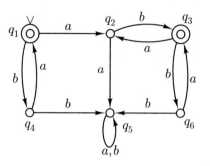

Figure 2-20

merged into one state. What does this mean, exactly? Intuitively, the reason we call these states equivalent is that, *from either state, precisely the same strings lead the automaton to acceptance.*

Our next definition captures a similar relation between strings that have "a common fate" with respect to a language.

Definition 2.5.1: Let $L \subseteq \Sigma^*$ be a language, and let $x, y \in \Sigma^*$. We say that x and y are **equivalent with respect to** L, denoted $x \approx_L y$, if for all $z \in \Sigma^*$, the following is true: $xz \in L$ if and only if $yz \in L$. Notice that $\approx_L$ is an equivalence relation.

That is, $x \approx_L y$ if either both strings belong to L or neither is in L; and moreover, appending any fixed string to both x and y results in two strings that are either both in L or both not in L.

Example 2.5.1: If x is a string, and when L is understood by context, we denote by $[x]$ the equivalence class with respect to L to which x belongs. For example, for the language $L = (ab \cup ba)^*$ accepted by the automaton in Figure 2-20, it is not hard to see that $\approx_L$ has *four* equivalence classes:

(1) $[e] = L$,
(2) $[a] = La$,
(3) $[b] = Lb$,
(4) $[aa] = L(aa \cup bb)\Sigma^*$.

In (1), for any string $x \in L$, including $x = e$, the z's that make $xz \in L$ are precisely the members of L. In (2), any $x \in La$ needs a z of the form bL in order for xz to be in L. Similarly, for (3) the z's are of the form aL. Finally, in (4) there is no z that can restore to L a string with a prefix in $L(aa \cup bb)$. In other words, all strings in set (1) have *the same fate* with respect to inclusion in L; and the same for (2), (3), and (4). Finally, it is easy to see that these four classes exhaust all of Σ^*. Hence these are the equivalence classes of $\approx_L$.◊

Notice that $\approx_L$ relates strings in terms of a language, not in terms of an automaton. Automata provide another, somewhat less fundamental, relation, described next.

Definition 2.5.2: Let $M = (K, \Sigma, \delta, s, F)$ be a deterministic finite automaton. We say that two strings $x, y \in \Sigma^*$ are **equivalent with respect to** M, denoted $x \sim_M y$, if, intuitively, they both drive M from s to the same state. Formally, $x \sim_M y$ if there is a state q such that $(s, x) \vdash_M^* (q, e)$ and $(s, y) \vdash_M^* (q, e)$.

Again, $\sim_M$ is an equivalence relation. Its equivalence classes can be identified by the states of M —more precisely, with those states that are reachable from s and therefore have at least one string in the corresponding equivalence class. We denote the equivalence class corresponding to state q of M as E_q.

Example 2.5.1 (continued): For example, for the automaton M in Figure 2-20, the equivalence classes of $\sim_M$ are these (where $L = (ab \cup ba)^*$ is the language accepted by M)

(1) $E_{q_1} = (ba)^*$,
(2) $E_{q_2} = abLa$,
(3) $E_{q_3} = abL$,
(4) $E_{q_4} = b(ab)^*$,
(5) $E_{q_5} = L(bb \cup aa)\Sigma^*$,
(6) $E_{q_6} = abLb$.

Again, they form a partition of Σ^*.◊

These two important equivalence relations, one associated with the language, the other with the automaton, are related as follows:

Theorem 2.5.1: *For any deterministic finite automaton* $M = (K, \Sigma, \delta, s, F)$ *and any strings* $x, y \in \Sigma^*$, *if* $x \sim_M y$, *then* $x \approx_{L(M)} y$.

Proof: For any string $x \in \Sigma^*$, let $q(x) \in K$ be the unique state such that $(s, x) \vdash_M^* (q(x), e)$. Notice that, for any $x, z \in \Sigma^*$, $xz \in L(M)$ if and only if $(q(x), z) \vdash_M^* (f, e)$ for some $f \in F$. Now, if $x \sim_M y$ then, by the definition of $\sim_M$, $q(x) = q(y)$, and thus $x \sim_M y$ implies that the following holds:

$$xz \in L(M) \text{ if and only if } yz \in L(M) \text{ for all } z \in \Sigma^*\},$$

which is the same as $x \approx_{L(M)} y$. ■

A very suggestive way of expressing Theorem 2.5.1 is to say that $\sim_M$ is a **refinement** of $\approx_{L(M)}$. In general, we say that an equivalence relation $\sim$ is a refinement of another $\approx$ if for all x, y $x \sim y$ implies $x \approx y$. If $\sim$ is a refinement of $\approx$, then each equivalence class with respect to $\sim$ is contained in some equivalence class of $\approx$; that is, each equivalence class of $\approx$ is the union of one or more equivalence classes of $\sim$. For example, the equivalence relation that relates any two cities of the United States that are in the same *county* is a refinement of the equivalence relation that relates any two cities that are in the same *state*.

Example 2.5.1 (continued): For an example that is more to the point, the equivalence classes of $\sim_M$ for the automaton M in Figure 2-20 "refine" in this sense the equivalence classes of $\approx_{L(M)}$, exactly as predicted by Theorem 2.5.1. For example, classes E_{q_5} and $[aa]$ coincide, while classes E_{q_1} and E_{q_3} are both subsets of $[e]$.◊

Theorem 2.5.1 implies something very important about M and any other automaton M accepting the same language $L(M)$: Its number of states must be *at least as large* as the number of equivalence classes of $L(M)$ under $\approx$. In other words, the number of equivalence classes of $L(M)$ is a natural *lower bound* on the number of states of any automaton equivalent to M. Can this lower bound be achieved? We next show that indeed it can.

Theorem 2.5.2 (The Myhill-Nerode Theorem): Let $L \subseteq \Sigma^*$ be a regular language. Then there is a deterministic finite automaton with precisely as many states as there are equivalence classes in $\approx_L$ that accepts L.

Proof: As before, we denote the equivalence class of string $x \in \Sigma^*$ in the equivalence relation $\approx_L$ by $[x]$. Given L, we shall construct a deterministic finite automaton (the **standard automaton for** L) $M = (K, \Sigma, \delta, s, F)$ such that $L = L(M)$. M is defined as follows:

$K = \{[x] : x \in \Sigma^*\}$, the set of equivalence classes under $\approx_L$.
$s = [e]$, the equivalence class of e under $\approx_L$.
$F = \{[x] : x \in L\}$.
Finally, for any $[x] \in K$ and any $a \in \Sigma$, define $\delta([x], a) = [xa]$.

How do we know that the set K is finite, that is, that $\approx_L$ has finitely many equivalent classes? L is regular, and so it is surely accepted by some deterministic finite automaton M'. By the previous theorem, $\sim_{M'}$ is a refinement of $\approx_L$, and so there are fewer equivalence classes in L than there are equivalence classes of $\sim_{M'}$ —that is to say, states of M'. Hence K is a finite set. We also have to argue that δ is *well defined*, that is, $\delta([x], a) = [xa]$ is independent of the string $x \in [x]$. But this is easy to see, because $x \approx_L x'$ if and only if $xa \approx_L x'a$.

We next show that $L = L(M)$. First we show that for all $x, y \in \Sigma^*$, we have

$$([x], y) \vdash_M^* ([xy], e). \tag{1}$$

This is established by induction on $|y|$. It is trivial when $y = e$, and, if it holds for all y's of length up to n and $y = y'a$, then by induction $([x], y'a) \vdash_M^* ([xy'], a) \vdash_M^* ([xy], e)$.

Now (1) completes the proof: For all $x \in \Sigma^*$, we have that $x \in L(M)$ if and only if $([e], x) \vdash (q, e)$ for some $q \in F$, which is by (1) the same as saying $[x] \in F$, or, by the definition of F, $[x \in L]$. ∎

Example 2.5.1 (continued): The standard automaton corresponding to the language $L = (ab \cup ba)^*$ accepted by the six-state deterministic finite automaton in Figure 2-20 is shown in Figure 2-21. It has *four* states. Naturally, it is the smallest deterministic finite automaton that accepts this language.◊

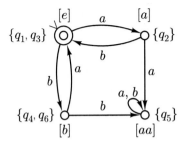

Figure 2-21

Incidentally, Theorems 2.5.2 immediately imply the following characterization of regular languages, sometimes itself called *the Myhill-Nerode Theorem*:

Corollary: *A language L is regular if and only if $\approx_L$ has finitely many equivalence classes.*

Proof: If L is regular, then $L = L(M)$ for some deterministic finite automaton M, and M has at least as many states as $\approx_L$ has equivalence classes. Hence there are finitely many equivalence classes in $\approx_L$.

Conversely, if $\approx_L$ has finitely many equivalence classes, then the standard deterministic finite automaton M_L (recall the proof of Theorem 2.5.2) accepts L. ∎

Example 2.5.2: The corollary just proved is an interesting alternative way of specifying what it means for a language L to be regular. Furthermore, it provides another useful way for proving that a language is *not* regular —besides the Pumping Theorem.

For example, here is an alternative proof that $L = \{a^n b^n : n \geq 1\}$ is not regular: No two strings a^i and a^j, with $i \neq j$, are equivalent under $\approx_L$, simply because there is a string (namely, b^i) which, when affixed a^i gives a string in L, but when affixed to a^j produces a string not in L. Hence $\approx_L$ has infinitely many equivalence classes $[e], [a], [aa], [aaa], \ldots$, and hence by the corollary L is not regular.$\Diamond$

For any regular language L the automaton constructed in the proof of Theorem 2.5.2 is the deterministic automaton with the fewest states that accepts L —an object of obvious practical importance. Unfortunately, this automaton is defined in terms of the equivalence classes of $\approx_L$, and it is not clear how these equivalence classes can be identified for any given regular language L — especially if L is given in terms of a deterministic automaton M. We shall next develop an *algorithm* for constructing this minimal automaton, starting from *any deterministic finite automaton* M such that $L = L(M)$.

Let $M = (K, \Sigma, \delta, s, F)$ be a deterministic finite automaton. Define a relation $A_M \subseteq K \times \Sigma^*$, as follows: $(q, w) \in A_M$ if and only if $(q, w) \vdash_M^* (f, e)$ for some $f \in F$; that is, $(q, w) \in A_M$ means that w drives M from q to an accepting state. Let us call two states $q, p \in K$ **equivalent**, denoted $q \equiv p$, if the following holds for all $z \in \Sigma^*$: $(q, z) \in A_M$ if and only if $(p, z) \in A_M$. Thus, if two states are equivalent, then the corresponding equivalence classes of $\sim_M$ are subsets of the same equivalence class of $\approx_L$. In other words, the equivalence classes of $\equiv$ are precisely those sets of states of M that must be clumped together in order to obtain the standard automaton of $L(M)^\dagger$.

We shall develop an algorithm for computing the equivalence classes of $\equiv$. Our algorithm will compute $\equiv$ as the *limit* of a sequence of equivalence relations $\equiv_0, \equiv_1, \equiv_2, \ldots$, defined next. For two states $q, p \in K$, $q \equiv_n p$ if the following is true: $(q, z) \in A_M$ if and only if $(p, z) \in A_M$ for all strings z such that $|z| \leq n$. In other words, $\equiv_n$ is a *coarser* equivalence relation than $\equiv$, only requiring that states q and p behave the same with respect to acceptance when driven by strings *of length up to n*.

Obviously, each equivalence relation in $\equiv_0, \equiv_1, \equiv_2, \ldots$ is a refinement of the previous one. Also, $q \equiv_0 p$ holds if q and p are either both accepting, or both non-accepting. That is, there are precisely two equivalence classes of $\equiv_0$: F and $K - F$ (assuming they are both nonempty). It remains to show how $\equiv_{n+1}$ depends on $\equiv_n$. Here is how:

$\dagger$ The relation $\equiv$ can be called the *quotient* of $\sim_M$ by $\approx_L$. If $\sim$ is a refinement of $\approx$, then the **quotient** of $\approx$ by $\sim$, denoted $\approx / \sim$, is *an equivalence relation on the equivalence classes of* $\sim$. Two classes $[x]$ and $[y]$ of $\sim$ are related by $\approx / \sim$ if $x \approx y$ —it is easy to see that this is indeed an equivalence relation. To return to our geographic example, the quotient of the "same state" relation by the "same county" relation relates any two counties (each with at least one city in it) that happen to be in the same state.

Lemma 2.5.1: *For any two states $q, p \in K$ and any integer $n \geq 1$, $q \equiv_n p$ if and only if (a) $q \equiv_{n-1} p$, and (b) for all $a \in \Sigma$, $\delta(q, a) \equiv_n \delta(p, a)$.*

Proof: By definition of $\equiv_n$, $q \equiv_n p$ if and only if $q \equiv_{n-1} p$, and furthermore any string $w = av$ of length precisely n drives either both q and p to acceptance, or both to nonacceptance. However, the second condition is the same as saying that $\delta(q, a) \equiv_n \delta(p, a)$ for any $a \in \Sigma$. ∎

Lemma 2.5.1 suggests that we can compute $\equiv$, and from this the standard automaton for L, by the following algorithm:

> Initially the equivalence classes of $\equiv_0$ are F and $K - F$;
>> repeat for $n := 1, 2, \ldots$
>>> compute the equivalence classes of $\equiv_n$ from those $\equiv_{n-1}$
>> until $\equiv_n$ is the same as $\equiv_{n-1}$.

Each iteration can be carried out by applying Lemma 2.5.1: For each pair of states of M we test whether the conditions of the lemma hold, and if so we put the two states in the same equivalence class of $\equiv_n$. But how do we know that *this is an algorithm*, that the iteration will eventually terminate? The answer is simple: For each iteration at which the termination condition is not satisfied, $\equiv_n \neq \equiv_{n-1}$, $\equiv_n$ is a *proper refinement* of $\equiv_{n-1}$, and thus has at least one more equivalence class than $\equiv_{n-1}$. Since the number of equivalence classes cannot become more than the number of states of M, the algorithm will terminate after at most $|K| - 1$ iterations.

When the algorithm terminates, say at the nth iteration and having computed $\equiv_n = \equiv_{n-1}$, then the lemma implies that $\equiv_n = \equiv_{n+1} = \equiv_{n+2} = \equiv_{n+3} = \cdots$ Hence the relation computed is precisely $\equiv$. In the next section we give a more careful analysis of the complexity of this important algorithm, establishing that it is polynomial.

Example 2.5.3: Let us apply the state minimization algorithm to the deterministic finite automaton M in Figure 2-20 (of course, by the previous example, we know what to expect: the four-state standard automaton for $L(M)$). At the various iterations we shall have these equivalence classes of the corresponding $\equiv_i$:

> Initially, the equivalence classes of $\equiv_0$ are $\{q_1, q_3\}$ and $\{q_2, q_4, q_5, q_6\}$.
> After the first iteration, the classes of $\equiv_1$ are $\{q_1, q_3\}$, $\{q_2\}$, $\{q_4, q_6\}$, and $\{q_5\}$. The splitting happened because $\delta(q_2, b) \not\equiv_0 \delta(q_4, b), \delta(q_5, b)$, and $\delta(q_4, a) \not\equiv_0 \delta(q_5, a)$.
> After the second iteration, there is no further splitting of classes. The algorithm thus terminates, and the minimum-state automaton is shown in

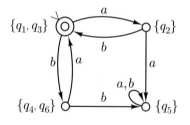

Figure 2-22

Figure 2-22. As expected, it is isomorphic with the standard automaton shown in Figure 2-21.◊

Example 2.5.4: Recall the language $L \subseteq \{a_1, \ldots, a_n\}^*$ of all strings that do not contain occurrences of all n symbols, and the corresponding deterministic finite automaton with 2^n states (Example 2.2.5). We can now show that these states are all necessary. The reason is that $\approx_L$ has 2^n equivalence classes. Namely, for each subset A of Σ, let L_A be the set of all strings containing occurrences of all symbols in A, and of no symbols in $\Sigma - A$ (for example, $L_\emptyset = \{e\}$). Then it is not hard to see that the 2^n sets L_A are precisely the equivalence classes of $\approx_L$. Because if $x \in L_A$ and $y \in L_B$ for two distinct subsets A and B of Σ, then for any $z \in L_{\Sigma-B}$, $xz \in L$, and $yz \notin L$ (here we assumed that B is not contained in A; otherwise, reverse the rôles of A and B).◊

Recall that there is a *nondeterministic* finite automaton with $n + 1$ states that accepts the same language (Example 2.2.2). Although deterministic automata are exactly as powerful as nondeterministic ones *in principle*, determinism comes with a price in the number of states which is, at worst, exponential. To put it in a different way, and in fact a way that anticipates the important issues of *computational complexity* discussed in Chapters 6 and 7: When the number of states is taken into account, *nondeterminism is exponentially more powerful than determinism in the domain of finite automata.*

Problems for Section 2.5

2.5.1. (a) Give the equivalence classes under $\approx_L$ for these languages:
  (i) $L = (aab \cup ab)^*$.
  (ii) $L = \{x : x \text{ contains an occurrence of } aababa\}$.
  (iii) $L = \{xx^R : x \in \{a, b\}^*\}$.
  (iv) $L = \{xx : x \in \{a, b\}^*\}$.
  (v) $L_n = \{a, b\}a\{a, b\}^n$, where $n > 0$ is a fixed integer.
  (vi) The language of balanced parentheses (Problem 2.4.6).

(b) For those languages in (a) for which the answer is finite, give a deterministic finite automaton with the smallest possible number of states that accepts the corresponding language.

2.5.2. Call a string $x \in \Sigma^*$ *square-free* if it cannot be written as $x = uvvw$ for some $u, v, w \in \Sigma^*$, $v \neq e$. For example, *lewis* and *christos* are square-free, but *harry* and *papadimitriou* are not. Show that, if $|\Sigma| > 1$, then the set of all square-free strings in Σ^* is not regular.

2.5.3. For each of the finite automata (deterministic or nondeterministic) considered in Problems 2.1.2 and 2.2.9, find the minimum-state equivalent deterministic finite automaton.

2.5.4. **A two-way finite automaton** is like a deterministic finite automaton, except that the reading head can go backwards as well as forwards on the input tape. If it tries to back up off the left end of the tape, it stops operating without accepting the input. Formally, a two-way finite automaton M is a quintuple $(K, \Sigma, \delta, s, F)$, where K, Σ, s, and F are as defined for deterministic finite automata, and δ is a function from $K \times \Sigma$ to $K \times \{\leftarrow, \rightarrow\}$; the $\leftarrow$ or $\rightarrow$ indicates the direction of head movement. A **configuration** is a member of $K \times \Sigma^* \times \Sigma^*$; configuration (p, u, v) indicates that the machine is in state p with the head on the first symbol of v and with u to the left of the head. If $v = e$, configuration (p, u, e) means that M has completed its operation on u, and ended up in state p.

We write $(p_1, u_1, v_1) \vdash_M (p_2, u_2, v_2)$ if and only if $v_1 = \sigma v$ for some $\sigma \in \Sigma$, $\delta(p_1, \sigma) = (p_2, \epsilon)$, and either

1. $\epsilon = \rightarrow$ and $u_2 = u_1 \sigma, v_2 = v$, or
2. $\epsilon = \leftarrow, u_1 = u\sigma'$ for some $u \in \Sigma^*$, and $v_2 = \sigma' v_1$.

As usual, $\vdash_M^*$ is the reflexive, transitive closure of $\vdash_M$. M accepts w if and only if $(s, e, w) \vdash_M^* (f, w, e)$ for some $f \in F$. In this problem you will use the Myhill-Nerode Theorem (Theorem 2.5.2 and its corollary) to show that a language accepted by a two-way finite automaton is accepted by a one-way finite automaton. Thus, the apparent power to move the head to the left does not enhance the power of finite automata.

Let M be a two-way finite automaton as just defined.

(a) Let $q \in K$ and $w \in \Sigma^*$. Show that there is at most one $p \in K$ such that $(q, e, w) \vdash_M^* (p, w, e)$.

(b) Let t be some fixed element *not* in K. For any $w \in \Sigma^*$, define a function $\chi_w : K \mapsto K \cup \{t\}$ as follows.

$$\chi_w(q) = \begin{cases} p, & \text{if } (q, e, w) \vdash_M^* (p, w, e) \\ t, & \text{otherwise} \end{cases}$$

By Part (a), χ_w is well defined. Also, for any $w \in \Sigma^*$, define $\theta_w :$ $K \times \Sigma \mapsto K \cup \{t\}$ as follows:

$$\theta_w(q, a) = \begin{cases} p, & \text{if } (q, w, a) \vdash_M^+ (p, w, a) \text{ but it is not the case that} \\ & \quad (q, w, a) \vdash_M^+ (r, w, a) \vdash_M^+ (p, w, a) \text{ for any } r \neq p, \\ t, & \text{if there is no } p \in K \text{ such that } (q, w, a) \vdash_M^+ (p, w, a) \end{cases}$$

(Here by $\vdash_M^+$ we mean the reflexive (not transitive) closure of $\vdash_M$, that is, the "yields in one or more steps" relation on configurations.) Now suppose that $w, v \in \Sigma^*$, $\chi_w = \chi_v$, and $\theta_w = \theta_v$. Show that, for any $u \in \Sigma^*$, M accepts wu if and only if M accepts vu.

(c) Show that, if $L(M)$ is the language accepted by a deterministic two-way automaton, then $L(M)$ is accepted by some ordinary (one-way) deterministic finite automaton. (*Hint:* Use (b) above to show that $\approx_{L(M)}$ has finitely many equivalence classes.)

(d) Conclude that there is an exponential algorithm which, given a deterministic two-way automaton M, constructs an equivalent deterministic finite automaton. (*Hint:* How many different functions χ_w and θ_w can there be, as a function of $|K|$ and $|\Sigma|$?)

(e) Design a deterministic two-way finite automaton with $\mathcal{O}(n)$ states accepting the language $L_n = \{a, b\}^* a\{a, b\}^n$ (recall Problem 2.5.1(a)(v)). Comparing with Problem 2.5.1(b)(v), conclude that the exponential growth in (d) above is necessary.

(f) Can the argument and construction in this problem be extended to *nondeterministic* two-way finite automata?

2.6 | ALGORITHMS FOR FINITE AUTOMATA

Many of the results in this chapter were concerned with different ways of representing a regular language: as a language accepted by a finite automaton, deterministic or nondeterministic, and as a language generated by a regular expression. In the previous section we saw how, given any deterministic finite automaton, we can find the equivalent deterministic finite automaton with the fewest possible states. All these results are constructive, in that their proofs immediately suggest *algorithms* which, given a representation of one kind, produce a representation of any one of the others. In this subsection we shall make such algorithms more explicit, and we shall analyze roughly their complexity.

We start from the algorithm for converting a nondeterministic finite automaton to a deterministic one (Theorem 2.2.1); let us pinpoint its complexity. The input to the algorithm is a nondeterministic finite automaton $M =$

$(K, \Sigma, \Delta, s, F)$; thus, we must calculate its complexity as a function of the cardinalities of K, Σ, and Δ. The basic challenge is to compute the transition function of the deterministic automaton, that is, for each $Q \subseteq K$, and each $a \in \Sigma$, to compute

$$\delta'(Q, a) = \bigcup \{E(p) : p \in K \text{ and } (q, a, p) \in \Delta \text{ for some } q \in Q\}.$$

It is more expedient to *precompute* all $E(p)$'s once and for all, using the closure algorithm explained in that proof. It is easy to see that this can be done in total time $\mathcal{O}(|K|^3)$ for all $E(p)$'s. Once we have the $E(p)$'s, the computation of $\delta'(Q, a)$ can be carried out by first collecting all states p such that $(q, a, p) \in \Delta$, and then taking the union of all $E(p)$'s —a total of $\mathcal{O}(|\Delta||K|^2)$ elementary operations such as adding an element to a subset of K. The total complexity of the algorithm is thus $\mathcal{O}(2^{|K|}|K|^3|\Sigma||\Delta||K|^2)$. It is no surprise that our complexity estimate is an exponential function of the size of the input (as manifested by the $2^{|K|}$ factor); we have seen that the output of the algorithm (the equivalent deterministic finite automaton) may in the worst case be exponential.

Converting a regular expression R into an equivalent *nondeterministic* finite automaton (Theorem 2.3.2) is in comparison efficient: It is very easy to show by induction on the length of R that the resulting automaton has no more than $2|R|$ states, and therefore no more than $4|R|^2$ transitions —a polynomial.

Turning a given finite automaton $M = (K, \Sigma, \Delta, s, F)$ (deterministic or not) into a regular expression generating the same language (Theorem 2.3.2) involves computing $|K|^3$ regular expressions $R(i, j, k)$. However, the *length* of these expressions is in the worst case exponential: During each iteration on the index k, the length of each regular expression is roughly *tripled*, as it is the concatenation of three regular expressions from the previous iteration. The resulting regular expressions may have length as large as $3^{|K|}$ —an exponential function of the size of the automaton.

The minimization algorithm in the previous section which, given any deterministic automaton $M = (K, \Sigma, \delta, s, F)$, computes an equivalent deterministic finite automaton with the smallest number of states, is *polynomial*. It proceeds in at most $|K| - 1$ iterations, with each iteration involving the determination, for each pair of states, whether they are related by $\equiv_n$; this test only takes $\mathcal{O}(|\Sigma|)$ elementary operations such as testing whether two states are related by a previously computed equivalence relation $\equiv_{n-1}$. Thus the total complexity of the minimization algorithm is $\mathcal{O}(|\Sigma||K|^3)$ —a polynomial.

Given two language generators or two language acceptors, one natural and interesting question to ask is whether they are *equivalent* that is, whether they generate or accept the same language. If the two acceptors are deterministic finite automata, the state minimization algorithm also provides a solution to the equivalence problem: Two deterministic finite automata are equivalent if and only if *their standard automata are identical.* This is because the standard automaton only depends on the language accepted, and is therefore a useful standardization for testing equivalence. To check whether two deterministic automata are identical is not a difficult isomorphism problem, because states can be identified starting from the initial states, with the help of the labels on the transitions.

In contrast, the only way we know how to tell whether two *nondeterministic* automata, or two regular expressions, are equivalent is by converting them into two deterministic finite automata, and then testing *them* for equivalence. The algorithm is, of course, exponential.

We summarize our discussion of the algorithmic problems related to regular languages and their representations as follows:

Theorem 2.6.1: *(a) There is an exponential algorithm which, given a nondeterministic finite automaton, constructs an equivalent deterministic finite automaton.*

(b) There is a polynomial algorithm which, given a regular expression, constructs an equivalent nondeterministic finite automaton.

(c) There is an exponential algorithm which, given a nondeterministic finite automaton, constructs an equivalent regular expression.

(d) There is a polynomial algorithm which, given a deterministic finite automaton, constructs an equivalent deterministic finite automaton with the smallest possible number of states.

(e) There is a polynomial algorithm which, given two deterministic finite automata, decides whether they are equivalent.

(f) There is an exponential algorithm which, given two nondeterministic finite automata, decides whether they are equivalent; similarly for the equivalence of two regular expressions.

We know that the exponential complexity in (a) and (c) above is necessary, because, as Example 2.2.5 and Problem 2.3.8 indicate, the output of the algorithm (in (a), the deterministic automaton; in (c), the equivalent regular expression) may have to be exponential. There are, however, three important questions that remain unresolved in Theorem 2.6.1:

(1) Is there a polynomial algorithm for determining whether two given nondeterministic finite automata are equivalent, or is the exponential complexity in (f) inherent?

(2) Can we find in polynomial time the nondeterministic automaton with the fewest states that is equivalent to a given nondeterministic automaton? We can certainly do so in exponential time: Try all possible nondeterministic automata with fewer states than the given one, testing equivalence in each case using the exponential algorithm in (f).

(3) More intriguingly, suppose that we are given a nondeterministic finite automaton and we wish to find the equivalent deterministic finite automaton with the fewest states. This can be accomplished by combining the algorithms for (a) and (d) above. However, the number of steps may be exponential in the size of the given nondeterministic automaton, even though the end result may be small —simply because the intermediate result, the unoptimized deterministic automaton produced by the subset construction, may have exponentially more states than necessary. Is there an algorithm that produces *directly* the minimum-state equivalent deterministic automaton in time which is bounded by a polynomial in the input *and the final output?*

As we shall see in Chapter 7 on $\mathcal{NP}$-completeness, we strongly suspect that all three of these questions have negative answers *although at present nobody knows how to prove it.*

Finite Automata as Algorithms

There is something very basic that can be said about deterministic finite automata in connection with algorithms: A deterministic finite automaton M *is an efficient algorithm for deciding whether a given string is in $L(M)$.* For example, the deterministic finite automaton in Figure 2-23 can be rendered as the following algorithm:

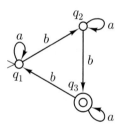

Figure 2-23

q_1:   Let $\sigma :=$ get-next-symbol;
     if $\sigma =$ end-of-file then reject;
     else if $\sigma = a$ then goto q_1;
     else if $\sigma = b$ then goto q_2;
q_2:   Let $\sigma :=$ get-next-symbol;
     if $\sigma =$ end-of-file then reject;
     else if $\sigma = a$ then goto q_2;
     else if $\sigma = b$ then goto q_3;
q_3:   Let $\sigma :=$ get-next-symbol;

if σ = end-of-file then accept;
else if $\sigma = a$ then goto q_3;
else if $\sigma = b$ then goto q_1;

To render a deterministic finite automaton $M = (K, \Sigma, \delta, s, F)$ as an algorithm, for each state in K we have $|\Sigma| + 2$ instructions, of which the first obtains the next input symbol, and each of the others is responsible for performing the correct action for a particular value of the input symbol —or for the case in which we have reached the end of the input string, an event that we call "end-of-file." We can express formally the discussion above as follows:

Theorem 2.6.2: *If L is a regular language, then there is an algorithm which, given $w \in \Sigma^*$, tests whether it is in L in $\mathcal{O}(|w|)$ time.*

But how about nondeterministic finite automata? They are definitely a powerful notational simplification, and they are the most natural and direct way of rendering regular expressions as automata (recall the constructions in the proof of Theorem 2.3.1), but they do not obviously correspond to algorithms. Of course, we can always transform a given nondeterministic finite automaton to the equivalent deterministic one by the subset construction in the proof of Theorem 2.2.1, but the construction itself (and the ensuing automaton) may be exponential. The question arises, *can we "run" a nondeterministic finite automaton directly,* very much the same way we run deterministic ones? We next point out that, with a modest loss in speed, we can.

Recall the idea behind the subset construction: After having read part of the input, a nondeterministic automaton can be in any one of a *set of states.* The subset construction computes all these possible sets of states. But when we are only interested in running a single string through the automaton, perhaps a better idea is this: *We can calculate the sets of states "on the fly,"* as needed and suggested by the input string.

Concretely, suppose that $M = (K, \Sigma, \Delta, s, F)$ is a nondeterministic finite automaton, and consider the following algorithm:

$S_0 := E(s), n := 0$;
repeat the following
    set $n := n + 1$, and let σ be the nth input symbol;
    if $\sigma \neq$ end-of-file then
        $S_n := \bigcup \{E(q) : \text{ for some } p \in S_{n-1}, (p, \sigma, q) \in \Delta\}$
until $\sigma =$ end-of-file
if $S_{n-1} \cap F \neq \emptyset$ then accept else reject

Here $E(q)$ stands for the set $\{p : (q, e) \vdash^*_M (p, e)\}$, as in the subset construction.

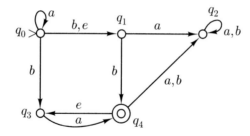

Figure 2-24

Example 2.6.1: Let us "run," using this algorithm, the nondeterministic finite automaton in Figure 2-24 on the input string $aaaba$. The various values for the set S_n are shown below.

$$S_0 = \{q_0, q_1\},$$
$$S_1 = \{q_0, q_1, q_2\},$$
$$S_2 = \{q_0, q_1, q_2\},$$
$$S_3 = \{q_0, q_1, q_2\},$$
$$S_4 = \{q_2, q_3, q_4\},$$
$$S_5 = \{q_2, q_3, q_4\}.$$

The machine ends up accepting the input $aaaba$, because S_5 contains a final state.◇

It is easy to prove by induction on the length of the input string that this algorithm maintains the set S_n of all states of M that could be reached by reading the first n symbols of the input. In other words, it simulates the equivalent deterministic finite automaton *without ever constructing it*. And its time requirements are quite modest, as the following theorem states (for a proof of the time bound, as well as an improvement, see Problem 2.6.2).

Theorem 2.6.3: If $M = (K, \Sigma, \Delta, s, F)$ is a nondeterministic finite automaton, then there is an algorithm which, given $w \in \Sigma^*$, tests whether it is in $L(M)$ in time $\mathcal{O}(|K|^2 |w|)$.

Suppose next that we are given a *regular expression* α over the alphabet Σ, and we wish to determine whether a given string $w \in \Sigma^*$ is in $L[\alpha]$, the language generated by α. Since α can be easily transformed into an equivalent nondeterministic finite automaton M, of size comparable to that of α (recall the constructions in Theorem 2.3.1), the algorithm above is also useful for answering such questions.[†]

A related computational problem, which also can be solved by methods based on finite automata, is that of **string matching**, a most central problem in computer systems and their applications. Let us fix a string $x \in \Sigma^*$, which we shall call the *pattern*. We wish to devise an efficient algorithm which, given any string w, the *text* (presumably much longer than x), determines whether x occurs as a substring of w. Notice that we are not interested in an algorithm that takes both x and w as inputs and tells us if x occurs in w; we want our algorithm, call it A_x, to specialize in discovering the pattern x in all possible longer strings. Our strategy is, naturally enough, to design a finite automaton that accepts the language $L_x = \{w \in \Sigma^* : x \text{ is a substring of } w\}$.

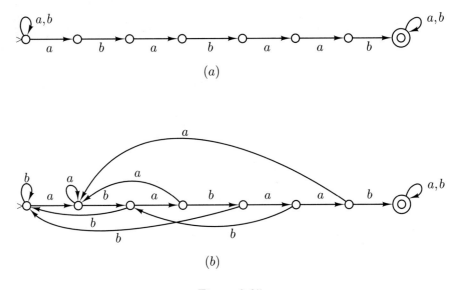

Figure 2-25

In fact, it is trivial to design a *nondeterministic* finite automaton for accepting L_x. For example, if $\Sigma = \{a, b\}$ and $x = ababaab$, the corresponding nondeterministic finite automaton is shown in Figure 2-25(a). But in order to turn this into a useful algorithm we would have to resort to the direct simulation of Theorem 2.6.3 —with its running time $\mathcal{O}(|x|^2|w|)$, polynomial but very slow for this application— or convert it into an equivalent deterministic automaton

—a construction which we know is potentially exponential. Fortunately, in the case of nondeterministic automata arising in string-matching applications, the subset construction *is always efficient*, and the resulting deterministic automaton M_x has exactly the same number of states as the original nondeterministic one (see Figure 2-25(b)). It is clearly the minimal equivalent automaton. This automaton M_x is therefore an algorithm for testing whether $w \in L_x$ in time $\mathcal{O}(|w|)$, for any string $w \in \Sigma^*$.

Still, this algorithm has a drawback that makes it unsuitable for the many practical applications of string matching. In real applications, the underlying alphabet Σ has several dozens, often hundreds, of symbols. A deterministic finite automaton rendered as an algorithm must execute for each input symbol a long sequence of if statements, one for each symbol of the alphabet (recall the first algorithm in this subsection). In other words, the $\mathcal{O}$ notation in the $\mathcal{O}(|w|)$ running time of the algorithm "hides" a potentially large constant: the running time is in fact $\mathcal{O}(|\Sigma||w|)$. For a clever remedy, see Problem 2.6.3.

Problems for Section 2.6

2.6.1. Show that these two regular expressions do not represent the same language: $aa(a \cup b)^* \cup (bb)^* a^*$ and $(ab \cup ba \cup a)^*$. Do so
   (a) by subjecting them to a general algorithm; and
   (b) by finding a string generating by one and not by the other.

2.6.2. (a) What is the sequence of S_i's produced if the nondeterministic finite automaton in Example 2.6.1 is presented with input *bbabbabba*?
   (b) Prove that the algorithm for running a nondeterministic finite automaton with m states on an input of length n takes time $\mathcal{O}(m^2 n)$.
   (c) Suppose that the given nondeterministic finite automaton has at most p transitions from each state. Show that an $\mathcal{O}(mnp)$ algorithm is possible.

2.6.3. Let Σ be an alphabet, $x = a_1 \ldots a_n \in \Sigma^*$, and consider the nondeterministic finite automaton $M_x = (K, \Sigma, \Delta, s, F)$, where $K = \{q_0, q_1, \ldots, q_n\}$, $\Delta = \{(q_{i-1}, a_i, q_i) : i = 0, \ldots, n-1\} \cup \{(q_i, a, q_i) : a \in \Sigma, i \in \{0, n\}\}$ (recall Figure 2-25).
   (a) Show that $L(M_x) = \{w \in \Sigma^* : x \text{ is a substring of } w\}$.
   (b) Show that the deterministic finite automaton M'_x with the fewest states that is equivalent to M_x also has $n + 1$ states. What is the worst-case time required for its construction, as a function of n?
   (c) Show that there is a nondeterministic finite automaton M''_x equivalent to M_x, also with $n + 1$ states $\{q_0, q_1, \ldots, q_n\}$, and with the following important property: *Each state except q_0 and q_n has exactly two transitions out of it, of which one is an e-transition.* (*Hint:* Replace each

backwards transition in the deterministic finite automaton on Figure
2-25 by an appropriate e-transition; generalize.)

(d) Argue that M_x'' remedies the problem of the hidden constant $|\Sigma|$ dis-
cussed in the last paragraph of the text.

(e) Give an algorithm for constructing M_x'' from x. What is the complexity
of your algorithm as a function of n?

(f) Devise an $\mathcal{O}(n)$ algorithm for the problem in (e) above. (*Hint:* Suppose
that the e-transitions of M_x'' are $(q_i, e, q_{f(i)}), i = 1, \ldots, n-1$. Show
how to compute $f(i)$, based on the values $f(j)$ for $j < i$. A clever
"amortized" analysis of this computation gives the $\mathcal{O}(n)$ bound.)

(g) Suppose that $\Sigma = \{a, b\}$ and $x = aabbaab$. Construct M_x, M_x', and
M_x''. Run each of these automata on the input $aababbaaabbaaabbaabb$.

REFERENCES

Some of the first papers on finite automata were

o G. H. Mealy   "A method for synthesizing sequential circuits," *Bell System Technical Journal, 34,* 5 , pp. 1045–1079, 1955, and

o E. F. Moore   "Gedanken experiments on sequential machines," *Automata Studies,* ed. C. E. Shannon and J. McCarthy, pp. 129–53. Princeton: Princeton
University Press, 1956.

The classical paper on finite automata (containing Theorem 2.2.1) is

o M. O. Rabin and D. Scott   "Finite automata and their decision problems," *IBM
Journal of Research and Development, 3,* pp. 114–25, 1959.

Theorem 2.3.2, stating that finite automata accept regular languages, is due to Kleene:

o S. C. Kleene   "Representation of events by nerve nets," in *Automata Studies,*
ed. C. E. Shannon and J. McCarthy, pp. 3–42. Princeton: Princeton University
Press, 1956.

Our proof of this theorem follows the paper

o R. McNaughton and H. Yamada   "Regular expressions and state graphs for automata," *IEEE Transactions on Electronic Computers, EC-9,* 1 pp. 39–47, 1960.

Theorem 2.4.1 (the "pumping lemma") is from

o V. Bar-Hillel, M. Perls, and E. Shamir   "On formal properties of simple phrase
structure grammars," *Zeitschrift fur Phonetik, Sprachwissenschaft, und Kommunikationsforschung, 14,* pp. 143–172, 1961.

Finite-state transducers (Problem 2.1.4) were introduced in

o S. Ginsburg   "Examples of abstract machines," *IEEE Transactions on Electronic
Computers, EC-11,* 2, pp. 132–135, 1962.

Two-tape finite state automata (Problems 2.1.5 and 2.4.7) are examined in

o M. Bird   "The equivalence problem for deterministic two-tape automata," *Journal of Computer and Systems Sciences, 7,* pp. 218–236, 1973.

The Myhill-Nerode Theorem (Theorem 2.5.2) is from

o A. Nerode "Linear automaton transformations," *Proc. AMS, 9*, pp.541–544, 1958.

The algorithm for minimizing finite automata is from Moore's paper cited above. A more efficient algorithm is given in

o J. E. Hopcroft "An $n \log n$ algorithm for minimizing the states in a finite automaton," in *The Theory of Machines and Computations*, ed. Z. Kohavi. New York: Academic Press, 1971.

The simulation of nondeterministic automata (Theorem 2.6.3) is based on

o K. Thompson "Regular expression search algorithms," *Communications of the ACM, 11*, 6, pp. 419–422, 1968.

The fast pattern matching algorithm in Problem 2.6.3 is from

o D. E. Knuth, J. H. Morris, Jr, V. R. Pratt "Fast pattern matching in strings," *SIAM J. on Computing, 6*, 2, pp. 323–350, 1976.

The equivalence of one-way and two-way finite automata (Problem 2.5.4) is shown in

o J. C. Shepherdson "The reduction of two-way automata to one-way automata," *IBM Journal of Research and Development, 3*. pp. 198–200, 1959.

3 | Context-Free Languages

3.1 CONTEXT-FREE GRAMMARS

Think of yourself as a language processor. You can recognize a legal English sentence when you hear one; "the cat is in the hat" is at least syntactically correct (whether or not it says anything that happens to be the truth), but "hat the the in is cat" is gibberish. However you manage to do it, you can immediately tell when reading such sentences whether they are formed according to generally accepted rules for sentence structure. In this respect you are acting as a **language recognizer**: a device that accepts valid strings. The finite automata of the last chapter are formalized types of language recognizers.

You also, however, are capable of producing legal English sentences. Again, why you would want to do so and how you manage to do it are not our concern; but the fact is that you occasionally speak or write sentences, and in general they are syntactically correct (even when they are lies). In this respect you are acting as a **language generator**. In this section we shall study certain types of formal language generators. Such a device begins, when given some sort of "start" signal, to construct a string. Its operation is not completely determined from the beginning but is nevertheless limited by a set of rules. Eventually this process halts, and the device outputs a completed string. The language defined by the device is the set of all strings that it can produce.

Neither a recognizer nor a generator for the English language is at all easy to produce; indeed, designing such devices for large subsets of natural languages has been a challenging research front for several decades. Nevertheless the idea of a language generator has some explanatory force in attempts to discuss human language. More important for us, however, is the theory of generators of formal, "artificial" languages, such as the regular languages and the important class of "context-free" languages introduced below. This theory will neatly complement the study of automata, which recognize languages, and is also of practical value in the specification and analysis of computer languages.

Regular expressions can be viewed as language generators. For example, consider the regular expression $a(a^* \cup b^*)b$. A verbal description of how to generate a string in accordance with this expression would be the following

> First output an a. Then do one of the following two things:
> Either output a number of a's or output a number of b's.
> Finally output a b.

The language associated with this language generator —that is, the set of all strings that can be produced by the process just described —is, of course, exactly the regular language defined in the way described earlier by the regular expression $a(a^* \cup b^*)b$.

In this chapter we shall study certain more complex sorts of language generators, called **context-free grammars**, which are based on a more complete understanding of the structure of the strings belonging to the language. To take again the example of the language generated by $a(a^* \cup b^*)b$, note that any string in this language consists of a leading a, followed by a *middle part* —generated by $(a^* \cup b^*)$— followed by a trailing b. If we let S be a new symbol interpreted as "a string in the language," and M be a symbol standing for "middle part," then we can express this observation by writing

$$S \to aMb,$$

where $\to$ is read "can be." We call such an expression a **rule**. What can M, the middle part, be? The answer is: either a string of a's or a string of b's. We express this by adding the rules

$$M \to A \text{ and } M \to B,$$

where A and B are new symbols that stand for strings of a's and b's, respectively. Now, what is a string of a's? It can be the empty string

$$A \to e,$$

or it may consist of a leading a followed by a string of a's:

$$A \to aA.$$

Similarly, for B:

$$B \to e \text{ and } B \to bB.$$

The language denoted by the regular expression $a(a^* \cup b^*)b$ can then be defined alternatively by the following language generator.

Start with the string consisting of the single symbol S. Find a symbol in the current string that appears to the left of $\rightarrow$ in one of the rules above. Replace an occurrence of this symbol with the string that appears to the right of $\rightarrow$ in the same rule. Repeat this process until no such symbol can be found.

For example, to generate the string $aaab$ we start with S, as specified; we then replace S by aMb according to the first rule, $S \rightarrow aMb$. To aMb we apply the rule $M \rightarrow A$ and obtain aAb. We then twice apply the rule $A \rightarrow aA$ to get the string $aaaAb$. Finally, we apply the rule $A \rightarrow e$. In the resulting string, $aaab$, we cannot identify any symbol that appears to the left of $\rightarrow$ in some rule. Thus the operation of our language generator has ended, and $aaab$ was produced, as promised.

A **context-free grammar** is a language generator that operates like the one above, with some such set of rules. Let us pause to explain at this point why such a language generator is called context-free. Consider the string $aaAb$, which was an intermediate stage in the generation of $aaab$. It is natural to call the strings aa and b that surround the symbol A the **context** of A in this particular string. Now, the rule $A \rightarrow aA$ says that we can replace A by the string aA no matter what the surrounding strings are; in other words, *independently of the context of A*. In Chapter 4 we examine more general grammars, in which replacements may be conditioned on the existence of an appropriate context.

In a context-free grammar, some symbols appear to the left of $\rightarrow$ in rules —S, M, A, and B in our example— and some —a and b— do not. Symbols of the latter kind are called **terminals**, since the production of a string consisting solely of such symbols signals the termination of the generation process. All these ideas are stated formally in the next definition.

Definition 3.1.1: A **context-free grammar** G is a quadruple (V, Σ, R, S), where

V is an alphabet,
Σ (the set of **terminals**) is a subset of V,
R (the set of **rules**) is a finite subset of $(V - \Sigma) \times V^*$, and
S (the **start symbol**) is an element of $V - \Sigma$.

The members of $V - \Sigma$ are called **nonterminals**. For any $A \in V - \Sigma$ and $u \in V^*$, we write $A \rightarrow_G u$ whenever $(A, u) \in R$. For any strings $u, v \in V^*$, we write $u \Rightarrow_G v$ if and only if there are strings $x, y \in V^*$ and $A \in V - \Sigma$ such that $u = xAy$, $v = xv'y$, and $A \rightarrow_G v'$. The relation $\Rightarrow_G^*$ is the reflexive, transitive closure of $\Rightarrow_G$. Finally, $L(G)$, the **language generated** by G, is $\{w \in \Sigma^* : S \Rightarrow_G^* w\}$; we also say that G **generates** each string in $L(G)$. A language L is said to be a **context-free language** if $L = L(G)$ for some context-free grammar G.

When the grammar to which we refer is obvious, we write $A \to w$ and $u \Rightarrow v$ instead of $A \to_G w$ and $u \Rightarrow_G v$.

We call any sequence of the form

$$w_0 \Rightarrow_G w_1 \Rightarrow_G \cdots \Rightarrow_G w_n$$

a **derivation** in G of w_n from w_0. Here $w_0, \cdots, w_n$ may be any strings in V^*, and n, the **length** of the derivation, may be any natural number, including zero. We also say that the derivation has n **steps**.

Example 3.1.1: Consider the context-free grammar $G = (V, \Sigma, R, S)$, where $V = \{S, a, b\}$, $\Sigma = \{a, b\}$, and R consists of the rules $S \to aSb$ and $S \to e$. A possible derivation is

$$S \Rightarrow aSb \Rightarrow aaSbb \Rightarrow aabb.$$

Here the first two steps used the rule $S \to aSb$, and the last used the rule $S \to e$. In fact, it is not hard to see that $L(G) = \{a^n b^n : n \geq 0\}$. Hence some context-free languages are not regular.$\diamondsuit$

We shall soon see, however, that all regular languages are context-free.

Example 3.1.2: Let G be the grammar $(W, \Sigma, R, S,)$, where

$$W = \{S, A, N, V, P\} \cup \Sigma,$$
$$\Sigma = \{\text{Jim, big, green, cheese, ate}\},$$
$$R = \{P \to N,$$
$$\quad P \to AP,$$
$$\quad S \to PVP,$$
$$\quad A \to \text{big},$$
$$\quad A \to \text{green},$$
$$\quad N \to \text{cheese},$$
$$\quad N \to \text{Jim},$$
$$\quad V \to \text{ate}\}$$

Here G is designed to be a grammar for a part of English; S stands for *sentence*, A for *adjective*, N for *noun*, V for *verb*, and P for *phrase*. The following are some strings in $L(G)$.

> Jim ate cheese
> big Jim ate green cheese
> big cheese ate Jim

Unfortunately, the following are also strings in $L(G)$:

big cheese ate green green big green big cheese
green Jim ate green big Jim

Example 3.1.3: Computer programs written in any programming language must satisfy some rigid criteria in order to be syntactically correct and therefore amenable to mechanical interpretation. Fortunately, the syntax of most programming languages can, unlike that of human languages, be captured by context-free grammars. We shall see in Section 3.7 that being context-free is extremely helpful when it comes to *parsing* a program, that is, analyzing it to understand its syntax. Here, we give a grammar that generates a fragment of many common programming languages. This language consists of all strings over the alphabet $\{(,),+,*,\mathsf{id}\}$ that represent syntactically correct arithmetic expressions involving $+$ and $*$. id stands for any *identifier*, that is to say, variable name.[†] Examples of such strings are id and $\mathsf{id} * (\mathsf{id} * \mathsf{id} + \mathsf{id})$, but not $*\mathsf{id} + ($ or $+ * \mathsf{id}$.

Let $G = (V, \Sigma, R, E)$ where V, Σ, and R are as follows.

$$V = \{+, *, (,), \mathsf{id}, T, F, E\},$$
$$\Sigma = \{+, *, (,), \mathsf{id}\},$$

$R = \{E \rightarrow E + T,$		$(R1)$
$E \rightarrow T,$		$(R2)$
$T \rightarrow T * F,$		$(R3)$
$T \rightarrow F,$		$(R4)$
$F \rightarrow (E),$		$(R5)$
$F \rightarrow \mathsf{id}\}.$		$(R6)$

The symbols E, T, and F are abbreviations for *expression*, *term*, and *factor*, respectively.

The grammar G generates the string $(\mathsf{id} * \mathsf{id} + \mathsf{id}) * (\mathsf{id} + \mathsf{id})$ by the following derivation.

$E \Rightarrow T$	by Rule R2
$\Rightarrow T * F$	by Rule R3
$\Rightarrow T * (E)$	by Rule R5
$\Rightarrow T * (E + T)$	by Rule R1

[†] Incidentally, discovering such identifiers (or reserved words of the language, or numerical constants) in the program is accomplished at the earlier stage of *lexical analysis*, by algorithms based on regular expressions and finite automata.

$$\Rightarrow T * (T + T) \qquad \text{by Rule R2}$$
$$\Rightarrow T * (F + T) \qquad \text{by Rule R4}$$
$$\Rightarrow T * (\text{id} + T) \qquad \text{by Rule R6}$$
$$\Rightarrow T * (\text{id} + F) \qquad \text{by Rule R4}$$
$$\Rightarrow T * (\text{id} + \text{id}) \qquad \text{by Rule R6}$$
$$\Rightarrow F * (\text{id} + \text{id}) \qquad \text{by Rule R4}$$
$$\Rightarrow (E) * (\text{id} + \text{id}) \qquad \text{by Rule R5}$$
$$\Rightarrow (E + T) * (\text{id} + \text{id}) \qquad \text{by Rule R1}$$
$$\Rightarrow (E + F) * (\text{id} + \text{id}) \qquad \text{by Rule R4}$$
$$\Rightarrow (E + \text{id}) * (\text{id} + \text{id}) \qquad \text{by Rule R6}$$
$$\Rightarrow (T + \text{id}) * (\text{id} + \text{id}) \qquad \text{by Rule R2}$$
$$\Rightarrow (T * F + \text{id}) * (\text{id} + \text{id}) \qquad \text{by Rule R3}$$
$$\Rightarrow (F * F + \text{id}) * (\text{id} + \text{id}) \qquad \text{by Rule R4}$$
$$\Rightarrow (F * \text{id} + \text{id}) * (\text{id} + \text{id}) \qquad \text{by Rule R6}$$
$$\Rightarrow (\text{id} * \text{id} + \text{id}) * (\text{id} + \text{id}) \qquad \text{by Rule R6}$$

See Problem 3.1.8 for context-free grammars that generate larger subsets of programming languages.$\Diamond$

Example 3.1.4: The following grammar generates all strings of properly balanced left and right parentheses: every left parenthesis can be paired with a unique subsequent right parenthesis, and every right parenthesis can be paired with a unique preceding left parenthesis. Moreover, the string between any such pair has the same property. We let $G = (V, \Sigma, R, S)$, where

$$V = \{S, (,)\},$$
$$\Sigma = \{(,)\},$$
$$R = \{S \rightarrow e,$$
$$\quad S \rightarrow SS,$$
$$\quad S \rightarrow (S)\}.$$

Two derivations in this grammar are

$$S \Rightarrow SS \Rightarrow S(S) \Rightarrow S((S)) \Rightarrow S(()) \Rightarrow ()(())$$

and

$$S \Rightarrow SS \Rightarrow (S)S \Rightarrow ()S \Rightarrow ()(S) \Rightarrow ()(())$$

Thus the same string may have several derivations in a context-free grammar; in the next subsection we discuss the intricate ways in which such derivations may be related.

Incidentally, $L(G)$ is another context-free language that is not regular (that it is not regular was the object of Problem 2.4.6).◊

Example 3.1.5: Obviously, there are context-free languages that are not regular (we have already seen two examples). However, *all regular languages are context-free*. In the course of this chapter we shall encounter several proofs of this fact. For example, we shall see in Section 3.3 that context-free languages are precisely the languages accepted by certain language acceptors called *pushdown automata*. Now we shall also point out that the pushdown acceptor is a generalization of the finite automaton, in the sense that any finite automaton can be trivially considered as a pushdown automaton. Hence all regular languages are context-free.

For another proof, we shall see in Section 3.5 that the class of context-free languages is closed under union, concatenation, and Kleene star (Theorem 3.5.1); furthermore, the trivial languages $\emptyset$ and $\{a\}$ are definitely context-free (generated by the context-free grammars with no rules, or with only the rule $S \to a$, respectively). Hence the class of context-free languages must contain all regular languages, the closure of the trivial languages under these operations.

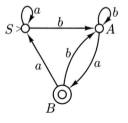

Figure 3-1

But let us now show that all regular languages are context-free *by a direct construction*. Consider the regular language accepted by the deterministic finite automaton $M = (K, \Sigma, \delta, s, F)$. The same language is generated by the grammar $G(M) = (V, \Sigma, R, S)$, where $V = K \cup \Sigma$, $S = s$, and R consists of these rules:

$$R = \{q \to ap : \delta(q, a) = p\} \cup \{q \to e : q \in F\}.$$

That is, the nonterminals are the states of the automaton; as for rules, for each transition from q to p on input a we have in R the rule $q \to ap$. For example, for the automaton in Figure 3-1 we would construct this grammar:

$$S \to aS, S \to bA, A \to aB, A \to bA, B \to aS, B \to bA, B \to e.$$

It is left as an exercise to show that the resulting context-free grammar generates precisely the language accepted by the automaton (see Problem 3.1.10 for
a general treatment of context-free grammars such as $G(M)$ above, and their
relationship with finite automata).◊

Problems for Section 3.1

3.1.1. Consider the grammar $G = (V, \Sigma, R, S)$, where

$$V = \{a, b, S, A\},$$
$$\Sigma = \{a, b\},$$
$$R = \{S \rightarrow AA,$$
$$\qquad A \rightarrow AAA, .$$
$$\qquad A \rightarrow a,$$
$$\qquad A \rightarrow bA,$$
$$\qquad A \rightarrow Ab\}.$$

(a) Which strings of $L(G)$ can be produced by derivations of four or fewer
steps?
(b) Give at least four distinct derivations for the string $babbab$.
(c) For any $m, n, p > 0$, describe a derivation in G of the string $b^m a b^n a b^p$.

3.1.2. Consider the grammar (V, Σ, R, S), where V, Σ, and R are defined as follows:

$$V = \{a, b, S, A\},$$
$$\Sigma = \{a, b\},$$
$$R = \{S \rightarrow aAa,$$
$$\qquad S \rightarrow bAb,$$
$$\qquad S \rightarrow e,$$
$$\qquad A \rightarrow SS\}.$$

Give a derivation of the string $baabbb$ in G. (Notice that, unlike all other
context-free languages we have seen so far, this one is very difficult to describe in English.)

3.1.3. Construct context-free grammars that generate each of these languages.
(a) $\{wcw^R : w \in \{a, b\}^*\}$
(b) $\{ww^R : w \in \{a, b\}^*\}$
(c) $\{w \in \{a, b\}^* : w = w^R\}$

3.1.4. Consider the alphabet $\Sigma = \{a, b, (,), \cup, ^{\star}, \oslash\}$. Construct a context-free grammar that generates all strings in Σ^* that are regular expressions over $\{a, b\}$.

3.1.5. Consider the context-free grammar $G = (V, \Sigma, R, S)$, where

$$
\begin{aligned}
V &= \{a, b, S, A, B\}, \\
\Sigma &= \{a, b\}, \\
R &= \{S \to aB, \\
&\quad\ S \to bA, \\
&\quad\ A \to a, \\
&\quad\ A \to aS, \\
&\quad\ A \to BAA, \\
&\quad\ B \to b, \\
&\quad\ B \to bS, \\
&\quad\ B \to ABB\}.
\end{aligned}
$$

(a) Show that $ababba \in L(G)$.
(b) Prove that $L(G)$ is the set of all strings in $\{a, b\}$ that have equal numbers of occurrences of a and b.

3.1.6. Let G be a context-free grammar and let $k > 0$. We let $L_k(G) \subseteq L(G)$ be the set of all strings that have a derivation in G with k or fewer steps.
(a) What is $L_5(G)$, where G is the grammar of Example 3.1.4
(b) Show that, for all context-free grammars G and all $k > 0$, $L_k(G)$ is finite.

3.1.7. Let $G = (V, \Sigma, R, S)$, where $V = \{a, b, S\}$, $\Sigma = \{a, b\}$, and $R = \{S \to aSb, S \to aSa, S \to bSa, S \to bSb, S \to e\}$. Show that $L(G)$ is regular.

3.1.8. A program in a real programming language, such as C or Pascal, consists of statements, where each statement is one of several types:
  (1) assignment statement, of the form id $:= E$, where E is any arithmetic expression (generated by the grammar of Example 3.1.3).
  (2) conditional statement, of the form, say, if $E < E$ then statement, or a while statement of the form while $E < E$ do statement.
  (3) goto statement; furthermore, each statement could be preceded by a label.
  (4) compound statement, that is, many statements preceded by a begin, followed by an end, and separated by a ";".
Give a context-free grammar that generates all possible statements in the simplified programming language described above.

3.1.9. Show that the following languages are context-free by exhibiting context-free grammars generating each.

(a) $\{a^m b^n : m \geq n\}$

(b) $\{a^m b^n c^p d^q : m + n = p + q\}$

(c) $\{w \in \{a, b\}^* : w \text{ has twice as many } b\text{'s as } a\text{'s}\}$

(d) $\{uawb : u, w \in \{a, b\}^*, |u| = |w|\}$

(e) $w_1 c w_2 c \ldots c w_k c c w_j^R : k \geq 1, 1 \leq j \leq k, w_i \in \{a, b\}^+ \text{ for } i = 1, \ldots, k\}$

(f) $\{a^m b^n : m \leq 2n\}$

3.1.10. Call a context-free grammar $G = (V, \Sigma, R, S)$ **regular** (or **right-linear**) if $R \subseteq (V - \Sigma) \times \Sigma^*(V - \Sigma \cup \{e\})$; that is, if each transition has a right-hand side that consists of a string of terminals followed by at most one nonterminal.

(a) Consider the regular grammar $G = (V, \Sigma, R, S)$, where

$$V = \{a, b, A, B, S\}$$
$$\Sigma = \{a, b\}$$
$$R = \{S \to abA, S \to B, S \to baB, S \to e,$$
$$A \to bS, B \to aS, A \to b\}.$$

Construct a nondeterministic finite automaton M such that $L(M) = L(G)$. Trace the transitions of M that lead to the acceptance of the string $abba$, and compare with a derivation of the same string in G.

(b) Prove that a language is regular if and only if there is a regular grammar that generates it. (*Hint:* Recall Example 3.1.5.)

(c) Call a context-free grammar $G = (V, \Sigma, R, S)$ **left-linear** if and only if $R \subseteq (V - \Sigma) \times (V - \Sigma) \cup \{e\})\Sigma^*$. Show that a language is regular if and only if it is the language generated by some left-linear grammar.

(d) Suppose that $G = (V, \Sigma, R, S)$ is a context-free grammar such that each rule in R is *either* of the form $A \to wB$ or of the form $A \to Bw$ or of the form $A \to w$, where in each case $A, B \in V - \Sigma$ and $w \in \Sigma^*$. Is $L(G)$ necessarily regular? Prove it or give a counter-example.

3.2 | PARSE TREES

Let G be a context-free grammar. A string $w \in L(G)$ may have many derivations in G. For example, if G is the context-free grammar that generates the language of balanced parentheses (recall Example 3.1.4), then the string ()() can be derived from S by at least two distinct derivations, namely,

$$S \Rightarrow SS \Rightarrow (S)S \Rightarrow ()S \Rightarrow ()(S) \Rightarrow ()()$$

and
$$S \Rightarrow SS \Rightarrow S(S) \Rightarrow (S)(S) \Rightarrow (S)() \Rightarrow ()()$$

However, these two derivations are in a sense "the same." The rules used are the same, and they are applied at the same places in the intermediate string. The only difference is in the *order* in which the rules are applied. Intuitively, both derivations can be pictured as in Figure 3-2.

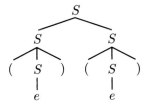

Figure 3-2

We call such a picture a **parse tree**. The points are called **nodes**; each node carries a **label** that is a symbol in V. The topmost node is called the **root**, and the nodes along the bottom are called **leaves**. All leaves are labeled by *terminals*, or possibly the empty string e. By concatenating the labels of the leaves from left to right, we obtain the derived string of terminals, which is called the **yield** of the parse tree.

More formally, for an arbitrary context-free grammar $G = (V, \Sigma, R, S)$, we define its parse trees and their roots, leaves, and yields, as follows.

1.   ∘ a

This is a parse tree for each $a \in \Sigma$. The single node of this parse tree is both the root and a leaf. The yield of this parse tree is a.

2. If $A \to e$ is a rule in R, then

is a parse tree; its root is the node labeled A, its sole leaf is the node labeled e, and its yield is e.

3. If

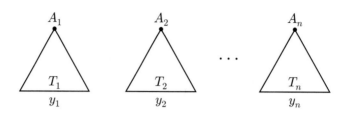

Are parse trees, where $n \geq 1$, with roots labeled $A_1, \ldots, A_n$ respectively, and with yields $y_1, \ldots, y_n$, and $A \to A_1 \ldots A_n$ is a rule in R, then

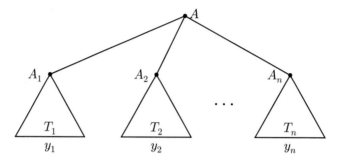

is a parse tree. Its root is the new node labeled A, its leaves are the leaves of its constituent parse trees, and its yield is $y_1 \ldots y_n$.

4. Nothing else is a parse tree.

Example 3.2.1: Recall the grammar G that generates all arithmetic expressions over id (Example 3.1.3). A parse tree with yield id $*$ (id $+$ id) is shown in Figure 3-3.◊

Intuitively, parse trees are ways of representing derivations of strings in $L(G)$ so that the superficial differences between derivations, owing to the order of application of rules, are suppressed. To put it otherwise, parse trees represent *equivalence classes of derivations*. We make this intuition precise below.

Let $G = (V, \Sigma, R, S)$ be a context-free grammar, and let $D = x_1 \Rightarrow x_2 \Rightarrow \cdots \Rightarrow x_n$ and $D' = x'_1 \Rightarrow x'_2 \Rightarrow \cdots \Rightarrow x'_n$ be two derivations in G, where $x_i, x'_i \in V^*$ for $i = 1, \ldots, n$, $x_1, x'_1 \in V - \Sigma$, and $x_n, x'_n \in \Sigma^*$. That is, they are both derivations of terminal strings from a single nonterminal. We say that D **precedes** D', written $D \prec D'$, if $n > 2$ and there is an integer k, $1 < k < n$ such that

(1) for all $i \neq k$ we have $x_i = x'_i$;
(2) $x_{k-1} = x'_{k-1} = uAvBw$, where $u, v, w \in V^*$, and $A, B, \in V - \Sigma$;

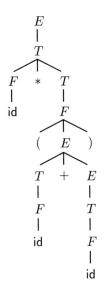

Figure 3-3

(3) $x_k = uyvBw$, where $A \to y \in R$;
(4) $x'_k = uAvzw$ where $B \to z \in R$;
(5) $x_{k+1} = x'_{k+1} = uyvzw$.

In other words, the two derivations are identical except for two consecutive steps, during which the same two nonterminals are replaced by the same two strings *but in opposite orders in the two derivations*. The derivation in which the leftmost of the two nonterminals is replaced first is said to precede the other.

Example 3.2.2: Consider the following three derivations D_1, D_2, and D_3 in the grammar G generating all strings of balanced parentheses:

$$D_1 = S \Rightarrow SS \Rightarrow (S)S \Rightarrow ((S))S \Rightarrow (())S \Rightarrow (())(S) \Rightarrow (())()$$
$$D_2 = S \Rightarrow SS \Rightarrow (S)S \Rightarrow ((S))S \Rightarrow ((S))(S) \Rightarrow (())(S) \Rightarrow (())()$$
$$D_3 = S \Rightarrow SS \Rightarrow (S)S \Rightarrow ((S))S \Rightarrow ((S))(S) \Rightarrow ((S))() \Rightarrow (())()$$

We have that $D_1 \prec D_2$ and $D_2 \prec D_3$. However, it is *not* the case that $D_1 \prec D_3$, since the two latter derivations differ in more than one intermediate string. Notice that all three derivations have the same parse tree, the one shown in Figure 3-4.◊

We say that two derivations D and D' are **similar** if the pair (D, D') belongs in the *reflexive, symmetric, transitive closure* of $\prec$. Since the reflexive,

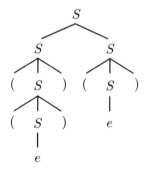

Figure 3-4

symmetric, transitive closure of any relation is by definition reflexive, symmetric, and transitive, similarity is an equivalence relation. To put it otherwise, two derivations are similar if they can be transformed into another via a sequence of "switchings" in the order in which rules are applied. Such a "switching" can replace a derivation either by one that precedes it, or by one that it precedes.

Example 3.2.2 (continued): Parse trees capture exactly, via a natural isomorphism, the equivalence classes of the "similarity" equivalence relation between derivations of a string defined above. The equivalence class of the derivations of $(())()$ corresponding to the tree in Figure 3-4 contains the derivations D_1, D_2, D_3 shown above, and also these seven:

$$D_4 = S \Rightarrow SS \Rightarrow (S)S \Rightarrow (S)(S) \Rightarrow ((S))(S) \Rightarrow (())(S) \Rightarrow (())()$$
$$D_5 = S \Rightarrow SS \Rightarrow (S)S \Rightarrow (S)(S) \Rightarrow ((S))(S) \Rightarrow ((S))() \Rightarrow (())()$$
$$D_6 = S \Rightarrow SS \Rightarrow (S)S \Rightarrow (S)(S) \Rightarrow (S)() \Rightarrow ((S))() \Rightarrow (())()$$
$$D_7 = S \Rightarrow SS \Rightarrow S(S) \Rightarrow (S)(S) \Rightarrow ((S))(S) \Rightarrow (())(S) \Rightarrow (())()$$
$$D_8 = S \Rightarrow SS \Rightarrow S(S) \Rightarrow (S)(S) \Rightarrow ((S))(S) \Rightarrow ((S))() \Rightarrow (())()$$
$$D_9 = S \Rightarrow SS \Rightarrow S(S) \Rightarrow (S)(S) \Rightarrow (S)() \Rightarrow ((S))() \Rightarrow (())()$$
$$D_{10} = S \Rightarrow SS \Rightarrow S(S) \Rightarrow S() \Rightarrow (S)() \Rightarrow ((S))() \Rightarrow (())()$$

These ten derivations are related by $\prec$ as shown in Figure 3-5.

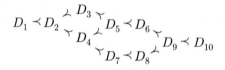

Figure 3-5

All these ten derivations are similar, because, informally, they represent applications of the same rules at the same positions in the strings, only differing in the relative order of these applications; equivalently, one can go from any one of them to any other by repeatedly following either a $\prec$, or an inverted $\prec$. There are no other derivations similar to these.

There are, however, other derivations of $(())()$ that are not similar to the ones above —and thus are not captured by the parse tree shown in Figure 3-5. An example is the following derivation: $S \Rightarrow SS \Rightarrow SSS \Rightarrow S(S)S \Rightarrow S((S))S \Rightarrow S(())S \Rightarrow S(())(S) \Rightarrow S(())() \Rightarrow (())()$. Its parse tree is shown in Figure 3-6 (compare with Figure 3-4).$\diamondsuit$

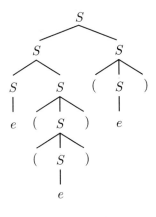

Figure 3-6

Each equivalence class of derivations under similarity, that is to say, each parse tree, contains a derivation that is *maximal* under $\prec$; that is, it is not preceded by any other derivation. This derivation is called a **leftmost derivation**. A leftmost derivation exists in every parse tree, and it can be obtained as follows. Starting from the label of the root A, repeatedly replace the *leftmost* nonterminal in the current string according to the rule suggested by the parse tree. Similarly, a **rightmost derivation** is one that does not precede any other derivation; it is obtained from the parse tree by always expanding the rightmost nonterminal in the current string. Each parse tree has exactly one leftmost and exactly one rightmost derivation. This is so because the leftmost derivation of a parse tree is uniquely determined, since at each step there is one nonterminal to replace: the leftmost one. Similarly for the rightmost derivation. In the example above, D_1 is a leftmost derivation, and D_{10} is a rightmost one.

It is easy to tell when a step of a derivation can be a part of a leftmost derivation: the leftmost nonterminal must be replaced. We write $x \overset{L}{\Rightarrow} y$ if and only if $x = wA\beta$, $y = w\alpha\beta$, where $w \in \Sigma^*$, $\alpha, \beta \in V^*$, $A \in V - \Sigma$, and $A \rightarrow \alpha$ is a rule of G. Thus, if $x_1 \Rightarrow x_2 \Rightarrow \cdots \Rightarrow x_n$ is a leftmost derivation, then in fact $x_1 \overset{L}{\Rightarrow} x_2 \overset{L}{\Rightarrow} \cdots \overset{L}{\Rightarrow} x_n$. Similarly for rightmost derivations (the notation is $x \overset{R}{\Rightarrow} y$).

To summarize our insights into parse trees and derivations in this section, we state without formal proof the following theorem.

Theorem 3.2.1: *Let $G = (V, \Sigma, R, S)$ be a context-free grammar, and let $A \in V - \Sigma$, and $w \in \Sigma^*$. Then the following statements are equivalent:*

(a) $A \Rightarrow^* w$.

(b) There is a parse tree with root A and yield w.

(c) There is a leftmost derivation $A \overset{L}{\Rightarrow}^* w$.

(d) There is a rightmost derivation $A \overset{R}{\Rightarrow}^* w$.

Ambiguity

We saw in Example 3.2.2 that there may be a string in the language generated by a context-free grammar with two derivations that are *not* similar —that is to say, *with two distinct parse trees*, or, equivalently, with two distinct rightmost derivations (and two distinct leftmost derivations). For a more substantial example, recall the grammar G that generates all arithmetic expressions over id in Example 3.1.3, and consider another grammar, G', that generates the same language, with these rules:

$$E \rightarrow E + E, \quad E \rightarrow E * E, \quad E \rightarrow (E), \quad E \rightarrow \text{id}.$$

It is not hard to see that $L(G') = L(G)$. Still, there are important differences between G and G'. Intuitively, the variant G', by "blurring the distinction" between factors (F) and terms (T) "risks getting wrong" the precedence of multiplication over addition. Indeed, there are two parse trees for the expression id $+$ id $*$ id in G', both shown in Figure 3-7. One of them, 3-7(a), corresponds to the "natural" meaning of this expression (with $*$ taking precedence over $+$), the other is "wrong."

Grammars such as G', with strings that have two or more distinct parse trees, are called **ambiguous**. As we shall see extensively in Section 3.7, assigning a parse tree to a given string in the language —that is to say, *parsing* the string— is an important first step towards understanding the structure of the string, the reasons why it belongs to the language —ultimately its "meaning." This is of course of special importance in the case of grammars such as G and G' above that generate fragments of programming languages. Ambiguous grammars such

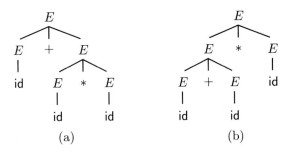

Figure 3-7

as G' are of no help in parsing, since they assign no unique parse tree —no unique "meaning"— to each string in the language.

Fortunately, in this case there is a way to "disambiguate" G' by introducing the new nonterminals T and F (recall the grammar G of Example 3.1.3). That is, there is an *unambiguous* grammar that generates the same language (namely, the grammar G defined in Example 3.1.3; for a proof that the grammar G is indeed unambiguous see Problem 3.2.1). Similarly, the grammar given in Example 3.1.4 for generating balanced strings of parentheses, which is also ambiguous (as discussed at the end of Example 3.2.2, can be easily made unambiguous (see Problem 3.2.2). In fact, there are context-free languages with the property that *all* context-free grammars that generate them must be ambiguous. Such languages are called **inherently ambiguous**. Fortunately, programming languages are never inherently ambiguous.

Problems for Section 3.2

3.2.1. Show that the context-free grammar G given in Example 3.1.3, which generates all arithmetic expressions over id, is unambiguous.

3.2.2. Show that the context-free grammar given in Example 3.1.4, which generates all strings of balanced parentheses is ambiguous. Give an equivalent unambiguous grammar.

3.2.3. Consider the grammar of Example 3.1.3. Give two derivations of the string id $*$ id $+$ id, one which is leftmost and one which is not leftmost.

3.2.4. Draw parse trees for each of the following.
(a) The grammar of Example 3.1.2 and the string "big Jim ate green cheese."
(b) The grammar of Example 3.1.3 and the strings id $+$ (id $+$ id) $*$ id and (id $*$ id $+$ id $*$ id).

3.3 | PUSHDOWN AUTOMATA

Not every context-free language can be recognized by a finite automaton, since, as we have already seen, some context-free languages are not regular. What sort of more powerful device could be used for recognizing arbitrary context-free languages? Or, to be a bit more specific, what extra features do we need to add to the finite automata so that they accept any context-free language?

To take a particular example, consider $\{ww^R : w \in \{a, b\}^*\}$. It *is* context-free, since it is generated by the grammar with rules $S \to aSa$, $S \to bSb$, and $S \to e$. It would seem that any device that recognizes the strings in this language by reading them from left to right must "remember" the first half of the input string so that it can check it —in reverse order— against the second half of the input. It is not surprising that this function cannot be performed by a finite automaton. If, however, the machine is capable of accumulating its input string as it is read, appending symbols one at a time to a stored string (see Figure 3-8), then it could nondeterministically guess when the center of the input has been reached and thereafter check the symbols off from its memory one at a time. The storage device need not be a general-purpose one. A sort of "stack" or "pushdown store," allowing read and write access only to the top symbol, would do nicely.

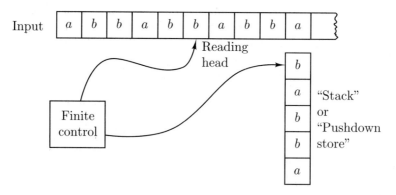

Figure 3-8

To take another example, the set of strings of balanced parentheses (Example 3.1.4) is also nonregular. However, computer programmers are familiar with a simple algorithm for recognizing this language: Start counting at zero, add one for every left parenthesis, and subtract one for every right parenthesis. If the count either goes negative at any time, or ends up different from zero, then the string should be rejected as unbalanced; otherwise it should be accepted. Now, a counter can be considered as a special case of a stack, on which only one kind of symbol can be written.

To address this question from yet another point of view, rules such as $A \to aB$ are easy to simulate by a finite automaton, as follows: "If in state A reading a, go to state B." But what about a rule whose right-hand side is not a terminal followed by a nonterminal, say the rule $A \to aBb$? Certainly the machine must again go from state A to state B reading a, but what about b? What further action would allow us to remember the presence of b in this rule? A stack would be handy here: By pushing b on the top of a stack, we resolve to remember it and act upon it when it resurfaces again —presumably to be checked against a b in the input.

The idea of an automaton with a stack as auxiliary storage can be formalized as follows.

Definition 3.3.1: Let us define a **pushdown automaton** to be a sextuple $M = (K, \Sigma, \Gamma, \Delta, s, F)$, where

K is a finite set of **states**,
Σ is an alphabet (the **input symbols**),
Γ is an alphabet (the **stack symbols**),
$s \in K$ is the **initial state**,
$F \subseteq K$ is the set of **final states**, and
Δ, the **transition relation**, is a finite subset of $(K \times (\Sigma \cup \{e\}) \times \Gamma^*) \times (K \times \Gamma^*)$.

Intuitively, if $((p, a, \beta), (q, \gamma)) \in \Delta$, then M, whenever it is in state p with β at the top of the stack, may read a from the input tape (if $a = e$, then the input is not consulted), replace β by γ on the top of the stack, and enter state q. Such a pair $((p, a, \beta), (q, \gamma))$ is called a **transition** of M; since several transitions of M may be simultaneously applicable at any point, the machines we are describing are nondeterministic in operation. (We shall later alter this definition to define a more restricted class, the deterministic pushdown automata.)

To **push** a symbol is to add it to the top of the stack; to **pop** a symbol is to remove it from the top of the stack. For example, the transition $((p, u, e), (q, a))$ pushes a, while $((p, u, a), (q, e))$ pops a.

As is the case with finite automata, during a computation the portion of the input already read does not affect the subsequent operation of the machine. Accordingly, a **configuration** of a pushdown automaton is defined to be a member of $K \times \Sigma^* \times \Gamma^*$: The first component is the state of the machine, the second is the portion of the input yet to be read, and the third is the contents of the pushdown store, read top-down. For example, if the configuration were (q, w, abc), the a would be on the top of the stack and the c on the bottom. If (p, x, α) and (q, y, ζ)

are configurations of M, we say that (p, x, α) **yields in one step** (q, y, ζ) (notation: $(p, x, \alpha) \vdash_M (q, x, \zeta)$) if there is a transition $((p, a, \beta), (q, \gamma)) \in \Delta$ such that $x = ay$, $\alpha = \beta\eta$, and $\zeta = \gamma\eta$ for some $\eta \in \Gamma^*$. We denote the reflexive, transitive closure of $\vdash_M$ by $\vdash_M^*$. We say that M **accepts** a string $w \in \Sigma^*$ if and only if $(s, w, e) \vdash_M^* (p, e, e)$ for some state $p \in F$. To put it another way, M accepts a string w if and only if there is a sequence of configurations $C_0, C_1, \ldots, C_n$ $(n > O)$ such that $C_0 \vdash_M C_1 \vdash_M \cdots \vdash_M C_n$, $C_0 = (s, w, e)$, and $C_n = (p, e, e)$ for some $p \in F$. Any sequence of configurations $C_0, C_1, \ldots, C_n$ such that $C_i \vdash_M C_{i+1}$ for $i = 0, \ldots, n-1$ will be called a **computation** by M; it will be said to have **length** n, or to have n **steps**. The **language accepted** by M, denoted $L(M)$, is the set of all strings accepted by M.

When no confusion can result, we write $\vdash$ and $\vdash^*$ instead of $\vdash_M$ and $\vdash_M^*$.

Example 3.3.1: Let us design a pushdown automaton M to accept the language $L = \{wcw^R : w \in \{a, b\}^*\}$. For example, $ababcbaba \in L$, but $abcab \notin L$, and $cbc \notin L$. We let $M = (K, \Sigma, \Gamma, \Delta, s, F)$, where $K = \{s, f\}$, $\Sigma = \{a, b, c\}$, $\Gamma = \{a, b\}$, $F = \{f\}$, and Δ contains the following five transitions.

(1) $((s, a, e), (s, a))$
(2) $((s, b, e), (s, b))$
(3) $((s, c, e), (f, e))$
(4) $((f, a, a), (f, e))$
(5) $((f, b, b), (f, e))$

This automaton operates in the following way. As it reads the first half of its input, it remains in its initial state s and uses transitions 1 and 2 to transfer symbols from the input string onto the pushdown store. Note that these transitions are applicable regardless of the current content of the pushdown store, since the "string" to be matched on the top of the pushdown store is the empty string. When the machine sees a c in the input string, it switches from state s to state f without operating on its stack. Thereafter only transitions 4 and 5 are operative; these permit the removal of the top symbol on the stack, provided that it is the same as the next input symbol. If the input symbol does not match the top symbol on the stack, no further operation is possible. If the automaton reaches in this way the configuration (f, e, e) —final state, end of input, empty stack —then the input was indeed of the form wcw^R, and the automaton accepts. On the other hand, if the automaton detects a mismatch between input and stack symbols, or if the input is exhausted before the stack is emptied, then it does not accept.

To illustrate the operation of M, we describe a sequence of transitions for the input string $abbcbba$.

Example 3.3.2: Now we construct a pushdown automaton to accept $L = \{ww^R : w \in \{a, b\}^*\}$. That is, the strings accepted by this machine are the

State	Unread Input	Stack	Transition Used
s	$abbcbba$	e	–
s	$bbcbba$	a	1
s	$bcbba$	ba	2
s	$cbba$	bba	2
f	bba	bba	3
f	ba	ba	5
f	a	a	5
f	e	e	4

same as those accepted by the machine of the previous example, except that the symbol c that marked the center of the strings is missing. Therefore the machine must "guess" when it has reached the middle of the input string and change from state s to state f in a nondeterministic fashion. Thus $M = (K, \Sigma, \Gamma, \Delta, s, F)$, where $K = (s, f)$, $\Sigma = \{a, b\}$, $F = \{f\}$, and Δ is the set of the following five transitions.

(1) $((s, a, e), (s, a))$
(2) $((s, b, e), (s, b))$
(3) $((s, e, e), (f, e))$
(4) $((f, a, a), (f, e))$
(5) $((f, b, b), (f, e))$

Thus this machine is identical to that of the last example, except for transition 3. Whenever the machine is in state s, it can nondeterministically choose either to push the next input symbol onto the stack, or to switch to state f without consuming any input. Therefore even starting from a string of the form ww^R, M has computations that do not lead it to the accepting configuration (f, e, e); but there is some computation that leads M to this configuration if and only if the input string is of this form.$\Diamond$

Example 3.3.3: This pushdown automaton accepts the language $\{w \in \{a, b\}^* :$ w has the same number of a's and b's$\}$. Either a string of a's or a string of b's is kept by M on its stack. A stack of a's indicates the excess of a's over b's thus far read, if in fact M has read more a's than b's; a stack of b's indicates the excess of b's over a's. In either case, M keeps a special symbol c on the bottom of the stack as a marker. Let $M = (K, \Sigma, \Gamma, \Delta, s, F)$, where $K = \{s, q, f\}$, $\Sigma = \{a, b\}$, $\Gamma = \{a, b, c\}$, $F = \{f\}$, and Δ is listed below.

(1) $((s, e, e), (q, c))$
(2) $((q, a, c), (q, ac))$
(3) $((q, a, a), (q, aa))$

(4) $((q, a, b), (q, e))$
(5) $((q, b, c), (q, bc))$
(6) $((q, b, b), (q, bb))$
(7) $((q, b, a), (q, e))$
(8) $((q, e, c), (f, e))$

Transition 1 puts M in state q while placing a c on the bottom of the stack. In state q, when M reads an a, it either starts up a stack of a's from the bottom, while keeping the bottom marker (transition 2), or pushes an a onto a stack of a's (transition 3), or pops a b from a stack of b's (transition 4). When reading a b from the input, the machine acts analogously, pushing a b onto a stack of b's or a stack consisting of just a bottom marker, and popping an a from a stack of a's (transitions 5, 6, and 7). Finally, when c is the topmost (and therefore the only) symbol on the stack, the machine may remove it and pass to a final state (transition 8). If at this point all the input has been read, then the configuration (f, e, e) has been reached, and the input string is accepted.

The following table contains an illustration of the operation of M.

State	Unread Input	Stack	Transition	Comments
s	$abbbabaa$	e	–	Initial configuration.
q	$abbbabaa$	c	1	Bottom marker.
q	$bbbabaa$	ac	2	Start a stack of a's.
q	$bbabaa$	c	7	Remove one a.
q	$babaa$	bc	5	Start a stack of b's.
q	$abaa$	bbc	6	
q	baa	bc	4	
q	aa	bbc	6	
q	a	bc	4	
q	e	c	4	
f	e	e	8	Accepts.

$\Diamond$

Example 3.3.4: Every finite automaton can be trivially viewed as a pushdown automaton that never operates on its stack. To be precise, let $M = (K, \Sigma, \Delta, s, F)$ be a nondeterministic finite automaton, and let M' be the pushdown automaton $(K, \Sigma, \emptyset, \Delta', s, F)$, where $\Delta' = \{((p, u, e), (q, e)) : (p, u, q) \in \Delta\}$. In other words, M' always pushes and pops an empty string on its stack, and otherwise simulates the transitions of M. Then it is immediate that M and M' accept precisely the same language.$\Diamond$

Problems for Section 3.3

3.3.1. Consider the pushdown automaton $M = (K, \Sigma, \Gamma, \Delta, s, F)$, where

$$K = \{s, f\},$$
$$F = \{f\},$$
$$\Sigma = \{a, b\},$$
$$\Gamma = \{a\},$$
$$\Delta = \{((s, a, e), (s, a)), ((s, b, e), (s, a)), ((s, a, e), (f, e)),$$
$$((f, a, a), (f, e)), ((f, b, a), (f, e))\}.$$

(a) Trace all possible sequences of transitions of M on input aba.
(b) Show that $aba, aa, abb \in L(M)$, but $baa, bab, baaaa \notin L(M)$.
(c) Describe $L(M)$ in English.

3.3.2. Construct pushdown automata that accept each of the following.
(a) The language generated by the grammar $G = (V, \Sigma, R, S)$, where

$$V = \{S, (,), [,]\},$$
$$\Sigma = \{(,), [,]\},$$
$$R = \{S \to e,$$
$$S \to SS,$$
$$S \to [S],$$
$$S \to (S)\}.$$

(b) The language $\{a^m b^n : m \le n \le 2m\}$.
(c) The language $\{w \in \{a, b\}^* : w = w^R\}$.
(d) The language $\{w \in \{a, b\}^* : w \text{ has twice as many } b\text{'s as } a\text{'s}\}$.

3.3.3. Let $M = (K, \Sigma, \Gamma, \Delta, s, F)$ be a pushdown automaton. The **language accepted by** M **by final state** is defined as follows:

$$L_f(M) = \{w \in \Sigma^* : (s, w, e) \vdash_M^* (f, e, \alpha) \text{ for some } f \in F, \alpha \in \Gamma^*\}.$$

a) Show that there is a pushdown automaton M' such that $L(M') = L_f(M)$.
b) Show that there is a pushdown automaton M'' such that $L_f(M'') = L(M)$.

3.3.4. Let $M = (K, , \Sigma, \Gamma, \Delta, s, F)$ be a pushdown automaton. The **language accepted by M by empty store** is defined as follows:

$$L_e(M) = \{w \in \Sigma^* : (s, w, e) \vdash_M^* (q, e, e) \text{ for some } q \in K\}.$$

(a) Show that there is a pushdown automaton M' such that $L_e(M') = L(M)$.

(b) Show that there is a pushdown automaton M'' such that $L(M'') = L_e(M)$.

(c) Show by a counterexample that it is not necessarily the case that $L_e(M) = L(M) \cup \{e\}$.

3.4 | PUSHDOWN AUTOMATA AND CONTEXT-FREE GRAMMARS

In this section we show that the pushdown automaton is exactly what is needed to accept arbitrary context-free languages. This fact is of mathematical and practical significance: mathematical, because it knits together two different formal views of the same class of languages; and practical, because it lays the foundation for the study of syntax analyzers for "real" context-free languages such as programming languages (more on this in Section 3.7).

Theorem 3.4.1: *The class of languages accepted by pushdown automata is exactly the class of context-free languages.*

Proof: We break this proof into two parts.

Lemma 3.4.1: *Each context-free language is accepted by some pushdown automaton.*

Proof: Let $G = (V, \Sigma, R, S)$ be a context-free grammar; we must construct a pushdown automaton M such that $L(M) = L(G)$. The machine we construct has only two states, p and q, and remains permanently in state q after its first move. Also, M uses V, the set of terminals and nonterminals, as its stack alphabet. We let $M = (\{p, q\}, \Sigma, V, \Delta, p, \{q\})$, where Δ contains the following transitions:

(1) $((p, e, e), (q, S))$

(2) $((q, e, A), (q, x))$ for each rule $A \to x$ in R.

(3) $((q, a, a), (q, e))$ for each $a \in \Sigma$.

The pushdown automaton M begins by pushing S, the start symbol of G, on its initially empty pushdown store, and entering state q (transition 1). On each subsequent step, it either replaces the topmost symbol A on the stack, provided that it is a nonterminal, by the right-hand side x of some rule $A \to x$ in R (transitions of type 2), or pops the topmost symbol from the stack, provided that it is a terminal symbol that matches the next input symbol (transitions of type 3). The transitions of M are designed so that the pushdown store during an accepting computation mimics a leftmost derivation of the input string; M intermittently carries out a step of such a derivation on the stack, and between such steps it strips away from the top of the stack any terminal symbols and matches them against symbols in the input string. Popping the terminals from the stack has in turn the effect of exposing the leftmost nonterminal, so that the process can continue.

Example 3.4.1: Consider the grammar $G = (V, \Sigma, R, S)$ with $V = \{S, a, b, c\}$, $\Sigma = \{a, b, c\}$, and $R = \{S \to aSa, S \to bSb, S \to c\}$, which generates the language $\{wcw^R : w \in \{a, b\}^*\}$. The corresponding pushdown automaton, according to the construction above, is $M = (\{p, q\}, \Sigma, V, \Delta, p, \{q\})$, with

$$\begin{aligned}
\Delta = \{&((p, e, e), (q, S)), & (T1)\\
&((q, e, S), (q, aSa)), & (T2)\\
&((q, e, S), (q, bSb)), & (T3)\\
&((q, e, S), (q, c)), & (T4)\\
&((q, a, a), (q, e)), & (T5)\\
&((q, b, b), (q, e)), & (T6)\\
&((q, c, c), (q, e))\} & (T7).
\end{aligned}$$

The string $abbcbba$ is accepted by M through the following sequence of moves.

State	Unread Input	Stack	Transition Used
p	$abbcbba$	e	–
q	$abbcbba$	S	T1
q	$abbcbba$	aSa	T2
q	$bbcbba$	Sa	T5
q	$bbcbba$	$bSba$	T3
q	$bcbba$	Sba	T6
q	$bcbba$	$bSbba$	T3
q	$cbba$	$Sbba$	T6
q	$cbba$	$cbba$	T4
q	bba	bba	T7
q	ba	ba	T6
q	a	a	T6
q	e	e	T5

Compare this to the operation, on the same string, of the pushdown automaton of Example 3.3.1.◊

To continue the proof of the Lemma, in order to establish that $L(M) = L(G)$, we prove the following claim.

Claim. Let $w \in \Sigma^*$ and $\alpha \in (V - \Sigma)V^* \cup \{e\}$. Then $S \overset{L}{\Rightarrow}{}^* w\alpha$ if and only if $(q, w, S) \vdash_M^* (q, e, \alpha)$.

This claim will suffice to establish Lemma 3.4.1, since it will follow (by taking $\alpha = e$) that $S \overset{L}{\Rightarrow}{}^* w$ if and only if $(q, e, S) \vdash_M^* (q, e, e)$ —in other words, $w \in L(G)$ if and only if $w \in L(M)$.

(Only if) Suppose that $S \overset{L}{\Rightarrow}{}^* w\alpha$, where $w \in \Sigma^*$, and $\alpha \in (V - \Sigma)V^* \cup \{e\}$. We shall show by induction on the length of the leftmost derivation of w from S that $(q, w, S) \vdash_M^* (q, e, \alpha)$.

Basis Step. If the derivation is of length 0, then $w = e$, and $\alpha = S$, and hence indeed $(q, w, S) \vdash_M^* (q, e, \alpha)$.

Induction Hypothesis. Assume that if $S \overset{L}{\Rightarrow}{}^* w\alpha$ by a derivation of length n or less, $n \geq 0$, then $(q, w, S) \vdash_M^* (q, e, \alpha)$.

Induction Step. Let

$$S = u_0 \overset{L}{\Rightarrow} u_1 \overset{L}{\Rightarrow} \cdots \overset{L}{\Rightarrow} u_n \overset{L}{\Rightarrow} u_{n+1} = w\alpha$$

be a leftmost derivation of $w\alpha$ from S. Let A be the leftmost nonterminal of u_n. Then $u_n = xA\beta$, and $u_{n+1} = x\gamma\beta$, where $x \in \Sigma^*$, $\beta, \gamma \in V^*$, and $A \to \gamma$ is a rule in R. Since there is a leftmost derivation of length n of $u_n = xA\beta$ from S, by the induction hypothesis

$$(q, x, S) \vdash_M^* (q, e, A\beta). \tag{2}$$

Since $A \to \gamma$ is a rule in R,

$$(q, e, A\beta) \vdash_M (q, e, \gamma\beta), \tag{3}$$

by a transition of type 2.

Now notice that u_{n+1} is $w\alpha$, but it is also $x\gamma\beta$. Hence, there is a string $y \in \Sigma^*$ such that $w = xy$ and $y\alpha = \gamma\beta$. Thus, we can rewrite (2) and (3) above as

$$(q, w, S) \vdash_M^* (q, y, \gamma\beta). \tag{4}$$

However, Since $y\alpha = \gamma\beta$,

$$(q, y, \gamma\beta) \vdash_M^* (q, e, \alpha), \tag{5}$$

by a sequence of $|y|$ transitions of type 3. Combining (4) and (5) completes the induction step.

(If) Now suppose that $(q, w, S) \vdash_M^* (q, e, \alpha)$ with $w \in \Sigma^*$ and $\alpha \in (V - \Sigma)V^* \cup \{e\}$; we show that $S \overset{*}{\underset{L}{\Rightarrow}} w\alpha$. Again, the proof is by induction, but this time *on the number of transitions of type 2* in the computation by M.

Basis Step. Since the first move in any computation is by a transition of type 2, if $(q, w, S) \vdash_M^* (q, e, \alpha)$ with no type-2 transitions, then $w = e$ and $\alpha = S$, and the result is true.

Induction Hypothesis. If $(q, w, S) \vdash_M^* (q, e, \alpha)$ by a computation with n type 2 steps or fewer, $n \geq 0$, then $S \overset{*}{\underset{L}{\Rightarrow}} w\alpha$.

Induction Step. Suppose that $(q, w, S) \vdash_M^* (q, e, \alpha)$ in $n + 1$ type-2 transitions, and consider the next-to-last such transition, say,

$$(q, w, S) \vdash_M^* (q, y, A\beta) \vdash_M (q, y, \gamma\beta) \vdash_M^* (q, e, \alpha),$$

where $w = xy$ for some $x, y \in \Sigma^*$, and $A \to \beta$ is a rule of the grammar. By the induction hypothesis we have that $S \overset{*}{\underset{L}{\Rightarrow}} xA\beta$, and thus $S \overset{*}{\underset{L}{\Rightarrow}} x\gamma\beta$. Since however $(q, y, \gamma\beta) \vdash_M^* (q, e, \alpha)$, presumably by transitions of type 3, it follows that $y\alpha = \gamma\beta$, and thus $S \overset{*}{\underset{L}{\Rightarrow}} xy\alpha = w\alpha$. This completes the proof of Lemma 3.4.1, and with it half the proof of Theorem 3.4.1. ∎

We now turn to the proof of the other half of Theorem 3.4.1.

Lemma 3.4.2: *If a language is accepted by a pushdown automaton, it is a context-free language.*

Proof: It will be helpful to restrict somewhat the pushdown automata under consideration. Call a pushdown automaton **simple** if the following is true:

> Whenever $((q, a, \beta), (p, \gamma))$ is a transition of the pushdown automaton and q is *not* the start state, then $\beta \in \Gamma$, and $|\gamma| \leq 2$.

In other words, the machine always consults its topmost stack symbol (and no symbols below it), and replaces it either with e, or with a single stack symbol, or with two stack symbols. Now it is easy to see that no interesting pushdown automaton can have only transitions of this kind, because then it would not be able to operate when the stack is empty (for example, it would not be able to *start* the computation, since in the beginning the stack is empty). This is why we do not restrict transitions from the start state.

We claim that if a language is accepted by an unrestricted pushdown automaton, then it is accepted by a simple pushdown automaton. To see this, let $M = (K, \Sigma, \Gamma, \Delta, s, F)$ be any pushdown automaton; we shall construct a simple pushdown automaton $M = (K', \Sigma, \Gamma \cup \{Z\}, \Delta', s', \{f'\})$ that also accepts $L(M)$;

here s' and f' are new states not in K, and Z is a new stack symbol, the *stack bottom symbol*, also not in Γ. We first add to Δ the transition $((s', e, e), (s, Z))$; this transition starts the computation by placing the stack bottom symbol in the bottom of the stack, where it will remain throughout the computation. No rule of Δ will ever push a Z in the stack —except to replace it at the bottom of the stack. We also add to Δ the transitions $((f, Z, e), (f', e))$ for each $f \in F$. These transitions end the computation by removing Z from the bottom of the stack and accepting the input seen so far.

Initially, Δ' consists of the start and final transitions described above, and all transitions of Δ. We shall next replace all transitions in Δ' that violate the simplicity condition by equivalent transitions that satisfy the simplicity condition. We shall do this in three stages: First we shall replace transitions with $|\beta| \geq 2$. Then we shall get rid of transitions with $|\gamma| > 2$, without introducing any transitions with $|\beta| \geq 2$. Finally, we shall get rid of transitions with $\beta = e$, without introducing any transitions with $|\beta| \geq 2$ or $|\gamma| > 2$.

Consider any transition $((q, a, \beta), (p, \gamma)) \in \Delta'$, where $\beta = B_1 \cdots B_n$ with $n > 1$. It is replaced by new transitions that pop sequentially the individual symbols in $B_1 \cdots B_n$, rather than removing them all in a single step. Specifically, we add to Δ' these transitions:

$$((q, e, B_1), (q_{B_1}, e)),$$
$$((t_1, e, B_2), (q_{B_1 B_2}, e)),$$

$$\vdots$$

$$((t_{n-2}, e, B_{n-1}), (q_{B_1 B_2 \ldots B_{n-1}}, e)),$$
$$((t_{n-1}, a, B_n), (p, \gamma)),$$

where, for $i = 1, \ldots, n - 1$, $q_{B_1 B_2 \ldots B_i}$ is a new state with the intuitive meaning "state q after symbols $B_1 B_2 \ldots B_i$ have been popped. We repeat this with all transitions $((q, u, \beta), (p, \gamma)) \in \Delta'$ with $|\beta| > 1$. It is clear that the resulting pushdown automaton is equivalent to the original one.

Similarly, we replace transitions $((q, u, \beta), (p, \gamma))$ with $\gamma = C_1 \ldots, C_m$ and $m \geq 2$ by the transitions

$$(q, a, \beta), (r_1, C_m)),$$
$$(r_1, e, e), (r_2, C_{m-1})),$$

$$\vdots$$

$$(r_{m-2}, e, e), (r_{m-1}, C_2)),$$
$$(r_{m-1}, e, e), (p, C_1)),$$

where $r_1, \ldots, r_{m-1}$ are new states. Notice that all transitions $((q, a, \beta), (p, \gamma)) \in \Delta$ have now $|\gamma| \leq 1$ —a more stringent requirement than simplicity (and actually one that *would be* a loss of generality). It will be restored to $|\gamma| \leq 2$ in the next stage. Also, no transitions $((q, u, \beta), (p, \gamma))$ with $|\beta| > 1$ were added.

Finally, consider any transition $((q, a, e), (p, \gamma))$ with $q \neq s'$ —the only possible remaining violations of the simplicity condition. Replace any such transition by all transitions of the form $((q, a, A), (p, \gamma A))$, for all $A \in \Gamma \cup \{Z\}$. That is, if the automaton could move without consulting its stack, it can also move by consulting the top stack symbol, whatever it may be, and replace it immediately. And we know that *there is* at least one symbol in the stack: throughout the main computation —apart from the start and final transitions— the stack never becomes empty. Notice also that at this stage we may introduce γ's of length two —this does not violate the simplicity condition, but is necessary for obtaining general pushdown automata.

It is easy to see that this construction results in a simple pushdown automaton M' such that $L(M) = L(M')$. To continue the proof of the lemma, we shall exhibit a context-free grammar G such that $L(G) = L(M')$; this would conclude the proof of the lemma, and with it of Theorem 3.4.1.

We let $G = (V, \Sigma, R, S)$, where V contains, in addition to a new symbol S and the symbols in Σ, a new symbol $\langle q, A, p \rangle$ for all $q, p \in K$ and each $A \in \Gamma \cup \{e, Z\}$. To understand the role of the nonterminals $\langle q, A, p \rangle$, remember that G is supposed to generate all strings accepted by M. Therefore the nonterminals of G stand for different parts of the input strings that are accepted by M. In particular, if $A \in \Gamma$, then the nonterminal $\langle q, A, p \rangle$ represents any portion of the input string that might be read between a point in time when M is in state q with A on top of its stack, and a point in time when M removes that occurrence of A from the stack and enters state p. If $A = e$, then $\langle q, e, p \rangle$ denotes a portion of the input string that might be read between a time when M is in state q and a time when it is in state p with the same stack, without in the interim changing or consulting that part of the stack.

The rules in R are of four types.

(1) The rule $S \rightarrow \langle s, Z, f' \rangle$, where s is the start state of the *original* pushdown automaton M and f' the new final state.
(2) For each transition $((q, a, B), (r, e))$, where $q, r \in K$, $a \in \Sigma \cup \{e\}$, $B, C \in \Gamma \cup \{e\}$, *and for each* $p \in K$, we add the rule $\langle q, B, p \rangle \rightarrow a \langle r, C, p \rangle$.
(3) For each transition $((q, a, B), (r, C_1 C_2))$, where $q, r \in K$, $a \in \Sigma \cup \{e\}$, $B \in \Gamma \cup \{e\}$, and $C_1, C_2 \in \Gamma$ *and for each* $p, p' \in K$, we add the rule $\langle q, B, p \rangle \rightarrow a \langle r, C_1, p' \rangle \langle p', C_2, p \rangle$.
(4) For each $q \in K$, the rule $\langle q, e, q \rangle \rightarrow e$.

Note that, because M is simple, either type 2 or type 3 applies to each transition of M.

A rule of type 1 states essentially that any input string which can be read by M' passing from state s to the final state, while at the same time the net effect on the stack is that the stack bottom symbol was popped, is a string in the language $L(M)$. A rule of type 4 says that no computation is needed to go from a state to itself without changing the stack. Finally, a rule of type 2 or 3 says that, if $((q, a, B), (p, \gamma)) \in \Delta'$, then one of the possible computations that lead from state q to state p while consuming B (possibly empty) from the top of the stack, starts by reading input a, replacing B by γ, passing to sate r, and *then* going on to consume γ and end up in state p —reading whatever input is appropriate during such computation. If $\gamma = C_1 C_2$, this last computation can in principle pass through any state p' immediately after C_1 is popped (this is a type-3 rule).

These intuitive remarks are formalized in the following claim.

Claim. For any $q, p \in K$, $A \in \Gamma \cup \{e\}$, and $x \in \Sigma^*$,

$$\langle q, A, p \rangle \Rightarrow^*_G x \text{ if and only if } (q, x, A) \vdash_M (p, e, e).$$

Lemma 3.4.2, and with it Theorem 3.4.1, follows readily from the claim, since then $\langle s, e, f \rangle \Rightarrow^*_G x$ for some $f \in F$ if and only if $(s, x, e) \vdash^*_M (f, e, e)$; that is, $x \in L(G)$ if and only if $x \in L(M)$.

Both directions of the claim can be proved by induction on the length either of the derivation of G or the computation of M; they are left as an exercise (Problem 3.4.5). ∎

Problems for Section 3.4

3.4.1. Carry out the construction of Lemma 3.4.1 for the grammar of Example 3.1.4. Trace the operation of the automaton you have constructed on the input string $(()())$.

3.4.2. Carry out the construction of Lemma 3.4.2 for the pushdown automaton of Example 3.3.2, and let G be the resulting grammar. What is the set $\{w \in \{a, b\}^* : \langle q, a, p \rangle \Rightarrow^*_G w\}$? Compare with the proof of Lemma 3.4.2.

3.4.3. Carry out the construction of Lemma 3.4.2 for the pushdown automaton of Example 3.3.3. The resulting grammar will have 25 rules, but many can be eliminated as useless. Show a derivation of the string $aababbba$ in this grammar. (You may change the names of the nonterminals for clarity.)

3.4.4. Show that if $M = (K, \Sigma, \Gamma, \Delta, s, F)$ is a pushdown automaton, then there is another pushdown automaton $M' = (K', \Sigma, \Gamma, \Delta', s, F)$ such that $(M') = L(M)$ and for all $((q, u, \beta), (p, \gamma)) \in \Delta'$, $|\beta| + |\gamma| \leq 1$.

3.4.5. Complete the proof of Lemma 3.4.2.

3.4.6. A context-free grammar is **linear** if and only if no rule has as its right-hand side a string with more than one nonterminal. A pushdown automaton $(K, \Sigma, \Gamma, \Delta, s, F)$ is said to be **single-turn** if and only if whenever $(s, w, e) \vdash^* (q_1, w_1, \gamma_1) \vdash (q_2, w_2, \gamma_2)$ and $|\gamma_2| < |\gamma_1|$, then $|\gamma_3| \leq |\gamma_2|$—. (That is, once the stack starts to decrease in height, it never again increases in height.) Show that a language is generated by a linear context-free grammar if and only if it is accepted by a single-turn pushdown automaton.

3.5 | LANGUAGES THAT ARE AND ARE NOT CONTEXT-FREE

Closure Properties

In the last section, two views of context-free languages —as languages generated by context-free grammars and as languages accepted by pushdown automata— were shown to be equivalent. These characterizations enrich our understanding of the context-free languages, since they provide two different methods for recognizing when a language is context-free. For example, the grammatical representation is more natural and compelling in the case of a programming language fragment such as that of Example 3.1.3; but the representation in terms of pushdown automata is easier to see in the case of $\{w \in \{a, b\}^* : w \text{ has equal numbers of } a\text{'s and } b\text{'s}\}$ (see Example 3.3.3). In this subsection we shall provide further tools for establishing context-freeness: we show some *closure* properties of the context-free languages under language operations —very much in the spirit of the closure properties of regular languages. In the next subsection we shall prove a more powerful *pumping theorem* which enables us to show that certain languages are *not* context-free.

Theorem 3.5.1: *The context-free languages are closed under union, concatenation, and Kleene star.*

Proof: . Let $G_1 = (V_1, \Sigma_1, R_1, S_1)$ and $G_2 = (V_2, \Sigma_2, R_2, S_2)$ be two context-free grammars, and without loss of generality assume that they have disjoint sets of nonterminals —that is, $V_1 - \Sigma_1$ and $V_2 - \Sigma_2$ are disjoint.

Union. Let S be a new symbol and let $G = (V_1 \cup V_2 \cup \{S\}, \Sigma_1 \cup \Sigma_2, R, S)$, where $R = R_1 \cup R_2 \cup \{S \to S_1, S \to S_2\}$. Then we claim that $L(G) = L(G_1) \cup L(G_2)$. For the only rules involving S are $S \to S_1$ and $S \to S_2$, so $S \Rightarrow_G^* w$ if and only if either $S_1 \Rightarrow_G^* w$ or $S_2 \Rightarrow_G^* w$; and since G_1 and G_2 have disjoint sets of nonterminals, the last disjunction is equivalent to saying that $w \in L(G_1) \cup L(G_2)$.

Concatenation. The construction is similar: $L(G_1)L(G_2)$ is generated by the grammar

$$G = (V_1 \cup V_2 \cup \{S\}, \Sigma_1 \cup \Sigma_2, R_1 \cup R_2 \cup \{S \to S_1 S_2\}, S).$$

Kleene Star. $L(G_1)^*$ is generated by

$$G = (V_1 \cup \{S\}, \Sigma_1, R_1 \cup \{S \to e, S \to SS_1\}, S).$$

∎

As we shall see shortly, the class of context-free languages is *not* closed under intersection or complementation. This is not very surprising: Recall that our proof that regular languages are closed under intersection depended on closure under complementation; and that construction required that the automaton be *deterministic*. And not all context-free languages are accepted by deterministic pushdown automata (see the corollary to Theorem 3.7.1).

There is an interesting direct proof of the closure under intersection of regular languages, not relying on closure under complement, but on a direct construction of a finite automaton whose set of states is the *Cartesian product* of the sets of states of the constituent finite automata (recall Problem 2.3.3). This construction cannot of course be extended to pushdown automata —the product automaton would have needed *two stacks*. However, it can be made to work *when one of the two automata is finite:*

Theorem 3.5.2: *The intersection of a context-free language with a regular language is a context-free language.*

Proof: If L is a context-free language and R is a regular language, then $L = L(M_1)$ for some pushdown automaton $M_1 = (K_1, \Sigma, \Gamma_1, \Delta_1, s_1, F_1)$, and $R = L(M_2)$ for some deterministic finite automaton $M_2 = (K_2, \Sigma, \delta, s_2, F_2)$. The idea is to combine these machines into a single pushdown automaton M that carries out computations by M_1 and M_2 *in parallel* and accepts only if both would have accepted. Specifically, let $M = (K, \Sigma, \Gamma, \Delta, s, F)$, where

$K = K_1 \times K_2$, the Cartesian product of the state sets of M_1 and M_2;
$\Gamma = \Gamma_1$;
$s = (s_1, s_2)$;
$F = F_1 \times F_2$, and
Δ, the transition relation, is defined as follows. For each transition of the pushdown automaton $((q_1, a, \beta), (p_1, \gamma)) \in \Delta_1$, and for each state $q_2 \in K_2$, we add to Δ the transition $(((q_1, q_2), a, \beta), ((p_1, \delta(q_2, a)), \gamma))$; and for each transition of the form $((q_1, e, \beta), (p_1, \gamma)) \in \Delta_1$ and each state $q_2 \in K_2$, we add to Δ the transition $(((q_1, q_2), e, \beta), ((p_1, q_2), \gamma))$. That is, M passes from state (q_1, q_2) to state (p_1, p_2) in the same way that M_1 passes from state q_1 to p_1, except that in addition M keeps track of the change in the state of M_2 caused by reading the same input.

It is easy to see that indeed $w \in L(M)$ if and only if $w \in L(M_1) \cap L(M_2)$. ∎

Example 3.5.1: Let L consist of all strings of a's and b's with equal numbers of a's and b's but containing no substring $abaa$ or $babb$. Then L is context-free, since it is the intersection of the language accepted by the pushdown automaton in Example 3.3.3 with the regular language $\{a, b\}^* - \{a, b\}^*(abaa \cup babb)\{a, b\}^*$. ◇

A Pumping Theorem

Infinite context-free languages display periodicity of a somewhat subtler form than do regular languages. To understand this aspect of context-freeness we start from a familiar quantitative fact about parse trees. Let $G = (V, \Sigma, R, S)$ be a context-free grammar. The **fanout** of G, denoted $\phi(G)$, is the largest number of symbols on the right-hand side of any rule in R. A **path** in a parse tree is a sequence of distinct nodes, each connected to the previous one by a line segment; the first node is the root, and the last node is a leaf. The **length** of the path is the number of line segments in it. The **height** of a parse tree is the length of the longest path in it.

Lemma 3.5.1: *The yield of any parse tree of G of height h has length at most* $\phi(G)^h$.

Proof: The proof is by induction on h. When $h = 1$, then the parse tree is a rule of the grammar (this is Case 2 of the definition of a parse tree), and thus its yield has at most $\phi(G)^h = \phi(G)$ symbols.

Suppose then that the result is true for parse trees of height up to $h \geq 1$. For the induction step, any parse tree of height $h+1$ consists of a root, connected to at most $\phi(G)$ smaller parse trees of height at most h (this is Case 3 of the definition of a parse tree). By induction, all these parse "subtrees" have yields of length at most $\phi(G)^h$ each. It follows that the total yield of the overall parse tree is indeed at most $\phi(G)^{h+1}$, completing the induction. ∎

To put it another way, the parse tree of any string $w \in L(G)$ with $|w| > \phi(G)^h$ must have a path longer than h. This is crucial in proving the following *pumping theorem* for context-free languages.

Theorem 3.5.3: *Let $G = (V, \Sigma, R, S)$ be a context-free grammar. Then any string $w \in L(G)$ of length greater than $\phi(G)^{|V-\Sigma|}$ can be rewritten as $w = uvxyz$ in such a way that either v or y is nonempty and uv^nxy^nz is in $L(G)$ for every $n \geq 0$.*

Proof: Let w be such a string, and let T be the parse tree with root labeled S and with yield w *that has the smallest number of leaves* among all parse trees with the same root and yield. Since T's yield is longer than $\phi(G)^{|V-\Sigma|}$, it follows that T has a path of length at least $|V - \Sigma| + 1$, that is, with at least $|V - \Sigma| + 2$ nodes. Only one of these nodes can be labeled by a terminal, and thus the remaining are labeled by nonterminals. Since there are more nodes in the path than there are nonterminals, there are two nodes on the path labeled with the same member A of $V - \Sigma$. Let us look at this path in more detail (see Figure 3-9).

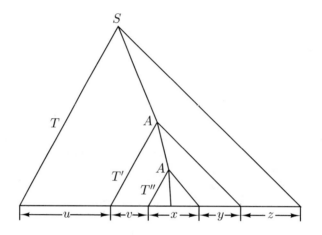

Figure 3-9

Let us call u, v, x, y, and z the parts of the yield of T as they are shown in the figure. That is, x is the yield of the subtree T'' whose root is the lower node labeled A; v is the part of the yield of the tree T' rooted at the higher A up to where the yield of T'' starts; u is the yield of T up to where the yield of T' starts; and z is the rest of the yield of T.

It is now clear that the part of T' excluding T'' can be repeated any number of times, *including zero times*, to produce other parse trees of G, whose yield is any string of the form $uv^n xy^n z, n \geq 0$. This completes the proof, except for the requirement that $vy \neq e$. But if $vy = e$, then there is a tree with root S and yield w with fewer leaves than that of T —namely, the one that results if we omit from T the part of T' that excludes T''— contrary to our assumption that T is the smallest tree of this kind. ∎

Example 3.5.2: Just like the pumping theorem for regular languages (Theorem 2.4.1), this theorem is useful for showing that certain languages are not context-free. For example, $L = \{a^n b^n c^n : n \geq 0\}$ is not. For suppose that $L = L(G)$ for some context-free grammar $G = (V, \Sigma, R, S)$. Let $n > \frac{\phi(G)^{|V-\Sigma|}}{3}$. Then $w = a^n b^n c^n$ is in $L(G)$ and has a representation $w = uvxyz$ such that v or

y is nonempty and $uv^n xy^n z$ is in $L(G)$ for each $n = 0, 1, 2, \ldots$ There are two cases, both leading to a contradiction. If vy contains occurrences of all three symbols a, b, c, then at least one of v, y must contain occurrences of at least two of them. But then $uv^2 xy^2 z$ contains two occurrences out of their correct order —a b before an a, or a c before an a or b. If vy contains occurrences of some but not all of the three symbols, then $uv^2 xy^2 z$ has unequal numbers of a's, b's, and c's.$\Diamond$

Example 3.5.3: $L = \{a^n : n \geq 1 \text{ is a prime}\}$ is not context-free. To see this, take a prime p greater than $\phi(G)^{|V - \Sigma|}$, where $G = (V, \Sigma, R, S)$ is the context-free grammar allegedly generating L. Then $w = a^p$ can be written as prescribed by the theorem, $w = uvxyz$, where all components of w are strings of a's and $vy \neq e$. Suppose that $vy = a^q$, and $uxz = a^r$, where p an q are natural numbers, and $q > 0$. Then the theorem states that $r + nq$ is a prime, for all $n \geq 0$. This was found absurd in Example 2.4.3.

It was no accident that, in our proof that $\{a^n : n \geq 1 \text{ is a prime}\}$ is not context-free, we resorted to an argument very similar to that in Example 2.4.3, showing that the same language is not regular. It turns out that *any* context-free language over a single-letter alphabet is regular; thus, the result of the present example follows immediately from this fact and Example 2.4.3.$\Diamond$

Example 3.5.4: We shall next show that the language $L = \{w \in \{a, b, c\}^* : w \text{ has an equal number of } a\text{'s, } b\text{'s, and } c\text{'s}\}$ is not context-free. This time we need both Theorems 3.5.3 and 3.5.2: If L were context-free, then so would be its intersection with the regular set $a^* b^* c^*$. But this language, $\{a^n b^n c^n : n \geq 0\}$, was shown to be non-context-free in Example 3.5.2 above.$\Diamond$

These negative facts also expose the poverty in closure properties of the class of context-free languages:

Theorem 3.5.4: *The context-free languages are not closed under intersection or complementation.*

Proof: Clearly $\{a^n b^n c^m : m, n \geq 0\}$ and $\{a^m b^n c^n : m, n \geq 0\}$ are both context-free. The intersection of these two context-free languages is the language $\{a^n b^n c^n : n \geq 0\}$ just shown not to be context-free. And, since

$$L_1 \cap L_2 = \overline{\overline{L_1} \cup \overline{L_2}},$$

if the context-free languages were closed under complementation, they would also be closed under intersection (we know they are closed under union, Theorem 3.5.1). $\blacksquare$

Problems for Section 3.5

3.5.1. Use closure under union to show that the following languages are context-free.
(a) $\{a^m b^n : m \neq n\}$
(b) $\{a, b\}^* - \{a^n b^n : n \geq 0\}$
(c) $\{a^m b^n c^p d^q : n = q, \text{ or } m \leq p \text{ or } m + n = p + q\}$
(d) $\{a, b\}^* - L$, where L is the language
$$L = \{babaabaaab \ldots ba^{n-1}ba^n b : n \geq 1\}$$
(e) $\{w \in \{a, b\}^* : w = w^R\}$

3.5.2. Use Theorems 3.5.2 and 3.5.3 to show that the following languages are not context-free.
(a) $\{a^p : p \text{ is a prime}\}$
(b) $\{a^{n^2} : n \geq 0\}$
(c) $\{www : w \in \{a, b\}^*\}$
(d) $\{w \in \{a, b, c\}^* : w \text{ has equal numbers of } a\text{'s, } b\text{'s, and } c\text{'s}\}$

3.5.3. Recall that a **homomorphism** is a function h from strings to strings such that for any two strings v and w, $h(vw) = h(v)h(w)$. Thus a homomorphism is determined by its values on single symbols: if $w = a_1 \ldots a_n$ with each a_i a symbol, then $h(w) = h(a_1) \ldots h(a_n)$. Note that homomorphisms can "erase": $h(w)$ may be e, even though w is not. Show that if L is a context-free language and h is a homomorphism, then
(a) $h[L]$ is context-free;
(b) $h^{-1}[L]$ (that is, $\{w \in \Sigma^* : h(w) \in L\}$) is context-free. (*Hint:* Start from a pushdown automaton M accepting L. Construct another pushdown automaton, similar to M, except that it reads its input not from the input tape, but from a finite buffer that is occasionally replenished in some way. You supply the rest of the intuition and the formal details.)

3.5.4. In the proof of Theorem 3.5.2, why did we assume that M_2 was deterministic?

3.5.5. Show that the language $L = \{babaabaaab \ldots ba^{n-1}ba^n b : n \geq 1\}$ is not context-free
(a) by applying the Pumping Theorem (3.5.3);
(b) by applying the result of Problem 3.5.3. (Hint: What is $h[L]$, where $h(a) = aa$, and $h(b) = a$?)

3.5.6. If $L_1, L_2 \subseteq \Sigma^*$ are languages, the **right quotient of L_1 by L_2** is defined as follows.

$$L_1/L_2 = \{w \in \Sigma^* : \text{ there is a } u \in L_2 \text{ such that } wu \in L_1\}$$

(a) Show that if L_1 is context-free and R is regular, then L_1/R is context-free.

(b) Prove that $\{a^p b^n : p \text{ is a prime number and } n > p\}$ is not context-free.

3.5.7. Prove the following stronger version of the Pumping Theorem (Theorem 3.5.3): Let G be a context-free grammar. Then there are numbers K and k such that any string $w \in L(G)$ with $w \geq K$ can be rewritten as $w = uvxyz$ with $vxy \leq k$ in such a way that either v or y is nonempty and $uv^n xy^n z \in L(G)$ for every $n \geq 0$.

3.5.8. Use Problem 3.5.7 to show that the language $\{ww : w \in \{a, b\}^*\}$ is not context-free.

3.5.9. Let $G = (V, \Sigma, R, S)$ be a context-free grammar. A nonterminal A of G is called **self-embedding** if and only if $A \Rightarrow_G^+ uAv$ for some $u, v \in V^*$.

(a) Give an algorithm to test whether a specific nonterminal of a given context-free grammar is self-embedding.

(b) Show that if G has no self-embedding nonterminal, then $L(G)$ is a regular language.

3.5.10. A context-free grammar $G = (V, \Sigma, R, S)$ is said to be in **Greibach normal form** if every rule is of the form or $A \rightarrow w$ for some $w \in \Sigma(V - \Sigma)^*$.

(a) Show that for every context-free grammar G, there is a context-free grammar G' in Greibach normal form such that $L(G') = L(G') - \{e\}$.

(b) Show that if M is constructed as in the proof of Lemma 3.4.1 from a grammar in Greibach normal form, then the number of steps in any computation of M on an input w can be bounded as a function of the length of w.

3.5.11. Deterministic finite-state transducers were introduced in Problem 2.1.4. Show that if L is context-free and f is computed by a deterministic finite-state transducer, then

(a) $f[L]$ is context-free;

(b) $f^{-1}[L]$ is context-free.

3.5.12. Develop a version of the Pumping Theorem for context-free languages in which the length of the "pumped part" is as long as possible.

3.5.13. Let M_1 and M_2 be pushdown automata. Show how to construct pushdown automata accepting $L(M_1) \cup L(M_2)$, $L(M_1)L(M_2)$, and $L(M_1)^*$, thus providing another proof of Theorem 3.5.1.

3.5.14. Which of the following languages are context-free? Explain briefly in each case.

(a) $\{a^m b^n c^p : m = n \text{ or } n = p \text{ or } m = p\}$

(b) $\{a^m b^n c^p : m \neq n \text{ or } n \neq p \text{ or } m \neq p\}$

(c) $\{a^m b^n c^p : m = n$ and $n = p$ and $m = p\}$

(d) $\{w \in \{a, b, c\}^* : w$ does not contain equal numbers of occurrences of a, b, and $c\}$

(e) $\{w \in \{a, b\}^* : w = w_1 w_2 \ldots w_m$ for some $m \geq 2$ and $w_1, \ldots, w_m$ such that $|w_1| = |w_2| = \cdots = |w_m| \geq 2\}$

3.5.15. Suppose that L is context-free and R is regular. Is $L - R$ necessarily context-free? What about $R - L$? Justify your answers.

3.6 | ALGORITHMS FOR CONTEXT-FREE GRAMMARS

In this section we consider the computational problems related to context-free languages, we develop algorithms for these problems, and we analyze their complexity. All in all, we establish the following results.

Theorem 3.6.1: *(a) There is a polynomial algorithm which, given a context-free grammar, constructs an equivalent pushdown automaton.*

(b) There is a polynomial algorithm which, given a pushdown automaton, constructs an equivalent context-free grammar.

(c) There is a polynomial algorithm which, given a context-free grammar G and a string x, decides whether $x \in L(G)$.

It is instructive to compare Theorem 3.6.1 with the corresponding statement summarizing the algorithmic aspects of finite automata (Theorem 2.6.1). To be sure, there are certain similarities: in both cases there are algorithms which transform acceptors to generators and vice versa —then finite automata to regular expressions and back, now pushdown automata to context-free grammars and back. But the differences are perhaps more striking. First, in Theorem 2.6.1 there was no need for an analog of part (c) above, since regular languages are represented in terms of an efficient algorithm for deciding precisely the membership question in (c): a deterministic finite automaton. In contrast, for context-free languages we have so far introduced only non-algorithmic, nondeterministic acceptors —pushdown automata. In order to establish part (c), we show in the next subsection that for any context-free language we can construct a deterministic acceptor; the construction is rather indirect and sophisticated, and the resulting algorithm, although polynomial, is no longer linear in the length of the input.

A second major difference between Theorem 2.6.1 and Theorem 3.6.1 is that in the present case we do not mention any algorithms for testing whether two given context-free grammars (or two pushdown automata) are equivalent; neither do we claim that there are algorithms for minimizing the number of states in a pushdown automaton. We shall see in Chapter 5 that such questions about context-free grammars and pushdown automata are not amenable to solution *by any algorithm* —however inefficient!

The Dynamic Programming Algorithm

We turn now to proving part (c) of the Theorem (parts (a) and (b) are straightforward consequences of the constructions in the proofs of the Lemmata 3.4.1 and 3.4.2). Our algorithm for deciding context-free languages is based on a useful way of "standardizing" context-free grammars.

Definition 3.6.1: A context-free grammar $G = (V, \Sigma, R, S)$ is said to be in **Chomsky normal form** if $R \subseteq (V - \Sigma) \times V^2$.

In other words, the right-hand side of a rule in a context-free grammar in Chomsky normal form must have length two. Notice that no grammar in Chomsky normal form would be able to produce strings of length less than two, such as a, b, or e; therefore, context-free languages containing such strings cannot be generated by grammars in Chomsky normal form. However, the next result states that this is the only loss of generality that comes with Chomsky normal form:

Theorem 3.6.2: *For any context-free grammar G there is a context-free grammar G' in Chomsky normal form such that $L(G') = L(G) - (\Sigma \cup \{e\})$. Furthermore, the construction of G' can be carried out in time polynomial in the size of G.*

In other words, G' generates exactly the strings that G does, with the possible exception of strings of length less than two —since G' is in Chomsky normal form, we know that it cannot generate such strings.

Proof: We shall show how to transform any given context-free grammar $G = (V, \Sigma, R, S)$ into a context-free grammar in Chomsky normal form. There are three ways in which the right-hand side of a rule $A \to x$ may violate the constraints of Chomsky normal form: *long rules* (those whose right-hand side has length three or more), *e-rules* (of the form $A \Rightarrow e$), and *short rules* (of the form $A \Rightarrow a$ or $A \Rightarrow B$). We shall show how to remove these violations one by one.

We first deal with the long rules of G. Let $A \to B_1 B_2 \ldots B_n \in R$, where $B_1, \ldots, B_n \in V$ and $n \geq 3$. We replace this rule with $n - 1$ new rules, namely:

$$A \to B_1 A_1,$$
$$A_1 \to B_2 A_2,$$
$$\vdots$$
$$A_{n-2} \to B_{n-1} B_n,$$

where $A_1, \ldots, A_{n-2}$ are new nonterminals, not used anywhere else in the grammar. Since the rule $A \to B_1 B_2 \ldots B_n$ can be simulated by the newly inserted rules, and this is the only way in which the newly added rules can be used, it should be clear that the resulting context-free grammar is equivalent to the original one. We repeat this for each long rule of the grammar. The resulting grammar is equivalent to the original one, and has rules with right-hand sides of length two or less.

Example 3.6.1: Let us take the grammar generating the set of balanced parentheses, with rules $S \to SS, S \to (S), S \to e$. There is only one long rule, $S \to (S)$. It is replaced by the two rules $S \to (S_1$ and $S_1 \to S).\Diamond$

We must next take on the e-rules. To this end, we first determine *the set of erasable nonterminals*

$$\mathcal{E} = \{A \in V - \Sigma : A \Rightarrow^* e\},$$

that is, the set of all nonterminals that may derive the empty string. This is done by a simple closure calculation:

$\mathcal{E} := \emptyset$
while there is a rule $A \Rightarrow \alpha$ with $\alpha \in \mathcal{E}^*$ and
    $A \notin \mathcal{E}$ do add A to $\mathcal{E}$.

Once we have the set $\mathcal{E}$, we delete from G all e-rules, and repeat the following: For each rule of the form $A \to BC$ or $A \to CB$ with $B \in \mathcal{E}$ and $C \in V$, we add to the grammar the rule $A \to C$. Any derivation in the original grammar can be simulated in the new, and vice versa —with one exception: e cannot be derived in the language any longer, since we may have omitted the rule $S \to e$ during this step. Fortunately, the statement of the Theorem allows for this exclusion.

Example 3.6.1 (continued): Let us continue from the grammar with rules

$$S \to SS, \quad S \to (S_1, \quad S_1 \to S), \quad S \to e.$$

We start by computing the set $\mathcal{E}$ of vanishing nonterminals: Initially $\mathcal{E} = \emptyset$; then $\mathcal{E} = \{S\}$, because of the rule $S \to e$; and this is the final value of $\mathcal{E}$. We omit from the grammar the e-rules (of which there is only one, $S \to e$), and add variants of all rules with an occurrence of S, with that occurrence omitted. The new set of rules is

$$S \to SS, \quad S \to (S_1, \quad S_1 \to S), \quad S \to S, \quad S_1 \to).$$

The rule $S \rightarrow S$ was added because of the rule $S \rightarrow SS$ with $S \in \mathcal{E}$; it is of course useless and can be omitted. The rule $S_1 \rightarrow)$ was added because of the rule $S_1 \rightarrow S)$ with $S \in \mathcal{E}$.

For example, the derivation in the original grammar

$$S \Rightarrow SS \Rightarrow S(S) \Rightarrow S() \Rightarrow ()$$

can now simulated by

$$S \Rightarrow (S_1$$

—omitting the $S \Rightarrow SS$ part, since the first S would be eventually erased— and finally

$$(S_1 \Rightarrow ()$$

—using the $S_1 \Rightarrow)$ rule to anticipate the erasing of the S in the rule $S_1 \Rightarrow S)$. $\Diamond$

Our grammar now has only rules whose right-hand sides have length one and two. We must next get rid of the short rules, those with right-hand sides with length one. We accomplish this as follows: For each $A \in V$ we compute, again by a simple closure algorithm, *the set $\mathcal{D}(A)$ of symbols that can be derived from A in the grammar, $\mathcal{D}(A) = \{B \in V : A \Rightarrow^* B\}$,* as follows:

$\mathcal{D}(A) := \{A\}$
while there is a rule $B \Rightarrow C$ with $B \in \mathcal{D}(A)$ and
   $C \notin \mathcal{D}(A)$ do add C to $\mathcal{D}(A)$.

Notice that for all symbols A, $A \in \mathcal{D}(A)$; and if a is a terminal, then $\mathcal{D}(a) = \{a\}$.

In our third and final step of the transformation of our grammar to one in Chomsky normal form, we omit all short rules from the grammar, and we replace each rule of the form $A \rightarrow BC$ with all possible rules of the form $A \rightarrow B'C'$ where $B' \in \mathcal{D}(B)$ and $C' \in \mathcal{D}(C)$. Such a rule simulates the effect of the original rule $A \rightarrow BC$, with the sequence of short rules that produce B' from B and C' from C. Finally, we add the rules $S \rightarrow BC$ for each rule $A \rightarrow BC$ such that $A \in \mathcal{D}(S) - \{S\}$.

Again, the resulting grammar is equivalent to the one before the omission of the short rules, since the effect of a short rule is simulated by "anticipating" its use when the left-hand side first appears in the derivation (if the left-hand side is S, and thus it starts the derivation, the rules $A \rightarrow BC$ added in the last part of the construction suffice to guarantee equivalence). There is again only one exception: we may have removed a rule $S \rightarrow a$, thus omitting the string a from the language generated by G. Once again, fortunately this omission is allowed by the statement of the theorem.

Example 3.6.1 (continued): In our modified grammar with rules

$$S \rightarrow SS, \quad S \rightarrow (S_1, \quad S_1 \rightarrow S), \quad S_1 \rightarrow)$$

we have $\mathcal{D}(S_1) = \{S_1,)\}$, and $\mathcal{D}(A) = \{A\}$ for all $A \in V - \{S_1\}$. We omit all length-one rules, of which there is only one, $S_1 \rightarrow)$. The only nonterminal with a nontrivial set $\mathcal{D}$, S_1, appears on the right-hand side of only the second rule. This rule is therefore replaced by the two rules $S \rightarrow (S_1, S \rightarrow ()$, corresponding to the two elements of $\mathcal{D}(S_1)$. The final grammar in Chomsky normal form is

$$S \rightarrow SS, \quad S \rightarrow (S_1, \quad S_1 \rightarrow S), \quad S \rightarrow ().$$

$\Diamond$

After the three steps, the grammar is in Chomsky normal form, and, except for the possible omission of strings of length less than two, it generates the same language as the original one.

In order to complete the proof of the theorem, we must establish that the whole construction can be carried out in time polynomial *in the size of the original grammar G*. By "size of G" we mean the length of a string that suffices to fully describe G —that is to say, the sum of the lengths of the rules of G. Let n be this quantity. The first part of the transformation (getting rid of long rules) takes time $\mathcal{O}(n)$ and creates a grammar of size again $\mathcal{O}(n)$. The second part, getting rid of e-rules, takes $\mathcal{O}(n^2)$ time for the closure computation ($\mathcal{O}(n)$ iterations, each doable in $\mathcal{O}(n)$ time), plus $\mathcal{O}(n)$ for adding the new rules. Finally, the third part (taking care of short rules) can also be carried out in polynomial time ($\mathcal{O}(n)$ closure computations, each taking time $\mathcal{O}(n^2)$). This completes the proof of the theorem. ∎

The advantage of Chomsky normal form is that it enables a simple polynomial algorithm for deciding whether a string can be generated by the grammar. Suppose that we are given a context-free grammar $G = (V, \Sigma, R, S)$ in Chomsky normal form, and we are asked whether the string $x = x_1 \cdots x_n$, with $n \geq 2$, is in $L(G)$. The algorithm is shown below. It decides whether $x \in L(G)$ *by analyzing all substrings of x*. For each i and s such that $1 \leq i \leq i+s \leq n$, define $N[i, i+s]$ to be the set of all symbols in V that can derive in G the string $x_i \cdots x_{i+s}$. The algorithm computes these sets. It proceeds computing $N[i, i+s]$ from short strings (s small) to longer and longer strings. This general philosophy of solving a problem by starting from minuscule subproblems and building up solutions to larger and larger subproblems until the whole problem is solved is known as **dynamic programming**.

for $i := 1$ to n do $N[i,i] := \{x_i\}$; all other $N[i,j]$ are initially empty
for $s := 1$ to $n - 1$ do
    for $i := 1$ to $n - s$ do
        for $k := i$ to $i + s - 1$ do
        if there is a rule $A \to BC \in R$ with $B \in N[i,k]$ and $C \in N[k + 1, i + s]$
        then add A to $N[i, i + s]$.
Accept x if $S \in N[1, n]$.

In order to establish that the algorithm above correctly determines whether $x \in L(G)$, we shall prove the following claim.

Claim: *For each natural number s with $0 \leq s \leq n$, after the sth iteration of the algorithm, for all $i = 1, \ldots, n - s$,*

$$N[i, i + s] = \{A \in V : A \Rightarrow^* x_i \cdots x_{i+s}\}.$$

Proof of the Claim: The proof of this claim is by induction on s.

Basis Step. When $s = 0$ —where by "the zeroth iteration of the algorithm" we understand the first (initialization) line— the statement is true: since G is in Chomsky normal form, the only symbol that can generate the terminal x_i is x_i itself.

Induction Step: Suppose that the claim is true for all integers less than $s > 0$. Consider a derivation of the substring $x_i \cdots x_{i+s}$, say from a nonterminal A. Since G is in Chomsky normal form, the derivation starts with a rule of the form $A \to BC$, that is,

$$A \Rightarrow BC \Rightarrow^* x_1 \cdots x_{i+s},$$

where $B, C \in V$. Therefore, for some k with $i < k \leq i + s$,

$$B \Rightarrow^* x_1 \cdots x_k, \text{ and } C \Rightarrow^* x_{k+1} \cdots x_{i+s}.$$

We conclude that $A \in \{A \in V : A \Rightarrow^* x_i \cdots x_{i+s}\}$ if and only if there is an integer k, $i \leq k < i + s$, and two symbols $B \in \{A \in V : A \Rightarrow^* x_i \cdots x_k\}$ and $C \in \{A \in V : A \Rightarrow^* x_{k+1} \cdots x_{i+s}\}$ such that $A \to BC \in R$. We can rewrite the string $x_i \cdots x_k$ as $x_i \cdots x_{i+s'}$, where $s' = k - i$, and the string $x_{k+1} \cdots x_{i+s}$ as $x_{k+1} \cdots x_{k+1+s''}$, where $s'' = i + s - k - 1$. Notice that, since $i \leq k < i + s$, we must have $s', s'' < s$. *Hence, the induction hypothesis applies!*

By the induction hypothesis, $\{A \in V : A \Rightarrow^* x_i \cdots x_k\} = N[i, k]$, and $\{A \in V : A \Rightarrow^* x_{k+1} \cdots x_{i+s}\} = N[k + 1, i + s]$. We conclude that $A \in \{A \in V : A \Rightarrow^* x_i \cdots x_{i+s}\}$ if and only if there is an integer k, $i \leq k < i + s$, and two symbols $B \in N[i, k]$ and $C \in N[k + 1, i + s]$ such that $A \to BC \in R$.

But these are precisely the circumstances under which our algorithm adds A to $N[i, i + s]$. Therefore the claim holds for s as well, and this concludes the proof of the induction hypothesis —and of the claim. ∎

It follows immediately from the claim that the algorithm above correctly decides whether $x \in L(G)$: At the end, the set $N[1, n]$ will contain all symbols that derive the string $x_1 \cdots x_n = x$. Therefore, $x \in L(G)$ if and only if $S \in N[1, n]$.

To analyze the time performance of the algorithm, notice that it consists of three nested loops, each with a range bounded by $|x| = n$. At the heart of the loop we must examine for each rule of the form $A \rightarrow BC$ whether $B \in N[i, j]$ and $C \in N[j + 1, i + s]$; this can be carried out in time proportional to the size of the grammar G —the length of its rules. We conclude that the total number of operations is $\mathcal{O}(|x|^3 |G|)$ —a polynomial in *both* the length of x and the size of G. For any *fixed* grammar G (that is, when we consider $|G|$ to be a constant), the algorithm runs in time $O(n^3)$. ∎

Example 3.6.1 (continued): Let us apply the dynamic programming algorithm to the grammar for the balanced parentheses, as was rendered in Chomsky normal form with rules

$$S \Rightarrow SS, S \Rightarrow (S_1, S_1 \rightarrow S), S \Rightarrow ().$$

Suppose we wish to tell whether the string $(()(()))$ can be generated by G. We display in Figure 3.10 the values of $N[i, i + s]$ for $1 \le i \le j \le n = 8$, resulting from the iterations of the algorithm. The computation proceeds along parallel diagonals of the table. The main diagonal, corresponding to $s = 0$, contains the string being parsed. To fill a box, say $[2, 7]$, we look at all pairs of boxes of the form $N[2, k]$ and $N[k + 1, 7]$ with $2 \le k < 7$. All these boxes lie either on the left of or above the box being filled. For $k = 3$, we notice that $S \in N[2, 3]$, $S \in N[4, 7]$, and $S \rightarrow SS$ is a rule; thus we must add the left-hand side S to the box $N[2, 7]$. And so on. The lower-right corner is $N[1, n]$, and it does contain S; therefore the string is indeed in $L(G)$. In fact, by inspecting this table it is easy to recover an actual derivation of the string $(()(()))$ in G. The dynamic programming algorithm can be easily modified to produce such a derivation; see Problem 3.6.2.◊

Part (c) of Theorem 3.6.1 now follows by combining Theorems 3.6.2 and the claim above: Given a context-free grammar G and a string x, we determine whether $x \in L(G)$ as follows: First, we transform G into an equivalent context-free grammar G' in Chomsky normal form, according to the construction in the proof of Theorem 3.6.2, in polynomial time. In the special case in which $|x| \le 1$, we can already decide whether $x \in L(G)$: It is if and only if during

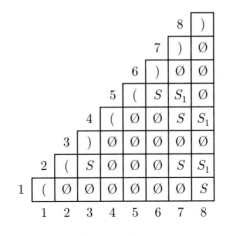

Figure 3-10

the transformation we had to delete a rule $S \to x$. Otherwise, we run the dynamic programming algorithm described above for the grammar G' and the string x. The total number of operations used by the algorithm is bounded by a polynomial in the size of the original grammar G and the length of the string x. ∎

Problems for Section 3.6

3.6.1. Convert the context-free grammar G given in Example 3.1.3 generating arithmetic expressions into an equivalent context-free grammar in Chomsky normal form. Apply the dynamic programming algorithm for deciding whether the string $x = (\mathsf{id} + \mathsf{id} + x3) * (\mathsf{id})$ is in $L(G)$.

3.6.2. How would you modify the dynamic programming algorithm in such a way that, when the input x is indeed in the language generated by G, then the algorithm produces an actual derivation of x in G?

3.6.3. (a) Let $G = (V, \Sigma, R, S)$ be a context-free language. Call a nonterminal $A \in V - \Sigma$ *productive* if $A \Rightarrow^*_G x$ for some $x \in \Sigma^*$. Give a polynomial algorithm for finding all productive nonterminals of G. (*Hint:* It is a closure algorithm.)
(b) Give a polynomial algorithm which, given a context-free grammar G, decides whether $L(G) = \emptyset$.

3.6.4. Describe an algorithm which, given a context-free grammar G, decides whether $L(G)$ is infinite. (*Hint:* One approach uses the Pumping Theorem.) What is the complexity of your algorithm? Can you find a polynomial-time algorithm?

3.7 | DETERMINISM AND PARSING

Context-free grammars are used extensively in modeling the syntax of programming languages, as was suggested by Example 3.1.3. A compiler for such a programming language must then embody a **parser**, that is, an algorithm to determine whether a given string is in the language generated by a given context-free grammar, and, if so, to construct the parse tree of the string. (The compiler would then go on to translate this parse tree into a program in a more basic language, such as assembly language.) The general context-free parser we have developed in the previous section, the dynamic programming algorithm, although perfectly polynomial, is far too slow for handling programs with tens of thousands of instructions (recall its *cubic* dependence on the length of the string). Many approaches to the parsing problem have been developed by compiler designers over the past four decades. Interestingly, the most successful ones among them are rooted in the idea of a pushdown automaton. After all, the equivalence of pushdown automata and context-free grammars, which was proved in Section 3.4, should be put to work. However, a pushdown automaton is not of immediate practical use in parsing, because it is a *nondeterministic* device. The question then arises, can we always make pushdown automata operate deterministically (as we were able to do in the case of finite automata)?

Our first objective in this section is to study the question of deterministic pushdown automata. We shall see that there are some context-free languages that cannot be accepted by deterministic pushdown automata. This is rather disappointing; it suggests that the conversion of grammars to automata in Section 3.4 cannot be the basis for any practical method. Nevertheless, all is not lost. It turns out that for most programming languages one can construct deterministic pushdown automata that accept all syntactically correct programs. Later in this section we shall give some *heuristic rules* —rules of thumb— that are useful for constructing deterministic pushdown automata from suitable context-free grammars. These rules will not invariably produce a useful pushdown automaton from any context-free grammar; we have already said that that would be impossible. But they are typical of the methods actually used in the construction of compilers for programming languages.

Deterministic Context-free Languages

A pushdown automaton M is **deterministic** if for each configuration there is at most one configuration that can succeed it in a computation by M. This condition can be rephrased in an equivalent way. Call two strings **consistent** if the first is a prefix of the second, or vice versa. Call two transitions $((p, a, \beta), (q, \gamma))$ and $((p, a', \beta'), (q', \gamma'))$ **compatible** if a and a' are consistent, and β and β' are also consistent —in other words, if there is a situation in which both transitions are applicable. Then M is deterministic if it has no two distinct compatible transitions.

For example, the machine we constructed in Example 3.3.1 to accept the language $\{wcw^R : w \in \{a, b\}^*\}$ is deterministic: For each choice of state and input symbol, there is only one possible transition. On the other hand, the machine we constructed in Example 3.3.2 to accept $\{ww^R : w \in \{a, b\}^*\}$ is not deterministic: Transition 3 is compatible with both Transitions 1 and 2; notice that these are the transitions that "guess" the middle of the string —an action which is intuitively nondeterministic.

Deterministic context-free languages are essentially those that are accepted by deterministic pushdown automata. However, for reasons that will become clear very soon, we have to modify the acceptance convention slightly. A language is said to be deterministic context-free if it is recognized by a deterministic pushdown automaton that also has the extra capability of *sensing the end of the input string*. Formally, we call a language $L \subseteq \Sigma^*$ **deterministic context-free** if $L\$ = L(M)$ for some deterministic pushdown automaton M. Here $\$$ is a new symbol, not in Σ, which is appended to each input string for the purpose of marking its end.

Every deterministic context-free language, as just defined, is a context-free language. To see this, suppose a deterministic pushdown automaton M accepts $L\$$. Then a (nondeterministic) pushdown automaton M' that accepts L can be constructed. At any point, M' may "imagine" a $\$$ in the input and jump to a new set of states from which it reads no further input.

If, on the other hand, we had not adopted this special acceptance convention, then many context-free languages that are deterministic intuitively would not be deterministic by our definition. One example is $L = a^* \cup \{a^n b^n : n \geq 1\}$. A deterministic pushdown automaton cannot both remember how many a's it has seen, in order to check the string of b's that may follow, and at the same time be ready to accept with empty stack in case no b's follow. However, one can easily design a deterministic pushdown automaton accepting $L\$$: If a $\$$ is met while the machine is still accumulating a's, then the input was a string in a^*. If this happens, the stack is emptied and the input accepted.

The natural question at this point is whether every context-free language is deterministic —just as every regular language is accepted by a deterministic finite automaton. It would be surprising if this were so. Consider, for example, the context-free language

$$L = \{a^n b^m c^p : m, n, p \geq 0, \text{ and } m \neq n \text{ or } m \neq p\}.$$

It would seem that a pushdown automaton could accept this language only by guessing which two blocks of symbols to compare: the a's with the b's, or the b's with the c's. Without so using nondeterminism, it would seem, the machine could not compare the b's with the a's, while at the same time preparing to compare the b's with the c's. However, to prove that L is not deterministic requires a more indirect argument: *The complement of L is not context-free.*

Theorem 3.7.1: *The class of deterministic context-free languages is closed under complement.*

Proof: Let $L \subseteq \Sigma^*$ be a language such that $L\$$ is accepted by the deterministic pushdown automaton $M = (K, \Sigma, \Gamma, \Delta, s, F)$. It will be convenient to assume, as in the proof of Lemma 3.4.2, that M is *simple*, that is, no transition of M pops more than one symbol from the stack, while an initial transition places a stack bottom symbol Z on the stack that is removed just before the end of the computation; it is easy to see that the construction employed to this end in the proof of Lemma 3.4.2 does not affect the deterministic nature of M.

Since M is deterministic, it would appear that all that is required in order to obtain a device that accepts $(\Sigma^* - L)\$$ is to reverse accepting and non-accepting states —as we have done with deterministic finite automata in the proof of Theorem 2.3.1(d), and will do again in the next chapter with more complex deterministic devices. In the present situation, however, this simple reversal will not work, because a deterministic pushdown automaton may reject an input not only by reading it and finally reaching a non-accepting state, but also by *never finishing reading its input*. This intriguing possibility may arise in two ways: First, M may enter a configuration C at which none of the transitions in Δ is applicable. Second, and perhaps more intriguingly, M may enter a configuration from which M executes a never-ending sequence of *e-moves* (transitions of the form $(q, e, \alpha)(p, \beta)$).

Let us call a configuration $C = (q, w, \alpha)$ of M a **dead end** if the following is true: If $C \vdash_M^* C'$ for some other configuration $C' = (q', w', \alpha')$, then $w' = w$ and $|\alpha'| \geq |\alpha|$. That is, a configuration is said to be a dead end if no progress can be made starting from it towards either reading more input, or reducing the height of the stack. Obviously, if M is at a dead-end configuration, then it will indeed fail to read its input to the end. Conversely, it is not hard to see that, if M has no dead-end configurations, then it will definitely read all its input. This is because, in the absence of dead-end configurations, at all times there is a time in the future in which either the next input symbol will be read, or the height of the stack will be decreased —and the second option can only be taken finitely many times, since the stack length cannot be decreased infinitely many times.

We shall show how to transform any simple deterministic pushdown automaton M into an equivalent deterministic pushdown automaton without dead-end configurations. The point is that, since M is assumed to be simple, whether a configuration is or is not a dead end *only depends on the current state, the next input symbol, and the top stack symbol*. In particular, let $q \in K$ be a state, $a \in \Sigma$

an input symbol, and $A \in \Gamma$ a stack symbol. We say that the triple (q, a, A) is a **dead end** if there is no state p and stack symbol string α such that the *configuration* (q, a, A) yields either (p, e, α) or (p, a, e). That is, a triple (q, a, A) is dead end if it is a dead end when considered as a configuration. Let $D \subseteq K \times \Sigma \times \Gamma$ denote the set of all dead-end triples. Notice that we are not claiming that we can effectively tell by examining a triple whether it is in D or not (although it can be done); all we are saying is that the set D is a well-defined, finite set of triples.

Our modification of M is the following: For each triple $(q, a, A) \in D$ we remove from Δ all transitions compatible with (q, a, A), and we add to Δ the transition $((q, a, A), (r, e))$, where r is a new, non-accepting state. Finally, we add to Δ these transitions: $((r, a, e), (r, e))$ for all $a \in \Sigma$, $((r, \$, e), (r', e))$, and $(r', e, A), (r', e))$ for each $A \in \Gamma \cup \{Z\}$, where r' is another new, non-accepting state. These transitions enable M', when in state r, to read the whole input (without consulting the stack), and, upon reading a \$, to empty the stack and reject. Call the resulting pushdown automaton M'.

It is easy to check that M' is deterministic, and accepts the same language as M (M' simply rejects explicitly whenever M would have rejected implicitly by failing to read the rest of the input). Furthermore, M' was constructed so that it has no dead end configurations —and hence, it will always end up reading its whole input. *Now* reversing the rôle of accepting and non-accepting states of M' produces a deterministic pushdown automaton that accepts $(\Sigma^* - L)\$$, and the proof is complete. ∎

Theorem 3.71 indeed establishes that the context-free language $L = \{a^n b^m c^p : m \neq n$ or $m \neq p\}$ above is not deterministic: If L were deterministic, then its complement, $\overline{L}$ would also be deterministic context-free —and therefore certainly context-free. Hence, the intersection of $\overline{L}$ with the regular language $a^* b^* c^*$ would be context-free, by Theorem 3.5.2. But it is easy to see that $\overline{L} \cap a^* b^* c^*$ is precisely the language $\{a^n b^n c^n : n \geq 0\}$, which we know is not context-free. We conclude that the context-free language L is not deterministic context-free:

Corollary: *The class of deterministic context free languages is properly contained in the class of context-free languages*

In other words, *nondeterminism is more powerful than determinism in the context of pushdown automata.* In contrast, we saw in the last chapter that nondeterminism adds nothing to the power of finite automata —unless the number of states is taken into account, in which case it is *exponentially* more powerful. This intriguing issue of the power of nondeterminism in various computational contexts is perhaps the single most important thread that runs through this book.

Top-Down Parsing

Having established that not every context-free language can be accepted by a deterministic pushdown automaton, let us now consider some of those that can. Our overall goal for the remainder of this chapter is to study cases in which context-free grammars can be converted into deterministic pushdown automata that can actually be used for "industrial grade" language recognition. However, our style here is rather different from that of the rest of this book; there are fewer proofs, and we do not attempt to tie up all the loose ends of the ideas we introduce. We present some guidelines —what we call "heuristic rules"— that will not be useful in all cases, and we do not even attempt to specify exactly when they will be useful. That is, we aim to introduce some suggestive applications of the theory developed earlier in this chapter, but this venture should not be taken as anything more than an introduction.

Let us begin with an example. The language $L = \{a^n b^n\}$ is generated by the context-free grammar $G = (\{a, b, S\}, \{a, b\}, R, S)$, where R contains the two rules $S \rightarrow aSb$ and $S \rightarrow e$. We know how to construct a pushdown automaton that accepts L: just carry out the construction of Lemma 3.4.1 for the grammar G. The result is

$$M_1 = (\{p, q\}, \{a, b\}, \{a, b, S\}\Delta_1, p, \{q\}),$$

where
$$\Delta_1 = ((p, e, e), (q, S)), ((q, e, S), (q, aSb))((q, e, S), (q, e)),$$
$$((q, a, a), (q, e)), ((q, b, b), (q, e))\}.$$

Since M_1 has two different transitions with identical first components —the ones corresponding to the two rules of G that have identical left-hand sides— it is not deterministic.

Nevertheless, L is a deterministic context-free language, and M_1 can be modified to become a deterministic pushdown automaton M_2 that accepts $L\$$. Intuitively, all the information that M_1 needs at each point in order to decide which of the two transitions to follow is the next input symbol. If that symbol is an a, then M_1 should replace S by aSb on its stack if hope of an accepting computation is to be retained. On the other hand, if the next input symbol is a b, then the machine must pop S. M_2 achieves this required anticipation or lookahead by consuming an input symbol ahead of time and incorporating that information into its state. Formally,

$$M_1 = (\{p, q, q_a, q_b, q_\$\}, \{a, b\}, \{a, b, S\}\Delta_2, p, \{q_\$\}),$$

where δ_2 contains the following transitions.

(1) $((p, e, e), (q, S))$
(2) $((q, a, e), (q_a, e))$
(3) $((q_a, e, a), (q, e))$
(4) $((q, b, e), (q_b, , e))$
(5) $((q_b, e, b), (q, e))$
(6) $((q, \$, e), (q_\$, e))$
(7) $((q_a, e, S), (q_a, aSb))$
(8) $((q_b, e, S), (q_b, e))$

From state q, M_2 reads one input symbol and, without changing the stack, enters one of the three new states q_a, q_b, or $q_\$$. It then uses that information to differentiate between the two compatible transitions $((q, e, S), (q, aSb))$ and $((q, e, S), (q, e))$: The first transition is retained only from state q_a and the second only from state q_b. So M_2 is deterministic. It accepts the input $ab\$$ as follows.

Step	State	Unread Input	Stack	Transition Used	Rule of G
0	p	$ab\$$	e	–	
1	q	$ab\$$	S	1	
2	q_a	$b\$$	S	2	
3	q_a	$b\$$	aSb	7	$S \to aSb$
4	q	$b\$$	Sb	3	
5	q_b	$\$$	Sb	4	
6	q_b	$\$$	b	8	$S \to e$
7	q	$\$$	e	5	
8	$q_\$$	e	e	6	

So M_2 can serve as a deterministic device for recognizing strings of the form $a^n b^n$. Moreover, by remembering which transitions of M_2 were derived from which rules of the grammar (this is the last column of the table above), we can use a trace of the operation of M_2 in order to reconstruct a leftmost derivation of the input string. Specifically, the steps in the computation where a nonterminal is replaced on top of the stack (Steps 3 and 6 in the example) correspond to the construction of a parse tree from the root towards the leaves (see Figure 3-11(a)).

Devices such as M_2, which correctly decide whether a string belongs in a context-free language, and, in the case of a positive answer, produce the corresponding parse tree are called **parsers**. In particular, M_2 is a **top-down parser** because tracing its operation at the steps where nonterminals are replaced on the stack reconstructs a parse tree in a *top-down, left-to-right* fashion (see Figure 3-11(b) for a suggestive way of representing how progress is made in a top-down parser). We shall see a more substantial example shortly.

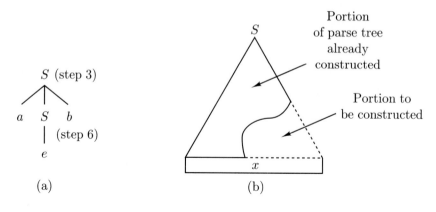

Figure 3-11

Naturally, not all context-free languages have deterministic acceptors that can be derived from the standard nondeterministic one via the lookahead idea. For example, we saw in the previous subsection that some context-free languages are not deterministic to begin with. Even for certain deterministic context-free languages, lookahead of just one symbol may not be sufficient to resolve all uncertainties. Some languages, however, are not directly amenable to parsing by lookahead for reasons that are superficial and can be removed by slightly modifying the grammar. We shall focus on these next.

Recall the grammar G that generates arithmetic expressions with operations $+$ and $*$ (Example 3.1.3). In fact, let us enrich this grammar by another rule,

$$F \to \mathsf{id}(E), \tag{R7}$$

designed to allow *function calls* —such as $sqrt(x * x + 1)$ and $f(z)$— to appear in our arithmetic expressions.

Let us try to construct a top-down parser for this grammar. Our construction of Section 3.4 would give the pushdown automaton

$$M_3 = (\{p, q\}, \Sigma, \Gamma, \Delta, p, \{f\}),$$

with

$$\Sigma = \{(,), +, *, \mathsf{id}\},$$
$$\Gamma = \Sigma \cup \{E, T, F\},$$

and Δ as given below.

(0) $((p, e, e), (q, E))$
(1) $((q, e, E), (q, E + T))$
(2) $((q, e, E), (q, T))$

(3) $((q, e, T), (q, T * F))$
(4) $((q, e, T), (q, F))$
(5) $((q, e, F), (q, (E)))$
(6) $((q, e, F), (q, \mathsf{id}))$
(7) $((q, e, F), (q, \mathsf{id}(E)))$

Finally, $((q, a, a), (q, e)) \in \Delta$ for all $a \in \Sigma$. The nondeterminism of M_3 is manifested by the sets of transitions 1–2, 3–4, and 5–6–7 that have identical first components. *What is worse, these decisions cannot be made based on the next input symbol.* Lets us examine more closely why this is so.

Transitions 6 and 7. Suppose that the configuration of M_3 is (q, id, F). At this point M_3 could act according to any one of transitions 5, 6, or 7. By looking at the next input symbol —id— M_3 could exclude transition 5, since this transition requires that the next symbol be (. Still, M_3 would not be able to decide between transitions 6 and 7, since they both produce a top of the stack that can be matched to the next input symbol —id. The problem arises because the rules $F \to \mathsf{id}$ and $F \to \mathsf{id}(E)$ of G have not only identical left-hand sides, but also the same first symbol on their right-hand sides.

There is a very simple way around this problem: Just replace the rules $F \to \mathsf{id}$ and $F \to \mathsf{id}(E)$ in G by the rules $F \to \mathsf{id}A$, $A \to e$, and $A \to (E)$, where A is a new nonterminal (A for *argument*). This has the effect of "procrastinating" on the decision between the rules $F \to \mathsf{id}$ and $F \to \mathsf{id}(E)$ until all needed information is available. A modified pushdown automaton M_3' now results from this modified grammar, in which transitions 6 and 7 are replaced by the following.

(6') $((q, e, F), (q, \mathsf{id}A))$
(7') $((q, e, A), (q, e))$
(8') $((q, e, A), (q, (E)))$

Now looking one symbol ahead is enough to decide the correct action. For example, configuration $(q, \mathsf{id}(\mathsf{id}), F)$ would yield $(q, \mathsf{id}(\mathsf{id}), \mathsf{id}A)$, $(q, (\mathsf{id}), A)$, $(q, (\mathsf{id}), (E))$, and so on.

This technique of avoiding nondeterminism is known as **left factoring**. It can be summarized as follows.

Heuristic Rule 1: *Whenever $A \to \alpha\beta_1, A \to \alpha\beta_2, \ldots, A \to \alpha\beta_m$ are rules with $\alpha \neq e$ and $n \geq 2$, then replace them by the rules $A \to \alpha A'$ and $A' \to \beta_i$ for $i = 1, \ldots, n$, where A' is a new nonterminal.*

It is easy to see that applying Heuristic Rule 1 does not change the language generated by the grammar.

We now move to examining the second kind of anomaly that prevents us from transforming M_3 into a deterministic parser.

Transitions 1 and 2. These transitions present us with a more serious problem. If the automaton sees id as the next input symbol and the contents of the stack are just E, it could take a number of actions. It could perform transition 2, replacing E by T (this would be justified in case the input is, say, id). Or it could replace E by $E + T$ (transition 1) and then the top E by T (this should be done if the input is id + id). Or it could perform transition 2 twice and transition 1 once (input id+id+id), and so on. It seems that there is no bound whatsoever on how far ahead the automaton must peek in order to decide on the right action. The culprit here is the rule $E \rightarrow E + T$, in which the nonterminal on the left-hand side is repeated as the first symbol of the right-hand side. This phenomenon is called **left recursion**, and can be removed by some further surgery on the grammar.

To remove left recursion from the rule $E \rightarrow E + T$, we simply replace it by the rules $E \rightarrow T E'$, $E' \rightarrow +T E'$, and $E' \rightarrow e$, where E' is a new nonterminal. It can be shown that such transformations do not change the language produced by the grammar. The same method must also be applied to the other left recursive rule of G, namely $T \rightarrow T * F$. We thus arrive at the grammar $G' = (V', \Sigma, R', E)$ where $V' = \Sigma \cup \{E, E', T, T', F, A\}$, and the rules are as follows.

(1) $E \rightarrow T E'$
(2) $E' \rightarrow +T E'$
(3) $E' \rightarrow e$
(4) $T \rightarrow F T'$
(5) $T' \rightarrow *F T'$
(6) $T' \rightarrow e$
(7) $F \rightarrow (E)$
(8) $F \rightarrow \text{id}A$
(9) $A \rightarrow e$
(10) $A \rightarrow (E)$

The above technique for removing left recursion from a context-free grammar can be expressed as follows.[†]

Heuristic Rule 2: *Let $A \rightarrow A\alpha_1, \ldots, A \rightarrow A\alpha_n$ and $A \rightarrow \beta_1, \ldots, A \rightarrow \beta_m$ be all rules with A on the left-hand side, where the β_i's do not start with an A and $m > 0$ (that is, there is at least one left-recursive rule). Then replace these rules by $A \rightarrow \beta_1 A', \ldots, A \rightarrow \beta_m A'$ and $A' \rightarrow \alpha_1 A', \ldots, A' \rightarrow \alpha_n A'$, and $A' \rightarrow e$, where A' is a new nonterminal.*

Still the grammar G' of our example has rules with identical left-hand sides, only now all uncertainties can be resolved by looking ahead at the next input

---

[†] We assume here that there are no rules of the form $A \rightarrow A$.

symbol. We can thus construct the following deterministic pushdown automaton M_4 that accepts $L(G)\$$.

$$M_4 = (K, \Sigma \cup \{\$\}, V', \Delta, p, \{q_\$\}),$$

where

$$K = \{p, q, q_{\mathsf{id}}, q_+, q_*, q_), q_(, q_\$\},$$

and Δ is listed below.

$$((p, e, e), (q, E))$$
$$((q, a, e), (q_a, e)) \qquad \text{for each } a \in \Sigma \cup \{\$\}$$
$$((q_a, e, a), (q, e)) \qquad \text{for each } a \in \Sigma$$
$$((q_a, e, E), (q_a, TE')) \qquad \text{for each } a \in \Sigma \cup \{\$\}$$
$$((q_+, e, E'), (q_+, +TE'))$$
$$((q_a, e, E'), (q_a, e)) \qquad \text{for each } a \in \{), \$\}$$
$$((q_a, e, T), (q_a, FT')) \qquad \text{for each } a \in \Sigma \cup \{\$\}$$
$$((q_*, e, T'), (q_*, *FT'))$$
$$((q_a, e, T'), (q_a, e)) \qquad \text{for each } a \in \{+,), \$\}$$
$$((q_(, e, F), (q_(, (E)))$$
$$((q_{\mathsf{id}}, e, F), (q_x, \mathsf{id}A))$$
$$((q_(, e, A), (q_(, (E)))$$
$$((q_a, e, A), (q_a, e)) \qquad \text{for each } a \in \{+, *,), \$\}$$

Then M_4 is a parser for G'. For example, the input string id $*$ (id)$\$$ would be accepted as shown in the table in the next page.

Here we have indicated the steps in the computation where a nonterminal has been replaced on the stack in accordance with a rule of G'. By applying these rules of G' in the last column of this table in sequence, we obtain a leftmost derivation of the input string:

$$E \Rightarrow TE' \Rightarrow FT'E' \Rightarrow \mathsf{id}T'E' \Rightarrow \mathsf{id} * FT'E' \Rightarrow \mathsf{id} * (E)T'E' \Rightarrow$$

$$\mathsf{id} * (TE')T'E' \Rightarrow \mathsf{id} * (FT'E')T'E' \Rightarrow \mathsf{id} * (\mathsf{id}T'E')T'E' \Rightarrow$$

$$\mathsf{id} * (\mathsf{id}E')T'E' \Rightarrow \mathsf{id} * (\mathsf{id})T'E' \Rightarrow \mathsf{id} * (\mathsf{id})E' \Rightarrow \mathsf{id} * (\mathsf{id})$$

In fact, a *parse tree* of the input can be reconstructed (see Figure 3-12; the step of the pushdown automaton corresponding to the expansion of each node of the parse tree is also shown next to the node). Notice that this parser constructs the parse tree of the input in a **top-down**, **left-first** manner, starting from E and repeatedly applying an appropriate rule to the leftmost nonterminal.

Step	State	Unread Input	Stack	Rule of G'
0	p	id $*$ (id)$\$$	e	
1	q	id $*$ (id)$\$$	E	
2	q_{id}	$*$(id)$\$$	E	
3	q_{id}	$*$(id)$\$$	TE'	1
4	q_{id}	$*$(id)$\$$	$FT'E'$	4
5	q_{id}	$*$(id)$\$$	id$AT'E'$	8
6	q	$*$(id)$\$$	$AT'E'$	
7	q_*	(id)$\$$	$AT'E'$	
8	q_*	(id)$\$$	$T'E'$	9
9	q_*	(id)$\$$	$*FT'E'$	5
10	q	(id)$\$$	$FT'E'$	
11	$q_($	id)$\$$	$FT'E'$	
12	$q_($	id)$\$$	$(E)T'E'$	7
13	q	id)$\$$	$E)T'E'$	
14	q_{id}	)$\$$	$E)T'E'$	
15	q_{id}	)$\$$	$TE')T'E'$	1
16	q_{id}	)$\$$	$FT'E')T'E'$	4
17	q_{id}	)$\$$	id$AT'E')T'E'$	8
18	q	)$\$$	$AT'E')T'E'$	
19	$q_)$	$\$$	$AT'E')T'E'$	
20	$q_)$	$\$$	$T'E')T'E'$	10
21	$q_)$	$\$$	$E')T'E'$	6
22	$q_)$	$\$$	$)T'E'$	3
23	q	$\$$	$T'E'$	6
24	$q_\$$	e	$T'E'$	
25	$q_\$$	e	E'	6
26	$q_\$$	e	e	3

In general, given a grammar G, one may try to construct a top-down parser for G as follows: Eliminate left recursion in G by repeatedly applying Heuristic Rule 2 to all left-recursive nonterminals A of G. Apply Heuristic Rule 1 to left-factor G whenever necessary. Then examine whether the resulting grammar has the property that one can decide among rules with the same left-hand side by looking at the next input symbol. Grammars with this property are called $LL(1)$. Although we have not specified exactly how to determine whether a grammar is indeed $LL(1)$ —nor how to construct the corresponding deterministic parser if it is $LL(1)$— there are systematic methods for doing so. In any case, inspection of the grammar and some experimentation will often be all that is needed.

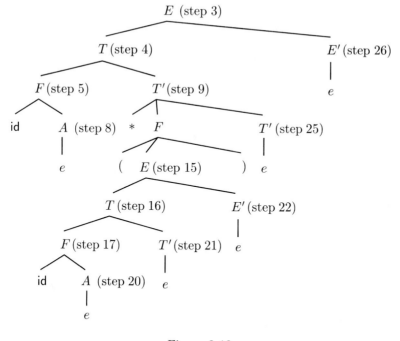

Figure 3-12

Bottom-Up Parsing

There is no one best way to parse context-free languages, and different methods are sometimes preferable for different grammars. We close this chapter by briefly considering methods quite dissimilar from those of top-down parsing. Nevertheless they, too, find their genesis in the construction of a pushdown automaton.

In addition to the construction of Lemma 3.4.1, there is a quite orthogonal way of constructing a pushdown automaton that accepts the language generated by a given context-free grammar. The automata of that construction (from which the top-down parsers studied in the last subsection are derived) operate by carrying out a leftmost derivation on the stack; as terminal symbols are generated, they are compared with the input string. In the construction given below, the automaton attempts to read the input first and, on the basis of the input actually read, deduce what derivation it should attempt to carry out. The general effect, as we shall see, is to reconstruct a parse tree from the leaves to the root, rather than the other way around, and so this class of methods is called **bottom-up**.

The bottom-up pushdown automaton is constructed as follows. Let $G = (V, \Sigma, R, S)$ be any context-free grammar; then let $M = (K, \Sigma, s, F)$, where $K = p, q$, $\Gamma = V$, $F = \{q\}$, and Δ contains the following.

(1) $((p, a, e), (p, a))$ for each $a \in \Sigma$.

(2) $((p, e, \alpha^R), (p, A))$ for each rule $A \to \alpha$ in R.

(3) $((p, e, S), (q, e))$.

Before moving to the proof itself, compare these types of transitions with those of the automaton constructed in the proof of Lemma 3.4.1. Transitions of type 1 here move input symbols onto the stack; transitions of type 3 in Lemma 3.4. pop terminal symbols off the stack when they match input symbols. Transitions of type 2 here replace the right-hand side of a rule on the stack by the corresponding left-hand side, the right-hand side being found reversed on the stack; those of type 2 of Lemma 3.4.1 replace the left-hand side of a rule on the stack by the corresponding right-hand side. Transitions of type 3 here end a computation by moving to the final state when only the start symbol remains on the stack; transitions of type 1 of Lemma 3.4.1 start off the computation by placing the start symbol on the initially empty stack. So the machine of this construction is in a sense perfectly orthogonal to the one of Lemma 3.4.1.

Lemma 3.7.1: *Let G and M be as just presented. Then $L(M) = L(G)$.*

Proof: . Any string in $L(G)$ has a rightmost derivation from the start symbol. Therefore proof of the following claim suffices to establish the lemma.

Claim: For any $x \in \Sigma^*$ and $\gamma \in \Gamma^*$, $(p, x, \gamma) \vdash_M^* (p, e, S)$ if and only if $S \overset{R}{\underset{G}{\Rightarrow}}{}^* \gamma^R x$.

For if we let x be an input to M and $\gamma = e$, then since q is the only final state and it can be entered only via transition 3, the claim implies that M accepts x if and only if G generates x. The *only if* direction of the claim can be proved by an induction on the number of steps in the computation of M, whereas the *if* direction can be proved by an induction on the number of steps in the rightmost derivation of x from S. ■

Let us consider again the grammar for arithmetic expressions (Example 3.1.3, without the rule $F \to \mathsf{id}(E)$ of the previous subsection). The rules of this grammar are the following.

$$E \to E + T \tag{R1}$$

$$E \to T \tag{R2}$$

$$T \to T * F \tag{R3}$$

$$T \to F \tag{R4}$$

$$F \to (E) \tag{R5}$$

$$F \to \mathsf{id} \tag{R6}$$

If our new construction is applied to this grammar, the following set of transitions is obtained.

$$(p, a, e), (p, a)) \qquad \text{for each } a \in \Sigma \qquad (\Delta 0)$$

$$(p, e, T + E), (p, E) \qquad (\Delta 1)$$

$$(p, e, T), (p, E) \qquad (\Delta 2)$$

$$(p, e, F * T), (p, T) \qquad (\Delta 3)$$

$$(p, e, F), (p, T) \qquad (\Delta 4)$$

$$(p, e,)E(), (p, F) \qquad (\Delta 5)$$

$$(p, e, \mathsf{id}), (p, F) \qquad (\Delta 6)$$

$$(p, e, E), (q, e) \qquad (\Delta 7)$$

Let us call this pushdown automaton M. The input $\mathsf{id} * (\mathsf{id})$ is accepted by M as shown in the table below.

Step	State	Unread Input	Stack	Transition Used	Rule of G
0	p	$\mathsf{id} * (\mathsf{id})$	e		
1	p	$*(\mathsf{id})$	id	$\Delta 0$	
2	p	$*(\mathsf{id})$	F	$\Delta 6$	R6
3	p	$*(\mathsf{id})$	T	$\Delta 4$	R4
4	p	(id)	$*T$	$\Delta 0$	
5	p	$\mathsf{id})$	$(*T$	$\Delta 0$	
6	p	$)$	$\mathsf{id}(*T$	$\Delta 0$	
7	p	$)$	$F(*T$	$\Delta 7$	R6
8	p	$)$	$T(*T$	$\Delta 4$	R4
9	p	$)$	$E(*T$	$\Delta 2$	R2
10	p	e	$)E(*T$	$\Delta 0$	
11	p	e	$F * T$	$\Delta 5$	R5
12	p	e	T	$\Delta 3$	R3
13	p	e	E	$\Delta 2$	R2
14	p	e	e	$\Delta 8$	

We see that M is certainly not deterministic: Transitions of type $\Delta 0$ are compatible with all the transitions of type $\Delta 1$ through $\Delta 8$. Still, its overall "philosophy" of operation is suggestive. At any point, M may **shift** a terminal symbol from its input to the top of the stack (transitions of type $\Delta 0$, used in the sample computation at Steps 1, 4, 5, 6, and 10). On the other hand, it may occasionally recognize the top few symbols on the stack as (the reverse of) the right-hand side of a rule of G, and may then **reduce** this string to the corresponding left-hand side (transitions of types $\Delta 2$ through $\Delta 6$, used in the sample computation where a "rule of G" is indicated in the rightmost column). The sequence of rules corresponding to the reduction steps turns out to mirror exactly, in reverse order, a rightmost derivation of the input string. In our example, the implied rightmost derivation is as follows.

$$E \Rightarrow T$$
$$\Rightarrow T * F$$
$$\Rightarrow T * (E)$$
$$\Rightarrow T * (T)$$
$$\Rightarrow T * (F)$$
$$\Rightarrow T * (\text{id})$$
$$\Rightarrow F * (\text{id})$$
$$\Rightarrow \text{id} * (\text{id})$$

This derivation can be read from the computation by applying the rules mentioned in the right-hand column, from bottom to top, always to the rightmost nonterminal. Equivalently, this process can be thought of as a bottom-to-top, left-to-right reconstruction of a parse tree (that is, exactly orthogonal to Figure 3-12(b)).

In order to construct a practically useful parser for $L(G)$, we must turn M into a deterministic device that accepts $L(G)\$$. As in our treatment of top-down parsers, we shall not give a systematic procedure for doing so. Instead, we carry through the example of G, pointing out the basic heuristic principles that govern this construction.

First, we need a way of deciding between the two basic kinds of moves, namely, *shifting* the next input symbol to the stack and *reducing* the few topmost stack symbols to a single nonterminal according to a rule of the grammar. One possible way of deciding this is by looking at two pieces of information: the next input symbol —call it b— and the top stack symbol —call it a. (The symbol a could be a nonterminal.) The decision between shifting and reducing is then done through a relation $P \subseteq V \times (\Sigma \cup \{\$\})$ called a **precedence relation** P. If $(a, b) \in P$, then we reduce; otherwise we shift b. The correct precedence relation for the grammar of our example is given in the table below. Intuitively, $(a, b) \in P$ means that there exists a rightmost derivation of the form

$$S \overset{R}{\underset{G}{\Rightarrow}}{}^{*} \beta Abx \overset{R}{\underset{G}{\Rightarrow}} \beta\gamma abx.$$

Since we are reconstructing rightmost derivations backwards, it makes sense to undo the rule $A \to \gamma a$ whenever we observe that a immediately precedes b. There are systematic ways to calculate precedence relations, as well as to find out when, as is the case in this example, a precedence relation suffices to

	(	)	id	+	*	$
(						
)		✓		✓	✓	✓
id		✓		✓	✓	✓
+						
*						
E						
T		✓		✓		✓
F		✓		✓	✓	✓

decide between shifting and reducing; however, in many cases inspection and experimentation will lead to the right table.

Now we must confront the other source of nondeterminism: when we decide to reduce, how do we choose which of the prefixes of the pushdown store to replace with a nonterminal? For example, if the pushdown store contains the string $F * T + E$ and we must reduce, we have a choice between reducing F to T (Rule R4) or reducing $F * T$ to T (Rule R3). For our grammar, the correct action is always to choose the *longest* prefix of the stack contents that matches the reverse of the right-hand side of a rule and reduce it to the left-hand side of that rule. Thus in the case above we should take the second option and reduce $F * T$ to T.

With these two rules (reduce when the top of the stack and the next input symbol are related by P, otherwise shift; and, when reducing, reduce the longest possible string from the top of the stack) the operation of the pushdown automaton M becomes completely deterministic. In fact, we could design a deterministic pushdown automaton that "implements" these two rules (see Problem 3.7.9).

Once again, bear in mind that the two heuristic rules we have described —namely, (1) use a precedence relation to decide whether to shift or reduce, and (2) when in doubt, reduce the longest possible string— do not work in all situations. The grammars for which they do work are called **weak precedence grammars**; in practice, many grammars related to programming languages are or can readily be converted into weak precedence grammars. And there are many, even more sophisticated methods for constructing top-down parsers, which work for larger classes of grammars.

Problems for Section 3.7

3.7.1. Show that the following languages are deterministic context-free.
   (a) $\{a^m b^n : m \neq n\}$
   (b) $\{wcw^R : w \in \{a, b\}^*\}$

(c) $\{ca^m b^m : m \neq n\} \cup \{da^m b^{2m} : m \geq 0\}$
(d) $\{a^m cb^m : m \neq n\} \cup \{a^m db^{2m} : m \geq 0\}$

3.7.2. Show that the class of deterministic context-free languages is not closed under homomorphism.

3.7.3. Show that if L is a deterministic context-free language, then L is not inherently ambiguous.

3.7.4. Show that the pushdown automaton M' constructed in Section 3.7.1 accepts the language L, given that M accepts $L\$$.

3.7.5. Consider the following context-free grammar: $G = (V, \Sigma, R, S)$, where $V = \{(,), ., a, S, A\}$, $\Sigma = \{(,), ., .\}$, and $R = \{S \rightarrow (), S \rightarrow a, S \rightarrow (A), A \rightarrow S, A \rightarrow A.S\}$ (For the reader familiar with the programming language LISP, $L(G)$ contains all atoms and lists, where the symbol a stands for any non-null atom.)
(a) Apply Heuristic Rules 1 and 2 to G. Let G' be the resulting grammar. Argue that G' is $LL(l)$. Construct a deterministic pushdown automaton M accepting $L(G)\$$. Study the computation of M on the string $((()).a)$.
(b) Repeat Part (a) for the grammar resulting from G if one replaces the first rule by $A \rightarrow e$.
(c) Repeat Part (a) for the grammar resulting from G if one replaces the last rule by $A \rightarrow S.A$ in G.

3.7.6. Consider again the grammar G of Problem 3.7.5. Argue that G is a weak precedence grammar, with the precedence relation shown below. Construct a deterministic pushdown automaton that accepts $L(G)\$$.

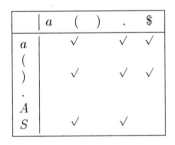

	a	(	)	.	$
a		✓		✓	✓
(					
)		✓		✓	✓
.					
A					
S		✓		✓	

3.7.7. Let $G' = (V, \Sigma, R', S)$ be the grammar with rules $S \rightarrow (A), S \rightarrow a, A \rightarrow S.A, A \rightarrow e$. Is G' weak precedence? If so, give an appropriate precedence relation; otherwise, explain why not.

3.7.8. Acceptance by final state is defined in Problem 3.3.3. Show that L is deterministic context-free if and only if L is accepted by final state by some deterministic pushdown automaton.

3.7.9. Give explicitly a deterministic pushdown automaton that accepts the language of arithmetic expressions, based on the nondeterministic pushdown automaton M and the precedence table P of the last subsection. Your automaton should look ahead in the input by absorbing the next input symbol, very much like the pushdown automaton M_4 of the previous section.

3.7.10. Consider the following classes of languages:
- (a) Regular
- (b) Context-free
- (c) The class of the *complements* of context-free languages
- (d) Deterministic context-free

Give a *Venn diagram* of these classes; that is, represent each class by a "bubble," so that inclusions, intersections, etc. of classes are reflected accurately. Can you supply a language for each non-empty region of your diagram?

REFERENCES

Context-free grammars are a creation of Noam Chomsky; see

- N. Chomsky   "Three models for the description of languages," *IRE Transactions on Information Theory, 2*, 3, pp. 113–124, 1956, and also

- N. Chomsky   "On certain formal properties of grammars," *Information and Control, 2*, 137–167, 1959.

In the last paper, Chomsky normal form was also introduced. A closely related notation for the syntax of programming languages, called BNF (for Backus Normal Form or Backus-Naur Form), was also invented in the late 1950s; see

- P. Naur, ed.   "Revised report on the algorithmic language Algol 60," *Communications of the ACM, 6*, 1, pp. 1–17, 1963, reprinted in S. Rosen, ed., *Programming Systems and Languages* New York: McGraw-Hill, pp. 79–118, 1967.

Problem 3.1.9 on the equivalence of regular grammars and finite automata is from

- N. Chomsky, G. A. Miller   "Finite-state languages," *Information and Control, 1*, pp. 91-112, 1958.

The pushdown automaton was introduced in

- A. G. Oettinger   "Automatic syntactic analysis and the pushdown store," *Proceedings of Symposia on Applied Mathematics, Vol. 12*, Providence, R.I.: American Mathematical Society, 1961.

Theorem 3.4.1 on the equivalence of context-free languages and pushdown automata was proved independently by Schutzenberger, Chomsky, and Evey.

- M. P. Schutzenberger   "On context-free languages and pushdown automata," *Information and Control, 6*, 3, pp. 246–264, 1963.

- N. Chomsky   "Context-free grammar and pushdown storage," Quarterly Progress Report, 65, pp. 187–194, M.I.T. Research Laboratory in Electronics, Cambridge, Mass., 1962 o J. Evey   "Application of pushdown store machines," *Proceedings of the 1963 Fall Joint Computer Conference*, pp. 215–217. Montreal: AFIPS Press, 1963.

The closure properties presented in subsection 3.5.1, along with many others, were pointed out in

o V. Bar-Hillel, M. Perles, and E. Shamir   "On formal properties of simple phrase structure grammars," *Zeitschrift für Phonetik, Sprachwissenschaft und Kommunikationsforschung, 14,* pp. 143–172, 1961.

In the same paper one finds a stronger version of Theorem 3.5.3 (the Pumping Theorem for context-free grammars; see also Problem 3.5.7). An even stronger version of that theorem appears in

o W. G. Ogden   "A helpful result for proving inherent ambiguity," *Mathematical Systems Theory, 2,* pp. 191–194, 1968.

The dynamic programming algorithm for context-free language recognition was discovered by

o T. Kasami   "An efficient recognition and syntax algorithm for context-free languages," Report AFCRL-65-758 (1965), Air Force Cambridge Research Laboratory, Cambridge, Mass., and independently by

o D. H. Younger   "Recognition and parsing of context-free languages in time n^3," *Information and Control, 10,* 2, pp. 189–208, 1967.

A variant of this algorithm is faster when the underlying grammar is unambiguous

o J. Earley   "An efficient context-free parsing algorithm," *Communications of the ACM, 13,* pp. 94–102, 1970.

The most efficient general context-free recognition algorithm known is due to Valiant. It runs in time proportional to the time required for multiplying two $n \times n$ matrices, currently $\mathcal{O}(n^{2.3\cdots})$.

o L. G. Valiant   "General context-free recognition in less than cubic time," *Journal of Computer and Systems Sciences, 10,* 2, pp. 308–315, 1975.

LL(1) parsers were introduced in

o P. M. Lewis II, R. E. Stearns   "Syntax-directed transduction," *Journal of the ACM, 15,* 3, pp. 465–488, 1968, and also in

o D. E. Knuth   "Top-down syntax analysis," *Acta Informatica, 1,* 2, pp. 79–110, 1971.

Weak precedence parsers were proposed in

o J. D. Ichbiah and S. P. Morse   "A technique for generating almost optimal Floyd-Evans productions for precedence grammars," *Communications of the ACM, 13,* 8, pp. 501–508, 1970.

The following is a standard book on compilers

o A. V. Aho, R. Sethi, J. D. Ullman   *Principles of Compiler Design*, Reading, Mass.: Addison-Wesley, 1985.

Ambiguity and inherent ambiguity were first studied in

o N. Chomsky and M. P. Schutzenberger   "The algebraic theory of context free languages," in *Computer Programming and Formal Systems* (pp. 118–161), ed. P. Braffort, D. Hirschberg. Amsterdam: North Holland, 1963, and o S. Ginsburg and J. S. Ullian   "Preservation of unambiguity and inherent ambiguity in context-free languages," *Journal of the ACM, 13,* 1, pp. 62–88, 1966,

respectively. Greibach normal form (Problem 3.5) is from

o S. Greibach   "A new normal form theorem for context-free phrase structure grammars," *Journal of the ACM, 12,* 1, pp. 42–52, 1965.

Two advanced books on context-free languages are

o S. Ginsburg   *The Mathematical Theory of Context-free Languages,* New York: McGraw-Hill, 1966, and

o M. A. Harrison   *Introduction to Formal Language Theory,* Reading, Massach.: Addison-Wesley, 1978.

4 | Turing Machines

4.1 THE DEFINITION OF A TURING MACHINE

We have seen in the last two chapters that neither finite automata nor pushdown automata can be regarded as truly general models for computers, since they are not capable of recognizing even such simple languages as $\{a^n b^n c^n : n \geq 0\}$. In this chapter we take up the study of devices that can recognize this and many more complicated languages. Although these devices, called **Turing machines** after their inventor Alan Turing (1912–1954), are more general than the automata previously studied, their basic appearance is similar to those automata. A Turing machine consists of a finite control, a tape, and a head that can be used for reading *or writing* on that tape. The formal definitions of Turing machines and their operation are in the same mathematical style as those used for finite and pushdown automata. So in order to gain the additional computational power and generality of function that Turing machines possess, we shall not move to an entirely new sort of model for a computer.

Nevertheless, Turing machines are not simply one more class of automata, to be replaced later on by a yet more powerful type. We shall see in this chapter that, as primitive as Turing machines seem to be, attempts to strengthen them do not have any effect. For example, we also study Turing machines with many tapes, or machines with fancier memory devices that can be read or written in a *random access* mode reminiscent of actual computers; significantly, these devices turn out to be no stronger in terms of computing power than basic Turing machines. We show results of this kind by simulation methods: We can convert any "augmented" machine into a standard Turing machine which functions in an analogous way. Thus any computation that can be carried out on the fancier type of machine can actually be carried out on a Turing machine of the standard variety. Furthermore, towards the end of this chapter we define a certain kind of language generator, a substantial generalization of context-free grammars, which is also shown to be equivalent to the Turing machine. From a totally different perspective, we also pursue the question of when to regard a numerical function (such as $2^x + x^2$) as computable, and end up with a notion that is once more equivalent to Turing machines!

So the Turing machines seem to form a *stable* and *maximal* class of computational devices, in terms of the computations they can perform. In fact, in the next chapter we shall advance the widely accepted view that any reasonable way of formalizing the idea of an "algorithm" must be ultimately equivalent to the idea of a Turing machine.

But this is getting ahead of our story. The important points to remember by way of introduction are that Turing machines are designed to satisfy simultaneously these three criteria:

(a) They should be automata; that is, their construction and function should be in the same general spirit as the devices previously studied.
(b) They should be as simple as possible to describe, define formally, and reason about.
(c) They should be as general as possible in terms of the computations they can carry out.

Now let us look more closely at these machines. In essence, a Turing machine consists of a finite-state control unit and a tape (see Figure 4-1). Communication between the two is provided by a single head, which reads symbols from the tape and is also used to change the symbols on the tape. The control unit operates in discrete steps; at each step it performs two functions in a way that depends on its current state and the tape symbol currently scanned by the read/write head:

(1) Put the control unit in a new state.
(2) *Either:*
    (a) Write a symbol in the tape square currently scanned, replacing the one already there; *or*
    (b) Move the read/write head one tape square to the left or right.

The tape has a left end, but it extends indefinitely to the right. To prevent the machine from moving its head off the left end of the tape, we assume that the leftmost end of the tape is always marked by a special symbol denoted by ▷; we assume further that all of our Turing machines are so designed that, whenever the head reads a ▷, it immediately moves to the right. Also, we shall use the distinct symbols ← and → to denote movement of the head to the left or right; we assume that these two symbols are not members of any alphabet we consider.

A Turing machine is supplied with input by inscribing that input string on tape squares at the left end of the tape, immediately to the right of the ▷

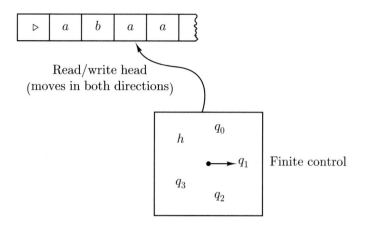

Figure 4-1

symbol. The rest of the tape initially contains **blank** symbols, denoted $\sqcup$. The machine is free to alter its input in any way it sees fit, as well as to write on the unlimited blank portion of the tape to the right. Since the machine can move its head only one square at a time, after any finite computation only finitely many tape squares will have been visited.

We can now present the formal definition of a Turing machine.

Definition 4.1.1: A Turing machine is a quintuple $(K, \Sigma, \delta, s, H)$, where
K is a finite set of **states**;
Σ is an alphabet, containing the **blank symbol** $\sqcup$ and the **left end symbol** $\rhd$, but not containing the symbols $\leftarrow$ and $\rightarrow$;
$s \in K$ is the **initial state**;
$H \subseteq K$ is the set of **halting states**;
δ, the **transition function**, is a function from $(K - H) \times \Sigma$ to $K \times (\Sigma \cup \{\leftarrow, \rightarrow\})$ such that,
(a) for all $q \in K - H$, if $\delta(q, \rhd) = (p, b)$, then $b = \rightarrow$
(b) for all $q \in K - H$ and $a \in \Sigma$, if $\delta(q, a) = (p, b)$ then $b \neq \rhd$.

If $q \in K - H$, $a \in \Sigma$, and $\delta(q, a) = (p, b)$, then M, when in state q and scanning symbol a, will enter state p, and (1) if b is a symbol in Σ, M will rewrite the currently scanned symbol a as b, or (2) if b is $\leftarrow$ or $\rightarrow$, M will move its head in direction b. Since δ is a function, the operation of M is deterministic and will stop only when M enters a halting state. Notice the requirement (a) on δ: When it sees the left end of the tape $\rhd$, it *must* move right. This way the leftmost $\rhd$ is never erased, and M never falls off the left end of its tape. By (b), M never writes a $\rhd$, and therefore $\rhd$ is the unmistakable sign of the left end of the tape. In other words, we can think of ▷ simply as a "protective barrier" that prevents the head of M from inadvertently falling off the left end, which does not interfere with the computation of M in any other way. Also notice that δ is *not* defined on states in H; when the machine reaches a halting state, then its operation stops.

Example 4.1.1: Consider the Turing machine $M = (K, \Sigma, \delta, s, \{h\})$, where

$$K = \{q_0, q_1, h\},$$
$$\Sigma = \{a, \sqcup, \triangleright\},$$
$$s = q_0,$$

and δ is given by the following table.

$q,$	σ	$\delta(q, \sigma)$
q_0	a	$(q_1, \sqcup)$
q_0	$\sqcup$	$(h, \sqcup)$
q_0	$\triangleright$	$(q_0, \rightarrow)$
q_1	a	(q_0, a)
q_1	$\sqcup$	$(q_0, \rightarrow)$
q_1	$\triangleright$	$(q_1, \rightarrow)$

When M is started in its initial state q_0, it scans its head to the right, changing all a's to $\sqcup$'s as it goes, until it finds a tape square already containing $\sqcup$; then it halts. (Changing a nonblank symbol to the blank symbol will be called **erasing** the nonblank symbol.) To be specific, suppose that M is started with its head scanning the first of four a's, the last of which is followed by a $\sqcup$. Then M will go back and forth between states q_0 and q_1 four times, alternately changing an a to a $\sqcup$ and moving the head right; the first and fifth lines of the table for δ are the relevant ones during this sequence of moves. At this point, M will find itself in state q_0 scanning $\sqcup$ and, according to the second line of the table, will halt. Note that the fourth line of the table, that is, the value of $\delta(q_1, a)$, is irrelevant, since M can never be in state q_1 scanning an a if it is started in state q_0. Nevertheless, *some* value must be associated with $\delta(q_1, a)$ since δ is required to be a function with domain $K \times \Sigma.\Diamond$

Example 4.1.2: Consider the Turing machine $M = (K, \Sigma, \delta, s, H)$, where

$$K = \{q_0, h\},$$
$$\Sigma = \{a, \sqcup, \triangleright\},$$
$$s = q_0,$$
$$H = \{h\},$$

$q,$	σ	$\delta(q,\sigma)$
q_0	a	$(q_0, \leftarrow)$
q_0	$\sqcup$	$(h, \sqcup)$
q_0	$\triangleright$	$(q_0, \rightarrow)$

and δ is given by this table.

This machine scans to the left until it finds a $\sqcup$ and then halts. If every tape square from the head position back to the left end of the tape contains an a, and of course the left end of the tape contains a $\triangleright$, then M will go to the left end of the tape, and from then on it will indefinitely go back and forth between the left end and the square to its right. Unlike other deterministic devices that we have encountered, *the operation of a Turing machine may never stop.*$\Diamond$

We now formalize the operation of a Turing machine.

To specify the status of a Turing machine computation, we need to specify the state, the contents of the tape, and the position of the head. Since all but a finite initial portion of the tape will be blank, the contents of the tape can be specified by a finite string. We choose to break that string into two pieces: the part to the left of the scanned square, including the single symbol in the scanned square; and the part, possibly empty, to the right of the scanned square. Moreover, so that no two such pairs of strings will correspond to the same combination of head position and tape contents, we insist that the second string not end with a blank (all tape squares to the right of the last one explicitly represented are assumed to contain blanks anyway). These considerations lead us to the following definitions.

Definition 4.1.2: A **configuration** of a Turing machine $M = (K, \Sigma, \delta, s, H)$ is a member of $K \times \triangleright\Sigma^* \times (\Sigma^*(\Sigma - \{\sqcup\}) \cup \{e\})$.

$\underset{\times \; \Sigma}{\underbrace{}_{\wedge}}$

That is, all configurations are assumed to start with the left end symbol, and never end with a blank —unless the blank is currently scanned. Thus $(q, \triangleright a, aba)$, $(h, \triangleright \sqcup \sqcup\sqcup, \sqcup a)$, and $(q, \triangleright \sqcup a \sqcup \sqcup, e)$ are configurations (see Figure 4-2), but $(q, \triangleright baa, a, bc\sqcup)$ and $(q, \sqcup aa, ba)$ are not. A configuration whose state component is in H will be called a **halted configuration**.

We shall use a simplified notation for depicting the tape contents (including the position of the head): We shall write $w\underline{a}u$ for the tape contents of the configuration (q, wa, u); the underlined symbol indicates the head position. For the three configurations illustrated in Figure 4-2, the tape contents would be represented as $\triangleright \underline{a}aba$, $\triangleright \sqcup\sqcup\underline{\sqcup}\sqcup a$, and $\triangleright \sqcup a\underline{\sqcup}\sqcup$. Also, we can write configurations by including the state together with the notation for the tape and head position. That is, we can write (q, wa, u) as $(q, w\underline{a}u)$. Using this convention, we would

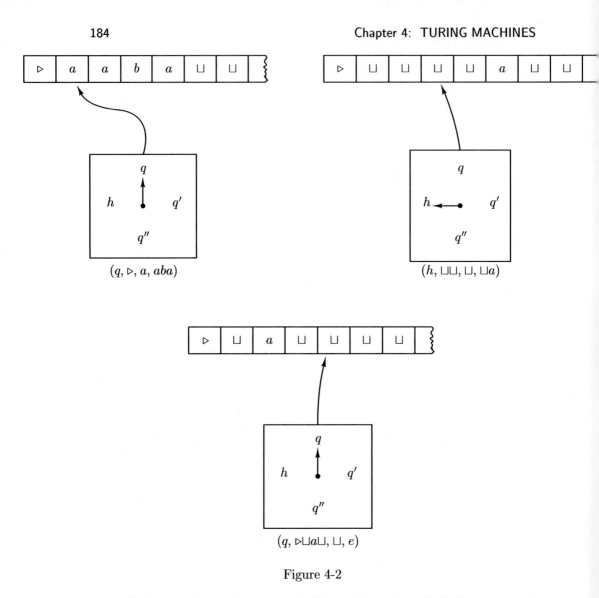

$(q, \triangleright, a, aba)$

$(h, \sqcup\sqcup, \sqcup, \sqcup a)$

$(q, \triangleright\sqcup a\sqcup, \sqcup, e)$

Figure 4-2

write the three configurations shown in Figure 4-2 as $(q, \triangleright\underline{a}aba)$, $(h, \triangleright \sqcup \sqcup\underline{\sqcup}\sqcup a)$, and $(q, \triangleright \sqcup a \sqcup \underline{\sqcup})$.

Definition 4.1.3: Let $M = (K, \Sigma, \delta, s, H)$ be a Turing machine and consider two configurations of M, $(q_1, w_1\underline{a_1}u_1)$ and $(q_2, w_2\underline{a_2}u_2)$, where $a_1, a_2 \in \Sigma$. Then

$$(q_1, w_1\underline{a_1}u_1) \vdash_M (q_2, w_2\underline{a_2}u_2)$$

if and only if, for some $b \in \Sigma \cup \{\leftarrow, \rightarrow\}$, $\delta(q_1, a_1) = (q_2, b)$, and either

1. $b \in \Sigma$, $w_1 = w_2$, $u_1 = u_2$, and $a_2 = b$, or
2. $b = \leftarrow$, $w_1 = w_2 a_2$, and either
    (a) $u_2 = a_1 u_1$, if $a \neq \sqcup$ or $u_1 \neq e$, or
    (b) $u_2 = e$, if $a = \sqcup$ and $u_1 = e$; or
3. $b = \rightarrow$, $w_2 = w_1 a_1$, and either
    (a) $u_1 = a_2 u_2$, or
    (b) $u_1 = u_2 = e$, and $a_2 = \sqcup$.

In Case 1, M rewrites a symbol without moving its head. In Case 2, M moves its head one square to the left; if it is moving to the left off blank tape, the blank symbol on the square just scanned disappears from the configuration. In Case 3, M moves its head one square to the right; if it is moving onto blank tape, a new blank symbol appears in the configuration as the new scanned symbol. Notice that all configurations, except for the halted ones, yield exactly one configuration.

Example 4.1.3: To illustrate these cases, let $w, u \in \Sigma^*$, where u does not end with a $\sqcup$, and let $a, b \in \Sigma$.

> *Case 1.* $\delta(q_1, a) = (q_2, b)$.
>   Example: $(q_1, w\underline{a}u) \vdash_M (q_2, w\underline{b}u)$.
> *Case 2.* $\delta(q_1, a) = (q_2, \leftarrow)$.
>   Example for (a): $(q_1, wb\underline{a}u) \vdash_M (q_2, w\underline{b}au)$.
>   Example for (b): $(q_1, wb\underline{\sqcup}) \vdash_M (q_2, w\underline{b})$.
> *Case 3.* $\delta(q_1, a) = (q_2, \rightarrow)$.
>   Example for (a): $(q_1, w\underline{a}bu) \vdash_M (q_2, wa\underline{b}u)$.
>   Example for (b): $(q_1, w\underline{a}) \vdash_M (q_2, wa\underline{\sqcup})$. $\Diamond$

Definition 4.1.4: For any Turing machine M, let, $\vdash_M^*$ be the reflexive, transitive closure of $\vdash_M$; we say that configuration C_1 **yields** configuration C_2 if $C_1 \vdash_M^* C_2$. A **computation** by M is a sequence of configurations $C_0, C_1, \ldots, C_n$, for some $n \geq 0$ such that

$$C_0 \vdash_M C_1 \vdash_M C_2 \vdash_M \cdots \vdash_M C_n.$$

We say that the computation is of **length** n or that it has n **steps**, and we write $C_0 \vdash_M^n C_n$.

Example 4.1.4: Consider the Turing machine M described in Example 4.1.1. If M is started in configuration $(q_0, \triangleright\underline{\sqcup}aaaa)$, its computation would be represented formally as follows.

$$(q_0, \triangleright \underline{\sqcup} aaaa) \vdash_M (q_0, \triangleright \sqcup \underline{a}aaa)$$
$$\vdash_M (q_1, \triangleright \sqcup \underline{\sqcup} aaa)$$
$$\vdash_M (q_0, \triangleright \sqcup \sqcup \underline{a}aa)$$
$$\vdash_M (q_1, \triangleright \sqcup \sqcup \underline{\sqcup} aa)$$
$$\vdash_M (q_0, \triangleright \sqcup \sqcup \sqcup \underline{a}a)$$
$$\vdash_M (q_1, \triangleright \sqcup \sqcup \sqcup \underline{\sqcup} a)$$
$$\vdash_M (q_0, \triangleright \sqcup \sqcup \sqcup \sqcup \underline{a})$$
$$\vdash_M (q_1, \triangleright \sqcup \sqcup \sqcup \sqcup \underline{\sqcup})$$
$$\vdash_M (q_0, \triangleright \sqcup \sqcup \sqcup \sqcup \sqcup \underline{\sqcup})$$
$$\vdash_M (h, \triangleright \sqcup \sqcup \sqcup \sqcup \sqcup \underline{\sqcup})$$

The computation has ten steps.$\Diamond$

A Notation for Turing Machines

The Turing machines we have seen so far are extremely simple —at least when compared to our stated ambitions in this chapter— and their tabular form is already quite complex and hard to interpret. Obviously, we need a notation for Turing machines that is more graphic and transparent. For finite automata, we used in Chapter 2 a notation that involved states and arrows denoting transitions. We shall next adopt a similar notation for Turing machines. However, the things joined by arrows will in this case be *themselves* Turing machines. In other words, we shall use a *hierarchical* notation, in which more and more complex machines are built from simpler materials. To this end, we shall define a very simple repertoire of *basic machines*, together with *rules for combining machines*.

The Basic Machines. We start from very humble beginnings: The *symbol-writing machines* and the *head-moving machines*. Let us fix the alphabet Σ of our machines. For each $a \in \Sigma \cup \{\rightarrow, \leftarrow\} - \{\triangleright\}$, we define a Turing machine $M_a = (\{s, h\}, \Sigma, \delta, s, \{h\})$, where for each $b \in \Sigma - \{\triangleright\}$, $\delta(s, b) = (h, a)$. Naturally, $\delta(s, \triangleright)$ is still always $(s, \rightarrow)$. That is, the only thing this machine does is to perform action a —writing symbol a if $a \in \Sigma$, moving in the direction indicated by a if $a \in \{\leftarrow, \rightarrow\}$— and then to immediately halt. Naturally, there is a unique exception to this behavior: If the scanned symbol is a $\triangleright$, then the machine will dutifully move to the right.

Because the symbol-writing machines are used so often, we abbreviate their names and write simply a instead of M_a. That is, if $a \in \Sigma$, then the *a-writing machine* will be denoted simply as a. The head-moving machines $M_\leftarrow$ and $M_\rightarrow$ will be abbreviated as L (for "left") and R (for "right").

The Rules for Combining Machines. Turing machines will be combined in a way suggestive of the structure of a finite automaton. Individual machines are like the states of a finite automaton, and the machines may be connected to each other in the way that the states of a finite automaton are connected together. However, the connection from one machine to another is not pursued until the first machine halts; the other machine is then started from its initial state with the tape and head position as they were left by the first machine. So if M_1, M_2, and M_3 are Turing machines, the machine displayed in Figure 4-3 operates as follows: *Start in the initial state of M_1; operate as M_1 would operate until M_1 would halt; then, if the currently scanned symbol is an a, initiate M_2 and operate as M_2 would operate; otherwise, if the currently scanned symbol is a b, then initiate M_3 and operate as M_3 would operate.*

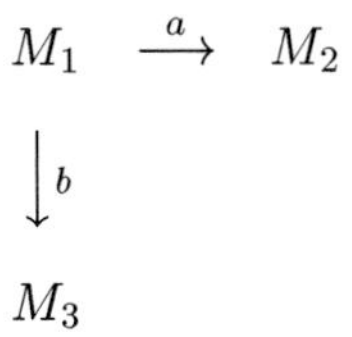

$$M_1 \quad \overset{a}{\longrightarrow} \quad M_2$$

$$\downarrow b$$

$$M_3$$

Figure 4-3

It is straightforward to give an explicit definition of the combined Turing machine from its constituents. Let us take the machine shown in Figure 4-3 above. Suppose that the three Turing machines M_1, M_2, and M_3 are $M_1 = (K_1, \Sigma, \delta_1, s_1, H_1)$, $M_2 = (K_2, \Sigma, \delta_2, s_2, H_2)$, and $M_3 = (K_3, \Sigma, \delta_3, s_3, H_3)$. We shall assume, as it will be most convenient in the context of combining machines, that *the sets of states of all these machines are disjoint.* The combined machine shown in Figure 4-3 above would then be $M = (K, \Sigma, \delta, s, H)$, where

$K = K_1 \cup K_2 \cup K_3$,

$s = s_1$,

$H = H_2 \cup H_3$.

For each $\sigma \in \Sigma$ and $q \in K - H$, $\delta(q, \sigma)$ is defined as follows:

(a) If $q \in K_1 - H_1$, then $\delta(q, \sigma) = \delta_1(q, \sigma)$.

(b) If $q \in K_2 - H_2$, then $\delta(q, \sigma) = \delta_2(q, \sigma)$.

(c) If $q \in K_3 - H_3$, then $\delta(q, \sigma) = \delta_3(q, \sigma)$.

(d) Finally, if $q \in H_1$ —the only case remaining— then $\delta(q, \sigma) = s_2$ if $\sigma = a$, $\delta(q, \sigma) = s_3$ if $\sigma = b$, and $\delta(q, \sigma) \in H$ otherwise.

All the ingredients of our notation are now in place. We shall be building machines by combining the basic machines, and then we shall further combine the combined machines to obtain more complex machines, and so on. We know that, if we wished, we could come up with a quintuple form of every machine we thus describe, by starting from the quintuples of the basic machines and carrying out the explicit construction exemplified above.

Example 4.1.5: Figure 4-4(a) illustrates a machine consisting of two copies of R. The machine represented by this diagram moves its head right one square; then, if that square contains an a, or a b, or a $\triangleright$, or a $\sqcup$, it moves its head one square further to the right.

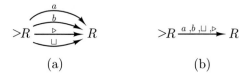

(a)   (b)

Figure 4-4

It will be convenient to represent this machine as in Figure 4-4(b). That is, an arrow labeled with several symbols is the same as several parallel arrows, one for each symbol. If an arrow is labeled by *all* symbols in the alphabet Σ of the machines, then the labels can be omitted. Thus, if we know that $\Sigma = \{a, b, \triangleright, \sqcup\}$, then we can display the machine above as

$$R \to R,$$

where, by convention, the leftmost machine is always the initial one. Sometimes an unlabeled arrow connecting two machines can be omitted entirely, by juxtaposing the representations of the two machines. Under this convention, the above machine becomes simply RR, or even $R^2.\diamondsuit$

Example 4.1.6: If $a \in \Sigma$ is any symbol, we can sometimes eliminate multiple arrows and labels by using $\bar{a}$ to mean "any symbol except a." Thus, the machine shown in Figure 4-5(a) scans its tape to the right until it finds a blank. We shall denote this most useful machine by $R_\sqcup$.

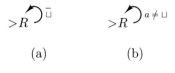

(a)   (b)

Figure 4-5

Another shorthand version of the same machine as in Figure 4-5(a) is shown in Figure 4-5(b). Here $a \neq \sqcup$ is read "any symbol a other than $\sqcup$." The advantage of this notation is that a may then be used elsewhere in the diagram as the name of a machine. To illustrate, Figure 4-6 depicts a machine that scans to the right

$$>R \overset{a \neq \sqcup}{\longrightarrow} La$$

Figure 4-6

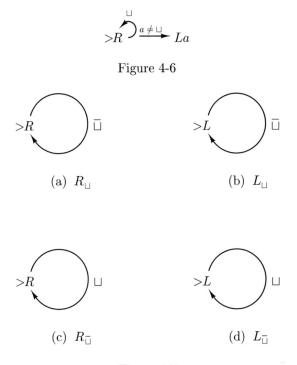

(a) $R_\sqcup$ (b) $L_\sqcup$

(c) $R_{\overline{\sqcup}}$ (d) $L_{\overline{\sqcup}}$

Figure 4-7

until it finds a nonblank square, then copies the symbol in that square onto the square immediately to the left of where it was found.◊

Example 4.1.7: Machines to find marked or unmarked squares are illustrated in Figure 4-7. They are the following.
(a) $R_\sqcup$, which finds the first blank square to the right of the currently scanned square.
(b) $L_\sqcup$, which finds the first blank square to the left of the currently scanned square.
(c) $R_{\overline{\sqcup}}$, which finds the first *non*blank square to the right of the currently scanned square.
(d) $L_{\overline{\sqcup}}$, which finds the first nonblank square to the left of the currently scanned square.◊

Example 4.1.8: The *copying machine* C performs the following function: If C starts with input w, that is, if string w, containing only nonblank symbols but possibly empty, is put on an otherwise blank tape with one blank square to its left, and the head is put on the blank square to the left of w, then the machine will eventually stop with $w \sqcup w$ on an otherwise blank tape. We say that C **transforms** $\sqcup w \sqcup$ **into** $\sqcup w \sqcup w \sqcup$.

A diagram for C is given in Figure 4-8.$\Diamond$

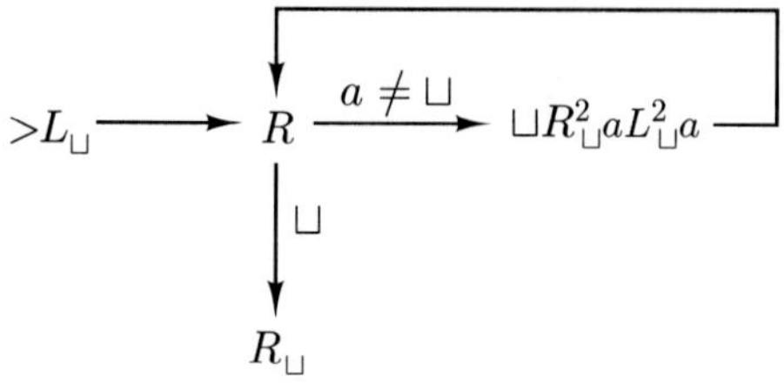

$$>L_\sqcup \longrightarrow R \xrightarrow{\ a \neq \sqcup\ } \sqcup R^2_\sqcup a L^2_\sqcup a$$

$$\downarrow \sqcup$$

$$R_\sqcup$$

Figure 4-8

Example 4.1.9: The left-shifting machine $S_\leftarrow$, transforms $\sqcup w \sqcup$, where w contains no blanks, into $w\sqcup$. It is illustrated in Figure 4-9.$\Diamond$

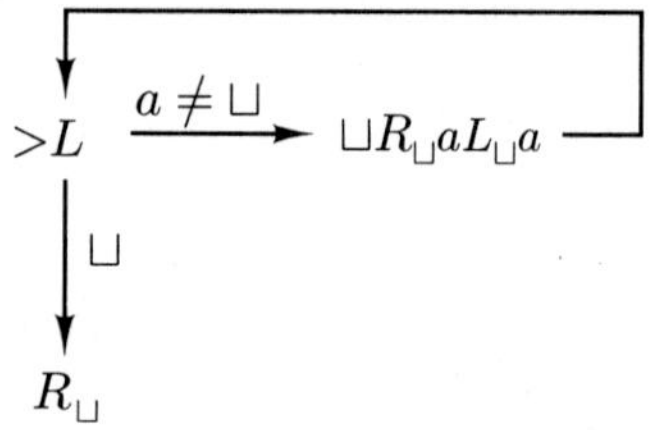

$$>L \xrightarrow{\ a \neq \sqcup\ } \sqcup R_\sqcup a L_\sqcup a$$

$$\downarrow \sqcup$$

$$R_\sqcup$$

Figure 4-9

Example 4.1.10: Figure 4-10 is the machine defined in Example 4.1.1, which erases the a's in its tape.

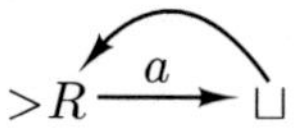

$$>R \xrightarrow{\ a\ } \sqcup$$

Figure 4-10

As a matter of fact, the fully developed transition table of this machine will differ from that of the machine given in Example 4.1.1 in ways that are subtle, inconsequential, and explored in Problem 4.1.8 —namely, the machine in Figure 4-10 will also contain certain extra states, which are final states of its constituents machines.$\Diamond$

Problems for Section 4.1

4.1.1. Let $M = (K, \Sigma, \delta, s, \{h\})$, where

$$K = \{q_0, q_1, h\},$$
$$\Sigma = \{a, b, \sqcup, \triangleright\},$$
$$s = q_0,$$

and δ is given by the following table.

$q,$	σ	$\delta(q, \sigma)$
q_0	a	(q_1, b)
q_0	b	(q_1, a)
q_0	$\sqcup$	$(h, \sqcup)$
q_0	$\triangleright$	$(q_0, \rightarrow)$
q_1	a	$(q_0, \rightarrow)$
q_1	b	$(q_0, \rightarrow)$
q_1	$\sqcup$	$(q_0, \rightarrow)$
q_1	$\triangleright$	$(q_1, \rightarrow)$

(a) Trace the computation of M starting from the configuration $(q_0, \triangleright\underline{a}abbba)$.

(b) Describe informally what M does when started in q_0 on any square of a tape.

4.1.2. Repeat Problem 4.1.1 for the machine $M = (K, \Sigma, \delta, s, \{h\})$, where

$$K = \{q_0, q_1, q_2, h\},$$
$$\Sigma = \{a, b, \sqcup, \triangleright\},$$
$$s = q_0,$$

and δ is given by the following table (the transitions on $\triangleright$ are $\delta(q, \triangleright) = (q, \triangleright)$, and are omitted).

$q,$	σ	$\delta(q, \sigma)$
q_0	a	$(q_1, \leftarrow)$
q_0	b	$(q_0, \rightarrow)$
q_0	$\sqcup$	$(q_0, \rightarrow)$
q_1	a	$(q_1, \leftarrow)$
q_1	b	$(q_2, \rightarrow)$
q_1	$\sqcup$	$(q_1, \leftarrow)$
q_2	a	$(q_2, \rightarrow)$
q_2	b	$(q_2, \rightarrow)$
q_2	$\sqcup$	$(h, \sqcup)$

Start from the configuration $(q_0, \triangleright a\underline{b}b \sqcup bb \sqcup \sqcup \sqcup aba)$.

4.1.3. Repeat Problem 4.1.1 for the machine $M = (K, \Sigma, \delta, s, \{h\})$, where

$$K = \{q_0, q_1, q_2, q_3, q_4, h\},$$
$$\Sigma = \{a, b, \sqcup, \triangleright\},$$
$$s = q_0,$$

and δ is given by the following table.

$q,$	σ	$\delta(q, \sigma)$
q_0	a	$(q_2, \rightarrow)$
q_0	b	(q_3, a)
q_0	$\sqcup$	$(h, \sqcup)$
q_0	$\triangleright$	$(q_0, \rightarrow)$
q_1	a	$(q_2, \rightarrow)$
q_1	b	$(q_2, \rightarrow)$
q_1	$\sqcup$	$(q_2, \rightarrow)$
q_1	$\triangleright$	$(q_1, \rightarrow)$
q_2	a	(q_1, b)
q_2	b	(q_3, a)
q_2	$\sqcup$	$(h, \sqcup)$
q_2	$\triangleright$	$(q_2, \rightarrow)$
q_3	a	$(q_4, \rightarrow)$
q_3	b	$(q_4, \rightarrow)$
q_3	$\sqcup$	$(q_4, \rightarrow)$
q_3	$\triangleright$	$(q_3, \rightarrow)$
q_4	a	$(q_2, \rightarrow)$
q_4	b	$(q_4, \rightarrow)$
q_4	$\sqcup$	$(h, \sqcup)$
q_4	$\triangleright$	$(q_4, \rightarrow)$

Start from the configuration $(q_0, \triangleright \underline{a}aabbbaa)$.

4.1.4. Let M be the Turing machine $(K, \Sigma, \delta, s, \{h\})$, where

$$K = \{q_0, q_1, q_2, h\},$$
$$\Sigma = \{a, \sqcup, \triangleright\},$$
$$s = q_0,$$

and δ is given by the following table.

Let $n \geq 0$. Describe carefully what M does when started in the configuration $(q_0, \triangleright \sqcup a^n \underline{a})$.

$q,\ \sigma$		$\delta(q,\sigma)$
q_0	a	$(q_1,\leftarrow)$
q_0	⊔	$(q_0,\text{⊔})$
q_0	▷	$(q_0,\rightarrow)$
q_1	a	$(q_2,\text{⊔})$
q_1	⊔	$(h,\text{⊔})$
q_1	▷	$(q_1,\rightarrow)$
q_2	a	(q_2,a)
q_2	⊔	$(q_0,\leftarrow)$
q_2	▷	$(q_2,\rightarrow)$

4.1.5. In the definition of a Turing machine, we allow rewriting a tape square without moving the head and moving the head left or right without rewriting the tape square. What would happen if we also allowed to leave the head stationary without rewriting the tape square?

4.1.6. (a) Which of the following could be configurations?
  (i) $(q,\triangleright a\ \text{⊔}\ a\text{⊔},\text{⊔},\text{⊔}a)$
  (ii) (q,abc,b,abc)
  (iii) $(p,\triangleright abc,a,e)$
  (iv) $(h,\triangleright,e,e)$
  (v) $(q,\triangleright a\ \text{⊔}\ ab,b,\text{⊔}aa\text{⊔})$
  (vi) $(p,\triangleright a,ab,\text{⊔}a)$
  (vii) $(q,\triangleright,e,\text{⊔}aa)$
  (viii) $(h,\triangleright a,a,\text{⊔}\ \text{⊔}\ \text{⊔}\ \text{⊔}\ \text{⊔}\ \text{⊔}\ a)$
(b) Rewrite those of Parts (i) through (viii) that are configurations using the abbreviated notation.
(c) Rewrite these abbreviated configurations in full.
  (i) $(q,\triangleright a\underline{b}cd)$
  (ii) $(q,\triangleright\underline{a})$
  (iii) $(p,\triangleright aa\ \text{⊔}\ \underline{\text{⊔}})$
  (iv) $(h,\triangleright\underline{\text{⊔}}abc)$

4.1.7. Design and write out in full a Turing machine that scans to the right until it finds two consecutive a's and then halts. The alphabet of the Turing machine should be $\{a,b,\text{⊔},\triangleright\}$.

4.1.8. Give the full details of the Turing machines illustrated.

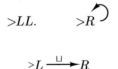

4.1.9. Do the machines LR and RL always accomplish the same thing? Explain.

4.1.10. Explain what this machine does.

$$>R \xrightarrow{a \neq \sqcup} R \xrightarrow{b \neq \sqcup} R_\sqcup a R_\sqcup b$$

4.1.11. Trace the operation of the Turing machine of Example 4.1.8 when started on $\triangleright \sqcup aabb$.

4.1.12. Trace the operation of the Turing machine of Example 4.1.9 on $\triangleright \sqcup aabb\sqcup$.

4.2 | COMPUTING WITH TURING MACHINES

We introduced Turing machines with the promise that they outperform, as language acceptors, all other kinds of automata we introduced in previous chapters. So far, however, we have presented only the "mechanics" of Turing machines, without any indication of how they are to be used in order to perform computational tasks —to recognize languages, for example. It is as though a computer had been delivered to you without a keyboard, disk drive, or screen —that is, without the means for getting information into and out of it. It is time, therefore, to fix some conventions for the use of Turing machines.

First, we adopt the following policy for presenting input to Turing machines: The input string, with no blank symbols in it, is written to the right of the leftmost symbol $\triangleright$, with a blank to its left, and blanks to its right; the head is positioned at the tape square containing the blank between the $\triangleright$ and the input; and the machine starts operating in its initial state. If $M = (K, \Sigma, \delta, s)$ is a Turing machine and $w \in (\Sigma - \{\sqcup, \triangleright\})^*$, then **the initial configuration of M on input** w is $(s, \triangleright\sqcup w)$. With this convention, we can now define how Turing machines are used as language recognizers.

Definition 4.2.1: Let $M = (K, \Sigma, \delta, s, H)$ be a Turing machine, such that $H = \{y, n\}$ consists of two distinguished halting states (y and n for "yes" and "no"). Any halting configuration whose state component is y is called an **accepting configuration**, while a halting configuration whose state component is n is called a **rejecting configuration**. We say that M **accepts** an input $w \in (\Sigma - \{\sqcup, \triangleright\})^*$ if $(s, \triangleright\sqcup w)$ yields an accepting configuration; we say that M **rejects** w if $(s, \triangleright\sqcup w)$ yields a rejecting configuration.

Let $\Sigma_0 \subseteq \Sigma - \{\sqcup, \triangleright\}$ be an alphabet, called the **input alphabet** of M; by fixing Σ_0 to be a subset of $\Sigma - \{\sqcup, \triangleright\}$, we allow our Turing machines to use extra symbols during their computation, besides those appearing in their inputs. We say that M **decides** a language $L \subseteq \Sigma_0^*$ if for any string $w \in \Sigma_0^*$ the following is true: If $w \in L$ then M accepts w; and if $w \notin L$ then M rejects w.

Finally, call a language L **recursive** if there is a Turing machine that decides it.

That is, a Turing machine decides a language L if, when started with input w, it always halts, and does so in a halt state that is the correct response to the input: y if $w \in L$, n if $w \notin L$. Notice that no guarantees are given about what happens if the input to the machine contains blanks or the left end symbol.

Example 4.2.1: Consider the language $L = \{a^n b^n c^n : n \geq 0\}$, which has heretofore evaded all types of language recognizers. The Turing machine whose diagram is shown in Figure 4-11 decides L. In this diagram we have also utilized two new basic machines, useful for deciding languages: Machine y makes the new state to be the accepting state y, while machine n moves the state to n.

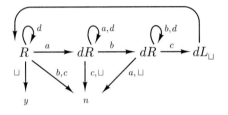

Figure 4-11

The strategy employed by M is simple: On input $a^n b^n c^n$ it will operate in n *stages*. In each stage M starts from the left end of the string and moves to the right in search of an a. When it finds an a, it replaces it by a d and then looks further to the right for a b. When a b is found, it is replaced by a d, and the machine then looks for a c. When a c is found and is replaced by a d, then the stage is over, and the head returns to the left end of the input. Then the next stage begins. That is, at each stage the machine replaces an a, a b, and a c by d's. If at any point the machine senses that the string is not in $a^* b^* c^*$, or that there is an excess of a certain symbol (for example, if it sees a b or c while looking for an a), then it enters state n and rejects immediately. If however it encounters the right end of the input while looking for an a, this means that all the input has been replaced by d's, and hence it was indeed of the form $a^n b^n c^n$, for some $n \geq 0$. The machine then accepts.$\Diamond$

There is a subtle point in relation to Turing machines that decide languages: With the other language recognizers that we have seen so far in this book (even the nondeterministic ones), one of two things could happen: either the machine accepts the input, or it rejects it. A Turing machine, on the other hand, even if it has only two halt states y and n, always has the option of evading an answer ("yes" or "no"), *by failing to halt*. Given a Turing machine, it might or it might not decide a language —and there is no obvious way to tell whether it does. The far-reaching importance —and *necessity*— of this deficiency will become apparent later in this chapter, and in the next.

Recursive Functions

Since Turing machines can write on their tapes, they can provide more elaborate output than just a "yes" or a "no:"

Definition 4.2.2: Let $M = (K, \Sigma, \delta, s, \{h\})$ be a Turing machine, let $\Sigma_0 \subseteq \Sigma - \{\sqcup, \triangleright\}$ be an alphabet, and let $w \in \Sigma_0^*$. Suppose that M halts on input w, and that $(s, \triangleright\sqcup w) \vdash_M^* (h, \triangleright\sqcup y)$ for some $y \in \Sigma_0^*$. Then y is called the **output of M on input** w, and is denoted $M(w)$. Notice that $M(w)$ is defined *only if* M halts on input w, and in fact does so at a configuration of the form $(h, \triangleright\sqcup y)$ with $y \in \Sigma_0^*$.

Now let f be any function from Σ_0^* to Σ_0^*. We say that M **computes** function f if, for all $w \in \Sigma_0^*$, $M(w) = f(w)$. That is, for all $w \in \Sigma_0^*$ M eventually halts on input w, and when it does halt, its tape contains the string $\triangleright \sqcup f(w)$. A function f is called **recursive**, if there is a Turing machine M that computes f.

Example 4.2.2: The function $\kappa : \Sigma^* \mapsto \Sigma^*$ defined as $\kappa(w) = ww$ can be computed by the machine $CS_{\leftarrow}$, that is, the copying machine followed by the left-shifting machine (both were defined towards the end of the last section).$\Diamond$

Strings in $\{0, 1\}^*$ can be used to represent the nonnegative integers in the familiar *binary notation*. Any string $w = a_1 a_2 \ldots a_n \in \{0, 1\}^*$ represents the number

$$\mathsf{num}(w) = a_1 \cdot 2^{n-1} + a_2 \cdot 2^{n-2} + \ldots + a_n.$$

And any natural number can be represented in a unique way by a string in $0 \cup 1(0 \cup 1)^*$ —that is to say, without redundant 0's in the beginning.

Accordingly, Turing machines computing functions from $\{0, 1\}^*$ to $\{0, 1\}^*$ can be thought of as computing functions from the natural numbers to the natural numbers. In fact, numerical functions with many arguments —such as addition and multiplication— can be computed by Turing machines computing functions from $\{0, 1, ; \}^*$ to $\{0, 1\}^*$, where ";" is a symbol used to separate binary arguments.

Definition 4.2.3: Let $M = (K, \Sigma, \delta, s, \{h\})$ be a Turing machine such that $0, 1, ; \in \Sigma$, and let f be any function from $\mathbf{N}^k$ to $\mathbf{N}$ for some $k \geq 1$. We say that M **computes** function f if for all $w_1, \ldots, w_k \in 0 \cup 1\{0,1\}^*$ (that is, for any k strings that are binary encodings of integers), $\mathsf{num}(M(w_1; \ldots; w_k)) = f(\mathsf{num}(w_1), \ldots, \mathsf{num}(w_k))$. That is, if M is started with the binary representations of the integers $n_1, \ldots, n_k$ as input, then it eventually halts, and when it does halt, its tape contains a string that represents number $f(n_1, \ldots, n_k)$ —the value of the function. A function $f : \mathbf{N}^k \mapsto \mathbf{N}$ is called **recursive** if there is a Turing machine M that computes f.

In fact, the term *recursive* used to describe both functions and languages computed by Turing machines originates in the study of such numerical functions. It anticipates a result we shall prove towards the end of this chapter, namely that the numerical functions computable by Turing machines coincide with those that can be defined *recursively* from certain basic functions.

Example 4.2.3: We can design a machine that computes the *successor* function $\mathsf{succ}(n) = n + 1$ (Figure 4.12; S_R is the *right-shifting machine*, the rightward analog of the machine in Example 4.1.9). This machine first finds the right end of the input, and then goes to the left as long as it sees 1's, changing all of them to 0's. When it sees a 0, it changes it into a 1 and halts. If it sees a ⊔ while looking for a 0, this means that the input number has a binary representation that is all 1's (it is a power of two minus one), and so the machine again writes a 1 in the place of the ⊔ and halts, after shifting the whole string one position to the right. Strictly speaking, the machine shown does not compute $n + 1$ because it fails to always halt with its head to the right of the result; but this can be fixed by adding a copy of $R_\sqcup$ (Figure 4-5).◇

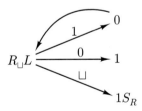

Figure 4-12

The last remark of the previous subsection, on our inability to tell whether a Turing machine decides a language, also applies to function computation. The price we must pay for the very broad range of functions that Turing machines can compute, is that we cannot tell whether a given Turing machine indeed computes such a function —that is to say, whether it halts on all inputs.

Recursively Enumerable Languages

If a Turing machine decides a language or computes a function, it can be reasonably thought of as an *algorithm* that performs correctly and reliably some computational task. We next introduce a third, subtler, way in which a Turing machine can define a language:

Definition 4.2.4: Let $M = (K, \Sigma, \delta, s, H)$ be a Turing machine, let $\Sigma_0 \subseteq \Sigma - \{\sqcup, \triangleright\}$ be an alphabet, and let $L \subseteq \Sigma_0^*$ be a language. We say that M **semidecides** L if for any string $w \in \Sigma_0^*$ the following is true: $w \in L$ if and only if M halts on input w. A language L is **recursively enumerable** if and only if there is a Turing machine M that semidecides L.

Thus when M is presented with input $w \in L$, it is required to halt eventually. We do not care precisely which halting configuration it reaches, as long as it does eventually arrive at a halting configuration. If however $w \in \Sigma_0^* - L$, then M must never enter the halting state. Since any configuration that is not halting yields some other configuration (δ is a fully defined function), the machine must in this case continue its computation indefinitely.

Extending the "functional" notation of Turing machines that we introduced in the previous subsection (which allows us to write equations such as $M(w) = v$), we shall write $M(w) = \nearrow$ if M fails to halt on input w. In this notation, we can restate the definition of semidecision of a language $L \subseteq \Sigma_0^*$ by Turing machine M as follows: For all $w \in \Sigma_0^*$, $M(w) = \nearrow$ if and only if $w \notin L$.

Example 4.2.4: Let $L = \{w \in \{a, b\}^* : w$ contains at least one $a\}$. Then L is semidecided by the Turing machine shown in Figure 4-13.

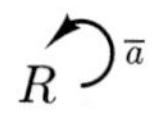

$$R \,\circlearrowright^{\bar{a}}$$

Figure 4-13

This machine, when started in configuration $(q0, \triangleright \sqcup w)$ for some $w \in \{a, b\}^*$, simply scans right until an a is encountered and then halts. If no a is found, the machine goes on forever into the blanks that follow its input, never halting. So L is exactly the set of strings w in $\{a, b\}^*$ such that M halts on input w. Therefore M semidecides L, and thus L is recursively enumerable.◊

"Going on forever into the blanks" is only one of the ways in which a Turing machine may fail to halt. For example, any machine with $\delta(q, a) = (q, a)$ will "loop forever" in place if it ever encounters an a in state q. Naturally, more complex looping behaviors can be designed, with the machine going indefinitely through a finite number of different configurations.

The definition of semidecision by Turing machines is a rather straightforward extension of the notion of acceptance for the deterministic finite automaton. There is a major difference, however. A finite automaton *always halts* when it has read all of its input —the question is whether it halts on a final or a nonfinal state. In this sense it is a useful computational device, an *algorithm* from which we can reliably obtain answers as to whether an input belongs in the accepted language: We wait until all of the input has been read, and we then observe the state of the machine. In contrast, a Turing machine that semidecides a language L cannot be usefully employed for telling whether a string w is in L, because, if $w \notin L$, then *we will never know when we have waited enough for an answer*.[†] Turing machines that semidecide languages are no algorithms.

We know from Example 4.2.1 that $\{a^n b^n c^n : n \geq 0\}$ is a recursive language. But is it recursively enumerable? The answer is easy: *Any recursive language is also recursively enumerable.* All it takes in order to construct another Turing machine that semidecides, instead of decides, the language is to make the rejecting state n a nonhalting state, from which the machine is guaranteed to never halt. Specifically, given any Turing machine $M = (K, \Sigma, \delta, s, \{y, n\})$ that decides L, we can define a machine M' that semidecides L as follows: $M = (K, \Sigma, \delta', s, \{y\})$, where δ' is just δ augmented by the following transitions related to n —no longer a halting state: $\delta'(n, a) = (n, a)$ for all $a \in \Sigma$. It is clear that if M indeed decides L, then M' semidecides L, because M' accepts the same inputs as M; furthermore, if M rejects an input w, then M' does not halt on w (it "loops forever" in state n). In other words, for all inputs w, $M'(w) = \nearrow$ if and only if $M(w) = n$.

We have proved the following important result:

Theorem 4.2.1: *If a language is recursive, then it is recursively enumerable.*

Naturally, the interesting (and difficult) question is the opposite: Can we always transform every Turing machine that semidecides a language (with our one-sided definition of semidecision that makes it virtually useless as a computational device) into an actual *algorithm* for *deciding* the same language? We shall see in the next chapter that the answer here is negative: *There are recursively enumerable languages that are not recursive.*

An important property of the class of recursive languages is that it is closed under complement:

Theorem 4.2.2: *If L is a recursive language, then its complement $\overline{L}$ is also*

[†] We have already encountered the same difficulty with pushdown automata (recall Section 3.7). A pushdown automaton can in principle reject an input by manipulating forever its stack without reading any further input —in Section 3.7 we had to remove such behavior in order to obtain computationally useful pushdown automata for certain context-free languages.

recursive.

Proof: If L is decided by Turing machine $M = (K, \Sigma, \delta, s, \{y, n\})$, then L is decided by the Turing machine $M' = (K, \Sigma, \delta', s, \{y, n\})$ which is identical to M *except that it reverses the rôles of the two special halting states y and n.* That is, δ' is defined as follows:

$$\delta'(q, a) = \begin{cases} n & \text{if } \delta(q, a) = y, \\ y & \text{if } \delta(q, a) = n, \\ \delta(q, a) & \text{otherwise.} \end{cases}$$

It is clear that $M'(w) = y$ if and only if $M(w) = n$, and therefore M' decides $\overline{L}$. ∎

Is the class of recursively enumerable languages also closed under complement? Again, we shall see in the next chapter that *the answer is negative.*

Problems for Section 4.2

4.2.1. Give a Turing machine (in our abbreviated notation) that computes the following function from strings in $\{a, b\}^*$ to strings in $\{a, b\}^*$: $f(w) = ww^R$.

4.2.2. Present Turing machines that decide the following languages over $\{a, b\}$:
  (a) $\emptyset$
  (b) $\{e\}$
  (c) $\{a\}$
  (d) $\{a\}^*$

4.2.3. Give a Turing machine that semidecides the language $a^* b a^* b$.

4.2.4. (a) Give an example of a Turing machine with one halting state that does not compute a function from strings to strings.
  (b) Give an example of a Turing machine with two halting states, y and n, that does not decide a language.
  (c) Can you give an example of a Turing machine with one halting state that does not *semidecide* a language?

4.3 | EXTENSIONS OF THE TURING MACHINE

The examples of the previous section make it clear that Turing machines can perform fairly powerful computations, albeit slowly and clumsily. In order to better understand their surprising power, we shall consider the effect of extending the Turing machine model in various directions. We shall see that in each case the additional features do not add to the classes of computable functions or decidable languages: the "new, improved models" of the Turing machine can in each instance be *simulated* by the standard model. Such results increase our confidence that the Turing machine is indeed the ultimate computational device, the end of our progression to more and more powerful automata. A side benefit of these results is that we shall feel free subsequently to use the additional features when designing Turing machines to solve particular problems, secure in the knowledge that our dependency on such features can, if necessary, be eliminated.

Multiple Tapes

One can think of Turing machines that have several tapes (see Figure 4-14). Each tape is connected to the finite control by means of a read/write head (one on each tape). The machine can in one step read the symbols scanned by all its heads and then, depending on those symbols and its current state, rewrite some of those scanned squares and move some of the heads to the left or right, in addition to changing state. For any *fixed* integer $k \geq 1$, a *k-tape Turing machine* is a Turing machine equipped as above with k tapes and corresponding heads. Thus a "standard" Turing machine studied so far in this chapter is just a k-tape Turing machine, with $k = 1$.

Definition 4.3.1: Let $k \geq 1$ be an integer. A **k-tape Turing machine** is a quintuple $(K, \Sigma, \delta, s, H)$, where K, Σ, s, and H are as in the definition of the ordinary Turing machine, and δ, the **transition function**, is a function from $(K - H) \times \Sigma^k$ to $K \times (\Sigma \cup \{\leftarrow, \rightarrow\})^k$. That is, for each state q, and each k-tuple of tape symbols $(a_1, \ldots, a_k)$, $\delta(q, (a_1, \ldots, a_k)) = (p, (b_1, \ldots, b_k))$, where p is, as before, the new state, and b_j is, intuitively, the action taken by M at tape j. Naturally, we again insist that if $a_j = \triangleright$ for some $j \leq k$, then $b_j = \rightarrow$.

Computation takes place in all k tapes of a k-tape Turing machine. Accordingly, a *configuration* of such a machine must include information about all tapes:

Definition 4.3.2: Let $M = (K, \Sigma, \delta, s, H)$ be a k-tape Turing machine. A **configuration** of M is a member of

$$K \times (\triangleright\Sigma^* \times (\Sigma^*(\Sigma - \{\sqcup\}) \cup \{e\}))^k.$$

That is, a configuration identifies the state, the tape contents, and the head position in each of the k tapes.

If $(q, (w_1\underline{a_1}u_1, \ldots, w_k\underline{a_k}u_k))$ is a configuration of a k-tape Turing machine (where we have used the k-fold version of the abbreviated notation for configurations), and if $\delta(p, (a_1, \ldots, a_k)) = (b_1, \ldots, b_k)$, then in one move the machine

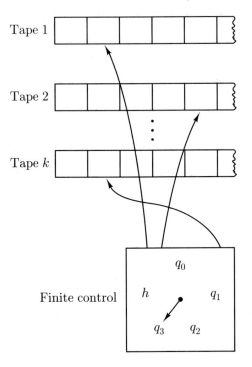

Figure 4-14

would move to configuration $(p, (w_1' a_1' u_1', \ldots, w_k' a_k' u_k'))$, where, for $i = 1, \ldots, k$, $w_i' a_i' u_i'$ is $w_i a_i u_i$ modified by action b_i, precisely as in Definition 4.1.3. We say that configuration $(q, (w_1 a_1 u_1, \ldots, w_k a_k u_k))$ *yields in one step* configuration $(p, (w_1' a_1' u_1', \ldots, w_k' a_k' u_k'))$.

Example 4.3.1: A k-tape Turing machine can be used for computing a function or deciding or semideciding a language in any of the ways discussed above for standard Turing machines. We adopt the convention that the input string is placed on the first tape, in the same way as it would be presented to a standard Turing machine. The other tapes are initially blank, with the head on the leftmost blank square of each. At the end of a computation, a k-tape Turing machine is to leave its output on its first tape; the contents of the other tapes are ignored.

Multiple tapes often facilitate the construction of a Turing machine to perform a particular function. Consider, for example, the task of the copying machine C given in Example 4.1.8: to transform $\triangleright \sqcup w\sqcup$ into $\triangleright \sqcup w \sqcup w\sqcup$, where $w \in \{a, b\}^*$. A 2-tape Turing machine can accomplish this as follows.

(1) Move the heads on both tapes to the right, copying each symbol on the first

tape onto the second tape, until a blank is found on the first tape. The first square of the second tape should be left blank.

(2) Move the head on the second tape to the left until a blank is found.

(3) Again move the heads on both tapes to the right, this time copying symbols from the second tape onto the first tape. Halt when a blank is found on the second tape.

This sequence of actions can be pictured as follows.

At the beginning: First tape   ▷⊔w
                   Second tape ▷⊔
After (1):   First tape   ▷ ⊔ w⊔
                   Second tape ▷ ⊔ w⊔
After (2):   First tape   ▷ ⊔ w⊔
                   Second tape ▷⊔w
After (3):   First tape   ▷ ⊔ w ⊔ w⊔
                   Second tape ▷ ⊔ w⊔

Turing machines with more than one tape can be depicted in the same way that single-tape Turing machines were depicted in earlier sections. We simply attach as a superscript to the symbol denoting each machine the number of the tape on which it is to operate; all other tapes are unaffected. For example, $\sqcup^2$ writes a blank on the second tape, $L^1_\sqcup$ searches to the left for a blank on the first tape, and $R^{1,2}$ moves to the right the heads of *both* the first and the second tape. A label a^1 on an arrow denotes an action taken if the symbol scanned in the first tape is an a. And so on. (When representing multi-tape Turing machines, we refrain from using the shorthand M^2 for MM.) Using this convention, the 2-tape version of the copying machine might be illustrated as in Figure 4-15. We indicate the submachines performing Functions 1 through 3 above.◊

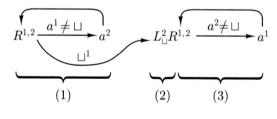

Figure 4-15

Example 4.3.2: We have seen (Example 4.2.3) that Turing machines can add 1 to any binary integer. It should come as no surprise that Turing machines can also *add arbitrary binary numbers* (recall Problem 2.4.3, suggesting that even finite automata, in a certain sense, can). With two tapes this task can be accomplished by the machine depicted in Figure 4-16. Pairs of bits such as 01 on an arrow label are a shorthand for, in this case, $a^1 = 0, a^2 = 1$.

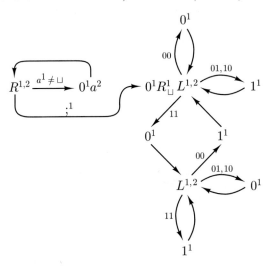

Figure 4-16

This machine first copies the first binary integer in its second tape, writing zeros in its place (and in the place of the ";" separating the two integers) in the first tape; this way the first tape contains the second integer, with zeros added in front. The machine then performs binary addition by the "school method," starting from the least significant bit of both integers, adding the corresponding bits, writing the result in the first tape, and "remembering the carry" in its state.◊

What is more, we can build a 3-tape Turing machine that *multiplies* two numbers; its design is left as an exercise (Problem 4.3.5).

Evidently, k-tape Turing machines are capable of quite complex computational tasks. We shall show next that any k-tape Turing machine can be *simulated* by a single-tape machine. By this we mean that, given any k-tape Turing machine, we can design a standard Turing machine that exhibits the same input-output behavior —decides or semidecides the same language, computes the same function. Such *simulations* are important ingredients of our methodology in studying the power of computational devices in this and the next chapters. Typically, they amount to a method for mimicking a single step of the simulated machine by several steps of the simulating machine. Our first result of this sort, and its proof, is quite indicative of this line of reasoning.

Theorem 4.3.1: *Let $M = (K, \Sigma, \delta, s, H)$ be a k-tape Turing machine for some $k \geq 1$. Then there is a standard Turing machine $M' = (K', \Sigma', \delta', s', H)$, where $\Sigma \subseteq \Sigma'$, and such that the following holds: For any input string $x \in \Sigma^*$, M on input x halts with output y on the first tape if and only if M' on input x halts at the same halting state, and with the same output y on its tape. Furthermore, if M halts on input x after t steps, then M' halts on input x after a number of steps which is $\mathcal{O}(t \cdot (|x| + t))$.*

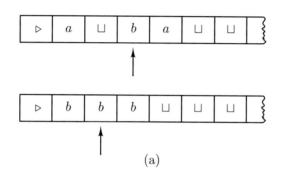

(a)

(b)

Figure 4-17

Proof: The tape of M' must somehow contain all information in all tapes of M. A simple way of achieving this is by thinking that the tape of M' is divided into several *tracks* (see Figure 4-18(b)), with each "track" devoted to the simulation of a different tape of M. In particular, except for the leftmost square, which contains as usual the left end symbol ▷, and the infinite blank portion of the tape to the right, the single tape of M' is split horizontally into $2k$ tracks. The first, third, ..., $(2k-1)$st tracks of the tape of M' correspond to the first, second, ..., kth tapes of M. The second, fourth, ..., $2k$th tracks of the tape of

M' are used to record the positions of the heads on the first, second, ..., kth tapes of M in the following way: If the head on the ith tape of M is positioned over the nth tape square, then the $2i$th track of the tape of M' contains a 1 in the $(n + 1)$st tape square and a 0 in all tape squares except the $(n + 1)$st. For example, if $k = 2$, then the tapes and heads of M shown in Figure 4-18(a) would correspond to the tape of M' shown in Figure 4-18(b).

Of course, the division of the tape of M' into tracks is a purely conceptual device; formally, the effect is achieved by letting

$$\Sigma' = \Sigma \cup (\Sigma \times \{0,1\})^k.$$

That is, the alphabet of M' consists of the alphabet of M (this enables M' to receive the same inputs as M and deliver the same output), plus all $2k$-tuples of the form $(a_1, b_1, \ldots, a_k, b_k)$ with $a_1, \ldots, a_k \in \Sigma$ and $b_1, \ldots, b_k \in \{0,1\}$. The translation from this alphabet to the $2k$-track interpretation is simple: We read any such $2k$-tuple as saying that the first track of M' contains a_1, the second b_1, and so on up to the $2k$th track containing b_k. This in turn means that the corresponding symbol of the ith tape of M contains a_i, and that this symbol is scanned by the ith head if and only if $b_i = 1$ (recall Figure 4-17(b)).

When given an input $w \in \Sigma^*$, M' operates as follows.

(1) Shift the input one tape square to the right. Return to the square immediately to the right of the $\triangleright$, and write the symbol $(\triangleright, 0, \triangleright, 0, \ldots, \triangleright, 0)$ on it —this will represent the left end of the k tapes. Go one square to the right and write the symbol $(\sqcup, 1, \sqcup, 1, \ldots, \sqcup, 1)$ —this signifies that the first squares of all k tapes contain a $\sqcup$, and are all scanned by the heads. Proceed to the right. At each square, if a symbol $a \neq \sqcup$ is encountered, write in its position the symbol $(a, 0, \sqcup, 0, \ldots, \sqcup, 0)$. If a $\sqcup$ is encountered, the first phase is over. The tape contents of M' faithfully represent the initial configuration of M.

(2) Simulate the computation by M, until M would halt (*if* it would halt). To simulate one step of the computation of M, M' will have to perform the following sequence operations (we assume that it starts each step simulation with its head scanning the first "true blank," that is, the first square of its tape that has not yet been subdivided into tracks):

   (a) Scan left down the tape, gathering information about the symbols scanned by the k tape heads of M. After all scanned symbols have been identified (by the 1's in the corresponding even tracks), return to the leftmost true blank. No writing on the tape occurs during this part of the operation of M', but when the head has returned to the right end, the state of the finite control has changed to reflect the k-tuple of symbols from Σ, in the k tracks at the marked head positions.

   (b) Scan left and then right down the tape to update the tracks in accordance with the move of M that is to be simulated. On each pair of tracks, this involves either moving the head position marker one square to the right or left, or rewriting the symbol from Σ.

(3) When M would halt, M' first converts its tape from tracks into single-symbol format, ignoring all tracks except for the first; it positions its head where M would have placed its first head, and finally it halts in the same state as M would have halted.

Many details have been omitted from this description. Phase 2, while by no means conceptually difficult, is rather messy to specify explicitly, and indeed there are several choices as to how the operations described might actually be carried out. One detail is perhaps worth describing. Occasionally, for some $n > |w|$, M may have to move one of its heads to the nth square of the corresponding tape *for the first time*. To simulate this, M' will have to extend the part of its tape that is divided into $2k$ tracks, and rewrite the first $\sqcup$ to the right as the $2k$-tuple $(\sqcup, 0, \sqcup, 0, \ldots, \sqcup, 0) \in \Sigma'$.

It is clear that M' can simulate the behavior of M as indicated in the statement of the theorem. It remains to argue that the number of steps required by M' for simulating t steps of M on input x is $\mathcal{O}(t \cdot (|x| + t))$. Phase 1 of the simulation requires $\mathcal{O}(|x|)$ steps of M'. Then, for each step of M, M' must carry out the maneuver in Phase 2, (a) and (b). This requires M' to scan the $2k$-track part of its tape twice; that is, it requires a number of steps by M' that is proportional to the length of the $2k$-track part of the tape of M'. The question is, how long can this part of M''s tape be? It starts by being $|x| + 2$ long, and subsequently it increases in length by no more than one for each simulated step of M. Thus, if t steps of M are simulated on input x, the length of the $2k$-track part of the tape of M' is at most $|x| + 2 + t$, and hence each step of M can be simulated by $\mathcal{O}(|x| + t)$ steps of M', as was to be shown. ∎

By using the conventions described for the input and output of a k-tape Turing machine, the following result is easily derived from the previous theorem.

Corollary: *Any function that is computed or language that is decided or semidecided by a k-tape Turing machine is also computed, decided, or semidecided, respectively, by a standard Turing machine.*

Two-way Infinite Tape

Suppose now that our machine has a tape that is infinite in both directions. All squares are initially blank, except for those containing the input; the head is initially to the left of the input, say. Also, our convention with the ▷ symbol would be unnecessary and meaningless for such machines.

It is not hard to see that, like multiple tapes, two-way infinite tapes do not add substantial power to Turing machines. A two-way infinite tape can be easily simulated by a 2-tape machine: one tape always contains the part of the tape to the right of the square containing the first input symbol, and the other contains the part of the tape to the left of this *in reverse*. In turn, this 2-tape machine can be simulated by a standard Turing machine. In fact, the simulation need only take *linear*, instead of quadratic, time, since at each step only one of the tracks is active. Needless to say, machines with *several* two-way infinite tapes could also simulated in the same way.

Multiple Heads

What if we allow a Turing machine to have one tape, but several heads on it? In one step, the heads all sense the scanned symbols and move or write independently. (Some convention must be adopted about what happens when two heads that happen to be scanning the same tape square attempt to write different symbols. Perhaps the head with the lower number wins out. Also, let us assume that the heads cannot sense each other's presence in the same tape square, except perhaps indirectly, through unsuccessful writes.)

It is not hard to see that a simulation like the one we used for k-tape machines can be carried out for Turing machines with several heads on a tape. The basic idea is again to divide the tape into tracks, all but one of which are used solely to record the head positions. To simulate one computational step by the multiple-head machine, the tape must be scanned twice: once to find the symbols at the head positions, and again to change those symbols or move the heads as appropriate. The number of steps needed is again *quadratic*, as in Theorem 4.3.1.

The use of multiple heads, like multiple tapes, can sometimes drastically simplify the construction of a Turing machine. A 2-head version of the copying machine C in Example 4.1.8 could function in a way that is much more natural than the one-head version (or even the two-tape version, Example 4.3.1); see Problem 4.3.3.

Two-Dimensional Tape

Another kind of generalization of the Turing machine would allow its "tape" to be an infinite two-dimensional grid. (One might even allow a space of higher dimension.) Such a device could be much more useful than standard Turing machines to solve problems such as "zigsaw puzzles" (see the *tiling* problem in the next chapter). We leave it as an exercise (Problem 4.3.6) to define in detail the operation of such machines. Once again, however, no fundamental increase in power results. Interestingly, the number of steps needed to simulate t steps of the two-dimensional Turing machine on input x by the ordinary Turing machine is again *polynomial* in t and $|x|$.

The above extensions on the Turing machine model can be *combined:* One can think of Turing machines with several tapes, all or some of which are two-way infinite and have more than one head on them, or are even multidimensional.

Again, it is quite straightforward to see that the ultimate capabilities of the Turing machine remain the same.

We summarize our discussion of the several variants of Turing machines discussed so far as follows.

Theorem 4.3.2: *Any language decided or semidecided, and any function computed by Turing machines with several tapes, heads, two-way infinite tapes, or multi-dimensional tapes, can be decided, semidecided, or computed, respectively, by a standard Turing machine.*

Problems for Section 4.3

4.3.1. Formally define:
   (a) M semidecides L, where M is a two-way infinite tape Turing machine;
   (b) M computes f, where M is a k-tape Turing machine and f is a function from strings to strings.

4.3.2. Formally define:
   (a) a k-head Turing machine (with a single one-way infinite tape);
   (b) a configuration of such a machine;
   (c) the yields in one step relation between configurations of such a machine. (There is more than one correct set of definitions.)

4.3.3. Describe (in an extension of our notation for k-tape Turing machines) a 2-head Turing machine that compute the function $f(w) = ww$.

4.3.4. The stack of a pushdown automaton can be considered as a tape that can be written and erased only at the right end; in this sense a Turing machine is a generalization of the deterministic pushdown automaton. In this problem we consider a generalization in another direction, namely the *deterministic pushdown automaton with two stacks*.
   (a) Define informally but carefully the operation of such a machine. Define what it means for such a machine to decide a language.
   (b) Show that the class of languages decided by such machines is precisely the class of recursive languages.

4.3.5. Give a three-tape Turing machine which, when started with two binary integers separated by a ';' on its first tape, computes their product. (*Hint:* Use the adding machine of Example 4.3.2 as a "subroutine."

4.3.6. Formally define a Turing machine with a 2-dimensional tape, its configurations, and its computation. Define what it means for such a machine to decide a language L. Show that t steps of this machine, starting on an input of length n, can be simulated by a standard Turing machine in time that is *polynomial* in t and n.

4.4 │ RANDOM ACCESS TURING MACHINES

Despite the apparent power and versatility of the variants of the Turing machines we have discussed so far, they all have a quite limiting common feature: Their memory is *sequential;* that is, in order to access the information stored at some location, the machine must first access, one by one, all locations between the current and the desired one. In contrast, real computers have *random access memories*, each element of which can be accessed in a single step, if appropriately addressed. What would happen if we equipped our machines with such a random access capability, enabling them to access any desired tape square in a single step? To attain such a capability, we must also equip our machines with *registers*, capable of storing and manipulating the *addresses* of tape squares. In this subsection we define such an extension of the Turing machine; significantly, we see that it too is equivalent in power to the standard Turing machine, with only a polynomial loss in efficiency.

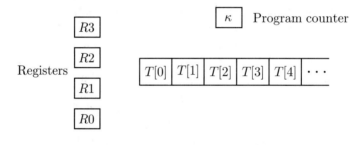

Figure 4-18

A *random access Turing machine* has a fixed number of *registers* and a one-way infinite tape (see Figure 4-18; we continue to call the machine's memory a "tape" for compatibility and comparison with the standard model, despite the fact that, as we shall see, it behaves much more like a random access memory chip). Each register and each tape square is capable of containing an arbitrary natural number. The machine acts on its tape squares and its registers as dictated by a fixed *program* —the analog of the transition function of ordinary Turing machines. The program of a random access Turing machine is a sequence of *instructions*, of a kind reminiscent of the instruction set of actual computers. The kinds of instructions allowed are enumerated in Figure 4-19.

Initially the register values are 0, the program counter is 1, and the tape contents encode the input string in a simple manner that will be specified shortly. Then the machine executes the first instruction of its program. This will change the contents of the registers or of the tape contents as indicated in Figure 4-19;

Instruction	Operand	Semantics
read	j	$R_0 := T[R_j]$
write	j	$T[R_j] := R_0$
store	j	$R_j := R_0$
load	j	$R_0 := R_j$
load	$= c$	$R_0 := c$
add	j	$R_0 := R_0 + R_j$
add	$= c$	$R_0 := R_0 + c$
sub	j	$R_0 := \max\{R_0 - R_j, 0\}$
sub	$= c$	$R_0 := \max\{R_0 - c, 0\}$
half		$R_0 := \lfloor \frac{R_0}{2} \rfloor$
jump	s	$\kappa := s$
jpos	s	if $R_0 > 0$ then $\kappa := s$
jzero	s	if $R_0 = 0$ then $\kappa := s$
halt		$\kappa := 0$

Notes: j stands for a register number, $0 \leq j < k$. $T[i]$ denotes the current contents of tape square i. R_j denotes the current contents of Register j. $s \leq p$ denotes any instruction number in the program. c is any natural number. All instructions change κ to $\kappa + 1$, unless explicitly stated otherwise.

Figure 4-19

also, the value of the *program counter* κ, an integer identifying the instruction to be executed next, will be computed as indicated in the figure. Notice the special role of Register 0: it is the *accumulator*, where all arithmetic and logical computation takes place. The κth instruction of the program will be executed next, and so on, until a halt instruction is executed —at this point the operation of the random access Turing machine ends.

We are now ready to define formally a random access Turing machine, its configurations, and its computation.

Definition 4.4.1: A random access Turing machine is a pair $M = (k, \Pi)$, where $k > 0$ is the number of **registers**, and $\Pi = (\pi_1, \pi_2, \ldots, \pi_p)$, the **program**, is a finite sequence of **instructions**, where each instruction π_i is of one of the types shown in Figure 4-19. We assume that the last instruction, π_p, is always a halt instruction (the program may contain other halt instructions as well).

A **configuration** of a random access Turing machine (k, Π) is a $k+2$-tuple $(\kappa, R_0, R_1, \ldots, R_{k-1}, T)$, where

$\kappa \in \mathbf{N}$ is the **program counter**, an integer between 0 and p. The configuration is a **halted configuration** if κ is zero.

For each j, $0 \leq j < k$, $R_j \in \mathbf{N}$ is the **current value of Register** j.

T, the **tape contents**, is a finite set of pairs of positive integers —that is, a finite subset of $(\mathbf{N} - \{0\}) \times (\mathbf{N} - \{0\})$— such that for all $i \geq 1$ there is at most one pair of the form $(i, m) \in T$.

Intuitively, $(i, m) \in T$ means that the ith tape square currently contains the integer $m > 0$. All tape squares not appearing as first components of a pair in T are assumed to contain 0.

Definition 4.4.1 (continued): Let $M = (k, \Pi)$ be a random access machine. We say that configuration $C = (\kappa, R_0, R_1, \ldots, R_{k-1}, T)$ of M **yields in one step** configuration $C' = (\kappa', R_0', R_1', \ldots, R_{k-1}', T')$, denoted $C \vdash_M C'$, if, intuitively, the values of κ', the R_j''s and T' correctly reflect the application to κ, the R_j's, and T of the "semantics" (as in Figure 4-19) of the current instruction π_κ. We shall indicate the precise definition for a only a few of the fourteen kinds of instructions in Figure 4-19.

If π_κ is of the form read j, where $j < k$, then the execution of this instruction has the following effect: The value contained in Register 0 becomes equal to the value stored in tape square number R_j —the tape square "addressed" by Register j. That is, $R_0' = T[R_j]$, where $T[R_j]$ is the unique value m such that $(R_j, m) \in T$, if such an m exists, and 0 otherwise. Also, $\kappa' = \kappa + 1$. All other components of the configuration C' are identical to those of C.

If π_κ is of the form add $= c$, where $c \geq 0$ is a fixed integer such as 5, then we have $R_0' = R_0 + c$, and $\kappa' = \kappa + 1$, with all other components remaining the same.

If π_κ is of the form write j, where $j < k$, then we have $\kappa' = \kappa + 1$, T' is T with any pair of the form (R_j, m), if one exists, deleted, and, if $R_0 > 0$, the pair (R_j, R_0) added; all other components remain the same.

If π_κ is of the form jpos s, where $1 \leq s \leq p$, then we have $\kappa' = s$ if $R_0 > 0$, and $\kappa' = c + 1$ otherwise; all other components remain the same.

Similarly for the other kinds of instructions. The relation **yields**, $\vdash_M^*$, is the reflexive transitive closure of $\vdash_M$.

Example 4.4.1: The instruction set of our random access Turing machine (recall Figure 4-19) has no *multiplication* instruction mply. As it happens, if we allowed this instruction as a primitive, our random access Turing machine, although still equivalent to the standard Turing machine, would be much more time-consuming to simulate (see Problem 4.4.4).

The omission of the multiplication instruction is no great loss, however, because this instruction can be emulated by the program shown in Figure 4-20. If[†] Register 0 initially contains a natural number x and Register 1 initially

---

[†] The computation of a random access Turing machine starts with all registers 0.

contains y, then this random access Turing machine will halt, and Register 0 will contain the product $x \cdot y$. Multiplication is done by successive additions, where the instruction half is used to reveal the binary representation of y (actually, our instruction set contains this unusual instruction precisely for this use).

1.	store 2
2.	load 1
3.	jzero 19
4.	half
5.	store 3
6.	load 1
7.	sub 3
8.	sub 3
9.	jzero 13
10.	load 4
11.	add 2
12.	store 4
13.	load 2
14.	add 2
15.	store 2
16.	load 3
17.	store 1
19.	load 4
18.	jump 2
19.	load 4
20.	halt

Figure 4-20

Here is a typical sequence of configurations (since this machine does not interact with tape squares, the T part of these configurations is empty; there are $k = 5$ registers):

$(1; 5, 3, 0, 0, 0; \emptyset) \vdash (2; 5, 3, 5, 0, 0; \emptyset) \vdash (3; 3, 3, 5, 0, 0; \emptyset) \vdash (4; 3, 3, 5, 0, 0; \emptyset) \vdash$
$(5; 1, 3, 5, 0, 0; \emptyset) \vdash (6; 1, 3, 5, 1, 0; \emptyset) \vdash (7; 3, 3, 5, 1, 0; \emptyset) \vdash (8; 2, 3, 5, 1, 0; \emptyset) \vdash$
$(9; 1, 3, 5, 1, 0; \emptyset) \vdash (10; 1, 3, 5, 1, 0; \emptyset) \vdash (11; 0, 3, 5, 1, 0; \emptyset) \vdash$
$(12; 5, 3, 5, 1, 0; \emptyset) \vdash (13; 5, 3, 5, 1, 5; \emptyset) \vdash (14; 5, 3, 5, 1, 5; \emptyset) \vdash$
$(15; 10, 3, 5, 1, 5; \emptyset) \vdash (16; 10, 3, 10, 1, 5; \emptyset) \vdash (17; 1, 3, 10, 1, 5; \emptyset) \vdash$
$(18; 1, 1, 10, 1, 5; \emptyset) \vdash (2; 1, 1, 10, 1, 5; \emptyset) \vdash^* (18; 0, 0, 20, 0, 15; \emptyset) \vdash$
$(2; 0, 0, 20, 0, 15; \emptyset) \vdash (3; 0, 0, 20, 0, 15; \emptyset) \vdash (19; 0, 0, 20, 0, 15; \emptyset) \vdash$
$(20; 15, 0, 20, 0, 15; \emptyset)]$

However, since the present program is intended to be used as a part of other random access Turing machines, it makes sense to explore what would happen if it were started at an arbitrary configuration.

Let x and y be the nonnegative integers stored in Registers 0 and 1, respectively, at the beginning of the execution of this program. We claim that the machine eventually halts with the product $x \cdot y$ stored in Register 0 —as if it had executed the instruction "mply 1." The program proceeds in several *iterations*. An iteration is an execution of the sequence of instructions π_2 through π_{18}. At the kth iteration, $k \geq 1$, the following conditions hold:

(a) Register 2 contains $x2^k$,
(b) Register 3 contains $\lfloor y/2^k \rfloor$,
(c) Register 1 contains $\lfloor y/2^{k-1} \rfloor$,
(d) Register 4 contains the "partial result" $x \cdot (y \bmod 2^k)$.

The iteration seeks to maintain these "invariants." So, instructions π_2 through π_5 enforce Invariant (b), assuming (c) held in the previous iteration. Instructions π_6 through π_8 compute the kth least significant bit of y, and, if this bit is *not* zero, instructions π_9 through π_{12} add $x2^{k-1}$ to Register 4, as mandated by Invariant (d). Then Register 2 is doubled by instructions π_{13} through π_{15}, enforcing Invariant (a), and finally Register 3 is transferred to Register 1, enforcing (c). The iteration is then repeated. If at some point it is seen that $\lfloor y/2^{k-1} \rfloor = 0$, then the process terminates, and the final result is loaded from Register 4 to the accumulator.

We can abbreviate this program as "mply 1," that is, an instruction with semantics $R_0 := R_0 \cdot R_1$. We shall therefore feel free to use the instruction "mply j" or "mply $= c$" in our programs, knowing that we can simulate them by the above program. Naturally, the instruction numbers would be different, reflecting the program of which this mply instruction is a part. If a random access Turing machine uses this instruction, then it is implicitly assumed that, in addition to its registers explicitly mentioned, it must have three more registers that play the role of Registers 2, 3, and 4 in the above program. ◇

In fact, we can avoid the cumbersome appearance of random access Turing machine programs such as the one in the previous example by adopting some useful abbreviations. For example, denoting the value stored in Register 1 by R_1, in Register 2 by R_2, and so on, we can write

$$R_1 := R_2 + R_1 - 1$$

as an abbreviation of the sequence

1.	load 1
2.	add 2
3.	sub =1
4.	store 1

Once we adopt this, we could use better-looking names for the quantities stored at Registers 1 and 2, and express this sequence of instructions simply as

$$x := y + x - 1.$$

Here x and y are just names for the contents of Registers 1 and 2. We can even use abbreviations like

while $x > 0$ do $x := x - 3,$

where x denotes the value of Register 1, instead of the sequence

1. load 1
2. jzero 6
3. sub =3
4. store 1
5. jump 1

Example 4.4.1 (continued): Here is a much more readable abbreviation of the mply program in Figure 4-20, where we are assuming that x and y are to be multiplied, and the result is w:

w := 0
while $y > 0$ do
    begin
    z := half(y)
    if $y - z - z \neq 0$ then $w := w + x$
    x := x + x
    y := z
    end
    halt

The correspondence between the form above and the original program in Figure 4-20 is this: y stands for R_1, x for R_2, z for R_3, and w for R_4. Notice that we have also omitted for clarity the explicit instruction numbers; if goto instructions were necessary, we could label instructions by symbolic instruction labels like a and b wherever necessary.

Naturally, it is quite mechanical from an abbreviated program such as the above to arrive to an equivalent full-fledged random access Turing machine program such as the original one.◇

Although we have explained the mechanics of random access Turing machines, we have not said how they receive their input and return their output. In order to facilitate comparisons with the standard Turing machine model, we shall assume that the input-output conventions of random access Turing machines are very much in the spirit of the input-output conventions for ordinary

$n := 1$
while $T[n \cdot n] \neq 0$ do $n := n + 1$
$n := n - 1$
$i := 0$
while $i < n$ do $i := i + 1, T[i \cdot n + i] := 2$
$i := j := k := 0$
while $j < n$ do $j := j + 1,$
   while $i < n$ do $i := i + 1,$
      while $k < n$ do $k := k + 1,$
         if $T[i \cdot n + j] = 2$ and $T[j \cdot n + k] = 2$ then $T[i \cdot n + k] := 2$
halt

agile model. How does its power compare to that of the standard Turing machine? It is very easy to see, and not at all surprising, that *the random access Turing machine is at least as powerful as the standard Turing machine.* Let $M = (K, \Sigma, \delta, s, H)$ be a Turing machine; we can design a random access Turing machine M' that simulates M. M' has a register, call it n, that keeps track of the head position of M on its tape. Initially n points to the beginning of the input. Each state $q \in K$ is simulated by a sequence of instructions in the program of M'. For example, suppose that $\Sigma = \{\sqcup, a, b\}$, $\mathbf{E}(a) = 1$, $\mathbf{E}(b) = 2$, and let q be a state of M such that $\delta(q, \sqcup) = (p, \rightarrow)$, $\delta(q, a) = (p, \leftarrow)$, $\delta(q, b) = (r, \sqcup)$, and $\delta(q, \triangleright) = (s, \rightarrow)$. The sequence of instructions simulating state q is this:

q: if $T[n] = 0$ then $n := n + 1$, goto p
      if $T[n] = 1$ then if $n > 0$ then $n := n - 1$, goto p
         else goto s
      if $T[n] = 2$ then $T[n] := 0$, goto r

The **else** clause in the third line (which should be present in any line simulating a $\leftarrow$ move) has the effect of the $\triangleright$ symbol, making sure that the head never falls off the left end of M''s tape. We have shown:

Theorem 4.4.1: *Any recursive or recursively enumerable language, and any recursive function, can be decided, semidecided, and computed, respectively, by a random access Turing machine.*

The remarkable direction is the opposite:

Theorem 4.4.2: *Any language decided or semidecided by a random access Turing machine, and any function computable by a random access Turing machine, can be decided, semidecided, and computed, respectively, by a standard Turing machine. Furthermore, if the machines halt on an input, then the number of steps taken by the standard Turing machine is bounded by a polynomial in the number of steps of the random access Turing machine on the same input.*

Proof: Let $M = (k, \Pi)$ be a random access Turing machine deciding or semideciding a language $L \subseteq \Sigma^*$ or computing a function from Σ^* to Σ^*. We will outline the design an ordinary Turing machine M' that simulates M. We shall describe M' as a $(k + 3)$-tape machine, where k is the number of registers of M, which simulates M; we know from Theorem 4.3.1 that such a machine can in turn be simulated by the basic model.

Turing machine M' keeps track of the current configuration of the random access Turing machine M, and repeatedly computes the next configuration. The first tape is used only for reading the input of M, and possibly for reporting the output at the end, in the case where M computes a function. The second tape is used for keeping track of the T part of the configuration —the tape contents of M. The relation T is maintained as a sequence of strings of the form $(111, 10)$, a left parenthesis followed by the binary representation of an integer, followed by a comma, followed by another binary integer, followed by a right parenthesis. The intended meaning of the above string is that the seventh tape square of M contains the integer 2. The pairs of integers in the sequence representing T are not in any particular order, and may be separated by arbitrarily long sequences of blanks (this necessitates an *endmarker,* such as \$, at the end of the representation of T, to help M' decide when it has seen all such pairs). Each of the next k tapes of M' maintain the contents of a register of M, also in binary. The current value of the program counter κ of M is maintained in the state of M' in a manner to be explained below.

The simulation has three phases. During the first phase, M' receives on its first tape the input $x = a_1 a_2 \ldots a_n \in \Sigma^*$, and converts it to the string $(1, \mathbf{E}(a_1)) \ldots (n, \mathbf{E}(a_n))$ on the second tape. Thus M' can start the second phase, the simulation of M, from the initial configuration of M on input x.

During the second phase M' repeatedly simulates a step of M by several steps of its own. The precise nature of the step to be simulated depends heavily on the program counter κ of M. As we said before, κ is maintained in the state of M'. That is, the set of states of M' that are used during this phase are separated into p disjoint sets $K_1 \cup K_1 \cup \cdots \cup K_p$, where p is the number of instructions in the program Π of M. The set of states K_j "specializes" in simulating the instruction π_j of Π. The precise nature of this part of M' depends of course on the kind of the instruction π_j. We shall give three indicative examples of how this is done.

Suppose first that π_j is **add** 4, requiring that the contents of Register 4 be added to those of Register 0. Then M' will perform binary addition (recall Example 4.3.2) between its two tapes representing Registers 4 and 0, will leave the result in the tape for Register 0, and then move to the first state of K_{j+1} to start the simulation of the next instruction. If the instruction is, say, **add** $= 33$, then M' will start by writing the integer 33 in binary on the $(k + 3)$rd tape (the one heretofore unassigned to parts of M); the binary representation of the fixed integer 33 is "remembered" by the states of K_j. Then it will add 33 to the contents of Register 0, and finally it will erase the last tape and will move to K_{j+1}.

Suppose next that π_j is write 2, requiring that the contents of the accumulator be copied to the tape square pointed at by Register 2. Then M' will add at the right end of the second tape —the one where the contents of the tape of M are kept in the (x, y) format— the pair (x, y), where x is the contents of Register 2 and y those of Register 0; both x and y are copied from the corresponding tapes of M'. M' will then scan all other pairs (x', y') on the second tape, comparing each x', bit by bit, with the contents of Register i. If a match is found, the pair is erased, thus maintaining the integrity of the table. Then the state moves to K_{j+1}, and the next instruction is executed.

Suppose now that π_j is jpos 19, requiring that instruction 19 be executed next if Register 0 contains a positive integer. Turing machine M' simply scans its tape representing Register 0; if a 1 is found in the binary representation of the integer in it, M moves to K_{19}; otherwise it moves to K_{j+1}.

It is straightforward to simulate, in a very similar manner, all other kinds of instructions in the table of Figure 4-19. Eventually, M may reach a halt instruction. If this happens, M' enters its third phase, translating M's output to the Turing machine output conventions. If M is deciding a language, then M' would read the contents of Register 0. If they are 1, it will halt at state y, if they are 0 it will halt at state n. If M is semideciding a language, then M' simply halts at state h. Finally, if M is computing a function, then M must translate the contents of the tape of M to a string in Σ^*, inverting the bijection $\mathbf{E}$, and then halt.

It is clear from the preceding discussion that a $k + 3$-tape Turing machine M' can be designed that performs the above tasks —and hence, by Theorem 4.3.1, a standard Turing machine can.

To prove the second part of the theorem, we shall establish that t steps of M on an input of size n can be simulated in $\mathcal{O}(t + n)^3$ time. Naturally, the constants in the $\mathcal{O}$ notation will, as usual, depend on the simulated machine M; for example they will depend on the largest constant (as in add $= 314159$) mentioned in the program of M.

The $\mathcal{O}(t + n)^3$ bound is based on the following three observations:

(a) At each step of M (including the addition and subtraction steps, see Problem 4.4.3) can be simulated in $\mathcal{O}(m)$ steps of M', where m is the total length of the nonblank parts of all tapes of M' —that is to say, the total length of the binary encodings of all integers in the current configuration of M.

(b) The parameter m defined above can at each step increase by at most $\mathcal{O}(r)$, where r is the length of the longest binary representation of any integer stored in the registers or tape squares of M. This is so because the increase comes either from an add instruction or from a store instruction, and in both cases it is trivial to see that the increase can only be linear in r.

(c) Finally, it is easy to see that $r = \mathcal{O}(t)$; that is, the length of the largest integer represented by M can only increase by a constant at each step. The claimed bound follows by putting these three facts together. ∎

Problems for Section 4.4

4.4.1. Give explicitly the full details of the random access Turing machine program of Example 4.4.2. Give the sequence of configurations of this machine on input *aabccc*.

4.4.2. Give (in our abbreviated notation) a random access Turing machine program that decides the language $\{wcw : w \in \{a, b\}^*\}$.

4.4.3. Show that, in the simulation in the proof of Theorem 4.4.2, each step can be simulated by $\mathcal{O}(m)$ steps of M', where m is the total length of M''s tapes. (You must establish that the 2-tape addition Turing machine in Example 4.3.2 operates in linear time.) Can you estimate the constant in $\mathcal{O}(m)$?

4.4.4. Suppose that our random access Turing machines had an explicit instruction mply. What goes wrong now in the second part of the proof of Theorem 4.4.2?

4.5 | NONDETERMINISTIC TURING MACHINES

We have added to our Turing machines many seemingly powerful features — multiple tapes and heads, even random access— with no appreciable increase in power. There is, however, an important and familiar feature that we have not tried yet: *nondeterminism*.

We have seen that when finite automata are allowed to act nondeterministically, no increase in computational power results (except that exponentially fewer states may be needed for the same task), but that nondeterministic pushdown automata are more powerful than deterministic ones. We can also imagine Turing machines that act nondeterministically: Such machines might have, on certain combinations of state and scanned symbol, more than one possible choice of behavior. Formally, a **nondeterministic Turing machine** is a quintuple $(K, \Sigma, \Delta, s, H)$, where K, Σ, s, and H are as for standard Turing machines, and Δ is a *subset* of $((K - H) \times \Sigma) \times (K \times (\Sigma \cup \{\leftarrow, \rightarrow\}))$, rather than a *function* from $(K - H) \times \Sigma$ to $K \times (\Sigma \cup \{\leftarrow, \rightarrow\})$. Configurations and the relations $\vdash_M$ and $\vdash_M^*$ are defined in the natural way. But now $\vdash_M$ need not be single-valued: One configuration may yield several others in one step.

When Turing machines are allowed to act nondeterministically, is there any increase in computational power? We must first define what it means for a nondeterministic Turing machine to compute something. Since a nondeterministic machine could produce two different outputs or final states from the same input, we have to be careful about what is considered to be the end result of a computation by such a machine. Because of this, it is easiest to consider at first nondeterministic Turing that *semidecide* languages.

Definition 4.5.1: Let $M = (K, \Sigma, \Delta, s, H)$ be a nondeterministic Turing machine. We say that M **accepts** an input $w \in (\Sigma - \{\triangleright, \sqcup\})^*$ if $(s, \triangleright\underline{\sqcup}w) \vdash^*_M (h, u\underline{a}w)$ for some $h \in H$ and $a \in \Sigma, u, w \in \Sigma^*$. Notice that a nondeterministic machine accepts an input even though it may have many nonhalting computations on this input input —as long as at least one halting computation exists. We say that M **semidecides a language** $L \subseteq (\Sigma - \{\triangleright, \sqcup\})^*$ if the following holds for all $w \in (\Sigma - \{\triangleright, \sqcup\})^*$: $w \in L$ if and only if M accepts w.

It is a little more subtle to define what it means for a nondeterministic Turing machine to decide a language, or to compute a function.

Definition 4.5.2: Let $M = (K, \Sigma, \Delta, s, \{y, n\})$ be a nondeterministic Turing machine. We say that M **decides** a language $L \subseteq (\Sigma - \{\triangleright, \sqcup\})^*$ if the following two conditions hold for all $w \in (\Sigma - \{\triangleright, \sqcup\})^*$:

(a) There is a natural number N, depending on M and w, such that there is no configuration C satisfying $(s, \triangleright\underline{\sqcup}w) \vdash^N_M C$.

(b) $w \in L$ if and only if $(s, \triangleright\underline{\sqcup}w) \vdash^*_M (y, u\underline{a}v)$ for some $u, v \in \Sigma^*, a \in \Sigma$.

Finally, we say that M **computes** a function $f : (\Sigma - \{\triangleright, \sqcup\})^* \mapsto (\Sigma - \{\triangleright, \sqcup\})^*$ if the following two conditions hold for all $w \in (\Sigma - \{\triangleright, \sqcup\})^*$:

(a) There is an N, depending on M and w, such that there is no configuration C satisfying $(s, \triangleright\underline{\sqcup}w) \vdash^N_M C$.

(b) $(s, \triangleright\underline{\sqcup}w) \vdash^*_M (h, u\underline{a}v)$ if and only if $ua = \triangleright\sqcup$, and $v = f(w)$.

These definitions reflect the difficulties associated with computing by nondeterministic Turing machines. First notice that, for a nondeterministic machine to decide a language and compute a function, we require that *all* of its computations halt; we achieve this by postulating that there is no computation continuing after N steps, where N is an "upper bound" depending on the machine and the input (this is condition (a) above). Second, for M to decide a language, we only require that *at least* one of its possible computations end up accepting the input. Some, most, or all of the remaining computations could end up rejecting —the machine accepts by the force of this single accepting computation. This is a very unusual, asymmetric, and counterintuitive convention. For example, to create a machine that decides the *complement* of the language, it is not enough to reverse the rôles of the y and n states (since the machine may have both accepting and rejecting computations for some inputs). As with nondeterministic finite automata, to show that the class of languages decided by nondeterministic Turing machines is closed under complement, we must go through an equivalent *deterministic* Turing machine —and our main result in this section (Theorem 4.5.1) states that an equivalent deterministic Turing machine must exist.

Finally, for a nondeterministic Turing machine to compute a *function*, we require that *all* possible computations agree on the outcome. If not, we would not be able to decide which one is the right value of the function (in the cases of deciding or semideciding a language, we resolve this uncertainty by postulating that the positive answer prevails).

Before showing that nondeterminism, like the features considered in the previous sections, can be eliminated from Turing machines, let us consider a classic example that demonstrates the power of nondeterminism in Turing machines as a conceptual device.

Example 4.5.1: A composite number is one that is the product of two natural numbers, each greater than one; for example, 4, 6, 8, 9, 10, and 12 are composite, but 1, 2, 3, 5, 7, and 11 are not. In other words, a composite number is a non-prime other than one or zero.

Let $C = \{100, 110, 1000, 1001, 1010, \ldots, 1011011, \ldots\}$ be the set of all binary representations of composite numbers. To design an "efficient" algorithm deciding C is an ancient, important, and difficult problem. To design such an algorithm it would seem necessary to come up with a clever way of discovering the *factors*, if any, of a number —a task that seems quite complex. Naturally, by searching exhaustively all numbers smaller than the given number (in fact, smaller than its *square root*) we would end up discovering its factors; the point is that *no more direct method is evident.*

However, if nondeterminism is available, we can design a machine to semidecide C rather simply, by guessing the factors, if there are any. This machine operates as follows, when given as input the binary representation of integer n:

(1) Nondeterministically choose two binary numbers p, q larger than one, bit by bit, and write their binary representation next to the input.

(2) Use the multiplication machine of Problem 4.3.5 (actually, the single-tape machine that simulates it) to replace the binary representations of p and q by that of their product.

(3) Check to see that the two integers, n and $p \cdot q$, are the same. This can be done easily by by comparing them bit by bit. Halt if the two integers are equal; otherwise continue forever in some fashion (recall that at present we are only interested in a machine that semidecides C).

This machine, on input 1000010 (the binary representation of 66) will have many rejecting (nonhalting) computations, corresponding to phase 1 above choosing pairs of binary integers, such as $101; 11101$, that *fail* to multiply to 66. The point is that, since 66 is a composite number, there will be *at least one* computation of M that will end up accepting —and that is all we need. In fact, there will be more than one (corresponding to $2 \cdot 33 = 6 \cdot 11 = 11 \cdot 6 = 33 \cdot 2 = 66$). If the input were 1000011, however, no computation would end up accepting —because 67 is a prime number.

This machine can be modified to a nondeterministic machine that *decides* the language C. The deciding machine has the same basic structure, except that in Phase (1) the new machine never guesses an integer with more bits than n itself —obviously, such an integer cannot be a factor of n. And in Phase 3, after comparing the input and the product, the new machine would halt at state y if they are equal, and at state n otherwise. As a result, *all computations will eventually halt* after some finite number of steps.

The upper bound N required by Definition 4.5.2 is now easy to compute explicitly. Suppose that the given integer n has ℓ bits. Let N_1 be the maximum number of steps in any computation by the multiplying machine on any input of length $2\ell+1$ or less; this is a finite number, the maximum of finitely many natural numbers. Let N_2 the number of steps it takes to compare two strings of length at most 3ℓ each. Then any computation by M' will halt after $N_1 + N_2 + 3\ell + 6$ steps, certainly a finite number depending only on the machine and the input.◊

Nondeterminism would seem to be a very powerful feature that cannot be eliminated easily. Indeed, there appears to be no easy way to simulate a nondeterministic Turing machine by a deterministic one in a step-by-step manner, as we have done in all other cases of enhanced Turing machines that we have examined so far. However, the languages semidecided or decided by nondeterministic Turing machines are in fact no different from those semidecided or decided, respectively, by deterministic Turing machines.

Theorem 4.5.1: *If a nondeterministic Turing machine M semidecides or decides a language, or computes a function, then there is a standard Turing machine M' semideciding or deciding the same language, or computing the same function.*

Proof: We shall describe the construction for the case in which M semidecides a language L; the constructions for the case of deciding a language or computing a function are very similar. So, let $M = (K, \Sigma, \Delta, s, H)$ be a nondeterministic Turing machine semideciding a language L. Given an input w, M' will attempt to run systematically through all possible computations by M, searching for one that halts. When and if it discovers a halting computation, it too will halt. So M' will halt if and only if M halts, as required.

But M may have an infinity of different computations starting from the same input; how can M explore them all? It does so by using a *dovetailing procedure* (recall the argument illustrated in Figure 1-8). The crucial observation is the following: Although for any configuration C of M there may be several configurations C' such that $C \vdash C'$, the *number* of such configurations C' is fixed and bounded in a way that depends only on M, not on C. Specifically, the number of quadruples $(q, a, p, b) \in \Delta$ that can be applicable at any point is finite; in fact, it cannot exceed $|K| \cdot (|\Sigma| + 2)$, since this is the maximum number of possible combinations (p, b) with $p \in K$ and $b \in \Sigma \cup \{\leftarrow, \rightarrow\}$. Let us call r the maximum number of quadruples that can be applicable at any point; the number r can be determined by inspection of M. In fact, we shall assume that for each state-symbol combination (q, a), and for each integer $i \in \{1, 2, \ldots, r\}$, there is a well-defined ith applicable quadruple (q, a, p_i, b_i). If for some state-symbol combination (q, a) there are fewer than r relevant quadruples in Δ, then some may be repeated.

Since M is nondeterministic, it has no definite way to decide at each step how to choose among its r available "choices." But suppose that *we help it decide*. To be precise, let M_d, the *deterministic version of M*, be a device with the same set of states as M, but with two tapes. The first tape is the tape of M, initially containing the input w, while the second tape initially contains a string of n integers in the range $1, \ldots, r$, say $i_1 i_2 \ldots i_n$. M_d then operates as follows for n steps: In the first step, among the r possible next state-action combinations $(p_1, b_1), \ldots, (p_r, b_r)$ that are applicable to the initial configuration, M_d chooses the i_1th —that is, (p_{i_1}, b_{i_1}), the one suggested by the currently scanned symbol in the second tape, i_1. M_d also moves its second tape head to the right, so that it next scans i_2. In the next step, M_d takes the i_2th combination, then the i_3th, and so on. When M_d sees a blank on its second tape, meaning that it has run out of "hints," it halts.

M_d is an important ingredient in our design of the deterministic Turing machine M' that simulates M. We shall describe M' as a 3-tape Turing machine; we know by Theorem 4.3.1 that M' can be converted into an equivalent single-tape Turing machine. The three tapes of M' are used as follows:

(1) The first tape is never changed; it always contains the original input w, so that each simulated computation of M can begin afresh with the same input.

(2) The second and the third tapes are used to simulate the computations of M_d, the deterministic version of M, with all strings in $\{1, 2, \ldots, r\}^*$. The input is copied from the first tape onto the second before M' begins to simulate each new computation. Initially, the third tape contains e, the empty string (and therefore the simulation of M_d will not even start the first time around).

(3) Between two simulations of M_d, M' uses a Turing machine N to generate the *lexicographically next* string in $\{1, 2, \ldots, r\}^*$. That is, N will generate from e the strings $1, 2, \ldots, r, 11, 12, \ldots, rr, 111, \ldots$. For $r = 2$, N is precisely the Turing machine that computes the binary successor function (Example 4.2.3); its generalization to $r > 2$ is rather straightforward.

M' is is the Turing machine given in Figure 4-22. By $C^{1 \to 2}$ we mean a simple Turing machine that erases the second tape and copies the first tape on the second. B^3 is the machine that generates the lexicographically next string in the third tape. Finally, $M_d^{2,3}$ is the deterministic version of M, operating on tapes 2 and 3. This completes the description of M'.

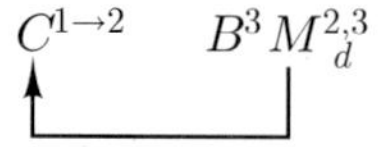

$$C^{1 \to 2} \qquad B^3 M_d^{2,3}$$

Figure 4-22

We claim that M' halts on an input w if and only if (some computation of) M does. Suppose that M' indeed halts on input w; by inspecting Figure 4-22, this means that M_d halts with its third tape head not scanning a blank. This implies that, for some string $i_1 i_2 \cdots i_n \in \{1, 2, \ldots, r\}^*$, M_d, when started with w on its first tape and $i_1 i_2 \cdots i_n$ on its second, halts before reaching the blank part of its second tape. This, however, means that there is a computation of M on input w that halts. Conversely, if there is a halting computation of M on input w, say with n steps, then M', after at most $r + r^2 + \cdots + r^n$ failed attempts, the string in $\{1, 2, \ldots, r\}^*$ corresponding to the choices of M's halting computation will be generated by B^3, and M_d will halt scanning the last symbol of this string. Thus M' will halt, and the proof is complete. ∎

As we had expected, the simulation of a nondeterministic Turing machine by a deterministic one is not a step-by-step simulation, as were all other simulations we have seen in this chapter. Instead, it goes through all possible computations of the nondeterministic Turing machine. As a result, it requires *exponentially many steps* in n to simulate a computation of n steps by the nondeterministic machine —whereas all other simulations described in this chapter are in fact *polynomial*. Whether this long and indirect simulation is an intrinsic feature of nondeterminism, or an artifact of our poor understanding of it, is a deep and important open question, explored in Chapters 6 and 7 of this book.

Problems for Section 4.5

4.5.1. Give (in abbreviated notation) nondeterministic Turing machines that accept these languages.

(a) $a^*abb^*baa^*$

(b) $\{ww^Ruu^R : w, u \in \{a, b\}^*\}$

4.5.2. Let $M = (K, \Sigma, \delta, s, \{h\})$ be the following nondeterministic Turing machine:

$$K = \{q_0, q_1, h\},$$
$$\Sigma = \{a, \triangleright, \sqcup\},$$
$$s = q_0,$$
$$\Delta = \{(q_0, \sqcup, q_1, a), (q_0, \sqcup, q_1, \sqcup), (q_1, \sqcup, q_1, \sqcup), (q_1, a, q_0, \rightarrow), (q_1, a, h, \rightarrow)\}$$

Describe all possible computations of five steps or less by M starting from the configuration $(q_0, \triangleright \sqcup)$. Explain in words what M does when started from this configuration. What is the number r (in the proof of Theorem 4.5.1) for this machine?

4.5.3. Although nondeterministic Turing machines are not helpful in showing closure under complement of the recursive languages, they are very convenient for showing other closure properties. Use nondeterministic Turing machines to show that the class of recursive languages is closed under union, concatenation, and Kleene star. Repeat for the class of recursively enumerable languages.

4.6 | GRAMMARS

In this chapter we have introduced several computational devices, namely the Turing machine and its many extensions, and we have demonstrated that *they are all equivalent in computational power*. All these various species of Turing machines can be reasonably called *automata*, like their weaker relatives —the finite automata and the pushdown automata— studied in previous chapters. Like those automata, Turing machines and their extensions act basically as *language acceptors*, receiving an input, examining it, and expressing in various ways their approval or disapproval of it. Two important families of languages, the recursive and the recursively enumerable languages, have resulted.

But in previous chapters we have seen that there is another important family of devices, very different in spirit from language acceptors, that can be used to define interesting classes of languages: *language generators*, such as regular expressions and context-free grammars. In fact, we have demonstrated that these two formalisms provide valuable *alternative characterizations* of the classes of languages defined by language acceptors. This chapter would not be complete without such a maneuver: We shall now introduce a new kind of language generator that is a generalization of the the context-free grammar, called the **grammar** (or **unrestricted grammar**, to contrast it with the context-free grammars) and show that the class of languages generated by such grammars is precisely the class of recursively enumerable ones.

Let us recall the essential features of a context-free grammar. It has an alphabet, V, which is divided into two parts, the set of terminal symbols, Σ, and the set of nonterminal symbols, $V - \Sigma$. It also has a finite set of rules, each of the form $A \rightarrow u$, where A is a nonterminal symbol and $u \in V^*$. A context-free grammar operates by starting from the start symbol S, a nonterminal, and repeatedly replacing the left-hand side of a rule by the corresponding right-hand side until no further such replacements can be made.

In a grammar all the same conventions apply, *except that the left-hand sides of rules need not consist of single nonterminals*. Instead, the left-hand side of a rule may consist of any string of terminals and nonterminals containing at least one nonterminal. A single step in a derivation entails removing the entire substring on the left-hand side of a rule and replacing it by the corresponding right-hand side. The final product is, as in context-free grammars, a string containing terminals only.

Definition 4.6.1: A **grammar** (or **unrestricted grammar**, or a **rewriting system**) is a quadruple $G = (V, \Sigma, R, S)$, where

> V is an alphabet;
>
> $\Sigma \subseteq V$ is the set of **terminal** symbols, and $V - \Sigma$ is called the set of **nonterminal** symbols;
>
> $S \in V - \Sigma$ is the **start** symbol; and
>
> R, the set of **rules**, is a finite subset of $(V^*(V - \Sigma)V^*) \times V^*$.

We write $u \rightarrow v$ if $(u, v) \in R$; we write $u \Rightarrow_G v$ if and only if, for some $w_1, w_2 \in V^*$ and some rule $u' \rightarrow v' \in R$, $u = w_1 u' w_2$ and $v = w_1 v' w_2$. As usual, $\Rightarrow_G^*$ is the reflexive, transitive closure of $\Rightarrow_G$. A string $w \in \Sigma^*$ is generated by G if and only if $S \Rightarrow_G^* w$; and $L(G)$, the **language generated by** G is the set of all strings in Σ^* generated by G.

We also use other terminology introduced originally for context-free grammars; for example, a **derivation** is a sequence of the form $w_0 \Rightarrow_G w_1 \Rightarrow_G \cdots \Rightarrow_G w_n$.

Example 4.6.1: Any context-free grammar is a grammar; in fact, a context-free grammar is a grammar such that the left-hand side of each rule is a member of $V - \Sigma$, rather than $V^*(V - \Sigma)V^*$. Thus, in a grammar, a rule might have the form $uAv \rightarrow uwv$, which could be read "replace A by w *in the context of u and v.*" Of course, the rules of a grammar may be of a form even more general than this; but it turns out that any language that can be generated by a grammar can be generated by one in which all rules are of this "context-dependent replacement" type (Problem 4.6.3).◊

Example 4.6.2: The following grammar G generates the language $\{a^n b^n c^n : n \geq 1\}$. $G = (V, \Sigma, R, S)$, where

$$V = \{S, a, b, c, A, B, C, T_a, T_b, T_c\},$$
$$\Sigma = \{a, b, c\}, \text{and}$$
$$R = \{S \rightarrow ABCS,$$
$$\quad S \rightarrow T_c,$$
$$\quad CA \rightarrow AC,$$
$$\quad BA \rightarrow AB,$$
$$\quad CB \rightarrow BC,$$
$$\quad CT_c \rightarrow T_c c,$$
$$\quad CT_c \rightarrow T_b c,$$
$$\quad BT_b \rightarrow T_b b,$$
$$\quad BT_b \rightarrow T_a b,$$
$$\quad AT_a \rightarrow T_a a,$$
$$\quad T_a \rightarrow e\}.$$

The first three rules generate a string of the form $(ABC)^n T_c$. Then the next three rules allow the A's, B's, and C's in the string to "sort out" themselves correctly, so that the string becomes $A^n B^n C^n T_c$. Finally, the remaining rules allow the T_c to "migrate" to the left, transforming all C's to c's, and then becoming T_b. In turn, T_b migrates to the left, transforming all B's into b's and becoming T_a, and finally T_a transforms all A's into a's and then is erased.

It is rather obvious that any string of the form $a^n b^n c^n$ can be produced this way. Of course, many more strings that contain nonterminals can be produced; however, it is not hard to see that the only way to erase all nonterminals is to follow the procedure outlined above. Thus, the only strings in $\{a, b, c\}$ that can be generated by G are those in $\{a^n b^n c^n : n \geq 1\}$.◊

Evidently, the class of languages generated by grammars contains certain non-context-free specimens. But precisely how large is this class of languages? More importantly, how does it relate to the other two important extensions of the context-free languages we have seen in this chapter, namely, the recursive and the recursively enumerable languages? As it happens, grammars play with respect to Turing machines precisely the same rôle that context-free grammars play in relation to pushdown automata, and regular expressions to finite automata:

Theorem 4.6.1: *A language is generated by a grammar if and only if it is recursively enumerable.*

Proof: *Only if.* Let $G = (V, \Sigma, R, S)$ be a grammar. We shall design a Turing machine M that semidecides the language generated by G. In fact, M will be *nondeterministic;* its conversion to a deterministic machine that semidecides the same language is guaranteed by Theorem 4.5.1.

M has three tapes. The first tape contains the input, call it w, and is never changed. In the second tape, M tries to reconstruct a derivation of w from S in the grammar G; M therefore starts by writing S on the second tape. Then M proceeds in steps, corresponding to the steps of the derivation being constructed. Each step starts with a nondeterministic transition, guessing one between $|R| + 1$ possible states. Each of the first $|R|$ of these $|R| + 1$ states is the beginning of a sequence of transitions that applies the corresponding rule to the current contents of the second tape. Suppose that the chosen rule is $u \to v$. M then scans its second tape from left to right, nondeterministically stopping at some symbol. It then checks that the next $|u|$ symbols match u, erases u, shifts the rest of the string appropriately to make just enough space for v, and writes v in u's place. If the check fails, M enters an unending computation —the present attempt at generating w has failed.

The $|R| + 1$st choice of M entails checking whether the current string equals w, the input. If so, M halts and accepts: w can indeed be generated by G. And if the strings are found unequal, M again loops forever.

It is clear that the only possible halting computations of M are those that correspond to a derivation of w in G. Thus M accepts w if and only if $w \in L(G)$, and the *only if* direction has been proved.

If. Suppose now that $M = (K, \Sigma, \delta, s, \{h\})$ is a Turing machine. It will be convenient to assume that Σ and K are disjoint, and that neither contains the new endmarker symbol $\triangleleft$. We also assume that M, if it halts, it always does so in the configuration $(h, \triangleright\underline{\sqcup})$ —that is, after having erased its tape. Any Turing machine that semidecides a language can be transformed into an equivalent one that satisfies the above conditions. We shall construct a grammar $G = (V, \Sigma - \{\sqcup, \triangleright\}, R, S)$ that generates the language $L \subseteq (\Sigma - \{\sqcup, \triangleright\})^*$ semidecided by M.

The alphabet V consists of all symbols in Σ and all states in K, plus the start symbol S and the endmarker $\triangleleft$. Intuitively, the derivations of G will simulate *backward computations* of M. We shall simulate configuration $(q, \triangleright u\underline{a}w)$ by the string $\triangleright uaqw\triangleleft$ —that is, by the tape contents, with the current state inserted immediately after the currently scanned symbol, and with the endmarker $\triangleleft$ appended at the end of the string. The rules of G simulate *backwards moves of M*. That is, for each $q \in K$ and $a \in \Sigma$, G has these rules, depending on $\delta(q, a)$.

(1) If $\delta(q, a) = (p, b)$ for some $p \in K$ and $b \in \Sigma$, then G has a rule $bp \to aq$.
(2) If $\delta(q, a) = (p, \to)$ for some $p \in K$, then G has a rule $abp \to aqb$ for all $b \in \Sigma$, and also the rule $a \sqcup p\triangleleft \to aq\triangleleft$ (the last rule reverses the extension

of the tape to the right by a new blank).

(3) If $\delta(q, a) = (p, \leftarrow)$ for some $p \in K$, and $a \neq \sqcup$, then G has a rule $pa \to aq$.

(4) If $\delta(q, \sqcup) = (p, \leftarrow)$ for some $p \in K$, then G has a rule $pab \to aqb$ for all $b \in \Sigma$, and also the rule $p\triangleleft \to \sqcup q\triangleleft$ that reverses the erasing of extraneous blanks.

Finally, G contains certain transitions for the beginning of the computation (the end of the derivation) and the end of the computation (the beginning of the derivation). The rule

$$S \to \triangleright \sqcup h\triangleleft$$

forces the derivation to start exactly where an accepting computation would end. The other rules are $\triangleright \sqcup s \to e$, erasing the part of the final string to the left of the input, and $\triangleleft \to e$, erasing the endmarker and leaving the input string.

The following result makes precise our notion that G simulates backward computations of M:

Claim: *For any two configurations $(q_1, u_1\underline{a_1}w_1)$ and $(q_2, u_2\underline{a_2}w_2)$ of M, we have that $(q_1, u_1\underline{a_1}w_1) \vdash_M (q_2, u_2\underline{a_2}w_2)$ if and only if $u_2a_2q_2w_2\triangleleft \Rightarrow_G u_1a_1q_1w_1\triangleleft$.*

The proof of the claim is a straightforward case analysis on the nature of the move M, and is left as an exercise.

We now complete the proof of the theorem, by showing that, for all $w \in (\Sigma - \{\triangleright, \sqcup\})^*$, M halts on w if and only if $w \in L(G)$. $w \in L(G)$ if and only if

$$S \Rightarrow_G \triangleright \sqcup h\triangleleft \Rightarrow_G^* \triangleright \sqcup sw\triangleleft \Rightarrow_G w\triangleleft \Rightarrow_G w,$$

because $S \to \triangleright \sqcup h\triangleleft$ is the only rule that involves S, and the rules $\triangleright \sqcup s \to e$ and $\triangleleft \to e$ are the only rules that allow for the eventual erasing of the state and the endmarker $\triangleleft$. Now, by the claim, $\triangleright \sqcup h\triangleleft \Rightarrow_G^* \triangleright \sqcup sw\triangleleft$ if and only if $(s, \triangleright\underline{b}w) \vdash_M^* (h, \triangleright\underline{\sqcup})$, which happens if and only if M halts on w. This completes the proof of the Theorem. ∎

Theorem 4.6.1 identifies grammars with an aspect of the Turing machines that we have deemed unrealistic —semidecision, with its one-sided definition that provides no information when the input is not in the language. This is consistent with what we know about grammars: If a string can be generated by the grammar, we can patiently search all possible derivations, starting from the shorter ones and proceeding to the longer ones, until we find the correct one. But if no derivation exists, this process will go on indefinitely, without giving us any useful information.

As it turns out, we can also identify grammars with the more useful modes of computation based on Turing machines.

Definition 4.6.2: Let $G = (V, \Sigma, R, S)$ be a grammar, and let $f : \Sigma^* \mapsto \Sigma^*$ be a function. We say that G **computes** f if, for all $w, v \in \Sigma^*$, the following is true:

$$SwS \Rightarrow^*_G v \text{ if and only if } v = f(w).$$

That is, the string consisting of the input w, with a starting symbol of G on each side, yields exactly one string in Σ^*: the correct value of $f(w)$.

A function $f : \Sigma^* \mapsto \Sigma^*$ is called **grammatically computable** if and only if there is a grammar G that computes it.

We leave the proof of the following result —a modification of the proof of Theorem 4.6.1— as an exercise, see Problem 4.6.4:

Theorem 4.6.2: *A function $f : \Sigma^* \mapsto \Sigma^*$ is recursive if and only if it is grammatically computable.*

Problems for Section 4.6

4.6.1. (a) Give a derivation of the string $aaabbbccc$ in the grammar of Example 4.6.2.

    (b) Prove carefully that the grammar in Example 4.6.2 generates the language $L = \{a^n b^n c^n : n \geq 1\}$.

4.6.2. Find grammars that generate the following languages:

  (a) $\{ww : w \in \{a, b\}^*\}$

  (b) $\{a^{2^n} : n \geq 0\}$

  (c) $\{a^{n^2} : n \geq 0\}$

4.6.3. Show that any grammar can be converted into an equivalent grammar with rules of the form $uAv \to uwv$, with $A \in V - \Sigma$, and $u, v, w \in V^*$.

4.6.4. Prove Theorem 4.6.2. (For the *only if* direction, given a grammar G, show how to construct a Turing machine which, on input w, outputs a string $u \in \Sigma^*$ such that $SwS \Rightarrow^*_G u$, if such a string u exists. For the *if* direction, use a simulation similar to the proof of Theorem 4.6.1, except in the opposite (forward) direction.)

4.6.5. An oddity in the use of grammars to compute functions is that the order in which rules are applied is indeterminate. In the following alternative, due to A. A. Markov (1903–1979), this indeterminacy is avoided. A **Markov system** is a quadruple $G = (V, \Sigma, R, R_1)$, where V is an alphabet; $\Sigma \subseteq V$; R is a finite *sequence* (not set) of rules $(u_1 \to v_1, \ldots, u_k \to v_k)$, where $u_i, v_i \in V^*$; and R_1 is a set of rules from R. The relation $w \Rightarrow_G w'$ is defined as follows: If there is an i such that u_i is a substring of w, then let

i be the smallest such number, and let w_1 be the shortest string such that $w = w_1 u_i w_2$; then $w \Rightarrow_G w'$ provided that $w' = w_1 v_i w_2$. Thus if a rule is applicable, then there is at most one rule, and it is applicable in exactly one position. We say that G **computes** a function $f : \Sigma^* \mapsto \Sigma^*$ if for all $u \in \Sigma^*$

$$u = u_0 \Rightarrow_G u_1 \rightarrow_G \cdots \Rightarrow_G u_{n-1} \Rightarrow_G u_n = f(u),$$

and the first time that a rule from R_1 was used was the last one, $u_{n-1} \Rightarrow_G u_n$. Show that a function is computable by a Markov system if and only if it is recursive. (The proof is similar to that of Theorem 4.6.2.)

4.7 | NUMERICAL FUNCTIONS

Let us now adopt a completely different point of view on computation, one that is not based on any explicit computational or information-processing formalism such as Turing machines or grammars, but instead focuses on what has to be computed: *functions from numbers to numbers.* For example, it is clear that the value of the function

$$f(m, n) = m \cdot n^2 + 3 \cdot m^{2 \cdot m + 17}$$

can be computed for any given values of m and n, because it is the composition of functions —addition, multiplication, and exponentiation, plus a few constants— that can be computed. And how do we know that exponentiation can be computed? Because it is *recursively defined* in terms of a simpler function (namely, multiplication) and values at smaller arguments. After all, m^n is 1 if $n = 0$, and otherwise it is $m \cdot m^{n-1}$. Multiplication itself can be defined recursively in terms of addition —and so on.

In principle, we should be able to start with functions from natural numbers to natural numbers that are so simple that they will be unequivocally considered computable (e.g., the identity function and the successor function $\mathsf{succ}(n) = n + 1$), and combine them slowly and patiently through combinators that are also very elementary and obviously computable —such as composition and recursive definition— and finally get a class of functions from numbers to numbers that are quite general and nontrivial. In this section we shall undertake this exercise. Significantly, the notion of computation thus defined will then be proved identical to the notions arrived at by the other approaches of this chapter —Turing machines, their variants, and grammars— that are so different in spirit, scope, and detail.

Definition 4.7.1: We start by defining certain extremely simple functions from $\mathbf{N}^k$ to $\mathbf{N}$, for various values of $k \geq 0$ (a 0-ary function is, of course, a constant, as it has nothing on which to depend). The **basic functions** are the following:

(a) For any $k \geq 0$, the **k-ary zero function** is defined as $\text{zero}_k(n_1, \ldots, n_k) = 0$ for all $n_1, \ldots, n_k \in \mathbf{N}$.

(b) For any $k \geq j > 0$, the **jth k-ary identity function** is simply the function $\text{id}_{k,j}(n_1, \ldots, n_k) = n_j$ for all $n_1, \ldots, n_k \in \mathbf{N}$.

(c) The **successor function** is defined as $\text{succ}(n) = n + 1$ for all $n \in \mathbf{N}$.

Next we introduce two simple ways of combining functions to get slightly more complex functions.

(1) Let $k, \ell \geq 0$, let $g : \mathbf{N}^k \mapsto \mathbf{N}$ be a k-ary function, and let $h_1, \ldots, h_k$ be ℓ-ary functions. Then the **composition of g with $h_1, \ldots, h_k$** is the ℓ-ary function defined as

$$f(n_1, \ldots, n_\ell) = g(h_1(n_1, \ldots, n_\ell), \ldots, h_k(n_1, \ldots, n_\ell)).$$

(2) Let $k \geq 0$, let g be a k-ary function, and let h be a $(k+2)$-ary function. Then the **function defined recursively by g and h** is the $(k+1)$-ary function f defined as

$$f(n_1, \ldots, n_k, 0) = g(n_1, \ldots, n_k),$$
$$f(n_1, \ldots, n_k, m+1) = h(n_1, \ldots, n_k, m, f(n_1, \ldots, n_k, m))$$

,

for all $n_1, \ldots, n_k, m \in \mathbf{N}$.

The **primitive recursive functions** are all basic functions, and all functions that can be obtained by them by any number of successive applications of composition and recursive definition.

Example 4.7.1: The function plus2, defined as $\text{plus2}(n) = n + 2$ is primitive recursive, as it can be obtained from the basic function succ by composition with itself. In particular, let $k = \ell = 1$ in (1) of Definition 4.7.1, and let $g = h_1 = \text{succ}$.

Similarly, the binary function plus, defined as $\text{plus}(m, n) = m + n$ is primitive recursive, because it can be recursively defined from functions obtained by combining identity, zero, and successor functions. In particular, in Part 2 of Definition 4.7.1 set $k = 1$, take g to be the $\text{id}_{2,1}$ function, and let h be the ternary function $h(m, n, p) = \text{succ}(\text{id}_{3,3}(m, n, p))$ —the composition of succ with $\text{id}_{3,3}$. The resulting recursively defined function is precisely the plus function:

$$\text{plus}(m, 0) = m,$$
$$\text{plus}(m, n+1) = \text{succ}(\text{plus}(m, n)).$$

Why stop? The function multiplication $\mathsf{mult}(m,n) = m \cdot n$ is defined recursively as

$$\mathsf{mult}(m,0) = \mathsf{zero}(m),$$
$$\mathsf{mult}(m,n+1) = \mathsf{plus}(m,\mathsf{mult}(m,n)),$$

and the function $\exp(m,n) = m^n$ is defined as

$$\exp(m,0) = \mathsf{succ}(\mathsf{zero}(m)),$$
$$\exp(m,n+1) = \mathsf{mult}(m,\exp(m,n)).$$

Hence all these functions are primitive recursive.

All *constant* functions of the form $f(n_1,\ldots,n_k) = 17$ are primitive recursive, since they can be obtained by composing an appropriate zero function with the succ function, in this example seventeen times. Also, the *sign* function $\mathsf{sgn}(n)$, which is zero if $n = 0$, and otherwise it is one, is also primitive recursive: $\mathsf{sgn}(0) = 0$, and $\mathsf{sgn}(n+1) = 1$.

For better readability, we shall henceforth use $m + n$ instead of $\mathsf{plus}(m,n)$, $m \cdot n$ instead of $\mathsf{mult}(m,n)$, and $m \uparrow n$ instead of $\exp(m,n)$. All numerical functions such as

$$m \cdot (n + m^2) + 178^m$$

are thus primitive recursive, since they are obtained from the ones above by successive compositions.

Since we are confined within the natural numbers, we cannot have true subtraction and division. However, we can define certain useful functions along these lines, such as $m \sim n = \max\{m - n, 0\}$, and the functions $\mathsf{div}(m,n)$ and $\mathsf{rem}(m,n)$ (the integer quotient and remainder of the division of m by n; assume that they are both 0 if $n = 0$). First define the *predecessor* function:

$$\mathsf{pred}(0) = 0,$$
$$\mathsf{pred}(n+1) = n,$$

from which we get our "nonnegative subtraction" function

$$m \sim 0 = m,$$
$$m \sim n + 1 = \mathsf{pred}(m \sim n).$$

The quotient and remainder functions will be defined in a subsequent example.◇

It is rather clear that we can calculate the value of any primitive recursive function for given values of its arguments. It is equally self-evident that we can calculate the validity of *assertions* about numbers such as

$$m \cdot n > m^2 + n + 7,$$

for any given values of m and n. It is convenient to define a **primitive recursive predicate** to be a primitive recursive function that only takes values 0 and 1. Intuitively, a primitive recursive predicate, such as greater-than(m, n), will capture a *relation* that may or may not hold between the values of m and n. If the relation holds, then the primitive recursive predicate will evaluate to 1, otherwise to 0.

Example 4.7.2: The function iszero, which is 1 if $n = 0$, and 0 if $n > 0$, is a primitive recursive predicate, defined recursively thus:

$$\text{iszero}(0) = 1,$$
$$\text{iszero}(m + 1) = 0.$$

Similarly, isone$(0) = 0$, and isone$(n + 1) = $ iszero(n). The predicate positive(n) is the same as the already defined sgn(n). Also, greater-than-or-equal(m, n), written $m \geq n$, can be defined as iszero$(n \sim m)$. Its *negation*, less-than(m, n) is of course $1 \sim$ greater-than-or-equal(m, n). In general, the negation of any primitive recursive predicate is also a primitive recursive predicate. In fact, so are the *disjunction* and *conjunction* of two primitive recursive predicates: $p(m, n)$ or $q(m, n)$ is $1 \sim$ iszero$(p(m, n) + q(m, n))$, and $p(m, n)$ and $q(m, n)$ is $1 \sim$ iszero$(p(m, n) \cdot q(m, n))$. For example, equals(m, n) can be defined as the conjunction of greater-than-or-equal(m, n) and greater-than-or-equal(n, m).

Furthermore, if f and g are primitive recursive functions and p is a primitive recursive predicate, all three with the same arity k, then the **function defined by cases**

$$f(n_1, \ldots, n_k) = \begin{cases} g(n_1, \ldots, n_k), & \text{if } p(n_1, \ldots, n_k); \\ h(n_1, \ldots, n_k), & \text{otherwise} \end{cases}$$

is also primitive recursive, since it can be rewritten as:

$$f(n_1, \ldots, n_k) = p(n_1, \ldots, n_k) \cdot g(n_1, \ldots, n_k) + (1 \sim p(n_1, \ldots, n_k)) \cdot h(n_1, \ldots, n_k).$$

As we shall see, definition by cases is a very useful shorthand.$\Diamond$

Example 4.7.3: We can now define div and rem.

$$\text{rem}(0, n) = 0,$$
$$\text{rem}(m + 1, n) = \begin{cases} 0 & \text{if equal}(\text{rem}(m, n), \text{pred}(n)); \\ \text{rem}(m, n) + 1 & \text{otherwise,} \end{cases}$$

and

$$\mathsf{div}(0, n) = 0,$$

$$\mathsf{div}(m + 1, n) = \begin{cases} \mathsf{div}(m + 1, n) + 1 & \text{if } \mathsf{equal}(\mathsf{rem}(m, n), \mathsf{pred}(n)); \\ \mathsf{div}(m, n) & \text{otherwise.} \end{cases}$$

Another interesting function that turns out to be primitive recursive is $\mathsf{digit}(m, n, p)$, *the m-th least significant digit of the base-p representation of n.* (As an illustration of the use of digit, the predicate $\mathsf{odd}(n)$, with the obvious meaning, can be written simply as $\mathsf{digit}(1, n, 2)$.) It is easy to check that $\mathsf{digit}(m, n, p)$ can be defined as $\mathsf{div}(\mathsf{rem}(n, p \uparrow m), p \uparrow (m \sim 1))$.$\Diamond$

Example 4.7.4: If $f(n, m)$ is a primitive recursive function, then the *sum*

$$\mathsf{sum}_f(n, m) = f(n, 0) + f(n, 1) + \cdots + f(n, m)$$

is also primitive recursive, because it can be defined as $\mathsf{sum}_f(n, 0) = 0$, and $\mathsf{sum}_f(n, m + 1) = \mathsf{sum}_f(n, m) + f(n, m + 1)$. We can also define this way the *unbounded conjunctions and disjunctions* of predicates. For example, if $p(n, m)$ is a predicate, the disjunction

$$p(n, 0) \text{ or } p(n, 1) \text{ or } p(n, 2) \text{ or } \cdots \text{ or } p(n, m)$$

is just $\mathsf{sgn}(\mathsf{sum}_p(n, m))$.$\Diamond$

Evidently, starting from the extremely simple materials of Definition 4.7.1, we can show that several quite complex functions are primitive recursive. However, primitive recursive functions fail to capture all functions that we should reasonably consider computable. This is best established in terms of a *diagonalization* argument:

Example 4.7.5: The set of primitive recursive functions is *enumerable*. This is because each primitive recursive function can in principle be defined in terms of the basic functions, and therefore can be represented as a string in a finite alphabet; the alphabet should contain symbols for the identity, successor, and zero functions, for primitive recursion and composition, plus parentheses and the symbols 0 and 1 used to index in binary basic functions such as $\mathsf{id}_{17,11}$ (see Section 5.2 for another use of such indexing, this time to represent all Turing machines). We could then enumerate all strings in the alphabet and keep only the ones that are legal definitions of primitive recursive functions —in fact, we could choose to keep only the *unary* primitive recursive functions, those with only one argument.

Suppose then that we list all unary primitive recursive functions, as strings, in lexicographic order

$$f_0, f_1, f_2, f_3, \ldots$$

In principle, given any number $n \geq 0$, we could find the n-th unary primitive recursive function in this list, f_n, and then use its definition to compute the number $f_n(n) + 1$. Call this number $g(n)$. Clearly, $g(n)$ is a computable function —we just outlined how to compute it. Still, g is *not* a primitive recursive function. Because if it were, say $g = f_m$ for some $m \geq 0$, then we would have $f_m(m) = f_m(m) + 1$, which is absurd.

This is a diagonalization argument. It depends on our having a sequential listing of all primitive recursive functions; from that listing one can define a function which differs from all those in the list, and which, therefore, cannot itself be in the list. Compare this argument with the proof of Theorem 1.5.2, stating that $2^{\mathbf{N}}$ is uncountable. There we started with a purported listing of all the members of $2^{\mathbf{N}}$, and obtained a member of $2^{\mathbf{N}}$ not in the listing.◇

Evidently, any way of defining functions so that they encompass everything we could reasonably call "computable" cannot be based only on simple operations such as composition and recursive definition, which produce functions that can always and reliably be recognized as such, and therefore enumerated. We have thus discovered an interesting truth about formalisms of computation: Any such formalism whose members (computational devices) are *self-evident* (that is, given a string we can decide easily whether it encodes a computational device in the formalism) must be either too weak (like finite-state automata and primitive recursive functions) or so general as to be useless in practice (like Turing machines that may or may not halt on an input). Any formalism that captures all computable functions, and just these, must include *functions that are not self-evident* (just as it is not self-evident whether a Turing machine halts on all inputs, and thus decides a language). Indeed, we define next a subtler operation on functions, corresponding to the familiar computational primitive of *unbounded iteration* —essentially the while loop. As we shall see, unbounded iteration does introduce the possibility that the result may *not* be a function.

Definition 4.7.2:   Let g be a $(k + 1)$-ary function, for some $k \geq 0$. The **minimalization** of g is the k-ary function f defined as follows:

$$f(n_1, \ldots, n_k) = \begin{cases} \text{the least } m \text{ such that } g(n_1, \ldots, n_k, m) = 1, \\ \quad \textit{if} \text{ such an } m \text{ exists;} \\ 0 \text{ otherwise.} \end{cases}$$

We shall denote the minimalization of g by $\mu\, m[g(n_1, \ldots, n_k, m) = 1]$.

Although the minimalization of a function g is always well-defined, there is no obvious method for computing it —even if we know how to compute g. The obvious method

> $m := 0$;
> while $g(n_1, \ldots, n_k, m) \neq 1$ do $m := m + 1$;
> output m

is not an algorithm, because it may fail to terminate.

Let us then call a function g **minimalizable** if the above method always terminates. That is, a $(k + 1)$-ary function g is *minimalizable* if it has the following property: For every $n_1, \ldots, n_k \in \mathbf{N}$, there is an $m \in \mathbf{N}$ such that $g(n_1, \ldots, n_k, m) = 1$.

Finally, call a function μ-**recursive** if it can be obtained from the basic functions by the operations of composition, recursive definition, *and minimalization of minimalizable functions.*

Note that now we cannot repeat the diagonalization argument of example 4.7.5 to show that there is a computable function that is not μ-recursive. The catch is that, given a purported definition of a μ-recursive function, *it is not clear at all whether indeed it defines a μ-recursive function* —that is, whether all applications of minimalization in this definition indeed acted upon minimalizable functions!

Example 4.7.6: We have defined an inverse of addition (the $\sim$ function), and an inverse of multiplication (the div function); but how about the inverse of exponentiation —the *logarithm?* Using minimalization,[†] we can define the *logarithm* function: $\log(m, n)$ is the smallest power to which we must raise $m + 2$ to get an integer at least as big as $n + 1$ (that is, $\log(m, n) = \lceil \log_{m+2}(n + 1) \rceil$; we have used $m + 2$ and $n + 1$ as arguments to avoid the mathematical pitfalls in the definition of $\log_m n$ when $m \leq 1$ or $n = 0$). The function log is defined as follows:

$$\log(m, n) = \mu\ p[\text{greater-than-or-equal}((m + 2) \uparrow p, n + 1)].$$

Note that this is a proper definition of a μ-recursive function, since the function $g(m, n, p) = \text{greater-than-or-equal}((m + 2) \uparrow p, n + 1)$ is minimalizable: indeed, for any $m, n \geq 0$ there is $p \geq 0$ such that $(m + 2)^p \geq n$ —because by raising an integer ≥ 2 to larger and larger powers we can obtain arbitrarily large integers.◊

We can now prove the main result of this section:

[†] The logarithm function can be defined without the minimalization operation, see Problem 4.7.2. Our use of minimalization here is only for illustration and convenience.

Theorem 4.7.1: *A function* $f : \mathbf{N}^k \mapsto \mathbf{N}$ *is μ-recursive if and only if it is recursive (that is, computable by a Turing machine).*

Proof: *Only if:* Suppose that f is a μ-recursive function. Then it is defined from the basic functions by applications of composition, recursive definition, and minimalization on minimalizable functions. We shall show that f is Turing computable.

First, it is easy to see that the basic functions are recursive: We have seen this for the successor function (Example 4.2.3), and the remaining functions only involve erasing some or all of the inputs.

So, suppose that $f : \mathbf{N}^k \mapsto \mathbf{N}$ is the composition of the functions $g : \mathbf{N}^\ell \mapsto \mathbf{N}$ and $h_1, \ldots, h_\ell : \mathbf{N}^k \mapsto \mathbf{N}$, where, by induction we know how to compute g and the h_i's. Then we can compute f as follows (in this and the other cases we give programs in the style of random access Turing machine programs that compute these functions; it is fairly easy to see that the same effect can be achieved by standard Turing machines):

$$m_1 := h_1(n_1, \ldots, n_k);$$
$$m_2 := h_2(n_1, \ldots, n_k);$$
$$\vdots$$
$$m_\ell := h_\ell(n_1, \ldots, n_k);$$
$$\text{output } g(m_1, \ldots, m_\ell).$$

Similarly, if f is defined recursively from g and h (recall the definition), then $f(n_1, \ldots, n_k, m)$ can be computed by the following program:

$$v := g(n_1, \ldots, n_k);$$
$$\text{if } m = 0 \text{ then output } v$$
$$\text{else for } i := 1, 2, \ldots, m \text{ do}$$
$$\quad v := h(n_1, \ldots, n_k, i - 1, v);$$
$$\text{output } v.$$

Finally, suppose that f is defined as $\mu\, m[g(n_1, \ldots, n_k, m)]$, where g is minimalizable and computable. Then f can be computed by the program

$$m := 0;$$
$$\text{while } g(n_1, \ldots, n_k, m) \neq 1 \text{ do } m := m + 1;$$
$$\text{output } m$$

Since we are assuming the g is minimalizable, the algorithm above will terminate and output a number.

We have therefore proved that all basic functions are recursive, and that the composition and the recursive definition of recursive functions, and the minimalization of minimalizable recursive functions, are recursive; we must conclude that all μ-recursive functions are recursive. This completes the *only if* direction of the proof.

If. Suppose that a Turing machine $M = (K, \Sigma, \delta, s, \{h\})$ computes a function $f : \mathbf{N} \mapsto \mathbf{N}$ —we are assuming for simplicity of presentation that f is unary; the general case is an easy extension (see Problem 4.7.5). We shall show that f is μ-recursive. We shall patiently define certain μ-recursive functions pertaining to M and its operation until we have accumulated enough materials to define f itself.

Assume without loss of generality that K and Σ are disjoint. Let $b = |\Sigma| + |K|$, and let us fix a mapping $\mathbf{E}$ from $\Sigma \cup K$ to $\{0, 1, \ldots, b-1\}$, such that $\mathbf{E}(0) = 0$ and $\mathbf{E}(1) = 1$ —recall that, since M computes a numerical function, its alphabet must contain 0 and 1. Using this mapping, we shall represent configurations of M as integers in base-b. The configuration $(q, a_1 a_2 \ldots \underline{a_k} \ldots a_n)$, where the a_i's are symbols in Σ, will be represented as the base-b integer $a_1 a_2 \ldots a_k q a_{k+1} \ldots a_n$, that is, as the integer

$$\mathbf{E}(a_1)b^n + \mathbf{E}(a_2)b^{n-1} + \cdots + \mathbf{E}(a_k)b^{n-k+1} + \mathbf{E}(q)b^{n-k} + \mathbf{E}(a_{k+1})b^{n-k-1} + \cdots + \mathbf{E}(a_n)$$

We are now ready to embark on the definition of f as a μ-recursive function. Ultimately, f will be defined as

$$f(n) = \mathsf{num}(\mathsf{output}(\mathsf{last}(\mathsf{comp}(n)))).$$

num is a function that takes an integer whose base-b representation is a string of 0's and 1's and outputs the binary value of that string. output takes the integer representing in base b a halted configuration of the form $\triangleright \sqcup hw$, and omits the first three symbols $\triangleright \sqcup h$. comp(n) is the number whose representation in base b is the juxtaposition of the unique sequence of configurations that starts with $\triangleright \sqcup sw$, where w is the binary encoding of n, and ends with $\triangleright \sqcup hw'$, where w' is the binary encoding of $f(n)$; such a sequence exists, since we are assuming that M computes a function —namely, f. And last takes an integer representing the juxtaposition of configurations, and extracts the last configuration in the sequence (the part between the last $\triangleright$ and the end).

Of course, we have to define all these functions. We give most of the definitions below, leaving the rest as an exercise (Problem 4.7.4). Let us start with, well, last. We can define lastpos(n), the last (rightmost, least significant) position in the string encoded by n in base b where a $\triangleright$ occurs:

$$\mathsf{lastpos}(n) = \mu\, m[\mathsf{equal}(\mathsf{digit}(m, n, b), \mathbf{E}(\triangleright))\ \mathsf{or}\ \mathsf{equal}(m, n)].$$

Notice that, in order to make the function within the brackets minimalizable, we allowed lastpos(n) to be n if no $\triangleright$ is found in n. Incidentally, this is another superficial use of minimalization, as this function can be easily redefined without the use of minimalization. We can then define $\mathsf{last}(n)$ as $\mathsf{rem}(n, b \uparrow \mathsf{lastpos}(n))$. We could also define $\mathsf{rest}(n)$, the sequence that remains after the deletion of $\mathsf{last}(n)$, as $\mathsf{div}(n, b \uparrow \mathsf{lastpos}(n))$.

$\mathsf{output}(n)$ is simply $\mathsf{rem}(n, b \uparrow \log(b \sim 2, n \sim 1) \sim 2)$ —recall our convention that the arguments of $\log$ must be decreased by 2 and 1, respectively.

The function $\mathsf{num}(n)$ can be written as the sum

$$\mathsf{digit}(1, n, b) \cdot 2 + \mathsf{digit}(2, n, b) \cdot 2 \uparrow 2 + \cdots$$
$$+ \mathsf{digit}(\log(b \sim 2, n \sim 1), n, b) \cdot 2 \uparrow \log(b \sim 2, n \sim 1).$$

This is a μ-recursive function since both the summand and the bound $\log(b \sim 2, n \sim 1)$ are. Its inverse function, $\mathsf{bin}(n)$, which maps any integer to the string that is its binary encoding, encoded again in as a base-b integer, is very similar, with the rôles of 2 and b reversed.

The most interesting (and hard to define) function in the definition of $f(n)$ above is $\mathsf{comp}(n)$, which maps n to the sequence of configurations of M that carries out the computation of $f(n)$ —in fact, the base-b integer that encodes this sequence. At the highest level, it is just

$$\mathsf{comp}(n) = \mu \, m[\mathsf{iscomp}(m, n) \text{ and } \mathsf{halted}(\mathsf{last}(m))], \tag{1}$$

where $\mathsf{iscomp}(m, n)$ is a predicate stating that m is the sequence of configurations in a computation, not necessarily halted, starting from $\triangleright \underline{s}\mathbf{b}(n)$. (Incidentally, this is *the only place in this proof in which minimalization is truly, inherently needed*.) Notice that the function within the brackets in (1) is indeed minimalizable: Since M is assumed to compute f, such a sequence m of configurations will exist for all n. $\mathsf{halted}(n)$ is simply $\mathsf{equal}(\mathsf{digit}(\log(b - 2, n \sim 1) \sim 2, n, b), \mathbf{E}(h))$.

We leave the precise definition of iscomp as an exercise (Problem 4.7.4).

It follows that f is indeed a μ-recursive function, and the proof of the theorem has been completed. ∎

Problems for Section 4.7

4.7.1. Let $f : \mathbf{N} \mapsto \mathbf{N}$ be a primitive recursive function, and define $F : \mathbf{N} \mapsto \mathbf{N}$ by

$$F(n) = f(f(f(\ldots f(n) \ldots))),$$

where there are n function compositions. Show that F is primitive recursive.

4.7.2. Show that the following functions are primitive recursive:
  (a) $\mathsf{factorial}(n) = n!$.
  (b) $\mathsf{gcd}(m, n)$, the greatest common divisor of m and n.
  (c) $\mathsf{prime(n)}$, the predicate that is 1 if n is a prime number.
  (d) $\mathsf{p(n)}$, the nth prime number, where $\mathsf{p}(0) = 2$, $\mathsf{p}(1) = 3$, and so on.
  (e) The function $\log$ defined in the text.

4.7.3. Suppose that f is a μ-recursive bijection from $\mathbf{N}$ to $\mathbf{N}$. Show that its inverse, f^{-1}, is also μ-recursive.

4.7.4. Show that the function iscomp described in the proof of Theorem 4.7.1 is primitive recursive.

4.7.5. Which modifications must be made to the construction in the proof of the *if* directions of Theorem 4.7.1 if M computes a function $f : \mathbf{N}^k \mapsto \mathbf{N}$ with $k > 1$?

4.7.6. Develop a representation of primitive recursive functions as strings in an alphabet Σ of your choice (see the next chapter for such a representation of Turing machines). Formalize the argument in Example 4.7.5 that not all computable functions can be primitive recursive.

REFERENCES

Turing machines were first conceived by Alan M. Turing:

○ A. M. Turing "On computable numbers, with an application to the Entscheidungsproblem," *Proceedings, London Mathematical Society, 2*, 42 pp. 230–265, and no. 43, pp. 544–546, 1936.

Turing introduced this model in order to argue that all detailed sets of instructions that can be carried out by a human calculator can also be carried out by a suitably defined simple machine. For the record, Turing's original machine has one two-way infinite tape and one head (see Section 4.5). A similar model was independently conceived by Post; see

○ E. L. Post "Finite Combinatory Processes. Formulation I," *Journal of Symbolic Logic, 1*, pp. 103–105, 1936.

The following books contain interesting introductions to Turing machines:

○ M. L. Minsky *Computation: Finite and Infinite Machines*, Englewood Cliffs, N.J.: Prentice-Hall, 1967.

○ F. C. Hennie *Introduction to Computability*, Reading, Mass.: Addison-Wesley, 1977.

The following are other advanced books on Turing machines and related concepts introduced in this and the three subsequent chapters:

○ M. Davis, ed., *The Undecidable*, Hewlett, N.Y.: Raven Press, 1965. (This book contains many original articles on several aspects of the subject, including the papers of Turing and Post cited above.)

○ M. Davis, ed., *Computability and Unsolvability* New York: McGraw-Hill, 1958.

○ S. C. Kleene, *Introduction to Metamathematics*, Princeton, N.J.: D. Van Nostrand, 1952,

○ W. S. Brainerd and L. H. Landweber, *Theory of Computation*, New York: John Wiley, 1974,

○ M. Machtey and P. R. Young,   *An Introduction to the General Theory of Algorithms*, New York: Elsevier North-Holland, 1978,

○ H. Rogers, Jr.,   *The Theory of Recursive Functions and Effective Computability*, New York: McGraw-Hill, 1967,

○ M. Sipser,   *Introduction to the Theory of Computation*, Boston, Mass.: PWS Publishers, 1996,

○ J. E. Hopcroft and J. D. Ullman   *Introduction to Automata Theory, Languages, and Computation*, Reading, Mass.: Addison Wesley, 1979.

○ C. H. Papadimitriou   *Computational Complexity*, Reading, Mass.: Addison Wesley, 1994.

○ H. Hermes,   *Enumerability, Decidability, Computability*, New York: Springer Verlag, 1969 (translated from the German edition, 1965).

Our notion and notation for combining Turing machines (Section 4.3) was influenced by this last book.

Random access machines, similar in spirit to our "random access Turing machines" in Section 2.4, were studied in

○ S. A. Cook and R. A. Reckhow   "Time-bounded random-access machines," *Journal of Computer and Systems Sciences, 7,* 4, pp. 354–375, 1973.

Primitive and μ-recursive functions are due to Kleene

○ S. C. Kleene   "General recursive functions of natural numbers," *Mathematische Annalen, 112,* pp. 727–742, 1936,

and Markov Algorithms (Problem 2.6.5) are from

○ A. A. Markov   *Theory of Algorithms*, Trudy Math. Inst. V. A.Steklova, 1954. English translation: Israel Program for Scientific Translations, Jerusalem, 1961.

5 | Undecidability

5.1 THE CHURCH-TURING THESIS

In this book we address this question: What can be computed? (And, more intriguingly, what *cannot* be computed?) We have introduced various and diverse mathematical models of computational processes that accomplish concrete computational tasks —in particular, decide, semidecide, or generate languages, and compute functions. In the previous chapter we saw that Turing machines can carry out surprisingly complex tasks of this sort. We have also seen that certain additional features that we might consider adding to the basic Turing machine model, including a random access capability, do not increase the set of tasks that can be accomplished. Also, following a completely different path (namely, trying to generalize context-free grammars), we arrived at a class of language generators with precisely the same power as Turing machines. Finally, by trying to formalize our intuitions on which numerical functions can be considered computable, we defined a class of functions that turned out to be precisely the recursive ones.

All this suggests that we have reached a natural upper limit on what a computational device can be designed to do; that our search for the ultimate and most general mathematical notion of a computational process, of an *algorithm*, has been concluded successfully —and the Turing machine is the right answer. However, we have also seen in the last chapter that not all Turing machines deserve to be called "algorithms:" We argued that Turing machines that semidecide languages, and thus reject by never halting, are not useful computational devices, whereas Turing machines that decide languages and compute functions (and therefore halt at all inputs) are. Our notion of an algorithm must

245

exclude Turing machines that may not halt on some inputs.

We therefore propose to adopt the Turing machine that halts on all inputs as the precise formal notion corresponding to the intuitive notion of an "algorithm." Nothing will be considered an algorithm if it cannot be rendered as a Turing machine that is guaranteed to halt on all inputs, and all such machines will be rightfully called algorithms. This principle is known as the **Church-Turing thesis**. It is a thesis, not a theorem, because it is not a mathematical result: It simply asserts that a certain informal concept (algorithm) corresponds to a certain mathematical object (Turing machine). Not being a mathematical statement, the Church-Turing thesis cannot be proved. It is theoretically possible, however, that the Church-Turing thesis could be *dis*proved at some future date, if someone were to propose an alternative model of computation that was publicly acceptable as a plausible and reasonable model of computation, and yet was provably capable of carrying out computations that cannot be carried out by any Turing machine. No one considers this likely.

Adopting a precise mathematical notion of an algorithm opens up the intriguing possibility of formally proving that certain computational problems *cannot* be solved by *any* algorithm. We already know enough to expect this. In Chapter 1 we argued that if strings are used to represent languages, not every language can be represented: there are only a countable number of strings over an alphabet, and there are uncountably many languages. Finite automata, pushdown automata, context-free grammars, unrestricted grammars, and Turing machines are all examples of finite objects that can be used for specifying languages, and that can be themselves described by strings (in the next section we develop in detail a particular way of representing Turing machines as strings). Accordingly, there are only countably many recursive and recursively enumerable languages over any alphabet. So although we have worked hard to extend the capabilities of computing machines as far as possible, in absolute terms they can be used for semideciding or deciding only an infinitesimal fraction of all the possible languages.

Using cardinality arguments to establish the limitation of our approach is trivial; finding particular examples of computational tasks that cannot be accomplished within a model is much more interesting and rewarding. In earlier chapters we did succeed in finding certain languages that are not regular or context-free; in this chapter we do the same for the recursive languages. There are two major differences, however. First, these new negative results are not just temporary setbacks, to be remedied in a later chapter where an even more powerful computational device will be defined: according to the Church-Turing thesis, computational tasks that cannot be performed by Turing machines are impossible, hopeless, *undecidable*. Second, our methods for proving that languages are not recursive will have to be different from the "pumping" theorems we used for exploiting the weaknesses of context-free grammars and finite automata. Rather, we must devise techniques for exploiting the considerable *power* of Turing machines in order to expose their limitations. The aspect of the power of Turing machines that we will explore is a kind of *introspective* ability they possess: We point out that Turing machines can receive encodings of Turing machines as inputs, and manipulate these encodings in interesting ways. We will then ask what happens when a Turing machine manipulates an encoding of itself —an ingenious yet simple application of the diagonalization principle. How to encode a Turing machine so it can be manipulated by another (or *the same!*) Turing machine is thus our next subject.

5.2 | UNIVERSAL TURING MACHINES

Is hardware or software the basis of computation? You may have an opinion on the matter —and on whether the question is meaningful and productive. But the fact is that the formalism for algorithms we introduced and developed in the last chapter —the Turing machine— is an "unprogrammable" piece of hardware, specialized at solving one particular problem, with instructions that are "hard-wired at the factory."

We shall now take the opposite point of view. We shall argue that Turing machines are also software. That is, we shall show that there is a certain "generic" Turing machine that can be programmed, about the same way that a general-purpose computer can, to solve *any* problem that can be solved by Turing machines. The "program" that makes this generic machine behave like a specific machine M will have to be *a description of M*. In other words, we shall be thinking of the formalism of Turing machines as a *programming language*, in which we can write programs. Programs written in this language can then be *interpreted* by a *universal Turing machine* —that is to say, another program in the same language. That a program written in a language can interpret any program in the same language is not a very novel idea —it is the basis of the classical method for "bootstrapping" language processors.[†] But to continue with

---

[†] Language implementors often write translators for a programming language in the same programming language. But how is the translator to be *itself* translated? One way to do this is the following: Write the translator in a *simple fragment* of the same language, leaving out the more sophisticated (and difficult to translate) features of the language. Then write a translator for this fragment —a much simplified task— in an even more stripped-down version of the language. Continue this way until your language is so simple and explicit that it resembles an assembly language, and so it can be directly translated in one.

our project in this book we must make this point precise in the context of Turing machines.

To begin, we must present a general way of specifying Turing machines, so that their descriptions can be used as input to other Turing machines. That is, we must define a language whose strings are all legal representations of Turing machines. One problem manifests itself already: No matter how large an alphabet we choose for this representation, there will be Turing machines that have more states and more tape symbols. Evidently, we must encode the states and tape symbols as strings over a fixed alphabet. We adopt the following convention: A string representing a Turing machine state is of the form $\{q\}\{0,1\}^*$; that is, the letter q followed by a binary string. Similarly, a tape symbol is always represented as a string in $\{a\}\{0,1\}^*$.

Let $M = (K, \Sigma, \delta, s, H)$ be a Turing machine, and let i and j be the smallest integers such that $2^i \geq |K|$, and $2^j \geq |\Sigma| + 2$. Then each state in K will be represented as a q followed by a binary string of length i; each symbol in Σ will be likewise represented as the letter a followed by a string of j bits. The head directions $\leftarrow$ and $\rightarrow$ will also be treated as "honorary tape symbols" (they were the reason for the "+2" term in the definition of j). We fix the representations of the special symbols $\sqcup, \triangleright, \leftarrow$, and $\rightarrow$ to be the lexicographically four smallest symbols, respectively: $\sqcup$ will always be represented as $a0^j$, $\triangleright$ as $a0^{j-1}1$, $\leftarrow$ as $a0^{j-2}10$, and $\rightarrow$ as $a0^{j-2}11$. The start state will always be represented as the lexicographically first state, $q0^i$. Notice that we require the use of leading zeros in the strings that follow the symbols a and q, to bring the total length to the required level.

We shall denote the representation of the whole Turing machine M as "M". "M", consists of the transition table δ. That is, it is a sequence of strings of the form (q, a, p, b), with q and p representations of states and a, b of symbols, separated by commas and included in parentheses. We adopt the convention that the quadruples are listed in *increasing lexicographic order*, starting with $\delta(s, \sqcup)$. The set of halting states H will be determined indirectly, by the absence of its states as first components in any quadruple of "M". If M decides a language, and thus $H = \{y, n\}$, we will adopt the convention that y is the lexicographically smallest of the two halt states.

This way, any Turing machine can be represented. We shall use the same method to represent *strings* in the alphabet of the Turing machine. Any string $w \in \Sigma^*$ will have a unique representation, also denoted "w", namely, the juxtaposition of the representations of its symbols.

Example 5.2.1: Consider the Turing machine $M = (K, \Sigma, \delta, s, \{h\})$, where $K = \{s, q, h\}$, $\Sigma = \{\sqcup, \triangleright, a\}$, and δ is given in this table.

state,	symbol	δ
s	a	$(q, \sqcup)$
s	$\sqcup$	$(h, \sqcup)$
s	$\triangleright$	$(s, \rightarrow)$
q	a	(s, a)
q	$\sqcup$	$(s, \rightarrow)$
q	$\triangleright$	$(q, \rightarrow)$

Since there are three states in K and three symbols in Σ, we have $i = 2$ and $j = 3$. These are the smallest integers such that $2^i \geq 3$ and $2^j \geq 3 + 2$. The states and symbols are represented as follows:

state/symbol	representation
s	$q00$
q	$q01$
h	$q11$
$\sqcup$	$a000$
$\triangleright$	$a001$
$\leftarrow$	$a010$
$\rightarrow$	$a011$
a	$a100$

Thus, the representation of the string $\triangleright aa \sqcup a$ is

$$\text{``}\triangleright aa \sqcup a\text{''} = a001a100a100a000a100.$$

The representation "M" of the Turing machine M is the following string:

"M" $= (q00, a100, q01, a000), (q00, a000, q11, a000), (q00, a001, q00, a011),$
$(q01, a100, q00, a011), (q01, a000, q00, a011), (q01, a001, q01, 011). \Diamond$

Now we are ready to discuss a *universal Turing machine* U, which uses the encodings of other machines as programs to direct its operation. Intuitively, U takes two arguments, a description of a machine M, "M", and a description of an input string w, "w". We want U to have the following property: U halts on input "M" "w" if and only if M halts on input w. To use the functional notation for Turing machines we developed in the last chapter,

$$U(\text{``}M\text{''}\,\text{``}w\text{''}) = \text{``}M(w)\text{''}.$$

We actually describe not the single-tape machine U, but a closely related 3-tape machine U' (then U will be the single-tape Turing machine that simulates U'). Specifically, U' uses its three tapes as follows: the first tape contains the encoding of the current tape contents of M; the second tape contains the encoding of M itself; and the third tape contains the encoding of the state of M at the current point in the simulated computation.

The machine U' is started with some string "M""w" on its first tape and the other two tapes blank. (It does not matter how U' behaves if its input string is not of this form.) First U' moves "M" onto the second tape and shifts "w" down to the left end of the first tape, preceding it by "$\triangleright \sqcup$". Thus at this point the first tape contains "$\triangleright \sqcup w$". U' writes in the third tape the encoding of the initial state s of M, always $q0^i$ (U' can easily determine i and j by examining "M"). Now U' sets about simulating the steps of the computation of M. Between such simulated steps, U' will keep the heads on the second and third tapes at their left ends, and the head of the first tape scanning the a of the encoded version of the symbol that M would be scanning at the corresponding time.

U' simulates a step of M as follows: It scans its second tape until it finds a quadruple whose first component matches the encoded state written in its third tape, and whose second component matches the encoded symbol scanned in the first tape. If it finds such a quadruple, it changes the state to the third component of that quadruple, and performs in the first tape the action suggested by the fourth component. If the fourth component encodes a symbol of the tape alphabet of M, this symbol is written in the first tape. If the fourth component is $a0^{j-2}10$, the encoding of $\leftarrow$, then U' moves its first head to the first a symbol to the left, and if it is the encoding of $\rightarrow$, to the right. If a $\sqcup$ is encountered, U' must convert it to $a0^j$, the encoding of a blank of M.

If at some step the state-symbol combination is not found in the second tape, this means that the state is a halting state. U' also halts at an appropriate state. This completes our description of the operation of U'.

Problems for Section 5.2

5.2.1. Recall the Turing machine M in Example 4.1.1
 (a) What is the string "M"?
 (b) What is the representation of the string aaa?
 (c) Suppose that the universal (3-tape) Turing machine U' described in this chapter simulates the operation of M on input aaa. What are the contents of the tapes of U' at the beginning of the simulation? At the beginning of the simulation of the third step of M?

5.2.2. By analogy to the universal Turing machine, we could hope to design a *universal finite automaton* U that accepts the language $\{$ "M""w" $: w \in L(M)\}$. Explain why universal finite automata cannot exist.

5.3 | THE HALTING PROBLEM

Suppose that you have written a program, in your favorite programming language, that performs the following remarkable feat: It takes as input any program P, written in the same language, and an input X of that program. By some clever analysis, your program always determines correctly whether the program P would halt on input X (it returns "yes" if it does), or whether it would run forever (it returns "no"). You have named this program halts(P, X).

This is a most valuable program. It discovers all sorts of subtle bugs that make other programs run forever on certain inputs. Using it you can achieve many remarkable things. Here is one somewhat subtle example: You can use it to write another program, with the ominous name diagonal(X) (recall the proof by diagonalization that $2^{\mathbf{N}}$ is not countable in Section 1.5):

    diagonal(X)
a : if halts(X, X) then goto a else halt

Notice what diagonal(X) does: If your halts program decides that program X would halt if presented with *itself* as input, then diagonal(X) loops forever; otherwise it halts.

And now comes the unanswerable question: *Does* diagonal(diagonal) *halt?* It halts if and only if the call halts(diagonal, diagonal) returns "no"; in other words, *it halts if and only if it does not halt.* This is a contradiction: we must conclude that the only hypothesis that started us on this path is false, that program halts(P, X) does not exist. That is to say, there can be *no program, no algorithm* for solving the problem halts would solve: to tell whether arbitrary programs would halt or loop.

This kind of argument should be familiar not only from your past exposure to computer science, but also from general twentieth-century culture. The point is that we have now introduced all the necessary machinery for presenting a formal, mathematically rigorous version of this paradox. We have a full-fledged notation for algorithms, a "programming language" of sorts: the Turing machine. In fact, in the last section we introduced one last feature we need: we have developed a framework that allows our "programs" to manipulate other programs and their inputs —exactly as our fictitious program halts(P, X) does. We are thus ready to define a language that is not recursive, and *prove* that it is not. Let

$$H = \{ \text{``}M\text{''\,``}w\text{''} : \text{Turing machine } M \text{ halts on input string } w\}.$$

Notice first that H is recursively enumerable: It is precisely the language semidecided by our universal Turing machine U in the previous section. Indeed, on input "M" "w", U halts precisely when the input is in H.

Furthermore, if H is recursive, then *every* recursively enumerable language is recursive. In other words, H holds the key to the question we asked in Section 4.2, whether all recursively enumerable languages are also Turing decidable: the answer is positive if and only if H is recursive. For suppose that H is indeed decided by some Turing machine M_0. Then given any particular Turing machine M semideciding a language $L(M)$, we could design a Turing machine M' that *decides* $L(M)$ as follows: First, M' transforms its input tape from $\triangleright \sqcup w\sqcup$ to $\triangleright$"M" "w"$\sqcup$ and then simulates M_0 on this input. By hypothesis, M_0 will correctly decide whether or not M accepts w. Anticipating the issues dealt with in Chapter 7, we could say that there are *reductions* from all recursively enumerable languages to H, and thus H is *complete* for the class of recursively enumerable languages.

But we can show, by formalizing the argument for $\mathsf{halts}(P, X)$ above, that H is *not* recursive. First, if H were recursive, then

$$H_1 = \{\text{"}M\text{"} : \text{Turing machine } M \text{ halts on input string "}M\text{"}\}$$

would also be recursive. (H_1 stands for the $\mathsf{halts}(X, X)$ part of the diagonal program.) If there were a Turing machine M_0 that could decide H, then a Turing machine M_1 to decide H_1 would only need to transform its input string $\triangleright \sqcup$ "M"$\sqcup$ to $\triangleright \sqcup$ "M" "M"$\sqcup$ and then yield control to M_0. Therefore, it suffices to show that H_1 is not recursive.

Second, if H_1, were recursive, then its complement would also be recursive:

$\overline{H_1} = \{w : \text{either } w \text{ is not the encoding of a Turing machine, or it is}$

the encoding "M" of a Turing machine M that does not halt on "M"$\}$.

This is so because the class of recursive languages is closed under complement (Theorem 4.2.2). Incidentally, $\overline{H_1}$ is the *diagonal* language, the analog of our diagonal program, and the last act of the proof.

But $\overline{H_1}$ cannot even be recursively enumerable —let alone recursive. For suppose M^* were a Turing machine that semidecided $\overline{H_1}$. Is "M^*" in $\overline{H_1}$? By definition of $\overline{H_1}$, "M^*" $\in \overline{H_1}$ if and only if M^* does not accept input string "M^*". But M^* is supposed to semidecide $\overline{H_1}$, so "M^*" $\in \overline{H_1}$ if and only if M^* accepts "M^*". We have concluded that M^* accepts "M^*" if and only if M^* does not accept "M^*". This is absurd, so the assumption that M_0 exists must have been in error.

Let us summarize the development of this section. We wanted to discover whether every recursively enumerable language is recursive. We observed that this would be true if and only if the particular recursively enumerable language H were recursive. From H we derived, in two steps, the language $\overline{H_1}$, which has to be recursive in order for H to be recursive. But the assumption that $\overline{H_1}$ is recursive led to a logical contradiction, by diagonalization. We have therefore proved the following most important theorem.

Theorem 5.3.1: *The language H is not recursive; therefore, the class of recursive languages is a strict subset of the class of recursively enumerable languages.*

We said earlier that this argument is an instance of the diagonalization principle used in Section 1.5 to show that $2^{\mathbf{N}}$ is not countable. To see why, and to underscore one more time the essence of the proof, let us define a binary relation R on strings over the alphabet used for the encoding of Turing machines: $(u, w) \in R$ if and only if $u =$ "M" for some Turing machine M that accepts w. (R is a version of H.) Now let, for each string u,

$$R_u = \{w : (u, w) \in R\}$$

(the R_u's correspond to the recursively enumerable languages), and consider the *diagonal* of R, that is,

$$D = \{w : (w, w) \notin R\}$$

(D is $\overline{H_1}$). By the diagonalization principle, $D \neq R_u$ for all u; that is, $\overline{H_1}$ is a language different from any recursively enumerable language.

And why is $D \neq R_u$ for any u? Because D differs, by its very construction, from each R_u (and therefore from each recursively enumerable language) on at least one string —namely, u.

Theorem 5.3.1 answers negatively the first of the two questions we posed in the end of Section 4.2 ("is every recursively enumerable language also recursive?" and "is the class of recursively enumerable languages closed under complement?"). But the same proof supplies the answer to the other question. It is easy to see that H_1, like H, is recursively enumerable, and we have shown that $\overline{H_1}$ is not recursively enumerable. Therefore we have also proved the following result.

Theorem 5.3.2: *The class of recursively enumerable languages is not closed under complement.*

Problems for Section 5.3

5.3.1. We can find a particular example of a nonrecursive function without using a diagonal argument. The **busy-beaver function** $\beta : \mathbf{N} \mapsto \mathbf{N}$ is defined as follows: For each integer n, $\beta(n)$ is the largest number m such that there is a Turing machine with alphabet $\{\triangleright, \sqcup, a, b\}$ and with exactly n states which, when started with the blank tape, eventually halts at configuration $(h, \triangleright \sqcup a^m)$.

   (a) Show that, if f is any recursive function, then there is an integer k_f such that $\beta(n + k_f) \geq f(n)$. (k_f is the number of states in the Turing machine M_f, which, when started with input a^n, halts with $a^{f(n)}$ on its tape.)

(b) Show that β is not recursive. (Suppose it were; then so would be $f(n) = \beta(2n)$. Apply the result in (a) above.)

5.3.2. We know that the class of recursively enumerable languages is not closed under complementation. Show that it is closed under union and intersection.

5.3.3. Show that the class of recursive languages is closed under union, complementation, intersection, concatenation, and Kleene star.

5.4 | UNDECIDABLE PROBLEMS ABOUT TURING MACHINES

We have proved a momentous result. Let us back off a bit and see what it says on the intuitive level, in light of the Church-Turing thesis. Since the proof establishes that H is not recursive, and we have accepted the principle that any algorithm can be turned into a Turing machine that halts on all inputs, we must conclude that *there is no algorithm that decides, for an arbitrary given Turing machine M and input string w, whether or not M accepts w.* Problems for which no algorithms exist are called **undecidable** or **unsolvable**; we shall see many of them in this chapter. The most famous and fundamental undecidable problem is the one of telling whether a given Turing machine halts on a given input —whose undecidability we just established. This problem is usually called **the halting problem for Turing machines**.

Note that the undecidability of the halting problem in no way implies that there may not be some circumstances under which it is possible to predict whether a Turing machine will halt on an input string. In Example 4.1.2 we were able to conclude that a certain simple machine is bound to never halt on a certain input. Or we might examine the transition table of the Turing machine, for example, to check whether a halt state is anywhere represented; if not, the machine cannot halt on any input string. This and more complex analyses may yield some useful information for certain cases; but our theorem implies that any such analysis must ultimately either be inconclusive or yield incorrect results: There is no completely general method that correctly decides all cases.

Once we have established, by diagonalization, that the halting problem is undecidable, the undecidability of a great variety of problems follows. These results are proved not by further diagonalizations, but by *reductions*: we show in each case that if some language L_2 were recursive, then so would be some language L_1, already known *not* to be recursive.

Definition 5.4.1: Let $L_1, L_2 \subseteq \Sigma^*$ be languages. A **reduction from L_1 to L_2** is a recursive function $\tau : \Sigma^* \mapsto \Sigma^*$ such that $x \in L_1$ if and only if $\tau(x) \in L_2$.

The reader must take care to understand the "direction" in which a reduction is to be applied. To show that a language L_2 is not recursive, we must identify a language L_1 that is known to be not recursive, and then reduce L_1 to L_2. To reduce L_2 to L_1 would achieve nothing: it would merely show that L_2 could be decided if we could decide L_1 —which we know we cannot.

Formally, the correct use of reductions in proofs of undecidability is the following:

Theorem 5.4.1: *If L_1 is not recursive, and there is a reduction from L_1 to L_2, then L_2 is also not recursive.*

Proof: Suppose that L_2 is recursive, say decided by Turing machine M_2, and let T be the Turing machine that computes the reduction τ. Then the Turing machine TM_2 would decide L_1. But L_1 is undecidable —a contradiction. ∎

We next use reductions to show that several problems about Turing machines are undecidable.

Theorem 5.4.2: *The following problems about Turing machines are undecidable.*

(a) Given a Turing machine M and an input string w, does M halt on input w?

(b) Given a Turing machine M, does M halt on the empty tape?

(c) Given a Turing machine M, is there any string at all on which M halts?

(d) Given a Turing machine M, does M halt on every input string?

(e) Given two Turing machines M_1 and M_2, do they halt on the same input strings?

(f) Given a Turing machine M, is the language that M semidecides regular? Is it context-free? Is it recursive?

(g) Furthermore, there is a certain fixed machine M, for which the following problem is undecidable: Given w, does M halt on w?

Proof: Part (a) was proved in the previous section.

(b) We describe a reduction from H to the language

$$L = \{ \text{``}M\text{''} : M \text{ halts on } e \}.$$

Given the description of a Turing machine M and an input x, our reduction simply constructs the description of a Turing machine M_w that operates as follows: M_w, when started on the empty tape (that is, in configuration $(s, \triangleright\sqcup)$), writes w on its tape and then starts to simulate M. In other words, if $w = a_1 \cdots a_n$, then M_w is simply the machine

$$R a_1 R a_2 R \ldots R a_n L_{\sqcup} M.$$

And it is easy to see that the function τ that maps "M" "w" to "M_w" is indeed recursive.

(c) We can reduce the language L shown to be nonrecursive in Part (b) to the language $L' = \{$ "M" : M halts on some input$\}$, as follows. Given the representation of any Turing machine M, our reduction constructs the representation of a Turing machine M' that erases any input it is given, and then simulates M on the empty string. Clearly, M' halts on some string if and only if it halts on all strings, if and only if M halts on the empty string.

(d) The argument for Part (c) works here as well, since M' is constructed so that it accepts some input if and only if it accepts every input.

(e) We shall reduce the problem in Part (d) to this one. Given the description of a machine M, our reduction constructs the string

$$\tau(\text{``}M\text{''}) = \text{``}M\text{''}\text{``}y\text{''},$$

where "y" is the description of the machine that immediately accepts any input. Clearly, the two machines M and y accept the same inputs if and only if M accepts all inputs.

(f) We reduce the problem in Part (b) above to the present one. We show how to modify any Turing machine M to obtain a Turing machine M' such that M' halts either on the strings in H or on no strings, depending on whether M halts on the empty string or not. Since there is no algorithm for telling whether M halts on the empty string, there can be none for telling whether $L(M)$ is $\emptyset$ (which is regular, context-free, and recursive) or H (which is none of the three). First, M' saves its input string and initiates whatever M would do on input e. When and if M would halt, M' restores its input and carries out on that input the operation of the universal Turing machine U. Thus M' either halts on no input, because it never finishes imitating M on input e, or else it halts on precisely the strings in H.

(g) The fixed machine M_0 alluded to in the statement of the theorem is precisely the universal Turing machine U. ■

Problems for Section 5.4

5.4.1. Say that Turing machine M **uses** k tape squares on input string w if and only if there is a configuration of M, $(q, u\underline{a}v)$, such that $(s, \triangleright \underline{\sqcup} w) \vdash_M^* (q, u\underline{a}v)$ and $|uav| \geq k$.
    (a) Show that the following problem is solvable: Given a Turing machine M, an input string w, and a number k, does M use k tape squares on input w?

(b) Suppose that $f : \mathbf{N} \mapsto \mathbf{N}$ is recursive. Show that the following problem is solvable: Given a Turing machine M and an input string w, does M use $f(|w|)$ tape squares on input w?

(c) Show that the following problem is undecidable: Given a Turing machine M and an input string w, does there exist a $k \geq 0$ such that M does not use k tape squares on input w? (That is, does M use a finite amount of tape on input w?)

5.4.2. Which of the following problems about Turing machines are solvable, and which are undecidable? Explain your answers carefully.

(a) To determine, given a Turing machine M, a state q, and a string w, whether M ever reaches state q when started with input w from its initial state.

(b) To determine, given a Turing machine M and two states p and q, whether there is any configuration with state p which yields a configuration with state q, where p is a particular state of M.

(c) To determine, given a Turing machine M and a state q, whether there is any configuration at all that yields a configuration with state q.

(d) To determine, given a Turing machine M and a symbol a, whether M ever writes the symbol a when started on the empty tape.

(e) To determine, given a Turing machine M, whether M ever writes a nonblank symbol when started on the empty tape.

(f) To determine, given a Turing machine M and a string w, whether M ever moves its head to the left when started with input w.

(g) To determine, given two Turing machines, whether one semidecides the complement of the language semidecided by the other.

(h) To determine, given two Turing machines, whether there is any string on which they both halt.

(i) To determine, given a Turing machine M, whether the language semidecided by M is finite.

5.4.3. Show that it is an undecidable problem to determine, given a Turing machine M, whether there is some string w such that M enters each of its states during its computation on input w.

5.4.4. Show that the halting problem for Turing machines remains undecidable even when restricted to Turing machines with some small, fixed number of states. (If the number is required to be fixed but not small, the existence of a universal Turing machine establishes the result. Show how any Turing machine can be simulated, in some suitable sense, by a Turing machine with about half a dozen states but a much larger alphabet. Actually, three states are enough; in fact, two would be enough if we allowed our machines to write and move in a single step.)

5.4.5. Show that any Turing machine can be simulated, in some sense we leave it to you to specify, by an automaton with no tape but with two **counters**. A counter is a pushdown store with only one symbol, except for a distinguishable bottom-marker, which is never removed. Thus a counter may be thought of as a register for containing a number in unary. The possible operations on a counter are the following: add 1; see if it contains 0; and if it does not contain 0, subtract 1. Conclude that the halting problem for these 2-counter machines is undecidable. (Hint: Start by showing how to simulate a Turing machine tape by two push-down stores with two symbols; show that these can be simulated by *four* counters, by encoding the pushdown store contents in unary; finally, simulate four counters by two, by encoding four numbers a, b, c, d as $2^a 3^b 5^c 7^d$.)

5.5	UNSOLVABLE PROBLEMS ABOUT GRAMMARS

Unsolvable problems do not occur only in the domain of Turing machines, but in virtually all fields of mathematics. For example, there are several undecidable problems related to grammars, summarized below.

Theorem 5.5.1: *Each of the following problems is undecidable.*

(a) For a given grammar G and string w, to determine whether $w \in L(G)$.
(b) For a given grammar G, to determine whether $e \in L(G)$.
(c) For two given grammars G_1 and G_2, to determine whether $L(G_1) = L(G_2)$.
(d) For an arbitrary grammar G, to determine whether $L(G) = \emptyset$.
(e) Furthermore, there is a certain fixed grammar G_0, such that it is undecidable to determine whether any given string w is in $L(G_0)$.

Proof: We shall show a reduction from the halting problem to (a); very similar reductions establish the remaining parts. Given any Turing machine M and string w, we simply apply to M the construction given in the proof of Theorem 4.6.1 to produce a grammar G such that $L(G)$ is the language semidecided by M. It follows that $w \in L(G)$ if and only if M halts on input w. ∎

Since we had already established that grammars are exactly as powerful as Turing machines (Theorem 4.6.1), the undecidability results above probably came as no surprise. What is much more astonishing, however, is that similar questions about *context-free grammars* and related systems —a rather simple and limited domain— are undecidable. Naturally, the undecidable problems cannot include telling whether $w \in L(G)$, or whether $L(G) = \emptyset$ —these problems can be solved by algorithms, and in fact efficient ones (recall Theorem 3.6.1). Several other problems, however, are not solvable.

Theorem 5.5.2: *Each of the following problems is undecidable.*

(a) *Given a context-free grammar G, is $L(G) = \Sigma^*$?*
(b) *Given two context-free grammars G_1 and G_2, is $L(G_1) = L(G_2)$?*
(c) *Given two pushdown automata M_1 and M_2, do they accept precisely the same language?*
(d) *Given a pushdown automaton M, find an equivalent pushdown automaton with as few states as possible.*

Proof: (a) The main technical difficulty is in proving Part (a); the other parts follow rather easily. We shall reduce to Part (a) the problem shown to be undecidable in Part (d) of Theorem 5.5.1, that is, the problem of deciding whether a given generalized grammar generates any string at all.

Let $G_1 = (V_1, \Sigma_1, R_1, S_1)$ be a generalized grammar. We first modify this grammar as follows: Let the rules of G_1 be $\alpha_i \to \beta_i$, for $i = 1, \ldots, |R_1|$. We add to V_1 $|R_1|$ new nonterminal symbols A_i, $i = 1, \ldots, |R_1|$, one for each rule in R_1, and replace the ith rule, for $i = 1, \ldots, |R_1|$, by the two rules $\alpha_i \to A_i$ and $A_i \to \beta_i$. Let us call the resulting grammar $G'_1 = (V'_1, \Sigma_1, R'_1, S_1)$. It is clear that $L(G'_1) = L(G_1)$; any derivation of a string in G_1 can be turned into a **standard derivation** of the same string in G'_1, in which each odd step applies a rule of the form $u_i \to A_i$, while the subsequent even step applies a rule of the form $A_i \to v_i$.

From G'_1 we shall construct a *context-free* grammar G_2 over an alphabet Σ such that $L(G_2) = \Sigma^*$ if and only $L(G_1) = \emptyset$. This reduction would then establish Part (a).

Suppose that there is a derivation of a terminal string in G'_1; by the remark above, we can assume that it is a standard derivation, namely,

$$S_1 \Rightarrow x_1 \Rightarrow x_2 \Rightarrow x_3 \Rightarrow \cdots \Rightarrow x_n,$$

where $x_i \in V'^*_1$ for all i, and $x_n \in \Sigma^*_1$, n is even, each x_i with i odd contains exactly one A_j nonterminal, while each x_i with i even contains no A_j nonterminal. Such a derivation can be represented as a string in the alphabet $\Sigma = V \cup \{\Rightarrow\}$, precisely the string displayed above. In fact, for reasons that will be clear soon, we shall be more interested in the **boustrophedon version**[†] of the string that corresponds to the standard derivation, in which the odd-numbered x_i's x_1, x_3, etc. are *reversed*:

$$S_1 \Rightarrow x_1^R \Rightarrow x_2 \Rightarrow x_3^R \Rightarrow \ldots \Rightarrow x_{n-1}^R \Rightarrow x_n.$$

[†] *Boustrophedon*, from a Greek word meaning "as the ox turns," is a way of writing alternate lines in opposite direction, from left to right and from right to left.

Consider now the language $D_{G_1'} \subseteq \Sigma^*$ consisting of all such boustrophedon versions of standard derivations of terminal strings in G_1'. It is clear that $D_{G_1'} = \emptyset$ if and only if $L(G_1) = \emptyset$. To put it otherwise, in terms of the complement $\overline{D_{G_1'}} = \Sigma^* - D_{G'}$,

$$\overline{D_{G_1'}} = \Sigma^* \text{ if and only if } L(G_1) = \emptyset.$$

Therefore, all we have to show in order to conclude the proof is that $\overline{D_{G_1'}}$ is context-free.

To this end, let us look closer at the language $\overline{D_{G_1'}}$. What does it take for a string w to be in this language? That is, when does a string w *fail* to be a boustrophedon version of a standard derivation of a terminal string in G_1'? It does if and only if at least one of the following conditions holds:

(1) w does not start with $S_1 \Rightarrow$.
(2) w does not end with $\Rightarrow v$, where $v \in \Sigma_1^*$.
(3) w contains an odd number of $\Rightarrow$'s.
(4) w is of the form $u \Rightarrow y \Rightarrow v$ or $u \Rightarrow y$, where
    (a) u contains an even number of occurrences of $\Rightarrow$,
    (b) y contains exactly one occurrence of $\Rightarrow$, and
    (c) y is *not* of the form $y = y_1 A_i y_2 \Rightarrow y_2^R \beta_i y_1^R$ for some $i \le |R_1|$ and $y_1, y_2 \in \Sigma_1^*$, where β_i is the right-hand side of the ith rule of G_1.
(5) w is of the form $u \Rightarrow y \Rightarrow v$, where
    (a) u contains an odd number of occurrences of $\Rightarrow$,
    (b) y contains exactly one occurrence of $\Rightarrow$, and
    (c) y is *not* of the form $y = y_1 \alpha_i y_2 \Rightarrow y_2^R A_i y_1^R$ for some $i \le |R_1|$ and $y_1, y_2 \in \Sigma_1^*$, where α_i is the left-hand side of the ith rule of G_1.

If w satisfies any one of these five conditions, and only then, w is in $\overline{D_{G_1'}}$. That is, $\overline{D_{G_1'}}$ is the union of the five languages L_1, L_2, L_3, L_4, and L_5 described in (1) through (5) above. *We claim that all five languages are context-free*, and in fact that we can construct context-free grammars that generate them. For the first three, which happen to be regular languages, this is trivial.

For L_4 and L_5, our argument is indirect: We shall argue that we can design a *nondeterministic pushdown automaton* for each, and rely on Theorem 3.6.1 Part (b), stating that there is an algorithm for constructing from any pushdown automaton M a context-free grammar G such that $L(G) = L(M)$.

The pushdown automaton M_4 accepting L_4 works in two phases. In the first phase, it scans input w from left to right, always remembering whether it has seen an odd or even number of $\Rightarrow$'s (this can be accomplished by two states). When an even-numbered $\Rightarrow$ is encountered, M_4 has two options, and chooses between them nondeterministically: It can either continue to count $\Rightarrow$'s modulo two, or it can enter the second phase.

In the second phase, M_4 accumulates its input in its stack until a $\Rightarrow$ is found. If no A_i symbol was pushed, or more than one, then M_3 can accept —the input is in L_4. Otherwise, M_4 compares its stack contents (a string of the form $y_2^R A_i y_1^R$ when read from the top down) with the part of the input up to the next $\Rightarrow$. If a mismatch is found before A_i is encountered, or if it is discovered that A_i is not replaced in the input by β_i^R (a string remembered by M_4 in its state space), or if a mismatch is found after this, or if the next $\Rightarrow$ (or the end of the input) is not found immediately after the stack becomes empty, then again M_4 accepts. Otherwise it rejects.

This concludes the description of M_4, and it is clear that $L(M_4) = L_4$. The construction for L_5 is very similar. We can thus design context-free grammars that generate each of the languages L_1 through L_5; hence we can design a context-free grammar G_2 for their union.

Thus, given any generalized grammar G_1, we can construct a context-free grammar G_2 such that $L(G_2) = \overline{D_{G_1'}}$. But we know that $\overline{D_{G_1'}} = \Sigma^*$ if and only if $L(G_1) = \emptyset$. We conclude that if we had an algorithm for deciding whether any given context-free grammar generates all of Σ^*, then we could use this algorithm for deciding whether a given generalized grammar generates the empty language, which we know is impossible. The proof of Part (a) is complete.

(b) If we could tell whether two context-free grammars generate the same language, then we would be able to tell if a context-free grammar generates Σ^*: take the second grammar to be a trivial grammar that does generate Σ^*.

(c) If we could tell whether any two pushdown automata are equivalent, then we would be able to tell if two given context-free grammars are equivalent by transforming them into two pushdown automata that accept the same language, and then testing them for equivalence.

(d) If there were an algorithm for minimizing the number of states of a pushdown automaton, just as there is for finite automata, then we would be able to tell if a given pushdown automaton accepts Σ^*: It does if and only if the optimized pushdown automaton has one state and accepts Σ^*. And it is decidable whether a one-state pushdown automaton accepts Σ^* (this is established in Problem 5.5.1). ∎

Problems for Section 5.5

5.5.1. Show that it is decidable, given a pushdown automaton M *with one state*, whether $L(M) = \Sigma^*$. (*Hint:* Show that such an automaton accepts all strings if and only if it accepts all strings of length *one*.)

5.5.2. A **Post correspondence system** is a finite set P of ordered pairs of nonempty strings; that is, P is a finite subset of $\Sigma^* \times \Sigma^*$. A **match** of P

is any string $w \in \Sigma^*$ such that, for some $n > 0$ and some (not necessarily distinct) pairs $(u_1, v_1), (u_2, v_2), \ldots, (u_n . v_n)$, $w = u_1 u_2 \ldots u_n = v_1 v_2 \ldots v_n$.

(a) Show that it is undecidable, given a Post correspondence system, to determine whether it has a match. (Start with a restricted version, in which matches must start with a distinguished pair in P.)

(b) Use (a) above to find an alternative proof of Theorem 5.5.2.

5.5.3. A (nondeterministic) **2-head finite automaton** (THFA) consists of a finite control, an input tape, and two heads that can read but not write on the tape and move only left to right. The machine is started in its initial state with both heads on the leftmost square of the tape. Each transition is of the form (q, a, b, p), where q and p are states, and a and b are symbols or e. This transition means that M may, when in state q, read a with its first head and b with its second and enter state p. M accepts an input string by moving both heads together off the right end of the tape while entering a designated final state.

(a) Show that it is solvable, given a THFA M and an input string w, whether M accepts w.

(b) Show that it is unsolvable, given a THFA M, whether there is any string that M accepts. (Use the previous problem.)

5.6 | AN UNSOLVABLE TILING PROBLEM

We are given a finite set of *tiles*, each one unit square. We are asked to tile the first quadrant of the plane with copies of these tiles, as shown in Figure 5-1. We have an infinite supply of copies of each tile.

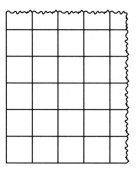

Figure 5-1

The only restrictions are that a special tile, the *origin tile*, must be placed in the lower left-hand corner; that only certain pairs of tiles may abut each other horizontally; and that only certain pairs of tiles may abut each other vertically. (Tiles may not be rotated or turned over.) Is there an algorithm for determining whether the first quadrant can be tiled, given a finite set of tiles, the origin tile, and the adjacency rules?

This problem can be formalized as follows. A **tiling system** is a quadruple $\mathcal{D} = (D, d_0, H, V)$, where D is a finite set of **tiles**, $d_0 \in D$, and $H, V \subseteq D \times D$. A **tiling** by $\mathcal{D}$ is a function $f : \mathbf{N} \times \mathbf{N} \mapsto D$ such that the following hold:

$$f(0,0) = d_0,$$
$$(f(m,n), f(m+1,n)) \in H \quad \text{for all } m, n \in \mathbf{N},$$
$$(f(m,n), f(m,n+1)) \in V \quad \text{for all } m, n \in \mathbf{N}.$$

Theorem 5.6.1: *The problem of determining, given a tiling system, whether there is a tiling by that system is undecidable.*

Proof: We reduce to this tiling problem the problem of determining, given a Turing machine M, whether M *fails to halt* on input e. This is simply the *complement* of the halting problem, and thus an undecidable problem. If this problem can be reduced to the tiling problem, the tiling problem is surely undecidable.

The basic idea is to construct from any Turing machine M a tiling system $\mathcal{D}$ such that a tiling by $\mathcal{D}$, if one exists, represents an infinite computation by M starting from the blank tape. Configurations of M are represented horizontally in a tiling; successive configurations appear one above the next. That is, the horizontal dimension represents the tape of M, while the vertical dimension stands for time. If M never halts on the empty input, successive rows can be tiled *ad infinitum;* but if M halts after k steps, it is impossible to tile more than k rows.

In constructing the relations H and V, it is helpful to think of the edges of the tiles as being marked with certain information; we allow tiles to abut each other horizontally or vertically only if the markings on the adjacent edges are identical. On the horizontal edges, these markings are either a symbol from the alphabet of M or a state-symbol combination. The tiling system is arranged so that if a tiling is possible, then by looking at the markings on the horizontal edges between the nth and $(n+1)$st rows of tiles, we can read off the configuration of M after $n - 1$ steps of its computation. Thus only one edge along such a border is marked with a state-symbol pair; the other edges are marked with single symbols.

The marking on a vertical edge of a tile is either absent (it only matches vertical edges also with no marking) or consists of a state of M, together with a "directional" indicator, which we indicate by an arrowhead. (Two exceptions

A language is **Turing-enumerable** if and only if it there is a Turing machine
that enumerates it.

That is, M enumerates L by starting from blank tape and computing away,
periodically passing through a special state q (*not* a halting state). Entering
state q signals that the string currently on M's tape is a member of L; M
may then leave state q and reenter it later on with some other member of L
on its tape. Notice that the members of L can be listed in any order and with
repetitions.

Theorem 5.7.2: *A language is recursively enumerable if and only if it is Turing-
enumerable.*

Proof: Suppose that L is semidecided by Turing machine M. Then we can
design a machine M' which, instead of taking a string as input, starts from the
empty tape, systematically generates (for instance, in lexicographic order) all
strings over the alphabet of L, and carries out on each the same computation
that M would carry out. Unfortunately, the obvious way to achieve this goal
may not work: Our new machine M' cannot hope to finish its computation on
each string before beginning to work on the next, since it may get "hung up"
forever on some string for which the calculation by M does not terminate, even
though there are other strings M would accept that have not yet been generated.
(This strategy would of course work if L were *decided* by M; see the proof of the
next theorem.)

The solution is based on a version of the the "dovetailing" procedure we used
in Section 1.4 to show that a union of countably many sets is countable. Instead
of attempting to complete the computation on each string as it is generated, M'
carries out the following sequence of operations:

(Phase 1) First M' carries out one step of the computation of M on the
(lexicographically) first string over the alphabet of M.

(Phase 2) Then it carries out two steps of the computation of M on each of
the first *two* strings.

(Phase 3) Then it carries out three steps of the computation of M on each
of the first three strings, and so on.

The first time M' discovers that M would accept a string, say w_1, M' writes
w_1 on its tape and pauses in state q to signal that $w_1 \in L$.

In general, after the ith string in L has been discovered, call it w_i, M' first
displays it at state q, and starts all over from Phase 1, and so on, *keeping w_i on
its tape*. Whenever it now discovers a string accepted by M, it first compares
it with w_i; if they are unequal, it continues. If it finds that the string just
discovered is the same as w_i, then it looks for *the next* string accepted by M.

This next string will be w_{i+1}. Again, w_{i+1} is displayed at state q, remembered, and compared. It is clear that any member of L will eventually be displayed.

The other direction is somewhat easier. If M enumerates L, then we can modify M to semidecide L as follows: Redesign M so that it saves any input supplied to it before beginning its enumeration process. Furthermore, every time M would enter the distinguished state q, the modified machine compares the current tape contents with the saved input string. If a match is found, the input string is accepted; otherwise, the enumeration process continues. The new machine then semidecides exactly the language enumerated by M. ∎

How about *recursive* languages? It turns out that they can be enumerated in a more orderly fashion.

Definition 5.7.2: Let M be a Turing machine enumerating a language L. We say that M **lexicographically enumerates** L if the following is true, where q is the special "display" state: Whenever $(q, \triangleright \sqcup w) \vdash_M^+ (q, \triangleright \sqcup w')$, then w' comes lexicographically after w. A language is **lexicographically Turing-enumerable** if and only if it there is a Turing machine that lexicographically enumerates it.

Theorem 5.7.3: *A language is recursive if and only if it is lexicographically Turing-enumerable.*

Proof: Suppose that M is a Turing machine that decides L. Then the following Turing machine M' (which was our first unsuccessful attempt at proving the same direction of Theorem 5.7.2) lexicographically enumerates L: M' generates one after the other in lexicographic order all strings in the alphabet of L, and runs M on each. Whenever M accepts, M' displays the string and continues to the next one. If M rejects, M' simply continues to the next string without passing through the display state.

For the other direction, suppose that L is lexicographically enumerated by a Turing machine M. There are two cases: If L is *finite*, then there is nothing to prove, since in this case L is certainly recursive (as well as context-free, regular, etc.). So, suppose that L is infinite. The following machine M' decides L: On input w, start the enumerating machine M. Wait until either w is displayed, or any string that comes lexicographically after w is displayed. In the first case, accept w; in the second, reject. Since there are finitely many strings that come lexicographically before w (fewer than $|\Sigma + 1|^{|w|}$) and L is infinite, we *know* that one of the two will happen. ∎

Every Turing machine M semidecides a unique language denoted $L(M)$ —namely, the set of all inputs on which it halts. But $L(M)$ is semidecided by many other Turing machines, ranging from trivial perturbations of M (for example, a version of M with its states renumbered, or a machine that performs a meaningless "dance" into new states just before halting, and is otherwise identical to M) to very subtle variants (the reader should be able to supply a few). In other words, this function from the set of all Turing machines to the class of recursively enumerable languages is far from an isomorphism, as it maps an infinity of wildly different machines to the same language. In fact, we know that it is undecidable whether two given machines are mapped to the same language by this mapping. The following result suggests that this mapping is so complicated, that, in some sense made precise below, *all conceivable problems about it are undecidable.*

Theorem 5.7.4 (Rice's Theorem):   Suppose that C is a proper, nonempty subset of the class of all recursively enumerable languages. Then the following problem is undecidable: Given a Turing machine M, is $L(M) \in C$?

Proof: We can assume that $\emptyset \notin C$ (otherwise, repeat the rest of the argument for the class of all recursively enumerable languages *not* in C, which is also a proper, nonempty subset of the recursively enumerable languages). Next, since C is nonempty, we can assume that there is a language $L \in C$ semidecided by machine M_L.

We shall reduce the halting problem to the problem of deciding whether the language semidecided by a given Turing machine is in C. Suppose then that we are given a Turing machine M, and input w, and we wish to decide whether M halts on w. To accomplish this, we construct a Turing machine $T_{M,w}$, such that the language semidecided by $T_{M,w}$ is either the language L fixed above or the language $\emptyset$. On input x, $T_{M,w}$ simulates the universal Turing machine U on input "M""w". If it halts, then $T_{M,w}$, instead of halting, goes on to simulate M_L on input x: It either halts and accepts, or never halts, depending on the behavior of M_L on x. Naturally, if $U($"M""w"$) = \nearrow$, $T_{M,w}(x) = \nearrow$ as well. To review, $T_{M,w}$ is this machine:

$$T_{M,w}(x) : \text{if } U(\text{``}M\text{''}\,\text{``}w\text{''}) \neq \nearrow \text{ then } M_L(x) \text{ else } \nearrow$$

Claim: The language semidecided by $T_{M,w}$ is in class C if and only if M halts on input w.

Notice that the claim states that the construction of $T_{M,w}$ from M and w is a *reduction* of the halting problem to the problem of telling, given a Turing machine, whether the language semidecided by it is in C. This would conclude the proof of the theorem

Proof of the claim: Suppose that M halts on input w. Then $T_{M,w}$ on input x determines this, and then always goes on to accept x if and only if $x \in L$. Hence, in this case, the language semidecided by $T_{M,w}$ is L —which is in C.

Suppose then that $M(w) = \nearrow$. In this case $T_{M,w}$ *never* halts, and thus M_x semidecides the language $\emptyset$, known not to be in $\mathcal{C}$. ∎

The undecidability of many problems follow from Rice's Theorem: Given a Turing machine M, is the language semidecided by it, $L(M)$, regular? context-free? finite? empty? Σ^*? recursive? —and so on.

Problems for Section 5.7

5.7.1. Show that L is recursively enumerable if and only if, for some nondeterministic Turing machine M, $L = \{w : (s \triangleright \sqcup) \vdash_M^* \triangleright \sqcup w)\}$, where s is the initial state of M.

5.7.2. Show that if a language is recursively enumerable, then there is a Turing machine that enumerates it without ever repeating an element of the language.

5.7.3. (a) Let Σ be an alphabet not containing the symbol ";", and suppose that $L \subseteq \Sigma^*; \Sigma^*$ is recursively enumerable. Show that the language $L' = \{x \in \Sigma^* : x; y \in L \text{ for some } y \in \Sigma^*\}$ is recursively enumerable.
(b) Is L' in (a) necessarily recursive if L is recursive?

5.7.4. A grammar is said to be **context-sensitive** if and only if each rule is of the form $u \to v$, where $|v| \geq |u|$. A **context-sensitive language** is one generated by a context-sensitive grammar.
(a) Show that every context-sensitive language is recursive. (*Hint:* How long can derivations be?)
(b) Show that a language is context-sensitive if and only if it is generated by a grammar such that every rule is of the form $uAv \to uwv$, where A is a nonterminal, and $w \neq e$.
(c) An **in-place acceptor** (or **linear-bounded automaton**) is a nondeterministic Turing machine such that the tape head never visits a blank square except for the two immediately to the right and to the left of the input. Show that a language is context-sensitive if and only if it is semidecided by an in-place acceptor. (*Hint:* Both directions are specializations of the proof of Theorem 4.6.1.)

5.7.5. The class of context-sensitive languages introduced in the previous problem, and characterized alternatively by nondeterministic in-place Turing acceptors in Part (c) above, completes the **Chomsky hierarchy,** an influential framework for thinking about the expressiveness of language generators and the power of automata, proposed by the linguist Noam Chomsky in the 1960s. The Chomsky hierarchy consists of these five classes of languages, in the order in which they were introduced in this book: *regular languages, context-free languages, recursive languages, recursively enumerable* *languages, context-sensitive languages.* Arrange these classes of languages in order of increasing generality (so that each class in the list properly includes all previous ones), and write next to each the corresponding class of automata and/or grammars.

5.7.6. Suppose that $f : \Sigma_0^* \mapsto \Sigma_1^*$ is a recursive *onto* function. Show that there is a recursive function $g : \Sigma_1^* \mapsto \Sigma_0^*$ such that $f(g(w)) = w$ for each $w \in \Sigma_0^*$.

5.7.7. Show that it is undecidable to tell whether the language semidecided by a given Turing machine is

  (a) finite.

  (b) regular.

  (c) context-free.

  (d) recursive.

  (e) equal to the language $\{ww^R : w \in \{a, b\}^*\}$.

5.7.8. The nonrecursive languages L exhibited in this chapter have the property that either L or $\overline{L}$ is recursively enumerable.

  (a) Show by a counting argument that there is a language L such that neither L nor $\overline{L}$ is recursively enumerable.

  (b) Give an example of such a language.

5.7.9. This problem continues Problem 3.7.10: Extend the Venn diagram of the (a) regular, (b) context-free, (c) deterministic context-free, and (d) complements of context-free languages, to include the following three new classes:

  (e) recursive,

  (f) recursively enumerable,

  (g) complements of recursively enumerable languages.

Give an example of a language in each region of the Venn diagram.

5.7.10. Describe a Turing machine M that has the property that, on any input, it outputs "M" —*its own description.* (*Hint:* First write a program in a programming language that prints itself. Or, for a more complicated argument, see the next problem.)

5.7.11. (a) Argue that there is a Turing machine G which, when presented with the description of a Turing machine M, it computes the description of another Turing machine M^2, which on any input x first simulates M on input "M", and then, if M halts with a valid description of a Turing machine N on its tape, it simulates N on input x.

(b) Argue that there is a Turing machine C which, when presented with the description of two Turing machines M_1 and M_2, it computes the Turing machine that is the *composition* of M_1 and M_2; that is, the machine which, on any input x, first simulates M_2 on x, and then it simulates M_1 on the result.

(c) Suppose that M is a Turing machine which, when its input is a valid description of a Turing machine, it outputs another valid description of a Turing machine. Show that any such M has a *fixpoint*, that is, a Turing machine F with the property that F and the machine represented by $M(``F")$ behave exactly the same on all inputs. (Suppose that the composition — recall Part (b)— of M and G —recall Part (a)— is presented as an input to G. Check that the machine whose description is output is the required fixpoint F.)

(d) Let M be any Turing machine. Argue that there is another Turing machine M' with the following property: For any input x, if M halts on input x with output y, then M' also halts on input x, and its output is $y``M'"$ —that is, M' pads the output of M with its own description, its "signature."

REFERENCES

The undecidability of the halting problem was proved by A. M. Turing in his 1936 paper referenced in the previous chapter. The undecidability of problems related to context-free grammars was proved in the paper by Bar-Hilel, Perles, and Shamir cited at the end of Chapter 3. Post's correspondence problem (see Problem 5.5.2) is from

o E. L. Post   "A variant of a recursively unsolvable problem," *Bulletin of the Americal Math. Society, 52*, pp. 264–268, 1946.

The Chomsky hierarchy (see Problem 5.7.5) is due to Noam Chomsky

o N. Chomsky   "Three models for the description of language," *IRE Transactions on Information Theory, 2*, 3, pp.113–124, 1956.

The tiling problem (Section 5.6) is from

o H. Wang   "Proving theorems by pattern recognition," *Bell System Technical Journal, 40*, pp. 1–141, 1961.

For many more unsolvable problems, see the references of the last chapter, especially the books by Martin Davis.

6 | Computational Complexity

6.1 THE CLASS P

In the previous chapter we saw that there exist well-defined decision problems that cannot be solved by algorithms, and gave some specific examples of such problems. We can therefore classify all computational problems into two categories: those that can be solved by algorithms, and those that cannot. With the great advances in computer technology of the last few decades, one may reasonably expect that all the problems of the former type can now be solved in a satisfactory way. Unfortunately, computing practice reveals that many problems, although in principle solvable, cannot be solved in any practical sense by computers *due to excessive time requirements*.

Suppose that it is your task to schedule the visits of a traveling sales representative to 10 regional offices. You are given a map with the 10 cities and distances in miles, and you are asked to produce the itinerary that minimizes the total distance traversed. This is surely the kind of task that you would like to use a computer to solve. And, from a theoretical standpoint, the problem is certainly solvable. If there are n cities to visit, the number of possible itineraries is finite —to be precise, $(n-1)!$, that is, $1 \cdot 2 \cdot 3 \cdots (n-1)$. Hence an algorithm can easily be designed that systematically examines all itineraries in order to find the shortest. Naturally, one can even design a Turing machine that computes the shortest tour.

Still, one gets an uneasy feeling about this algorithm. *There are too many tours to be examined.* For our modest problem of 10 cities, we would have to examine $9! = 362,880$ itineraries. With some patience, this can be carried out by a computer, but, what if we had 40 cities to visit? The number of itineraries is now gigantic: $39!$, which is larger than 10^{45}. Even if we could examine 10^{15} tours per second —a pace that is much too fast even for the most powerful supercomputers, existing or projected —the required time for completing this calculation would be several billion lifetimes of the universe!

Evidently, the fact that a problem is solvable in theory does not immediately imply that it can be solved realistically in practice. Our goal in this chapter is to develop a formal mathematical theory —a quantitative refinement of the Church-Turing thesis— that captures this intuitive notion of "a practically feasible algorithm." The question is, which algorithms —and which Turing machines— should we consider as practically feasible?

As the introductory example of the TRAVELING SALESMAN PROBLEM reveals, the limiting parameter here is the *time* or *number of steps* required by the algorithm on a given input. The $(n-1)!$ algorithm for the TRAVELING SALESMAN PROBLEM was deemed unrealistic exactly because of the excessive *exponential* growth of its time requirements (it is easy to see that the function $(n-1)!$ grows even faster than 2^n). In contrast, an algorithm with a *polynomial* rate of growth, like the algorithms we have developed in various parts of this book, would obviously be much more attractive.

It seems that, in order to capture the notion of "practically feasible algorithm" we must limit our computational devices to only run for a number of steps that is bounded by a **polynomial** in the length of the input. But which computational devices exactly should we choose as the basis of this important theory? The Turing machine, its multitape variant, the multidimensional one, or perhaps the random access model? The simulation results in Section 4.3 tell us that, since we are interested in polynomial growths, *the choice does not matter* —as long as we leave out the nondeterministic model with its apparent exponential power, recall Section 4.5 and see Section 6.4. If a Turing machine *of any one of these deterministic kinds* halts after a polynomial number of steps, there is an equivalent Turing machine *of any other kind* which also halts after a polynomial number of steps —only the polynomials will differ. So we might as well settle on the simplest model, the standard Turing machine. This "model independence" is an important side benefit of the choice of the polynomial rates of growth as our concept of "efficiency."

We are therefore led to the following definition:

Definition 6.1.1: A Turing machine $M = (K, \Sigma, \delta, s, H)$ is said to be **polynomially bounded** if there is a polynomial $p(n)$ such that the following is true: For any input x, there is no configuration C such that $(s, \triangleright \underline{\sqcup} x) \vdash_M^{p(|x|)+1} C$. In other words, the machine always halts after at most $p(n)$ steps, where n is the length of the input.

A language is called **polynomially decidable** if there is a polynomially bounded Turing machine that decides it. The class of all polynomially decidable languages is denoted $\mathcal{P}$.

Our quantitative refinement of the Church-Turing thesis can now be stated as follows: *Polynomially bounded Turing machines and the class $\mathcal{P}$ adequately capture the intuitive notions, respectively, of practically feasible algorithms and realistically solvable problems.*

In other words, we are proposing $\mathcal{P}$ as the quantitative analog of the class of recursive languages. In fact, $\mathcal{P}$ does indeed have some of the properties of the class of recursive languages:

Theorem 6.1.1: $\mathcal{P}$ *is closed under complement.*

Proof: If a language L is decidable by a polynomially bounded Turing machine M, then its complement is decided by the version of M that inverts y and n. Obviously, the polynomial bound is unaffected. ∎

Moreover, we can use diagonalization to exhibit certain simple recursive languages that are not in $\mathcal{P}$. Consider the following quantitative analog of the "halting" language H (recall Section 5.3):

$$E = \{\,\text{``}M\text{''}\,\text{``}w\text{''} : M \text{ accepts input } w \text{ after at most } 2^{|w|} \text{ steps}\}.$$

Theorem 6.1.2: $E \notin \mathcal{P}$.

Proof: The proof mimics rather faithfully that of the undecidability of the halting problem (Theorem 5.3.1). Suppose that $E \in \mathcal{P}$. Then the following language is also in $\mathcal{P}$:

$$E_1 = \{\,\text{``}M\text{''} : M \text{ accepts ``}M\text{''} \text{ after at most } 2^{|\text{``}M\text{''}|} \text{ steps}\},$$

and, by Theorem 6.1.1 so is its complement, $\overline{E_1}$. Therefore, there is a Turing machine M^* accepting all descriptions of Turing machines that *fail* to accept their own description within time 2^n (where n is the length of the description); M^* rejects all other inputs. Furthermore, M^* always halts within $p(n)$ steps, where $p(n)$ is a polynomial. We can assume that M^* is a single-tape machine because, otherwise, it can be converted to one with no loss of the polynomial property.

Recall that, since $p(n)$ is a polynomial, there is a positive integer n_0 such that $p(n) \leq 2^n$ for all $n \geq n_0$. Furthermore, we can assume that the length of the encoding of M^* is at least n_0, that is, $|\text{``}M^*\text{''}| \geq n_0$. If not, we can add to M^* n_0 useless states that are never reached in a computation.

The question is now this: *What does M^* do when presented with its own description, "M^*"?* Does it accept or reject? (It was constructed so that it does one of the two.) Both answers lead to a contradiction: If M^* accepts "M^*", then since M^* decides $\overline{E_1}$, this means that M^* does not accept "M^*" within $2^{|\text{"}M^*\text{"}|}$ steps; but M^* was constructed so that it always halts within $p(n)$ steps on inputs of length n, and $2^{|\text{"}M^*\text{"}|} > p(|\text{"}M^*\text{"}|)$; so it must reject. Similarly, by assuming that M^* rejects its own description, we deduce that it accepts it. Since the only assumption that led to this contradiction was that $E \in \mathcal{P}$, we must conclude that $E \notin \mathcal{P}$. ∎

Problems for Section 6.1

6.1.1. Show that $\mathcal{P}$ is also closed under union, intersection, and concatenation.

6.1.2. Show that $\mathcal{P}$ is closed under Kleene star. (This is harder than the proofs of the closure properties in the previous problem. To tell whether $x \in L^*$ for some $L \in \mathcal{P}$, you have to consider all substrings of x, starting with the ones of length one and progressing towards longer and longer ones —very much like the *dynamic programming* algorithm for context-free recognition; recall Section 3.6.)

6.2 | PROBLEMS, PROBLEMS...

How well does the class $\mathcal{P}$ capture the intuitive notion of "satisfactorily solvable problem?" How widely accepted is the thesis that polynomial algorithms are precisely the empirically feasible ones? It is fair to say that, while it is the only serious proposal in this arena, it can be challenged on various grounds[†]. For example, it can be argued that an algorithm with time requirements n^{100}, or even $10^{100}n^2$, is not at all "practically feasible," even though it is a polynomial-time one. Also, an algorithm with time requirements $n^{\log \log n}$ may be considered perfectly feasible in practice, despite the fact that its growth is not bounded by any polynomial. The empirical argument in defense of our thesis is that such extreme time bounds, though theoretically possible, *rarely come up in practice:* Polynomial algorithms that arise in computational practice usually have small exponents and palatable constant coefficients, while nonpolynomial algorithms are usually hopelessly exponential, and are therefore of quite limited use in practice.

[†] But even the Church-Turing thesis was challenged extensively during its time, and in fact from both sides: There were mathematicians who thought that Turing decidability is too restricted a notion, while others opined that it is too liberal. In fact, complexity theory, the subject of this and the next chapter, can be seen as the latest and most serious challenge of the latter type.

A further criticism of our thesis is that it categorizes an algorithm based only on its *worst-case* performance (the largest running time over all inputs of length n). Arguably, an *average-case* approach —for example, insisting that the time requirements of a Turing machine, when averaged over all possible inputs of length n, be bounded by $p(n)$— would be a better predictor of the practical utility of the algorithm. Although average-case analysis seems a very reasonable alternative, it is in fact itself open to even more devastating challenges. For example, which distribution on the inputs should we adopt in our average-case analysis? There seems to be no satisfactory answer.

Despite these reservations, however, polynomially bounded computation is an appealing and productive concept, and it leads to an elegant and useful theory. By focusing on the gray areas on its boundary, one often forgets what a useful classification tool it is, that it includes mostly practically feasible algorithms, and excludes mostly impractical ones. But the best way to get acquainted with polynomial-time computation, its true scope, and its limitations, is to introduce a variety of interesting computational problems that are known to belong in $\mathcal{P}$. It is also instructive to contrast such problems with certain examples of stubborn problems that *do not seem to be in* $\mathcal{P}$. Often the difficult and the easy problems look very similar.

We have already seen some very interesting specimens and subclasses of $\mathcal{P}$. For example, all regular languages and all context-free languages belong there (recall Theorems 2.6.2 and 3.6.1, part (c)). We also know that the *reflexive-transitive closure* of a relation can be computed in polynomial time (Section 1.6). We next examine an interesting variant of this latter problem.

The *reachability problem* is the following

REACHABILITY: Given a directed graph $G \subseteq V \times V$, where $V = \{v_1, \ldots, v_n\}$ is a finite set, and two nodes $v_i, v_j \in V$, is there a path from v_i to v_j?

(All graphs mentioned in the context of computational problems are, of course finite.) Is REACHABILITY in $\mathcal{P}$? Strictly speaking, since $\mathcal{P}$ contains only languages, REACHABILITY has no business there. REACHABILITY is what we call a **problem**. A problem is a set of *inputs*, typically infinite, together with a *yes-or-no question* asked of each input (a property an input may or may not have). In the example of REACHABILITY the set of inputs is the set of all triples (G, v_i, v_j), where G is a finite graph, and v_i, v_j are two nodes of G. The question asked is whether there is a path from v_i to v_j in G.

This is not the first time that we see problems. The HALTING PROBLEM is definitely a problem: Its inputs are Turing machines and strings, and the question asked is whether the given Turing machine halts when started on this input string:

HALTING PROBLEM: Given a Turing machine M and an input string w, does M accept w?

In Chapter 5 we studied the HALTING PROBLEM in terms of its "linguistic surrogate," the language

$$H = \{ \text{``}M\text{''}\,\text{``}w\text{''} : \text{Turing machine } M \text{ halts on string } w \}.$$

Similarly, we can study the REACHABILITY problem in terms of the language

$$R = \{ \kappa(G)\mathbf{b}(i)\mathbf{b}(j) : \text{There is a path from } v_i \text{ to } v_j \text{ in } G \},$$

where $\mathbf{b}(i)$ denotes the binary encoding of integer i, and κ is some reasonable way of encoding graphs as strings. Several natural encodings of graphs come to mind. Let us agree to encode a graph $G \subseteq V \times V$ by its *adjacency matrix*, linearized as a string (recall Example 4.4.3 and Figure 4-21). One of the main points that will emerge from the discussion that follows is that *the precise details of encodings rarely matter.*

Languages encode problems. But of course also any language $L \subseteq \Sigma^*$ can be thought of as a problem:

THE DECISION PROBLEM FOR L: Given a string $x \in \Sigma^*$, is $x \in L$?

It is productive to think of a problem and the associated language interchangeably. Languages are more appropriate in connection to Turing machines, while problems are more clear statements of practical computational tasks of interest, for which we must develop algorithms. In the following pages we shall introduce and discuss extensively many interesting problems; we shall treat a problem and the corresponding language as two different aspects of the same thing. For example, we shall next point out that REACHABILITY is in $\mathcal{P}$. By this we mean that the corresponding language R, defined above, is in $\mathcal{P}$.

Indeed, REACHABILITY can be solved by first computing the reflexive-transitive closure of G, in time $\mathcal{O}(n^3)$ by the random access Turing machine of Example 4.4.3. Inspecting the entry of the reflexive-transitive closure of G that corresponds to v_i and v_j would then tell us whether there is a path from v_i to v_j in G. Since we know that random access machines can be simulated by ordinary Turing machines in polynomial time, it follows that REACHABILITY is in $\mathcal{P}$.

Notice that, since we are only interested in determining whether the time bound is or is not a polynomial, we felt free to express it as a function *not of the length of the input*, which is $m = |\kappa(G)\mathbf{b}(i)\mathbf{b}(j)|$, but as a function of $n = |V|$, the number of nodes: Since it is easy to see that $m = \mathcal{O}(n^3)$, this is yet another inconsequential inaccuracy, one that will not interfere with the issues that we deem important.

Eulerian and Hamiltonian Graphs

Historically the first problem concerning graphs, studied and solved by the great mathematician of the eighteenth century Leonard Euler, is this:

EULER CYCLE: Given a graph G, is there a closed path in G that uses each edge exactly once?

The path sought can go through each node many times (or even not at all, if the graph has *isolated nodes*, nodes without edges in or out of them). A graph that contains such a path is called **Eulerian** or **unicursal**. For example, the graph shown in Figure 6-1(a) is Eulerian by virtue of the closed path $(v_1, v_2, v_3, v_4, v_3, v_2, v_4, v_1)$ while the graph in Figure 6-1(b) is not.

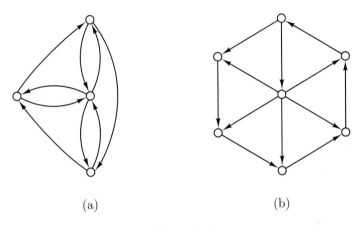

(a)   (b)

Figure 6-1

It is not difficult to see that EULER CYCLE is in $\mathcal{P}$ —by this we mean, of course, that the corresponding language

$$L = \{\kappa(G) : G \text{ is Eulerian}\}$$

is in $\mathcal{P}$. This follows from the following neat characterization of Eulerian graphs due to, well, Euler. Call a node in a graph *isolated* if and only if it has no edges incident upon it.

A graph G is Eulerian if and only if it has the following two properties:
(a) For any pair of nodes $u, v \in V$ neither of which is isolated, there is a path from u to v; and
(b) All nodes have equal numbers of incoming and outgoing edges.

It is rather immediate that both conditions are necessary for the graph to be Eulerian. We leave the proof of sufficiency as an exercise (Problem 6.2.1).

It is thus very easy to test whether a graph is Eulerian: We first make sure that all nodes, except for any isolated ones, are connected; this can be done in polynomial time by computing the reflexive-transitive closure of the graph, and then testing whether all nodes except for the isolated ones are connected in all possible ways (after all, the reflexive-transitive closure of a graph contains the answer to all possible connectivity questions on the graph). We know that the reflexive-transitive closure can be computed in a polynomial number of steps. We then test whether all nodes have an equal number of incoming and outgoing edges —this can be obviously done in polynomial time as well.

Incidentally, this is an instance of a pattern that will be repeated *ad nauseam* in the next pages: We show that a problem (EULER CYCLE) is in $\mathcal{P}$ by using the previously established fact that another problem (in our case REACHABILITY) in $\mathcal{P}$ —that is, by *reducing it to an already solved problem.*

Perhaps the main point of this and the next chapter is that there are many natural, decidable, simply stated problems that are *not known or believed to be in $\mathcal{P}$.* Very often, such a problem is very similar to another that is known to be in $\mathcal{P}$! Consider, for example, the following problem, studied by another famous mathematician, this time of the nineteenth century, William Rowan Hamilton —and many mathematicians after him:

> HAMILTON CYCLE: Given a graph G, is there a cycle that passes through each node of G exactly once?

Such a cycle is called a *Hamilton cycle,* and a graph that has one is called *Hamiltonian.* Notice the difference: Now it is the nodes, not the edges, that must be traversed exactly once; not all edges need be traversed. For example, the graph in Figure 6-1(b) is Hamiltonian but not Eulerian, while the one in Figure 6-1(a) is both Eulerian and Hamiltonian.

Despite the superficial similarity between the two problems EULER CYCLE and HAMILTON CYCLE, there appears to be a world of difference between them. After one and a half centuries of scrutiny by many talented mathematicians, no one has discovered a polynomial algorithm for HAMILTON CYCLE. Naturally, the following algorithm does solve the problem:

> Examine all possible permutations of the nodes;
> for each test whether it is a Hamilton cycle.

Unfortunately it fails to be polynomial, as do all simple ways of improving it and speeding it up.

Optimization Problems

The TRAVELING SALESMAN PROBLEM, introduced informally in the beginning of this chapter, is another simply stated problem for which, despite intense research efforts over several decades, no polynomial-time algorithm is known. We are given a set $\{c_1, c_2, \ldots, c_n\}$ of *cities,* and an $n \times n$ matrix of nonnegative integers d, where d_{ij} denotes the *distance* between city c_i and city c_j. We are assuming that $d_{ii} = 0$ and $d_{ij} = d_{ji}$ for all i, j. We are asked to find *the shortest tour* of the cities, that is, a bijection π from the set $\{1, 2, \ldots, n\}$ to itself (where $\pi(i)$ is, intuitively, the city visited ith in the tour), such that the quantity

$$c(\pi) = d_{\pi(1)\pi(2)} + d_{\pi(2)\pi(3)} + \cdots + d_{\pi(n-1)\pi(n)} + d_{\pi(n)\pi(1)}$$

is as small as possible.

There is a serious obstacle for studying the traveling salesman problem within our framework of problems and languages: Unlike all other problems we have seen in this chapter, the traveling salesman problem is not the kind of problem that requires a "yes" or "no" answer and can therefore be studied in terms of a language. It is an *optimization* problem, in that it requires us to find the best (according to some *cost function*) among many possible solutions.

There is a useful general method for turning optimization problems into languages, so that we can study their complexity: Supply each input with a *bound* on the cost function. In this case, consider the following problem:

TRAVELING SALESMAN PROBLEM: Given an integer $n \geq 2$, an $n \times n$ distance matrix d_{ij}, *and an integer* $B \geq 0$ (intuitively, the *budget* of the traveling salesman) find a permutation π of $\{1, 2, \ldots, n\}$ such that $c(\pi) \leq B$.

If we could solve the original optimization problem in polynomial time, that is, if we had an algorithm for computing the cheapest tour, then obviously we would be able to solve this "budget" version in polynomial time as well: Just compute the cost of the cheapest tour and compare it with B. Thus, any *negative* result about the complexity of the TRAVELING SALESMAN PROBLEM as defined just now will reflect negatively on our prospects for solving the original, optimization version of the problem.

We shall use this maneuver to bring many interesting optimization problems within our language framework. In the case of *maximization problems* we do not supply a budget B but instead a *goal* K. For example, the following is an important maximization problem transformed this way:

INDEPENDENT SET: Given an *undirected graph* G and an integer $K \geq 2$, is there a subset C of V with $|C| \geq K$ such that for all $v_i, v_j \in C$, there is no edge between v_i and v_j?

INDEPENDENT SET is yet another natural and simply stated problem for which, despite prolonged and intense interest by researchers, no polynomial-time algorithm has been found.

Let us introduce two more optimization problems on undirected graphs. The next problem is in some sense the exact opposite of INDEPENDENT SET:

CLIQUE: Given an undirected graph G and an integer $K \geq 2$, is there a subset C of V with $|C| \geq K$ such that for all $v_i, v_j \in C$, there is an edge between v_i and v_j?

For the next problem, let us say that a set of nodes *covers* an edge if it contains at least one endpoint of the edge.

NODE COVER: Given an undirected graph G and an integer $B \geq 2$, is there a subset C of V with $|C| \leq B$ such that C covers all edges of G?

We can think of the nodes of an undirected graph as the rooms of a museum, and each edge as a long straight corridor that joins two rooms. Then the NODE COVER problem may be useful in assigning as few as possible guards to the rooms, so that all corridors can be seen by a guard.

To illustrate these interesting problems, the largest independent set of the graph in Figure 6-2 has three nodes; the largest clique has four nodes; and the smallest node cover has six nodes. Can you find them? Can you convince yourself that they are optimal?

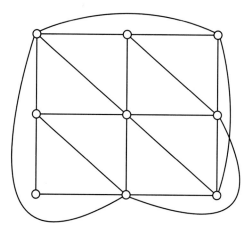

Figure 6-2

Integer Partitions

Suppose that we are given several positive integers, say $38, 17, 52, 61, 21, 88, 25$. We are asked whether they can be divided into two disjoint sets, which include between them all numbers, and both add up to the same number. In the above

example the answer is "yes," because $38 + 52 + 61 = 17 + 21 + 88 + 25 = 151$.
The general problem is this:

> PARTITION: Given a set n nonnegative integers $a_1, \ldots, a_n$ *represented in binary*, is there a subset $P \subseteq \{1, \ldots, n\}$ such that $\sum_{i \in P} a_i = \sum_{i \notin P} a_i$?

This problem can be solved by a simple algorithm explained next. First, let H be the sum of all integers in S divided by 2 (if this number is not an integer, then the numbers in S add up to an odd number and cannot be partitioned into two equal sums; so we can already answer "no"). For each i, $0 \le i \le n$, define this set of numbers:

$$B(i) = \{b \le H : b \text{ is the sum of some subset of the numbers } \{a_1, \ldots, a_i\}\}.$$

If we knew $B(n)$, we could solve the PARTITION problem easily by just testing whether $H \in B(n)$. If so, there is a partial sum that adds up to H and the answer is "yes"; otherwise, the answer is "no."

But notice that $B(n)$ can be computed by the following algorithm:

$B(0) := \{0\}$.
for $i = 1, 2, \ldots, n$ do
   $B(i) := B(i-1)$,
    for $j = a_i, a_i + 1, a_i + 2, \ldots, H$ do
      if $j - a_i \in B(i-1)$ then add j to $B(i)$

For example, in the instance of PARTITION shown above, with $a_1 = 38$, $a_2 = 17$, $a_3 = 52$, $a_4 = 61$, $a_5 = 21$, $a_6 = 88$, $a_7 = 25$, the $B(i)$ sets are as follows:

$B(0) = \{0\}$

$B(1) = \{0, 38\}$

$B(2) = \{0, 17, 38, 55\}$

$B(3) = \{0, 17, 38, 52, 55, 69, 90, 107\}$

$B(4) = \{0, 17, 38, 52, 55, 61, 69, 78, 90, 107, 113, 116, 130, 151\}$

$B(5) = \{0, 17, 21, 38, 52, 55, 59, 61, 69, 73, 76, 78, 82, 90, 99, 107, 111, 113, 116, 128, \\ 130, 134, 137, 151\}$

$B(6) = \{0, 17, 21, 38, 52, 55, 59, 61, 69, 73, 76, 78, 82, 88, 90, 99, 105, 107, 109, 111, \\ 113, 116, 126, 128, 130, 134, 137, 140, 143, 147, 149, 151\}$

$B(7) = \{0, 17, 21, 25, 38, 42, 46, 52, 55, 59, 61, 63, 69, 73, 76, 77, 78, 80, 82, 84, 86, \\ 88, 90, 94, 98, 99, 101, 103, 105, 107, 109, 111, 113, 115, 116, 124, 126, 128, \\ 130, 132, 134, 136, 137, 138, 140, 141, 143, 147, 149, 151\}$

This instance of PARTITION is a "yes" instance, because the half-sum $H = 151$ is contained in $B(7)$.

It is easy to prove by induction on i that this algorithm correctly computes $B(i)$, for $i = 0, \ldots, n$, and does so in $\mathcal{O}(nH)$ time (see Problem 6.2.5). Have we then proved that PARTITION is in $\mathcal{P}$?

The bound $\mathcal{O}(nH)$, despite its perfectly polynomial appearance, is *not polynomial in the length of the input*. The reason is that the integers $a_1, \ldots, a_n$ are given in binary, and thus their sum will in general be exponentially large when compared to the length of the input. For example, if all n integers in an instance of PARTITION are about 2^n, then H is approximately $\frac{n}{2} 2^n$, while the length of the input is only $\mathcal{O}(n^2)$. In fact, PARTITION is one of the notoriously hard problems, including the TRAVELING SALESMAN PROBLEM, HAMILTON CYCLE, and INDEPENDENT SET, for which no true polynomial algorithm is known or expected any time soon (and which are the subject of the next chapter).

However, the above algorithm does establish that the following problem is indeed in $\mathcal{P}$.

> UNARY PARTITION: Given a set of n natural numbers $\{a_1, \ldots, a_n\}$ *represented in unary*, is there a subset $P \subseteq \{1, \ldots, n\}$ such that $\sum_{i \in P} a_i = \sum_{i \notin P} a_i$?

This is because the input of the unary version has length about H, and so the $\mathcal{O}(nH)$ algorithm suddenly becomes "efficient."

This pair of problems, PARTITION and UNARY PARTITION, with their contrasting complexity, illustrates the following important fact about input representations: The precise representation of mathematical objects such as graphs, automata, Turing machines, and so on, as inputs to problems makes little difference in the membership of the corresponding language in $\mathcal{P}$, because the lengths of all reasonable representations of the same object are related by a polynomial. The only encoding convention whose violation leads to misleading results, is that *integers should be encoded in binary*,[†] and *not* in unary.

Equivalence of Finite Automata

In Chapter 2 we saw that the following important problem concerning finite automata is in $\mathcal{P}$ (Theorem 2.6.1, part (e)):

> EQUIVALENCE OF DETERMINISTIC FINITE AUTOMATA: Given two deterministic finite automata M_1 and M_2, is $L(M_1) = L(M_2)$?

In contrast, we noticed that we only know how to test *nondeterministic finite automata* for equivalence in exponential time. That is, we do not know whether either of the following two problems is in $\mathcal{P}$:

[†] Or in decimal, hexadecimal, or in any other radix system; all such representations of the same integer have lengths that are constant multiples of each other.

EQUIVALENCE OF NONDETERMINISTIC FINITE AUTOMATA: Given two non-deterministic finite automata M_1 and M_2, is $L(M_1) = L(M_2)$?

and

EQUIVALENCE OF REGULAR EXPRESSIONS: Given two regular expressions R_1 and R_2, is $L(R_1) = L(R_2)$?

One could solve either problem by transforming the two given nondeterministic automata (or regular expressions) to deterministic ones (Theorem 2.6.1), and then checking the resulting deterministic automata for equivalence. The problem is, of course, that the transformation from regular expressions or nondeterministic automata to deterministic may increase exponentially the number of states of the automaton (recall Example 2.5.4). Hence this approach fails to establish that either one of EQUIVALENCE OF NONDETERMINISTIC FINITE AUTOMATA and EQUIVALENCE OF REGULAR EXPRESSIONS is in $\mathcal{P}$ —as do, in fact, far more sophisticated approaches.

Problems for Section 6.2

6.2.1. Show that a graph is Eulerian if and only if it is connected and the in-degree of each node equals its out-degree. (*Hint:* One direction is easy. For the other, start at a node, and traverse an edge to get to another node. Continue traversing *new* edges until you cannot find a new one; at this point you are back at the starting node (why?). Show how you can start again and traverse the pieces of the graph you have left untraversed.)

6.2.2. Prove that the algorithm given in the text solves PARTITION in $\mathcal{O}(nH)$ steps.

6.2.3. Solve the traveling salesman problem for five cities A, B, C, D, and E with the following distance matrix:

$$
\begin{array}{c}
 & \begin{array}{cccc} B & C & D & E \end{array} \\
\begin{array}{c} A \\ B \\ C \\ D \end{array}
\left(\begin{array}{cccc}
8 & 4 & 5 & 9 \\
  & 1 & 7 & 3 \\
  &   & 6 & 2 \\
  &   &   & 5
\end{array}\right)
\end{array}
$$

6.2.4. We study optimization problems in terms of their language versions, defined in terms of a "budget" B or "target" K. Choose one of the optimization problems introduced in this section, and show that there is a polynomial algorithm for the original problem if and only if there is one for the "yes-no" version. (One direction is trivial. For the other, *binary search* is needed, plus a property of these problems that might be called *self-reducibility*.)

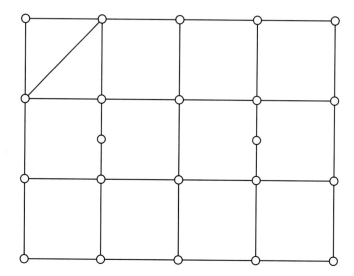

6.2.5. Does the undirected graph above have a Hamilton cycle? What is the largest clique, largest independent set, and smallest node cover of this graph?

6.3 | BOOLEAN SATISFIABILITY

In the previous section we saw many interesting computational problems that are in $\mathcal{P}$, and some others that are suspected not to be in $\mathcal{P}$. But perhaps the most fundamental problems of both kinds are related to **Boolean logic**.

Boolean logic is a familiar mathematical notation for expressing compound statements such as "either it is not raining now or the cane is not in the corner." In Boolean Logic we use **Boolean variables** $x_1, x_2, \ldots$ to stand for the individual statements such as "it is raining now." That is, each variable denotes a statement that can in principle be true or false independently of the truth value of the others. We then use **Boolean connectives** to combine Boolean variables and form more complicated **Boolean formulae**. For our purposes in this book we need only consider Boolean formulae of a specific kind, defined next.

Definition 6.3.1: Let $X = \{x_1, x_2, \ldots x_n\}$ be a finite set of **Boolean variables**, and let $\overline{X} = \{\overline{x_1}, \overline{x_2}, \ldots \overline{x_n}\}$, where the $\overline{x_1}, \overline{x_2}, \ldots, \overline{x_n}$ are new symbols standing for the **negations**, or opposites, of $x_1, x_2, \ldots, x_n$. We call the elements of $X \cup \overline{X}$ **literals**; variables are **positive literals**, whereas negations of variables are **negative literals**. A **clause** C is a nonempty set of literals: $C \subseteq X \cup \overline{X}$. Finally, a **Boolean formula in conjunctive normal form** (or simply **Boolean formula**, since we shall treat no other kind in this book) is a set of clauses defined on X.

Example 6.3.1: Let $X = \{x_1, x_2, x_3\}$, and therefore $\overline{X} = \{\overline{x_1}, \overline{x_2}, \overline{x_3}\}$. $C_1 = \{x_1, \overline{x_2}, x_3\}$ is a clause. Although a clause is a set of literals, we shall employ a special notation when writing clauses: We shall use parentheses instead of our usual set brackets; and we shall separate the various literals in the clause (if there are more than one) by the delimiter $\vee$ (pronounced **or**), instead of a comma. As always with sets, order is not important, and repetition of elements is not tolerated. For example, the clause C above will be written $C = (x_1 \vee \overline{x_2} \vee x_3)$.

The following is a Boolean formula in conjunctive normal form:

$$F = \{(x_1 \vee \overline{x_2} \vee x_3), (\overline{x_1}), (x_2 \vee \overline{x_2})\}. \tag{1}$$

It consists of three clauses, one of which is C above.◊

Definition 6.3.2: So far we have only defined the *syntax*, or apparent structure, of Boolean formulae. We next define the *semantics*, or meaning, of such a formula. Let F be a Boolean formula in conjunctive normal form defined over the variables in $X = \{x_1, x_2, \ldots x_n\}$. A **truth assignment** for F is a mapping from X to the set $\{\top, \bot\}$, where $\top$ and $\bot$ are two new symbols pronounced **true** and **false**, respectively. We say that a truth assignment T **satisfies** F if the following holds: For each clause $C \in F$ there is at least one variable x_i such that either (a) $T(x_i) = \top$, and $x_i \in C$, or (b) $T(x_i) = \bot$, and $\overline{x_i} \in C$. That is, a clause is satisfied if it contains *at least one true literal*, where x_i is considered true if and only if $T(x_i) = \top$, and $\overline{x_i}$ is considered true if and only if $T(x_i) = \bot$.

Finally, F is called **satisfiable** if there is a truth assignment that satisfies it.

Example 6.3.2: The Boolean formula F in (1) above is satisfied by the truth assignment T, where $T(x_1) = \bot$, $T(x_2) = \top$, and $T(x_3) = \top$. This truth assignment satisfies the clause $C_1 = (x_1 \vee \overline{x_2} \vee x_3)$ because $T(x_3) = \top$, and $x_3 \in C_1$; T satisfies the clause $C_2 = (\overline{x_1})$ because $\overline{x_1} \in C_2$, and $T(x_1) = \bot$; and it finally satisfies the third clause $C_3 = (x_2 \vee \overline{x_2})$ (this is not too surprising, as *any* truth assignment would satisfy C_3). There are many truth assignments that fail to satisfy F: For example, any truth assignment T' with $T'(x_1) = \bot$ would fail to satisfy C_2 and thus fail to satisfy F. Still, F is satisfiable, because there is at least one truth assignment that satisfies it.◊

Example 6.3.3: Consider now this formula:

$$F' = \{(x_1 \vee x_2 \vee x_3), (\overline{x_1} \vee x_2), (\overline{x_2} \vee x_3), (\overline{x_3} \vee x_1), (\overline{x_1} \vee \overline{x_2} \vee \overline{x_3})\}.$$

Is it satisfiable? The correct answer here is "no." Let us prove it.

The clause $(x_1 \lor x_2 \lor x_3)$ requires that at least one of the variables x_1, x_2, and x_3 be $\top$. Similarly, the last clause requires that at least one of them be $\bot$. Consider then the remaining three clauses, and suppose that $T(x_1) = \top$. Then in order for the clause $(\overline{x_1} \lor x_2)$ to be satisfied, $T(x_2)$ must be $\top$; and to satisfy $(\overline{x_2} \lor x_3)$ we must have $T(x_3) = \top$. On the other hand, if $T(x_1) = \bot$ then the $(\overline{x_3} \lor x_1)$ clause forces $T(x_3)$ to be $\bot$, and the $(\overline{x_2} \lor x_3)$ clause then makes $T(x_2)$ necessarily $\bot$. So, no matter what $T(x_1)$ is, *the truth values of the three variables must be the same* if the formula is to be satisfied.

To summarize, for a truth assignment to satisfy F' it must (a) map at least one variable to $\top$; (b) map at least one variable to $\bot$; and (c) map all three variables to the same truth value. This is clearly impossible, and thus F' encodes a contradiction: It is **unsatisfiable**.◊

> SATISFIABILITY: Given a Boolean formula F in conjunctive normal form, is it satisfiable?

This suggests the following important problem:

SATISFIABILITY: Given a Boolean formula F in conjunctive normal form, is it satisfiable?

As it perhaps became apparent in the previous example, it is a fairly tricky problem. Indeed, there is no known polynomial-time algorithm to date for this fundamental and very well-studied problem, and it is widely believed that no such algorithm exists.

2-SATISFIABILITY

Suppose that we restrict the instances of SATISFIABILITY to ones in which *all clauses have two or fewer literals*. What results is a new problem, which we call 2-SATISFIABILITY. We say that 2-SATISFIABILITY is a *special case* of SATISFIABILITY. By this we mean that the set of all possible inputs is a subset of the set of inputs for SATISFIABILITY, and the answers to each common input in the two problems are the same. A typical instance of 2-SATISFIABILITY is shown below.

$$\{(x_1 \lor x_2), (x_3 \lor \overline{x_2}), (x_1), (\overline{x_1} \lor \overline{x_2}), (x_3 \lor x_4), (\overline{x_3} \lor x_5), (\overline{x_4} \lor \overline{x_5}), (x_4 \lor \overline{x_3})\} \quad (2)$$

We shall next describe a sensible method for searching for a satisfying truth assignment for such a formula. During the course of our method, several variables will have been assigned $\top$ or $\bot$, while the rest are not yet assigned. Initially no variable is assigned a truth value.

Suppose that there is in our formula a clause with just one literal, say the third clause (x_1) in the example in (2). Then clearly this literal must be $\top$ in any satisfying truth assignment, and therefore we can immediately decide on the value of this variable. That is, in our example we immediately decide that $T(x_1) = \top$, and proceed. Now that we know that $T(x_1) = \top$, we can omit from the formula all clauses that contain x_1 as one of their literals, because these clauses are already satisfied (in our example we omit the first clause). If however a clause contains the opposite literal $\overline{x_1}$, then *we omit the literal from the clause*, because this literal is $\bot$ and thus it is of no use in satisfying the clause. In our example, the first clause is omitted, and the fourth clause is replaced by $(\overline{x_2})$. Thus, assigning a truth value to a literal that appears alone in a clause, may result in new single-literal clauses, and we must repeat (in our example (2) we next set $T(x_2) = \bot$).

We call this process of pursuing one-literal clauses until none exists a *purge*. If at any point of the purge the *empty clause* is produced —presumably because both clauses (x_i) and $(\overline{x_i})$, for some i, were present at the previous step— then we say that the purge has *failed*. In any event, after $\mathcal{O}(n)$ steps of this sort, where n is the number of clauses in the given formula, the purge must indeed either fail (in which case we decide that the formula is unsatisfiable), or halt with a set of clauses each of which has two distinct literals. In (2), for example, the initial purge ends up setting $T(x_1) = \top$, $T(x_2) = \bot$, and deleting the first four clauses.

We can therefore assume that we have a formula with precisely two literals in each clause. How can we look for a satisfying truth assignment? Here is a simple idea: Take any variable whose truth value has not been assigned yet, try setting its truth value to $\top$, and perform the purge; then restore the formula in its original form, set the same variable to $\bot$ and perform the purge again. If both purges fail, we give up; the formula is *unsatisfiable*. If however at least one of the two purges succeeds, then *we set the variable to the successful truth value and continue*. In our example trying the value $T(x_3) = \top$ in the four clauses that remain after the first purge,

$$\{(x_3 \vee x_4), (\overline{x_3} \vee x_5), (\overline{x_4} \vee \overline{x_5}), (x_4 \vee \overline{x_3})\} \tag{3}$$

starts a new purge that fails after setting $T(x_5) = \top$ (the clauses (x_4) and $(\overline{x_4})$ result); so we must restore the four clauses in (3) and try $T(x_3) = \bot$. This succeeds in finding a satisfying truth assignment for the whole formula (there are no clauses left), namely $T(x_4) = \top$ and $T(x_5) = \bot$.

It is easy to see (Problem 6.3.2) that this simple algorithm correctly solves the satisfiability problem when there are at most two literals per clause. Since the algorithm performs at most two purges for each variable, and each purge can be performed in polynomial time, it follows that 2-SATISFIABILITY is in $\mathcal{P}$.

Problems for Section 6.3

6.3.1. Find all satisfying truth assignments of the Boolean formula consisting of these clauses: $(x_1 \vee \overline{x_2} \vee x_3), (\overline{x_1} \vee x_4), (x_2 \vee \overline{x_3} \vee \overline{x_4})$.

6.3.2. (a) Show that the purge algorithm described in the text correctly solves any instance of 2-SATISFIABILITY in polynomial time. (*Hint:* Suppose the purge algorithm decides the formula is unsatisfiable, and yet a satisfying truth assignment exists. How did the purge algorithm miss this assignment?)
   (b) What is the lowest polynomial bound you can show for this algorithm?
   (c) How would the purge algorithm work on this formula? $(x_1 \vee \overline{x_2}), (\overline{x_1} \vee \overline{x_4}), (x_2 \vee \overline{x_3})(x_1 \vee x_4), (x_3 \vee x_4)$.

6.3.3. This is an alternative proof that 2-SATISFIABILITY is in $\mathcal{P}$. Any clause with two literals, say $(x \vee y)$, can be thought of as two *implications*, namely $(\overline{x} \rightarrow y)$ and $(\overline{y} \rightarrow x)$ (the clause (x) can be thought of as $(\overline{x} \rightarrow x)$). Thus, starting from any instance of 2-SATISFIABILITY, we can construct a directed graph with all literals as nodes that depicts all these implications. Show that an instance of 2-SATISFIABILITY is unsatisfiable if and only if there is a variable x such that there is a path from x to $\overline{x}$ *and* a path from $\overline{x}$ to x in this graph. Conclude that 2-SATISFIABILITY is in $\mathcal{P}$.

6.4 | THE CLASS NP

One of the main goals of complexity theory is to discover mathematical methods that will help us prove that problems of interest are not in $\mathcal{P}$. We have already seen such a method: The *diagonalization argument* used to establish, in full analogy with the unsolvability of the halting problem H, that $E \notin \mathcal{P}$, where E is the language

$$E = \{ \text{``}M\text{''} \text{``}w\text{''} : M \text{ accepts input } w \text{ after at most } 2^{|w|} \text{ steps} \}$$

(Theorem 6.1.2). However, this result is hardly satisfying. The reason is that, unlike the notion of decidability, $\mathcal{P}$ and polynomial-time computation are concepts of earthy, practical motivation. It is not enough to exhibit an artificial halting-like problem like E and argue that it is not in $\mathcal{P}$. We want to identify natural, reasonable, practically important problems that are not in $\mathcal{P}$.

   We saw in the last section a plethora of natural, reasonable problems, quite plausibly of practical interest, that appear not to belong in $\mathcal{P}$: HAMILTON CYCLE, the TRAVELING SALESMAN PROBLEM, INDEPENDENT SET, PARTITION, SATISFIABILITY. Despite prolonged, intense efforts by mathematicians and computer scientists to discover a polynomial-time algorithm for each of these problems, none has been found. It would be most worthwhile, then, to use the ideas and methods of computational complexity to establish that no such polynomial-time algorithm is possible, thus saving our fellow scientists from further ill-fated attempts.

Unfortunately, there is a subtle difficulty in coming up with such an impossibility proof. The reason is that, as we shall see next, *all of these problems can be solved by polynomially bounded nondeterministic Turing machines.* And separating determinism from nondeterminism at the polynomial-time level is one of the most important and deep unsolved problems in computer science today.

It was established in Chapter 4 that if a language L is decidable in polynomial time by a Turing machine of one of several varieties (single-tape, multiple-tape, two-dimensional, even random access), then L is decidable in polynomial time by a machine of any of the other kinds. What about the last variant of the Turing machine model that we have introduced in Chapter 4, namely the *nondeterministic Turing machine* (Section 4.6)? Is it also equivalent to the remaining kinds, up to a polynomial? In order to discuss this important issue, let us first define formally what we mean by saying that a language is decided by a nondeterministic Turing machine within a polynomial time bound; the definition is a straightforward extension of that for deterministic machines.

Definition 6.4.1: A nondeterministic Turing machine $M = (K, \Sigma, \Delta, H)$ is said to be **polynomially bounded** if there is a polynomial $p(n)$ such that for any input x, there is no configuration C of M with $(s, \triangleright \underline{\sqcup} x) \vdash_M^{p(|x|)+1} C$; that is, no computation of this machine continues for more than polynomially many steps. And define $\mathcal{NP}$ (for **nondeterministic polynomial**) to be the class of all languages that are decided by a polynomially bounded nondeterministic Turing machine.

It is important at this point to recall the peculiar definition of what it means for a nondeterministic machine to decide a language L: For each input *not in* L, *all* computations of the machine must reject the input; for each input in L, we only require that there be *at least one computation* that accepts the input —none, some, most, or all of the other computations may reject the input, as long as there is at least one accepting one.

The set of all possible computations of a nondeterministic Turing machine on a given input is best pictured by a treelike structure (see Figure 6-3). Nodes represent configurations, and downward lines are steps. Nondeterministic choices are represented by nodes that have more than one downward line leaving them. Time is measured in the vertical dimension. In Figure 6-3, for example, the input is accepted after five steps.

Such a picture makes it transparent why nondeterminism is such a powerful mode of computation: There are astronomically many configurations that are produced in very short time (vertical distance from the root). As we shall see in the next examples, this power of nondeterminism can be put to use in "solving" some of the formidable problems we have seen in the last section.

Example 6.4.1: We mentioned in the previous section that it is widely believed

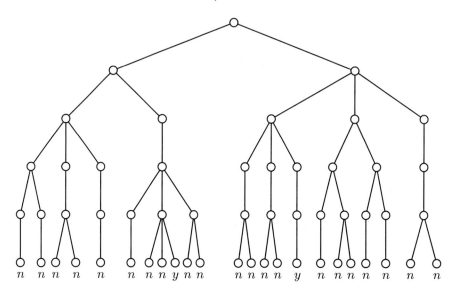

Figure 6-3

that SATISFIABILITY is not in $\mathcal{P}$. Let us now show that it is in $\mathcal{NP}$. We shall design a nondeterministic Turing machine M that decides in polynomial nondeterministic time all encodings of satisfiable Boolean formulae in conjunctive normal form.

M operates as follows: On input w, it first checks to see whether w is indeed the encoding of a Boolean formula in conjunctive normal form (if not, it rejects immediately), and counts the number of variables, n, that appear in it. This is easy to accomplish deterministically in polynomial time. At the end of this first stage, the second tape of M contains the string $\triangleright I^n$, with as many I's as the formula has variables.

Then M goes into a *nondeterministic phase*, during which it writes on its second tape a sequence of n $\top$'s and $\perp$'s over the I's. Which sequence of $\top$'s and $\perp$'s, exactly? The answer is "*any sequence, nondeterministically.*" A more precise answer is perhaps "*all sequences, each in a different branch of the tree of nondeterministic computations.*" It is easy to design a nondeterministic machine that does this: Just add a new state q to K, and add to Δ the transitions (ignoring the other tapes, where no activity takes place) $(q, I, q, \top), (q, I, q, \perp), (q, \top, q, \rightarrow), (q, \perp, q, \rightarrow), (q, \sqcup, q', \sqcup)$, where q' is the state that continues the computation.

The final phase of M is deterministic: M interprets the string in $\{\top, \perp\}^n$ in its second tape as a *truth assignment* for the input formula. It then visits each clause of the input one by one, and checks whether it contains a literal that is

⊤ under the truth assignment. If it finds that all clauses have a ⊤ literal, M accepts. Otherwise, if an unsatisfied clause is found, M rejects.

It is straightforward to see that M, as described above, establishes that SATISFIABILITY is in $\mathcal{NP}$. First, all computations are of length bounded by some small polynomial. For the crucial part, if the input encodes a satisfiable Boolean formula, then M will "guess" the satisfying truth assignment at some branch of the nondeterministic computation, and will therefore have at least one accepting computation —in addition to possibly many rejecting ones. Hence the input will be accepted. If the input formula is unsatisfiable, or not a formula at all, then all computations will end up rejecting. ◊

Example 6.4.2: The TRAVELING SALESMAN PROBLEM (as defined in Section 6.2 with the "budget" B given) is also in $\mathcal{NP}$. The nondeterministic Turing machine that achieves this writes in its second tape, nondeterministically, a string of zeros, ones, and ⊔'s of length equal to that of the input. Then the machine enters a deterministic phase, in which it checks to see if the string written on its second tape happens to be *the encoding of a bijection π* of the integers $1, \ldots, n$ where n is the number of cities in the given input —bijection π is encoded by writing $\pi(1), \pi(2), \ldots$ in binary, separated by ⊔'s. If the string is indeed the encoding of a bijection, the machine goes on to deterministically calculate the cost of the tour, and compare it with the "budget" B in its input. If the cost is smaller, the machine accepts; in all other eventualities (if the guessed string is not the encoding of a bijection, or if it represents a tour with cost greater than B) the machine rejects. It is clear that a string is in the language decided by this machine if and only if it encodes a "yes" instance of the TRAVELING SALESMAN PROBLEM.

Similarly, it is easy to show that the other apparently difficult problems we encountered in the previous section, INDEPENDENT SET, HAMILTON CYCLE, and PARTITION (though *not* EQUIVALENCE OF NONDETERMINISTIC FINITE AUTOMATA) are also in $\mathcal{NP}$.◊

Notice how cleverly the nondeterministic "algorithms" of the two previous examples exploit the *fundamental asymmetry* in the definition of nondeterministic time-bounded computation. They try out all possible solutions to the problem in hand in independent computations, and accept as soon as they discover one that works —oblivious of the others that do not.

The analogy with the class of recursively enumerable languages, another class whose definition had an asymmetry of a similar kind between acceptance and rejection, is tempting here. As with that class, it is not at all clear that $\mathcal{NP}$ is closed under complement (while it is clear in the case of $\mathcal{P}$, as well as the class of recursive functions). Also, it *is* immediate that $\mathcal{P} \subseteq \mathcal{NP}$ (the analog of the fact that every recursive language is recursively enumerable). This is because deterministic machines are simply nondeterministic ones in which the transition relation happens to be a function.

Is $\mathcal{P}$ equal to $\mathcal{NP}$? In other words, are nondeterministic Turing machines yet another version of Turing machines equivalent to the rest with respect to the class of languages decided in polynomial time? At first glance, one gets the intuitive feeling that nondeterminism is such a strong and "different" feature that this should not be the case. The trees that represent the set of computations of a nondeterministic Turing machine (recall Figure 6-3) have many nodes (that is, configurations), all at a moderate depth. The only way that a deterministic Turing machine can compete with the nondeterministic one with respect to the number of reachable configurations is by operating for an exponential number of steps. The nondeterministic machines that decide SATISFIABILITY and the TRAVELING SALESMAN PROBLEM above search quite effortlessly an exponentially large population of possibilities; it would be truly remarkable if the same effect could be achieved in a methodical deterministic manner in polynomial time.

This difficulty of using a deterministic Turing machine to search a large set of "solutions" was also reflected in the proof of Theorem 4.5.1. It was shown there that a nondeterministic Turing machine can be simulated by a deterministic one; but that simulation was not a direct step-by-step simulation, like the ones of Theorems 4.3.1 and 4.3.2 (for which we were able to prove polynomial bounds). The simulation of a nondeterministic Turing machine resorted to an exhaustive examination of all possible computations. Again, one gets the intuitive feeling that this is inherent in nondeterminism, since it allows multiple choices at each step, and so there is an exponentially large multitude of possible computations to be checked.

In order to compare nondeterministic and deterministic machines in terms of their time performance, we must first define a much more general class of languages:

Definition 6.4.2: A Turing machine $M = (K, \Sigma, \delta, s, H)$ is said to be **exponentially bounded** if there is a polynomial $p(n)$ such that the following is true: For any input x, there is no configuration C such that $(s, \triangleright \sqcup x) \vdash_M^{2^{p(|x|)}+1} C$. That is, the machine always halts after at most *exponentially* many steps.

Finally, define $\mathcal{EXP}$ to be the class of all languages that are decided by some exponentially bounded Turing machine.

Theorem 6.4.1: *If $L \in \mathcal{NP}$, then $L \in \mathcal{EXP}$.*

Proof: Suppose that we are given a nondeterministic polynomially bounded Turing machine M deciding L with time bound $p(n)$. We shall show how to construct a deterministic Turing machine M' that decides the same language in time $c^{p(n)}$ for some constant c (the theorem then follows, by considering the polynomial $k \cdot p(n)$, for some k such that $2^k > c$). M' is precisely the machine constructed in the proof of Theorem 4.5.1. M' simulates M on all possible computations of length 1, then on all possible computations of length 2, and so on, up to length $p(n) + 1$, at which point either an accepting computation has been discovered, or all computations have halted rejecting. To simulate a computation of M of length ℓ, M' needs $\mathcal{O}(\ell)$ steps —to copy the input, to produce the next string in $\{1, 2, \ldots, r\}^\ell$ (where r is the *degree of nondeterminism* of M, a fixed number depending only on M and equal to the maximum possible number of quadruples in Δ that share the same first two components), and to simulate M following the choices suggested by this string. Thus, M' can carry out the simulation of M on an input of length n in time

$$\sum_{\ell=1}^{p(n)+1} r^\ell \leq (r+1)^{p(n)+1},$$

which completes the proof with $c = r + 2$. ∎

As we have already mentioned, whether $\mathcal{P} = \mathcal{NP}$ is a question of central importance to complexity theory that is presently unresolved. Whether $\mathcal{NP} = \mathcal{EXP}$, that is, whether the inclusion in the above corollary is proper, is another question which, although quite a bit less important, is equally open. We *do* know the following, however: In the chain of inclusions

$$\mathcal{P} \subseteq \mathcal{NP} \subseteq \mathcal{EXP},$$

the third class properly includes the first. The reason is that the language E, shown in Theorem 6.1.2 not to be in $\mathcal{P}$, is certainly in $\mathcal{EXP}$: A Turing machine can in exponential time simulate M on input w for $2^{|w|}$ steps. *Thus, although we suspect that both of the inclusions displayed above are proper, all we can currently prove is that at least one of them is proper —and we do not know which. . .*

Succinct Certificates

The nondeterministic Turing machines we devised in Examples 6.4.1–2 for deciding SATISFIABILITY and the TRAVELING SALESMAN PROBLEM are quite simple, and somewhat similar: They start by nondeterministically generating a string, and then check deterministically whether the generated string has a certain required property in relation to the input. If the input is in the language, then at least one appropriate string exists. If the input is not in the language, then no string with the required property can be found.

Such a string is called a **certificate**, or a **witness**. As we shall see, all problems in $\mathcal{NP}$ have certificates, and only problems in $\mathcal{NP}$ do. A certificate must be *polynomially succinct*, that is, of length that is at most a polynomial in the length of the input. It must also be *checkable* in polynomial time. In the case of SATISFIABILITY, checking the certificate entails testing whether the truth assignment satisfies all clauses of the input formula; in the case of the TRAVELING SALESMAN PROBLEM, testing whether the proposed tour has a total cost within the budget; for INDEPENDENT SET, whether the given set of nodes is of the right size and free of edges; and so on. Finally, all "yes" inputs of a problem must have at least one certificate, while all "no" inputs must have none.

The idea of certificates can be formalized in the domain of languages, providing an interesting alternative definition of $\mathcal{NP}$.

Definition 6.4.3: Let Σ be an alphabet, and let ";" be a symbol not in Σ. Consider a language $L' \subseteq \Sigma^*; \Sigma^*$. We say that L' is **polynomially balanced** if there exists a polynomial $p(n)$ such that if $x; y \in L'$, then $|y| \leq p(|x|)$.

Theorem 6.4.2: *Let $L \subseteq \Sigma^*$ be a language, where $; \notin \Sigma$, and $|\Sigma| \geq 2$. Then $L \in \mathcal{NP}$ if and only if there is a polynomially balanced language $L' \subseteq \Sigma^*; \Sigma^*$ such that $L' \in \mathcal{P}$, and $L = \{x : \text{there is a } y \in \Sigma^* \text{ such that } x; y \in L' \}$.*

Proof: Intuitively, language L' summarizes all certificates of all inputs. That is,

$$L = \{x; y : \ y \text{ is a certificate for } x\}.$$

For each $x \in \Sigma^*$, there is a set of y's such that $x; y \in L'$; this set is the set of certificates of x. If x is in L, then its set of certificates has at least one element; if $x \notin L$, then this set of certificates is empty.

If such a language L' exists, then a nondeterministic Turing machine could decide L by trying all certificates (very much like the nondeterministic Turing machine that decides SATISFIABILITY does) and then utilizing the deterministic Turing machine that decides L'. And conversely, any nondeterministic Turing machine M deciding L provides a solid framework for certificates for L: A certificate for an input x is precisely any accepting computation of M on input x —both concise and polynomially checkable.

The formal proof is left as an exercise (Problem 6.4.5). ∎

This concept of succinct certificates is best illustrated in terms of the set $C \subseteq \mathbf{N}$ of *composite numbers* (recall the discussion in Example 4.5.1). Suppose that we are given a natural number in its usual decimal representation —for instance, $4,294,967,297$ —and asked whether it is composite. There is no clear, efficient way of answering such questions. However, every number in C does have a succinct certificate. For example, the number $4,294,967,297$, which happens to be composite, has as a certificate the pair of integers $6,700,417$ and 641 that have a product of $4,294,967,297$. To check the validity of the certificate, one just has to carry out the multiplication to be convinced that $4,294,967,297 \in C$. And this is the subtlety of a certificate: Once you have found it, you can efficiently exhibit its validity. But finding it may not be easy: The above factorization of $4,294,967,297$ was first discovered by the mathematician Leonard Euler (1707–1783) in 1732, a full 92 years after Pierre de Fermat (1601–1665), another great mathematician, had conjectured that no such factorization existed!

Problems for Section 6.4

6.4.1. Show that $\mathcal{NP}$ is closed under union, intersection, concatenation, and Kleene star. (The proofs for $\mathcal{NP}$ are much simpler that those for $\mathcal{P}$.)

6.4.2. Define $co\mathcal{NP}$ to be the following class of languages $\{\overline{L} : L \in \mathcal{NP}\}$. It is an important open problem whether $\mathcal{NP} = co\mathcal{NP}$, that is, whether $\mathcal{NP}$ is closed under complement. Show that if $\mathcal{NP} \neq co\mathcal{NP}$, then $\mathcal{P} \neq \mathcal{NP}$.

6.4.3. Call a homomorphism h (recall Problems 2.3.11 and 3.5.3) **nonerasing** if it maps no symbol to e. Show that $\mathcal{NP}$ is closed under nonerasing homomorphisms.

You may want to think about these questions: Is $\mathcal{NP}$ closed under general homomorphisms? How about the class of recursive languages? How about the recursive enumerable ones? How about $\mathcal{P}$? See Problem 7.2.4 in the next chapter for the last one.

6.4.4. Define appropriate succinct certificates for PARTITION and CLIQUE.

6.4.5. Prove Theorem 6.4.2.

REFERENCES

The theory of computational complexity, much anticipated in the late 1950s and early 1960s, was formally developed by Hartmanis and Stearns in this paper

- J. Hartmanis and R. E. Stearns "On the computational complexity of algorithms," *Transactions of the American Mathematical Society, 117,* pp 285–305, 1965;

Theorem 6.1.2 follows from results in that paper. The thesis that the class $\mathcal{P}$ adequately captures the notion of an "efficiently solvable problem," also implicit in much earlier work, emerged in the mid 1960s mainly in these two works:

- A. Cobham "The intrinsic computational difficulty of functions," *Proceedings of the 1964 Congress for Logic, Mathematics and the Philosophy of Science,* pp. 24–30, New York: North Holland, 1964, and

o J. Edmonds   "Paths, trees and flowers," *Canadian Journal of Mathematics, 17,*
   3, pp. 449–467, 1965.

In the last paper, the class $\mathcal{NP}$ was also informally introduced (in terms of certificates, recall Theorem 6.4.2), and it was first conjectured that $P \neq \mathcal{NP}$. For a much more extensive treatment of computational complexity, see

o C. H. Papadimitriou   *Computational Complexity*, Reading, Massach.: Addison-
   Wesley, 1994.

7 | NP-completeness

7.1 POLYNOMIAL-TIME REDUCTIONS

Many of the concepts and techniques we use in complexity theory are time-bounded analogs of the concepts and techniques that we developed for studying undecidability. We have already seen in the proof of Theorem 6.1.2 that we can use the polynomial-time analog of diagonalization in order to show that certain languages are not in $\mathcal{P}$. We shall next introduce *polynomial-time reductions*, the analog of the reductions we employed for establishing undecidability in Chapter 5. We shall use polynomial-time reductions to study the complexity of several important and seemingly difficult problems in $\mathcal{NP}$ introduced in the previous chapter: SATISFIABILITY, the TRAVELING SALESMAN PROBLEM, INDEPENDENT SET, PARTITION, and others. As we shall see, these problems have the following important *completeness* property: *All* problems in $\mathcal{NP}$ can be reduced to them via polynomial-time reductions —in much the same way that all recursively enumerable languages reduce to the halting problem. We call such problems $\mathcal{NP}$-**complete**.

Unfortunately, the analogy with the halting problem breaks down after this point. There seems to be no simple diagonalization argument which establishes that these $\mathcal{NP}$-complete problems are not in $\mathcal{P}$; diagonalization arguments appear to apply only to languages that are too hard and unnatural to matter, such as the exponential-time language E in Theorem 6.1.2.

Despite the fact that these $\mathcal{NP}$-complete problems fail to provide a proof that $\mathcal{P} \neq \mathcal{NP}$, they do occupy an important place in our study of complexity: *If we assume that $\mathcal{P} \neq \mathcal{NP}$* —a conjecture that is very widely accepted, although still far from proved— then all $\mathcal{NP}$-complete problems are indeed not in $\mathcal{P}$ (this is articulated in Theorem 7.1.1 below). This somewhat indirect evidence of difficulty is the most we can expect for a problem in $\mathcal{NP}$, short of proving that

$\mathcal{P} \neq \mathcal{NP}$.

But we must now define the polynomial-time variant of reduction (compare with Definition 5.4.1):

Definition 7.1.1: A function $f : \Sigma^* \mapsto \Sigma^*$ is said to be **polynomial-time computable** if there is a polynomially bounded Turing machine M that computes it.

Let now $L_1, L_2 \subseteq \Sigma^*$ be languages. A polynomial-time computable function $\tau : \Sigma^* \mapsto \Sigma^*$ is called a **polynomial reduction from L_1 to L_2** if for each $x \in \Sigma^*$ the following holds: $x \in L_1$ if and only if $\tau(x) \in L_2$.

Polynomial reductions are important because they reveal interesting relationships between computational problems. Strictly speaking, a polynomial reduction as defined above relates two languages, not two problems. However, we know from the discussion in Section 6.2 that languages can be used to encode all kinds of important computational problems, such as HAMILTON CYCLE. SATISFIABILITY, and INDEPENDENT SET. In this sense we can say that τ is a **polynomial reduction from Problem A to Problem B** if it is a polynomial reduction between the corresponding languages. That is, τ transforms in polynomial time instances of Problem A to instances of Problem B in such a way that x is a "yes" instance of Problem A if and only if $\tau(x)$ is a "yes" instance of Problem B.

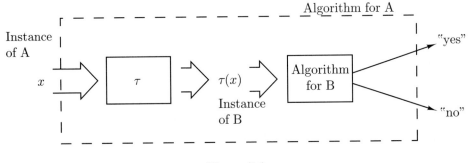

Figure 7-1

When a we have polynomial reduction τ from Problem A to Problem B, it is possible to adapt any polynomial-time algorithm for B to obtain one for A (see Figure 7-2). To tell whether any given instance x of Problem A is actually a "yes" instance of A, one can start by computing $\tau(x)$, and testing whether or not it is a "yes" instance of B. If we have a polynomial algorithm for B, this method for solving A is also polynomial, since both the reduction step and the algorithm for solving the resulting instance of B can be done in polynomial time. In other words, the existence of a polynomial reduction from A to B is evidence that B *is at least as hard as* A. If B is efficiently solvable, then so must be A; and, if A requires exponential time, then so does B.

We give several examples of reductions below.

Example 7.1.1: Let us describe a polynomial reduction from HAMILTON CYCLE to SATISFIABILITY. Suppose that we are given an instance of HAMILTON CYCLE, that is, a graph $G \subseteq V \times V$, where $V = \{1, 2, \ldots, n\}$. We shall describe an algorithm τ that produces a Boolean formula in conjunctive normal form $\tau(G)$, such that G has a Hamilton cycle (a closed path visiting each node of G exactly once) if and only if $\tau(G)$ is satisfiable.

Formula $\tau(G)$ will involve n^2 Boolean variables, which we shall denote x_{ij}, with $1 \le i, j \le n$. Intuitively, x_{ij} will be a Boolean variable with this *intended meaning:* "Node i of G is the jth node in the Hamilton cycle of G." The various clauses of $\tau(G)$ will then express in the language of Boolean logic the requirements that a Hamilton cycle must satisfy.

What requirements must the x_{ij}'s satisfy so that they indeed define a Hamilton cycle of G? We shall cast each such requirement as a clause. First, for $j = 1, \ldots, n$ we have the clause

$$(x_{1j} \vee x_{2j} \vee \ldots \vee x_{nj}).$$

For a truth assignment to satisfy this clause, it must set at least one of the variables $x_{1j}, x_{2j}, \ldots, x_{nj}$ to $\top$; thus this clause expresses, under the "intended meanings" of the Boolean variables, the requirement that at least one node should appear ith in the Hamilton cycle.

But of course, only one node of G can appear ith in the Hamilton cycle. Thus, we add to our Boolean formula all $\mathcal{O}(n^3)$ clauses of the form

$$(\overline{x_{ij}} \vee \overline{x_{ik}})$$

for $i, j, k = 1, \ldots, n$ and $j \ne k$. Since at least one literal in this clause must be satisfied, these clauses successfully express the requirement that not both node j and node k can appear ith on the cycle.

The clauses so far guarantee that exactly one node appears ith in the Hamilton cycle. But we must also require that node i appear exactly once in the cycle. This is done by the clauses

$$(x_{i1} \vee x_{i2} \vee \ldots \vee x_{in})$$

for $i = 1, \ldots, n$ and

$$(\overline{x_{ij}} \vee \overline{x_{kj}})$$

for $i, j, k = 1, \ldots, n$ and $i \ne k$.

So far these clauses express the requirement that the x_{ij}'s represent a *bijection* or *permutation* of the nodes of G. We must next express by new clauses the requirement that this permutation is indeed a cycle of G. We do this by adding the clause

$$(\overline{x_{ij}} \vee \overline{x_{k,j+1}}) \tag{1}$$

for $j = 1, \ldots, n$ and *for each pair* (i, k) *of nodes such that* (i, k) *is not an edge of G*. Here by $x_{k,n+1}$ we mean the Boolean variable x_{k1}; that is, addition in the second index is assumed to be modulo n. Intuitively, the clauses in (1) state that, if there is no (i, k) edge in G, then it cannot be the case that i and k appear consecutively in this order in the alleged Hamilton cycle. This completes the construction of $\tau(G)$.

It is easy to argue that the construction of $\tau(G)$ can be carried out in polynomial time. There are $\mathcal{O}(n^3)$ clauses to be constructed, with a total number of $\mathcal{O}(n^3)$ literals. The structure of these clauses is extremely simple, and either depends on n alone, or depends on the edges of G in a rather straightforward way. It would be straightforward to construct a polynomial-time Turing machine that computes the function τ.

Next we have to argue that G has a Hamilton cycle if and only if $\tau(G)$ is satisfiable. Suppose that there is a truth assignment T that satisfies $\tau(G)$. Since T must make at least one literal $\top$ in each of the clauses other than those in (1) above, it follows that T encodes a bijection on the nodes of G, that is, for each i exactly one $T(x_{ij})$ is $\top$, and for each j exactly one $T(x_{ij})$ is $\top$. Denote by $\pi(i)$ the unique j for which $T(x_{i,\pi(i)}) = \top$.

The set of clauses in (1) above must also be satisfied. This means that whenever $i = \pi(j)$ and $k = \pi(j + 1)$ (where again $n + 1$ means 1) then (j, k) must be an edge of G. It follows that $(\pi(1), \pi(2), \ldots, \pi(n))$ is indeed a Hamilton cycle of G. The *if* direction has been proved.

Conversely, suppose that G has a Hamilton cycle, say $(\pi(1), \pi(2), \ldots, \pi(n))$. Then it is easy to see that the truth assignment T, where $T(x_{ij}) = \top$ if and only if $j = \pi(i)$, satisfies all clauses of $\tau(G)$, and the proof is complete.

Later in this chapter we shall see a reduction *in the opposite direction* (Theorems 7.3.1 and 7.3.2).

Correctly interpreting polynomial reductions as to the information they reveal with respect to the difficulty of the problems involved can be confusing, and requires some care and experience. The reader is encouraged at this point to ponder these issues: Is this reduction good news or bad news about the complexity of HAMILTON CYCLE? of SATISFIABILITY? Suppose that we have a polynomial-time algorithm for HAMILTON CYCLE; what can we conclude about SATISFIABILITY in the light of this reduction? What if we had a polynomial-time algorithm for SATISFIABILITY? What can we conclude if we know that HAMILTON CYCLE is a difficult problem? that SATISFIABILITY is a difficult problem? $\Diamond$

Example 7.1.2: You must schedule n tasks on two machines. Both machines have the same speed, each task can be executed on either machine, and there are no restrictions on the order in which the tasks have to be executed. You are given the execution times $a_1, \ldots, a_n$ of the tasks and a deadline D, all in binary. Can you complete all these tasks on the two machines within this deadline?

Another way to state this question is the following: Is there a way to partition the given binary numbers into two sets so that the numbers in each set add up to D or less? We call this problem, whose relation to the PARTITION problem defined in the last chapter is perhaps clear, TWO-MACHINE SCHEDULING. We also introduce another problem, also closely related to PARTITION:

KNAPSACK: Given a set $S = \{a_1, \ldots, a_n\}$ of nonnegative integers, and an integer K, all represented in binary, is there a subset $P \subseteq S$ such that $\sum_{a_i \in P} a_i = K$?

(This graphic name is supposed to bring to mind a hiker who is trying to fill her knapsack to its limit with items of varying weights.)

How are these three problems (PARTITION, KNAPSACK, and TWO-MACHINE SCHEDULING) related by polynomial reductions? We shall show that *there are six polynomial reductions,* reducing any one of these three problems to any other!

Suppose that we have an instance of KNAPSACK, with integers $a_1, \ldots, a_n$ and K; we must reduce it to an equivalent instance of PARTITION. If K happens to be equal to $H = \frac{1}{2} \sum_{i=1}^{n} a_i$, the half-sum of the given integers, then all our reduction has to do is to erase K from the input: The resulting instance of partition is equivalent to the given instance of KNAPSACK. The problem is, of course, that K will not in general be equal to H. But this is easy to fix: Add to the set of a_i's two large new integers $a_{n+1} = 2H + 2K$ and $a_{n+2} = 4H$ (notice that these numbers are integers even if H fails to be one). Consider now the resulting set of integers $\{a_1, \ldots, a_{n+2}\}$ as an instance of PARTITION —the reduction is complete. It is obvious that this reduction can be carried out in polynomial time.

We must now show that the reduction works; that is, that the instance of partition has a solution if and only if the original instance of knapsack had one. Notice first that if the new set of integers can be partitioned into two sets with equal sums, then the two new integers a_{n+1} and a_{n+2} must be on opposite sides of the partition (their sum exceeds that of the remaining integers). Let P be the set of integers among the original ones $a_1, \ldots, a_n$ that are on the same side as $a_{n+2} = 4H$. We have that

$$4H + \sum_{a_i \in P} a_i = 2H + 2K + \sum_{a_i \in S - P} a_i.$$

Adding $\sum_{a_i \in P} a_i$ to both sides, we get (since $\sum_{a_i \in S} a_i = 2H$)

$$4H + 2 \sum_{a_i \in P} a_i = 4H + 2K,$$

or $\sum_{a_i \in P} a_i = K$. Hence, if the resulting instance of PARTITION has a solution, then the original instance of KNAPSACK has one. And conversely, if we have a solution of KNAPSACK, then adding a_{n+2} to it yields a solution of the instance of PARTITION.

This was the reduction from KNAPSACK to PARTITION. We started with an arbitrary instance of KNAPSACK and constructed an equivalent instance of PARTITION. A reduction in the opposite direction is trivial, because PARTITION is a *special case* of KNAPSACK. Given any instance of PARTITION with integers $a_1, \ldots, a_n$, the reduction to KNAPSACK transforms the given instance of PARTITION to the instance of KNAPSACK with the same numbers, and bound $K = \frac{1}{2} \sum_{i=1}^{n} a_i$.

But what if K is not an integer (that is, the given integers add to an odd number)? Then we can have the reduction produce any impossible instance of KNAPSACK we wish, such as the one with $n = 1$, $a_1 = 2$, and $K = 1$ —the given instance of PARTITION was also impossible.

The reduction from PARTITION to TWO-MACHINE SCHEDULING is also easy: Given an instance of PARTITION with integers $a_1, \ldots, a_n$, the reduction produces an instance of TWO-MACHINE SCHEDULING with n tasks, execution times $a_1, \ldots, a_n$, and deadline $D = \lfloor \frac{1}{2} \sum_{i=1}^{n} a_i \rfloor$ (if $\frac{1}{2} \sum_{i=1}^{n} a_i$ is not an integer, then this is already an impossible instance). It is easy to see that the resulting instance of TWO-MACHINE SCHEDULING is solvable if and only if the original instance of PARTITION was. This is because the tasks can be partitioned into two sets with sums at most D if and only if they can be partitioned into two sets with sums *exactly* D.

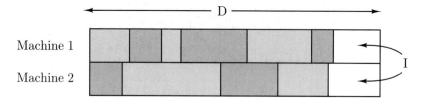

Figure 7-2

The reduction from TWO-MACHINE SCHEDULING to PARTITION is a little more involved. Suppose that we are given an instance of TWO-MACHINE SCHEDULING with task lengths $a_1, \ldots, a_n$, and deadline D. Consider the number $I = 2D - \sum_{i=1}^{n} a_i$. Intuitively, I is the total *idle time* in any legal schedule (see Figure 7-3). It is the amount of *slack* that we have in solving the scheduling problem. We add now several new numbers to the set of lengths of tasks, such that (a) the sum of these new numbers is I; and (b) moreover, we can make up any sum between 0 and I by adding a subset of these new numbers. It is not hard to see that, if we were able to do this, the resulting instance of PARTITION would be equivalent to the original instance of TWO-MACHINE SCHEDULING, because we could then transform any feasible schedule of the original tasks into an equitable partition of the new set of numbers by adding to each of the two sets a subset of the newly introduced numbers that will bring the sum of both to D.

All we have to do now is supply integers, adding up to I, so that any number between zero and I is the sum of a set of these numbers. Superficially, this looks trivial to do: Add I copies of the integer 1. What is wrong with this reduction, however, is that *it is not a polynomial-time reduction*, for the same reason for which the algorithm for PARTITION we sketched in the previous chapter failed to be polynomial: The integer I is not bounded by a polynomial in the size of the input —since the input consists of the task lengths and the deadline, all encoded in binary, the number I could be exponentially large in the size of the input.

The solution is a little more complicated: The numbers we add are all powers of 2 that are smaller than $\frac{1}{2}I$, plus another integer to bring the sum to I. For example, if $I = 56$, then the newly added integers would be $1, 2, 4, 8, 16,$ and 25. All integers between 0 and 56, and only these, can be made up as the sum of some subset of these integers. This completes the description of the reduction from TWO-MACHINE SCHEDULING to PARTITION; the reduction is polynomial, because the number of integers we introduce is bounded by *the logarithm of I* —which is less than the size of the input.$\Diamond$

In the above example we did not discuss direct reductions from KNAPSACK to TWO-MACHINE SCHEDULING and back. But there is no need: As we show next, polynomial reductions compose in a transitive fashion. Recall that the composition of two functions $f : A \mapsto B$ and $g : B \mapsto C$ is the function $f \circ g : A \mapsto C$, where for all $x \in A$, $f \circ g(x) = g(f(x))$.

Lemma 7.1.1: *If τ_1 is a polynomial reduction from L_1 to L_2 and τ_2 is a polynomial reduction from L_2 to L_3, then their composition $\tau_1 \circ \tau_2$ is a polynomial reduction from L_1 to L_3.*

Proof: Suppose that τ_1 is computed by a Turing machine M_1 in time p_1, a polynomial, and τ_2 is computed by M_2 in time p_2, also a polynomial. Then $\tau_1 \circ \tau_2$ can be computed by the machine $M_1 M_2$. On input $x \in \Sigma_1^*$, $M_1 M_2$ will output $\tau_1 \circ \tau_2(x)$ in time bounded by $p_1(|x|) + p_2(p_1(|x|))$ —a polynomial. The latter term reflects the fact that $|\tau_1(x)|$ cannot be larger than $p_1(|x|)$.

It remains to show that $x \in L_1$ if and only if $\tau_1 \circ \tau_2(x) \in L_3$. But this is trivial: $x \in L_1$ if and only if $\tau_1(x) \in L_2$, if and only if $\tau_1 \circ \tau_2(x) \in L_3$. ∎

We finally arrive at the following important definition.

Definition 7.1.2: A language $L \subseteq \Sigma^*$ is called $\mathcal{NP}$-**complete** if
(a) $L \in \mathcal{NP}$; and
(b) for every language $L' \in \mathcal{NP}$, there is a polynomial reduction from L' to L.

Just as the decidability of H captured the whole question of the decidability of Turing-acceptable languages, so the question of whether any one $\mathcal{NP}$-complete language is in $\mathcal{P}$ turns out to be equivalent to the whole $\mathcal{P} = \mathcal{NP}$ question:

Theorem 7.1.1: *Let L be an $\mathcal{NP}$-complete language. Then $\mathcal{P} = \mathcal{NP}$ if and only if $L \in P$.*

Proof: *(Only If)* Suppose that $\mathcal{P} = \mathcal{NP}$. Since L is $\mathcal{NP}$-complete, and hence $L \in \mathcal{NP}$ (recall that an $\mathcal{NP}$-complete language must be in $\mathcal{NP}$), it follows that $L \in \mathcal{P}$.

(If) Suppose that L is an $\mathcal{NP}$-complete language that is decided by a deterministic Turing machine M_1 in time $p_1(n)$, a polynomial, and let L' be any language in $\mathcal{NP}$; we shall show that $L' \in \mathcal{P}$.

Since L is $\mathcal{NP}$-complete and $L' \in \mathcal{NP}$, then there is a polynomial reduction τ from L' to L (we are now using the second part of the definition of an $\mathcal{NP}$-complete language). Suppose that τ is computed by some Turing machine M_2 in time $p_2(n)$, also a polynomial. Then we claim that the Turing machine $M_2 M_1$ decides L' in polynomial time. To see that $M_2 M_1$ decides L', notice that $M_2 M_1$ accepts input x if and only if $\tau(x) \in L$; and since τ is a polynomial reduction, $\tau(x) \in L$ if and only if $x \in L'$.

Finally, to analyze the time requirements of $M_2 M_1$, notice that its initial M_2 part takes, on input x, time $p_2(|x|)$ to produce an input for M_1. This input will have length at most $p_2(|x|)$, because M_2 cannot write more than one symbol per step. Hence, the computation of M_1 on this input will take time at most $p_1(p_2(|x|))$. The overall machine will halt, on input x, within time $p_2(|x|) + p_1(p_2(|x|) + |x|)$, and this is a polynomial in $|x|$.

Since L' was taken to be any language in $\mathcal{NP}$ and we concluded that $L' \in \mathcal{P}$, it follows that $\mathcal{NP} = \mathcal{P}$. ■

Problems for Section 7.1

7.1.1. In 3-COLORING we are given an undirected graph, and we are asked whether its nodes can be colored with three colors such that no two adjacent nodes have the same color.
(a) Show that 3-COLORING is in $\mathcal{NP}$.
(b) Describe a polynomial-time reduction from 3-COLORING to SATISFIABILITY.

7.1.2. Some authors define a more general notion of reduction, often called **polynomial Turing reduction**. Let L_1 and L_2 be languages. A **polynomial Turing reduction** from L_1 to L_2 is a 2-tape Turing machine with three distinguished states, $q_?$, q_1, and q_0, that decides L_2 in polynomial time, and whose computation is defined in a rather peculiar way. The yields relation of M for all configurations with states other than $q_?$ is defined exactly as for ordinary Turing machines. For $q_?$, however, we say that
$(q_?, \triangleright u_1 \underline{a_1} v_1, \triangleright u_2 \underline{a_2} v_2) \vdash_M (q, \triangleright u_1' \underline{a_1'} v_1', \triangleright u_2' \underline{a_2'} v_2')$ if and only if

(1) $u_1 = u_1'$, $a_1 = a_1'$, $v_1' = v_1$, $u_2 = u_2'$, $a_2' = a_2$, $v_2' = v_2$, and
(2) one of the following holds: either
    (2a) $u_2 a_2 v_2 \in L_1$ and $q' = q_1$, or
    (2b) $u_2 a_2 v_2 \notin L_1$ and $q' = q_0$.
In other words, from state $q_?$, M never changes anything on its tapes; it just goes to state q_1 or q_0, *depending on whether or not the string in its second tape is in L_1*. Furthermore, *this counts as one step of M*.

    (a) Show that if there is a polynomial Turing reduction from L_1 to L_2, and one from L_2 to L_3, then there is a polynomial Turing reduction from L_1 to L_3.

    (b) Show that if there is a polynomial Turing reduction from L_1 to L_2, and $L_2 \in \mathcal{P}$, then $L_1 \in \mathcal{P}$.

    (c) Give a polynomial Turing reduction from HAMILTON CYCLE to HAMILTON PATH (the version in which we are not requiring that the path that visits each node exactly once is closed). Can you find a direct (that is, not using the reduction in the proof of Theorem 7.3.2 below) polynomial reduction between the two problems?

7.2 | COOK'S THEOREM

We have not yet established that $\mathcal{NP}$-complete languages exist —but they do. During these past two decades research in computational complexity has discovered literally hundreds of such $\mathcal{NP}$-complete languages (or $\mathcal{NP}$-*complete problems*, as we shall continue to blur the distinction between computational problems such as SATISFIABILITY and HAMILTON CYCLE and the languages that encode them). Many of these $\mathcal{NP}$-complete problems are important practical problems from operations research, logic, combinatorics, artificial intelligence, and other seemingly unrelated application areas. Prior to the discovery of $\mathcal{NP}$-completeness, much research effort had been devoted in vain to finding polynomial algorithms for many of these problems. The concept of $\mathcal{NP}$-completeness unified the experiences of researchers in these diverse areas by showing that none of these problems is solvable by a polynomial-time algorithm unless $\mathcal{P} = \mathcal{NP}$ — a circumstance that appears to contradict both intuition and experience. This realization has had the beneficial effect of diverting the research effort previously focused on solving particular $\mathcal{NP}$-complete problems towards other, more tractable goals, which are the subject of Section 7.4. This redirection of research effort has been the most profound effect of the theory of computation on computational practice.

Bounded Tiling

Once we have proved the first $\mathcal{NP}$-complete problem, more problems can be shown $\mathcal{NP}$-complete by reducing to them a problem already known to be $\mathcal{NP}$-complete, and using the transitivity of polynomial reductions, recall Lemma 7.1.1. But the first $\mathcal{NP}$-completeness proof must be an application of the definition: We must establish that all problems in $\mathcal{NP}$ reduce to the problem in hand. Historically, the first problem to be shown $\mathcal{NP}$-complete by Stephen A. Cook in 1971 was SATISFIABILITY. Instead of giving that proof directly, we shall start with a version of the tiling problem that was shown to be undecidable in Chapter 5.

In the original tiling problem we were given a tiling system $\mathcal{D}$, and we were asked whether there is a way to tile the infinite first quadrant so that any two vertically or horizontally adjacent tiles are related as prescribed, and a given tile is placed at the origin. We can define a less ambitious problem, called BOUNDED TILING, in which we are asked whether there is a legal tiling, not of the whole quadrant, *but of an $s \times s$ square*, where $s > 0$ is a given integer. This time, instead of specifying only the tile placed at $(0,0)$, we specify the entire first row of tiles. That is, we are given a tiling system $\mathcal{D} = (D, H, V)$ (where we omit the starting tile d_0, which is now irrelevant), an integer $s > 0$, and a function $f_0 : \{0, \ldots, s-1\} \mapsto D$. We are asked whether there is an $s \times s$ tiling by $\mathcal{D}$ extending f_0, that is, a function $f : \{0, 1, \ldots, s-1\} \times \{0, 1, \ldots, s-1\} \mapsto D$ such that

$f(m, 0) = f_0(m)$ for all $m < s$;
$(f(m, n), f(m+1, n)) \in H$ for all $m < s-1, n < s$;
$(f(m, n), f(m, n+1)) \in V$ for all $m < s, n < s-1$.

The BOUNDED TILING problem is this:

> BOUNDED TILING Given a tiling system $\mathcal{D}$, an integer s, and a function $f_0 : \{0, \ldots, s-1\} \mapsto D$, represented by its sequence of values $(f_0(0), \ldots, f_0(s-1))$, is there an $s \times s$ tiling by $\mathcal{D}$ extending f_0?

Theorem 7.2.1: BOUNDED TILING *is $\mathcal{NP}$-complete.*

Proof: Let us first argue that it is in $\mathcal{NP}$. The certificate in this case is a complete listing of the s^2 values of a tiling function f. Such a function can be checked in polynomial time for compliance with the three requirements. Furthermore, it is succinct: Its total length is s^2 times the number of symbols it takes to represent a tile, and s is bounded from above by the length of the input *because the input includes the listing of f_0*. Actually, the purpose of this twist to our tiling formalism was precisely to ensure that the problem is in $\mathcal{NP}$; if we only specify one starting tile, the problem becomes much harder —it is *provably* not in $\mathcal{P}$; see Problem 7.2.2.

We must now show that all languages in $\mathcal{NP}$ reduce via polynomial reductions to BOUNDED TILING. So, consider any language $L \in \mathcal{NP}$. We must produce a polynomial reduction from L to BOUNDED TILING, that is, a polynomial-time computable function τ such that for each $x \in \Sigma^*$, $\tau(x)$ is the encoding of a tiling system $\mathcal{D} = (D, H, V)$, plus an integer $s > 0$ and the encoding of a function f_0, with this property: There is an $s \times s$ tiling with $\mathcal{D}$ extending f_0 if and only if $x \in L$.

To obtain this reduction, we must somehow exploit the little information we have about L. All we know about L is that it is a language in $\mathcal{NP}$; that is, we know that there is a nondeterministic Turing machine $M = (K, \Sigma, \delta, s)$ such that (a) all computations of M on input x halt within $p(|x|)$ steps for some polynomial p, and (b) there is an accepting computation on input x if and only if $x \in L$.

We start by describing the integer s constructed by τ on input x: it is $s = p(|x|) + 2$, two more than the time bound of M on input x.

The tiling system $\mathcal{D}$ described in $\tau(x)$ will be very similar to the one constructed in the proof of the undecidability of the unbounded tiling problem (Theorem 5.6.1). We shall describe the tiles in $\mathcal{D}$, as in that construction, by their edge markings; once more, the markings of the horizontal edges between rows t and $t + 1$ will represent the tape contents of M in a legal computation with input x right after the tth step (since M is nondeterministic, there may be several such computations, and therefore there may now be several possible legal ways to tile the $s \times s$ square).

The 0th row of the $s \times s$ square, prescribed by f_0, will be occupied by tiles spelling the initial configuration $(s, \triangleright \sqcup x)$. That is, $f_0(0)$ is a tile with upper edge marking $\triangleright$, $f_0(1)$ is a tile with upper edge marking $(s, \sqcup)$, and for $i = 1, \ldots, |x|$ $f_0(i + 1)$ is a tile with upper edge marking x_i, the ith letter of the input x. Finally, for all $i > |x| + 1$, $f_0(i)$ is a tile with upper edge marking $\sqcup$ (see Figure 7-3). Thus, the horizontal edge markings between the 0th and the first rows will spell the initial configuration of M on input x.

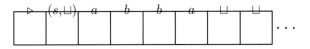

Figure 7-3

The remaining tiles in $\mathcal{D}$ are exactly as in the proof of Theorem 5.6.1. Since the machine is nondeterministic, there may be more than one tile with bottom horizontal marking $(q, a) \in K \times \Sigma$, corresponding to the possibly many choices of action when M scans an a in state q, and each of them is constructed as in that proof. There is only one minor difference: There is a tile with both upper and lower marking (y, a) for each symbol a, effectively allowing the tiling to continue after the computation has halted at state y —but not if it halts at state n. This completes the construction of the instance $\tau(x)$ of BOUNDED TILING. It should be clear that the construction of the instance can be carried out in time polynomial in $|x|$.

We must now show that there is an $s \times s$ tiling by $\mathcal{D}$ if and only if $x \in L$. Suppose that an $s \times s$ tiling exists. Our definition of f_0 ensures that the horizontal edge markings between the 0th and the first rows must spell the initial configuration of M on input x. It then follows by induction that the horizontal edge markings between the nth and the $n+1$st rows will spell the configuration right after the nth step of some legal computation of M on input x. Since no computation of M on input x continues for more than $p(|x|) = s - 2$ steps, the upper markings of the $s - 2$nd row must contain one of the symbols y and n. Since there is an $s - 1$st row, and there is no tile with lower marking n, we must conclude that the symbol y appears, and thus the computation is accepting. We conclude that if a tiling of the $s \times s$ square with $\mathcal{D}$ exists, then M accepts x.

Conversely, if an accepting computation of M on input x exists, it can be easily simulated by a tiling (possibly by repeating the last row several times, if the computation terminates in fewer than $p(|x|)$ steps at state y). The proof is complete. ∎

We can now use BOUNDED TILING to prove the main result of this section:

Theorem 7.2.2 (Cook's Theorem): SATISFIABILITY is $\mathcal{NP}$-complete.

Proof: We have already argued that the problem is in $\mathcal{NP}$; we shall next reduce BOUNDED TILING to SATISFIABILITY.

Given any instance of the BOUNDED TILING problem, say the tiling system $\mathcal{D} = (D, H, V)$, side s, and bottom row f_0, where $D = \{d_1, \ldots, d_k\}$, we shall show how to construct a Boolean formula $\tau(\mathcal{D}, s, f_0)$ such that there is an $s \times s$ tiling f by $\mathcal{D}$ if and only if $\tau(\mathcal{D}, s)$ is satisfiable.

The Boolean variables in $\tau(\mathcal{D}, s, f_0)$ are x_{mnd} for each $0 \leq m, n < s$ and $d \in D$. The intended correspondence between these variables and the tiling problem is that variable x_{mnd} is $\top$ if and only if $f(m, n) = d$. We shall next describe clauses which guarantee that f is indeed a legal $s \times s$ tiling by $\mathcal{D}$.

We first have, for each $m, n < s$, the clause

$$(x_{mnd_1} \lor x_{mnd_2} \lor \ldots \lor x_{mnd_k} \lor),$$

stating that each position has at least one tile. For each $m, n < s$ and each two distinct tiles $d \neq d' \in D$, we have the clause $(\overline{x_{mnd}} \vee \overline{x_{mnd'}})$, stating that a position cannot have more than one tile. The clauses described so far guarantee that the x_{mnd}'s represent a function f from $\{0, \ldots, s-1\} \times \{0, \ldots, s-1\}$ to D.

We must next construct clauses stating that the function described by the x_{mnd}'s is a legal tiling by $\mathcal{D}$. We first have clauses $(x_{i0f_0(i)})$ for $i = 0, \ldots, s-1$, forcing $f(i, 0)$ to be $f_0(i)$. Then, for each $n < s$ and $m < s - 1$, and for each $(d, d') \in D^2 - H$, we have the clause

$$(\overline{x_{mnd}} \vee \overline{x_{m+1, n, d'}}),$$

which forbids two tiles that are not horizontally compatible to be horizontally next to each other. For vertical compatibility, we have for each $n < s - 1$ and $m < s$, and for each $(d, d') \in D^2 - V$, the clause $(\overline{x_{mnd}} \vee \overline{x_{m, n+1, d'}})$. This completes the construction of the clauses in $\tau(\mathcal{D}, s)$. It remains to show that $\tau(\mathcal{D}, s, f_0)$ is satisfiable if and only if there is an $s \times s$ tiling by $\mathcal{D}$ that extends f_0.

Suppose then that $\tau(\mathcal{D}, s, f_0)$ is satisfiable, say by the truth assignment T. Since the big disjunctions are satisfied by T, for each m and n there is at least one $d \in D$ such that $T(x_{mnd}) = \top$. Since the clauses $(\overline{x_{mnd}} \vee \overline{x_{mnd'}})$ are all satisfied by T, there is no m and n such that two or more x_{mnd}'s are $\top$ under T. Hence T represents a function $f : \{0, \ldots, s-1\} \times \{0, \ldots, s-1\} \mapsto D$.

We claim that $f(m, n)$ is a legal $s \times s$ tiling that extends f_0. First, since the clauses $(x_{i0f_0(i)})$ are all satisfied, it must be the case that $f(i, 0) = f_0(i)$, as required. Then the horizontal adjacency constraint must be satisfied, because, if it is not satisfied at positions (m, n) and $(m + 1, n)$, then one of the clauses $(\overline{x_{mnd}} \vee \overline{x_{m+1, n, d'}})$ is left unsatisfied. Similarly for vertical adjacency; thus $f(m, n)$ is indeed a legitimate $s \times s$ tiling extending f_0.

Conversely, suppose that an $s \times s$ tiling f extending f_0 exists. Then define the following truth assignment T: $T(x_{mnd}) = \top$ if and only if $f(m, n) = d$. It is easy to check that T satisfies all clauses, and the proof is complete. ∎

Thus there is no polynomial-time algorithm for SATISFIABILITY, unless $\mathcal{P} = \mathcal{NP}$. As we have seen in Section 6.3, the special case of 2-SATISFIABILITY can be solved in polynomial time. The following theorem suggests that the immediately next most involved case is already intractable. In analogy with 2-SATISFIABILITY, let 3-SATISFIABILITY be the special case of SATISFIABILITY in which all clauses happen to involve three or fewer literals.

Theorem 7.2.3: 3-SATISFIABILITY *is $\mathcal{NP}$-complete.*

Proof: It is of course in $\mathcal{NP}$, as it is the special case of a problem in $\mathcal{NP}$.

To show completeness we shall reduce SATISFIABILITY to 3-SATISFIABILITY. This is a rather common kind of reduction, in which a problem is reduced to its own special case. Such reductions work by showing how, starting from any instance of the general problem, we can get rid of the features that prevent this instance from falling within the special case. In the present situation we must show how, starting from any set of clauses F, we can arrive in polynomial time at an *equivalent* set of clauses $\tau(F)$ with at most three literals in each clause.

The reduction is simple. For each clause in F with $k > 3$ literals, say

$$C = (\lambda_1 \vee \lambda_2 \vee \cdots \vee \lambda_k),$$

we do the following: We let $y_1, \ldots, y_{k-3}$ be new Boolean variables, appearing nowhere else in the Boolean formula $\tau(F)$, and we replace clause C with the following set of clauses:

$$(\lambda_1 \vee \lambda_2 \vee y_1), (\overline{y_1} \vee \lambda_3 \vee y_2), (\overline{y_2} \vee \lambda_4 \vee y_3), \ldots, (\overline{y_{k-4}} \vee \lambda_{k-2} \vee y_{k-3}), (\overline{y_{k-3}} \vee \lambda_{k-1} \vee \lambda_k).$$

We break up all "long" clauses of F this way, using a different set of y_i variables in each. We leave "short" clauses as they are. The resulting Boolean formula is $\tau(F)$. It is easy to see that τ can be carried out in polynomial time.

We claim that $\tau(F)$ is satisfiable if and only if F was satisfiable. The intuition is this: Interpret the variable y_i as saying, "at least one of the literals $\lambda_{i+2}, \ldots, \lambda_k$ is true," and the clause $(\overline{y_i} \vee \lambda_{i+2} \vee y_{i+1})$ as saying, "if y_i is true, then either λ_{i+2} is true, or y_{i+1} is true."

Formally, suppose that truth assignment T satisfies $\tau(F)$. We shall show that T also satisfies each clause of F. This is trivial for the short clauses; and if T maps all k literals of a long original clause to $\perp$, then the y_i variables would not be able by themselves to satisfy all resulting clauses: The first clause would force y_1 to be $\top$, the second y_2 to be $\top$, and finally the next-to-last clause would cause y_{k-3} to be $\top$, contradicting the last clause (incidentally, notice that this is precisely the *purge* algorithm solving this instance of 2-SATISFIABILITY).

Conversely, if there is a truth assignment T that satisfies F, then T can be extended to a truth assignment that satisfies $\tau(F)$, as follows: For each long clause $C = (\lambda_1 \vee \lambda_2 \vee \cdots \vee \lambda_k)$ of F, let j be the smallest index for which $T(\lambda_j) = \top$ (since T was assumed to satisfy F, such a j exists). Then we set the truth values of the new variables $y_1, \ldots, y_{k-3}$ to be $T'(y_i) = \top$ if $i \leq j - 2$, and to be $T'(y_i) = \perp$ otherwise. It is easy to see that T now satisfies $\tau(F)$, and the proof of equivalence is complete. ∎

Consider finally the following optimization version of SATISFIABILITY:

MAX SAT: Given a set F of clauses, and an integer K, is there a truth assignment that satisfies at least K of the clauses?

Theorem 7.2.4: MAX SAT *is* $\mathcal{NP}$-*complete.*

Proof: Membership in $\mathcal{NP}$ is obvious. We shall reduce SATISFIABILITY to MAX SAT.

This reduction is an extremely simple one, but of a kind that is very common and *very* useful in establishing $\mathcal{NP}$-completeness results (see Problem 7.3.4 for many more examples). We just have to observe that MAX SAT is a **generalization** of SATISFIABILITY; that is, every instance of SATISFIABILITY is a special kind of instance of MAX SAT. And this is true: An instance of SATISFIABILITY can be thought of as an instance of MAX SAT in which the parameter K *happens to be equal to the number of clauses.*

Formally, the reduction is this: Given an instance F of SATISFIABILITY with m clauses, we construct an equivalent instance (F, m) of MAX SAT by just apending to F the easily calculated parameter $K = m$. Obviously, there is a truth assignment satisfying at least $K = m$ clauses of F (of which there are exactly m) if and only if there is one that satisfies all clauses of F. ∎

As it turns out, the restriction of MAX SAT to clauses with at most two literals can be shown to be also $\mathcal{NP}$-complete (compare with 2-SATISFIABILITY).

Problems for Section 7.2

7.2.1. Let us consider what happens in the reduction from L to BOUNDED TILING when L is in $\mathcal{P}$ —that is to say, when the machine M in the proof of Theorem 7.2.1 is actually deterministic. It turns out that, in this case, the resulting tiling system can be expressed as a *closure* of a set under certain relations.

Let M be a deterministic Turing machine deciding language L in time $p(n)$, a polynomial; let x be an input of M; and let s, (D, H, V), and f_0 be the components of the bounded tiling instance resulting from the reduction in the proof of Theorem 7.2.1 applied to x. Consider the sets $P = \{0, 1, 2, \ldots, s - 1\}$ and $S = P \times P \times D$. Let $S_0 \subseteq S$ be the following set:

$$\{(m, 0, f_0(m)) : 0 \le m < s\}.$$

Let $R_H \subseteq S \times S$ be the following relation:

$$R\{((m - 1, n, d), (m, n, d')) : 1 \le m, n < s, (d, d') \in H\},$$

and $R_V \subseteq S \times S$ be this:

$$R\{((m, n - 1, d), (m, n, d')) : 0 \le m < s, 2 \le n < s, (d, d') \in V\}.$$

Show that $x \in L$ if and only if the closure of S_0 under R_H and R_V contains, for each $0 \leq i, j < s$, a triple (i, j, d) for some $d \in D$. In other words, not only can any closure property can be computed in polynomial time (this was shown near the end of Section 1.6), but also, conversely, *any polynomial computation can be expressed as a closure property.* Of course, the use of huge relations such as R_H makes this result seem a little artificial; but it turns out that it also holds in a much more meaningful setting (see the references at the end of the chapter).

7.2.2. Consider BINARY BOUNDED TILING, the version of BOUNDED TILING where we are not given the first row of tiles, but only the tile at the origin, d_0; the size of the square to be tiled, s, is given in binary.

(a) Show that there is a reduction from the language

$$E_1 = \{ \text{``}M\text{''} : M \text{ halts on the empty string within } 2^{|\text{``}M\text{''}|} \text{ steps} \}$$

to BINARY BOUNDED TILING.

(b) Conclude that BINARY BOUNDED TILING is not in $\mathcal{P}$.

(c) Let $\mathcal{NEXP}$ be the class of all languages decided by a *nondeterministic Turing machine* in time 2^{n^k} for some $k > 0$. Show that (i) BINARY BOUNDED TILING is in $\mathcal{NEXP}$, and (ii) all languages in $\mathcal{NEXP}$ are polynomially reducible to BINARY BOUNDED TILING. That is to say, BINARY BOUNDED TILING could be termed $\mathcal{NEXP}$-*complete*.

7.2.3. (a) Show that SATISFIABILITY remains $\mathcal{NP}$-complete even if it is restricted to instances in which each variable appears at most three times. (*Hint:* Replace the occurrences of variable, say, x, by new variables $x_1, \ldots, x_k$. Then add a formula in which each of these variables appears twice, stating that "all these variables are equivalent.")

(b) What happens if each variable appears at most twice?

7.2.4. Recall from Problem 6.4.3 that the class $\mathcal{NP}$ is closed under *nonerasing homomorphisms.* Show that $\mathcal{P}$ is closed under nonerasing homomorphisms if and only if $\mathcal{P} = \mathcal{NP}$. (*Hint:* One direction follows from (a). For the other, consider the following language, which is obviously in $\mathcal{P}$:

$$L = \{ xy : x \in \{0, 1\}^* \text{ is the encoding of a Boolean formula } F,$$
$$\text{and } y \in \{\top, \bot\}^* \text{ is a truth assignment that satisfies } F \}.)$$

7.2.5. Consider the following special case of MAX SAT:

MAX 2-SAT: Given a set F of clauses, with at most two literals each, and an integer K, is there a truth assignment that satisfies at least K of the clauses?

Show that MAX 2-SAT is $\mathcal{NP}$-complete. (This is hard. Consider the clauses $(x), (y), (z), (w), (\overline{x} \vee \overline{y}), (\overline{y} \vee \overline{z}), (\overline{z} \vee \overline{x}), (x \vee \overline{w}), (y \vee \overline{w}), (z \vee \overline{w})$. Show that this set of ten clauses has the following property: All satisfying truth assignment on x, y, z can be extended to satisfy seven clauses and no more, except for one, which can only be extended to satisfy six. Can you use this "gadget" to reduce 3-SATISFIABILITY to MAX 2-SAT?)

7.3 | MORE NP-COMPLETE PROBLEMS

Once we have proved our first $\mathcal{NP}$-complete problem, we can reduce it to other problems, and those to still others, proving them all $\mathcal{NP}$-complete. See Figure 7-4 for a depiction of the reductions proved in this section and the last, and see the problems and the references for many more $\mathcal{NP}$-complete problems.

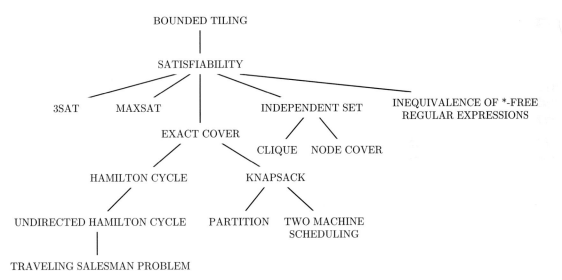

Figure 7-4

$\mathcal{NP}$-complete problems arise in all fields and applications in which sophisticated computation is done. It is an important skill to be able to spot $\mathcal{NP}$-complete problems —either by recognizing them as known $\mathcal{NP}$-complete problems,[†] or by proving them $\mathcal{NP}$-complete from scratch. Such knowledge

---

[†] This is not always easy, because $\mathcal{NP}$-complete problems tend to come up in applications under all sorts of confusing guises.

saves researchers and programmers from futile attempts at impossible goals, and redirects their efforts to more hopeful venues (reviewed in Section 7.4 on *coping with $\mathcal{NP}$-completeness*). $\mathcal{NP}$-complete problems such as GRAPH COLORING (see Problem 7.1.1), SATISFIABILITY, and INDEPENDENT SET are important because they come up frequently, and under various guises, in applications. Others, like the TRAVELING SALESMAN PROBLEM, are important not only because of their practical applications, but because they have been studied so much. Still others, such as the problem we introduce next, are important because they are often handy starting points for $\mathcal{NP}$-completeness reductions (SATISFIABILITY is important for all three reasons).

We are given a finite set $U = \{u_1, \ldots, u_n\}$ (the *universe*), and a family of m subsets of U, $\mathcal{F} = \{S_1, \ldots, S_m\}$. We are asked whether there is an *exact cover*, that is, subfamily $\mathcal{C} \subseteq \mathcal{F}$ such that that the sets in $\mathcal{C}$ are disjoint and have U as their union. We call this problem EXACT COVER.

For example, let the universe be $U = \{u_1, u_2, u_3, u_4, u_5, u_6\}$ and the family of subsets $\mathcal{F} = \{\{u_1, u_3\}, \{u_2, u_3, u_6\}, \{u_1, u_5\}, \{u_2, u_3, u_4\}, \{u_5, u_6\}, \{u_2, u_4\}\}$. An exact cover exists in this instance: It is $\mathcal{C} = \{\{u_1, u_3\}, \{u_5, u_6\}, \{u_2, u_4\}\}$.

Theorem 7.3.1: EXACT COVER *is $\mathcal{NP}$-complete.*

Proof: It is clear that EXACT COVER is $\mathcal{NP}$: Given an instance $(U, \mathcal{F})$ of the problem, the subfamily sought is a valid certificate. The certificate is polynomially concise in the size of the instance (since it is a subset of $\mathcal{F}$, which is a part of the input), and it can be checked in polynomial time whether indeed all elements of U appear exactly once in the sets of $\mathcal{C}$.

To prove $\mathcal{NP}$-completeness, we shall reduce SATISFIABILITY to the EXACT COVER problem. That is, we are given a Boolean formula F with clauses $\{C_1, \ldots, C_\ell\}$ over the Boolean variables $x_1, \ldots, x_n$, and we must show how to construct in polynomial time an equivalent instance $\tau(F)$ of the EXACT COVER problem. We shall denote the literals of clause C_j by λ_{jk}, $k = 1, \ldots, m_j$, where m_j is the number of literals in C_j.

The universe of $\tau(F)$ is the set

$$U = \{x_i : 1 \le i \le n\} \cup \{C_j : j = 1, \ldots, \ell\} \cup \{p_{jk} : 1 \le j \le \ell, k = 1, \ldots, m_j\}.$$

That is, there is one element for each Boolean variable, one for each clause, and also one element for each position in each clause.

Now for the sets in $\mathcal{F}$. First, for each element p_{jk}, we have in $\mathcal{F}$ a set $\{p_{jk}\}$. That is to say, the p_{jk}'s are very easy to cover. The difficulty lies in covering the elements corresponding to the Boolean variables and clauses. Each variable x_i belongs to two sets in $\mathcal{F}$, namely, the set

$$T_{i,\top} = \{x_i\} \cup \{p_{jk} : \lambda_{jk} = \overline{x_i}\},$$

which also contains all negative occurrences of x_i, and

$$T_{i,\perp} = \{x_i\} \cup \{p_{jk} : \lambda_{jk} = x_i\},$$

with the positive occurrences (notice the reversal in signs). Finally, each clause C_i belongs to m_j sets, one for each literal in it, namely $\{C_j, p_{jk}\}$, $k = 1, \ldots, m_j$. These are all the sets in $\mathcal{F}$, and this completes the description of $\tau(F)$.

Let us illustrate the reduction for the given Boolean formula F, with clauses $C_1 = (x_1 \vee \overline{x_2})$, $C_2 = (\overline{x_1} \vee x_2 \vee x_3)$, $C_3 = (x_2)$, and $C_4 = (\overline{x_2} \vee \overline{x_3})$. The universe of $\tau(F)$ is

$$U = \{x_1, x_2, x_3, C_1, C_2, C_3, C_4, p_{11}, p_{12}, p_{21}, p_{22}, p_{23}, p_{31}, p_{41}, p_{42}\},$$

and the family of sets $\mathcal{F}$ consists of these sets:

$$\{p_{11}\}, \{p_{12}\}, \{p_{21}\}, \{p_{22}\}, \{p_{23}\}, \{p_{31}, \}\{p_{41}\}, \{p_{42}\},$$
$$T_{1,\perp} = \{x_1, p_{11}\},$$
$$T_{1,\top} = \{x_1, p_{21}\},$$
$$T_{2,\perp} = \{x_2, p_{22}, p_{31}\},$$
$$T_{2,\top} = \{x_2, p_{12}, p_{41}\},$$
$$T_{3,\perp} = \{x_3, p_{23}\},$$
$$T_{3,\top} = \{x_2, p_{42}\},$$
$$\{C_1, p_{11}\}, \{C_1, p_{12}\}, \{C_2, p_{21}\}, \{C_2, p_{22}\},$$
$$\{C_2, p_{23}\}, \{C_3, p_{31}, \}, \{C_4, p_{41}\}, \{C_4, p_{42}\}.$$

We claim that $\tau(F)$ has an exact cover if and only if F is satisfiable. Suppose that an exact cover $\mathcal{C}$ exists. Since each x_i must be covered, exactly one of the two sets $T_{i,\top}$ and $T_{i,\perp}$ containing x_i must be in $\mathcal{C}$. Think of $T_{i,\top} \in \mathcal{C}$ as meaning that $T(x_i) = \top$, and $T_{i,\perp} \in \mathcal{C}$ as meaning that $T(x_i) = \perp$; this defines a truth assignment T. We claim that T satisfies F. In proof, consider a clause C_j. The element in U corresponding to this clause must be covered by a set $\{C_j, p_{jk}\}$, for $1 \le k \le m_j$. This means that the element p_{jk} is not contained in any other set in the exact cover $\mathcal{C}$; in particular, it is not in the set in $\mathcal{C}$ that contains the variable that occurs (negated or not) at the kth literal of C_j. But this means that T makes the kth literal of C_j $\top$, and thus C_j is satisfied by T. Hence F is satisfiable.

Conversely, suppose that there is a truth assignment T that satisfies F. We then construct the following exact cover $\mathcal{C}$: For each x_i, $\mathcal{C}$ contains the set $T_{i,\top}$ if $T(x_i) = \top$, and it contains the set $T_{i,\perp}$ if $T(x_i) = \perp$. Also, for each clause C_j, $\mathcal{C}$ contains a set $\{C_j, p_{jk}\}$ such that the kth literal of C_j is made $\top$ by T, and thus p_{jk} is not contained in any set selected in $\mathcal{C}$ so far —we know that such a k

exists by our assumption that T satisfies F. Finally, having covered all x_i's and C_j's, $\mathcal{C}$ includes enough singleton sets to cover any remaining p_{jk} elements that are not covered by the other sets. In the illustration above, the exact cover that corresponds to the satisfying truth assignment $T(x_1) = \top$, $T(x_2) = \top$, $T(x_3) = \bot$ contains these sets: $T_{1,\top}, T_{2,\top}, T_{3,\bot}, \{C_1, p_{11}\}, \{C_2, p_{22}\}, \{C_3, p_{31}\}, \{C_4, p_{42}\}$, plus the singletons $\{p_{12}\}, \{p_{21}\}, \{p_{23}\}, \{p_{41}\}$. We conclude that $\tau(F)$ has an exact cover, and the proof is complete. ■

The Traveling Salesman Problem

We can use the EXACT COVER problem to establish the $\mathcal{NP}$-completeness of HAMILTON CYCLE.

Theorem 7.3.2: HAMILTON CYCLE *is $\mathcal{NP}$-complete.*

Proof: We already know that it is $\mathcal{NP}$. We shall now show how to reduce EXACT COVER to HAMILTON CYCLE. We shall describe a polynomial-time algorithm which, given an instance $(U, \mathcal{F})$ of EXACT COVER, produces a directed graph $G = \tau(U, \mathcal{F})$ such that G has a Hamilton cycle if and only if $(U, \mathcal{F})$ has an exact cover.

The construction is based on a certain simple graph that has interesting properties *vis à vis* the Hamilton cycle problem —in $\mathcal{NP}$-completeness jargon such graphs are called **gadgets**. Figure 7-5(a) shows this gadget. Imagine that it is a part of a larger graph G, connected to the rest of G via the four nodes shown as solid dots. In other words, there are other nodes and edges to the graph, but no edges other than the ones shown are adjacent to the three nodes in the middle. Further, suppose that G has a Hamilton cycle, a cycle which traverses each node of G exactly once. The question is, via which edges is the Hamilton cycle going to traverse the three middle nodes? It is easy to see that there are really only two possibilities: Either the edges $(a, u), (u, v), (v, w), (w, b)$ are a part of the Hamilton cycle, or the edges $(c, w), (w, v), (v, u), (u, d)$ are. All other possibilities leave some of the three nodes untraversed by the Hamilton cycle, which therefore is not Hamilton at all.

To put it otherwise, this simple device can be thought of as *two edges* (a, b) and (c, d) with the following additional constraint: In any Hamilton cycle of the overall graph G, *either* (a, b) *is traversed, or* (c, d) *is, but not both.* This situation can be depicted as in Figure 7-5(b), where the two otherwise unrelated edges are connected by an *exclusive or* sign, meaning that exactly one of them is to be traversed by any Hamilton cycle. Whenever we show this construct in our depiction of a graph, we know that in fact the graph contains the full subgraph shown in Figure 7-5(a). In fact, we can have several edges connected by such subgraphs with the same edge (see Figure 7-5(c)). The result is the same: Either all edges on one side are traversed, or the edge on the other, but not both.

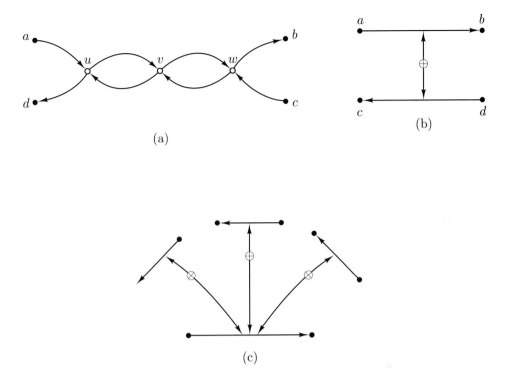

(a)

(b)

(c)

Figure 7-5

This device is central to our construction of the graph $G = \tau(U, \mathcal{F})$, corresponding to the instance of EXACT COVER with $U = \{u_1 \ldots, u_n\}$ and $\mathcal{F} = \{S_1, \ldots, S_m\}$. We describe the graph G next. There are nodes $u_0, u_1, \ldots, u_n$ and $S_0, S_1, \ldots, S_m$, that is, one for each element of the universe, and one for each set in the given instance, plus two more nodes. For $i = 1, \ldots, m$, there are *two* edges (S_{i-1}, S_i). Of course, in graphs it makes no sense to have two different edges connecting the same pair of nodes. The only reason we allow it in the present case is that the edges will be later joined by "exclusive or" subgraphs as in Figure 7-4, and thus there will be no "parallel" edges at the end of the construction. One of the two edges (S_{i-1}, S_i) is called the *long* edge, and the other is the *short* edge. For $j = 1, \ldots, n$, between the nodes u_{j-1} and u_j there are *as many edges as there are sets in $\mathcal{F}$ containing the element u_j*. This way, we can think that each copy of the edge (u_{j-1}, u_j) corresponds to an appearance of u_j in a set. Finally, we add the edges (u_n, S_0) and (S_m, u_0), thus "closing the cycle."

Notice that the construction so far only depends on the size of the universe and the number and sizes of the sets; it does not depend on *precisely which*

$$S_1 = \{u_3, u_4\}$$

$$S_2 = \{u_2, u_3, u_4\}$$

$$S_3 = \{u_1, u_2\}$$

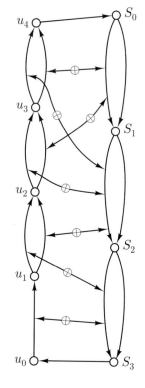

Figure 7-6

sets contain each element. This fine structure of the instance will influence our construction as follows: As each copy of edge (u_{j-1}, u_j) corresponds to an appearance of element u_j in some set $S_i \in \mathcal{F}$ such that $u_j \in S_i$, *we join by an "exclusive or" subgraph this copy of edge (u_{j-1}, u_j) with the long edge (S_{i-1}, S_i)* (see Figure 7-6 for an illustration). This completes the construction of the graph $\tau(U, \mathcal{F})$.

We claim that the graph $\tau(U, \mathcal{F})$ has a Hamilton cycle if and only if $\tau(U, \mathcal{F})$ has an exact cover. First, suppose that a Hamilton cycle exists. It must traverse the nodes corresponding to the sets in the order $S_0, S_1, \ldots, S_m$, then traverse the edge (S_m, u_0), then the nodes $u_0, u_1, \ldots, u_n$, and finally finish along the edge (u_n, S_0) (see Figure 7-6). The question is, will it traverse for each set S_j the short or the long edge (S_{j-1}, S_j)? Let $\mathcal{C}$ be the set of all sets T_j such that the short edge (S_{j-1}, S_j) is traversed by the Hamilton cycle. We shall show that $\mathcal{C}$ is a legitimate set cover; that is, it contains all elements without overlaps. But this is not hard to see: By the property of the "exclusive or" subgraph, the elements in the sets in $\mathcal{C}$ are precisely the copies of edges of the form (u_{i-1}, u_i) that are traversed by the Hamilton cycle; and the Hamilton cycle traverses exactly one such edge for each element $u_j \in U$. It follows that each $u_j \in U$ is contained in exactly one set in $\mathcal{C}$, and thus $\mathcal{C}$ is an exact cover.

Conversely, suppose that an exact cover $\mathcal{C}$ exists. Then a Hamilton cycle in the graph $\tau(U, \mathcal{F})$ can be constructed as follows: Traverse the short copies of all edges (S_{j-1}, S_j) where $S_j \in \mathcal{C}$, and the long edges for all other sets. Then for each element u_i, traverse the copy of the edge (u_{i-1}, u_i) that corresponds to the unique set in $\mathcal{C}$ that contains u_i. Complete the Hamilton cycle by the edges (u_n, S_0) and (S_m, u_0). ∎

Once a problem is shown to be $\mathcal{NP}$-complete, research often is focused on solving interesting yet tractable special cases of the problem. $\mathcal{NP}$-completeness proofs often produce instances of the target problem that are complex and "unnatural." The question often persists, whether the instances *that are of interest in practice*, being much less complex, may not be solvable by some efficient algorithm. Alternatively, it can be often shown that even substantially restricted versions of the problem remain $\mathcal{NP}$-complete. We have already seen both patterns in connection to SATISFIABILITY, whose special case 2-SATISFIABILITY can be solved in polynomial time, whereas the special case 3-SATISFIABILITY is $\mathcal{NP}$-complete. To introduce an interesting special case of HAMILTON CYCLE, define UNDIRECTED HAMILTON CYCLE to be the HAMILTON CYCLE problem restricted to graphs that are *undirected*, that is, symmetric without self-loops.

Theorem 7.3.3: UNDIRECTED HAMILTON CYCLE *is $\mathcal{NP}$-complete.*

Proof: We shall reduce the ordinary HAMILTON CYCLE problem to it. Given a graph $G \subseteq V \times V$, we shall construct a symmetric graph $G' \subseteq V' \times V'$, without self-loops, such that G has a Hamilton cycle if and only if G' has one. The construction, illustrated in Figure 7-7, is this: First, $V' = \{v_0, v_1, v_2 : v \in V\}$, that is, G' has three nodes v_0, v_1, and v_2 for each node v of G. Of these v_0 is, informally, the *entry* node, to which edges coming into v will be directed, and v_2 is the *exit* node, from which edges going out of v will emanate.

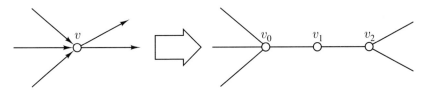

Figure 7-7

Thus, the edges in G' are these (see Figure 7-7; recall that undirected graphs are more conveniently depicted by undirected lines connecting the nodes):

$$\{(u_2, v_0), (v_0, u_2) : (u, v) \in G\} \cup \{(v_0, v_1), (v_1, v_0), (v_1, v_2), (v_2, v_1) : v \in V\}.$$

That is, the nodes v_0, v_1, v_2 are connected by a path in this order, and there is an undirected edge between u_2 and v_0 whenever $(u, v) \in G$. This completes the construction of G'.

We must now prove that G' has a Hamilton cycle if and only if G has one. Suppose that a Hamilton cycle of G' arrives at node v_0 from an edge of the form (u_2, v_0). If the Hamilton cycle leaves v_0 through an edge other than (v_0, v_1), then it cannot "pick up" node v_1 in any other way, and thus it was erroneously assumed to be a Hamilton cycle. Thus, edge (v_0, v_1) must be a part of the cycle, and so is (v_1, v_2). Then the cycle must continue through one of the edges (v_2, w_0), where $(v, w) \in G$, from there to w_1, w_2, to some z_0 where $(w, z) \in G$, and so on. Therefore, the edges of the form (u_0, v_2) in the Hamilton cycle of G' constitute in fact a Hamilton cycle of G. Conversely, any Hamilton cycle $(v^1, v^2, \ldots, v^{|V|})$ of G can be converted into a Hamilton cycle of G' as follows: $(v_0^1, v_1^1, v_2^1, v_0^2, v_1^2, v_2^2, \ldots, v_0^{|V|}, v_1^{|V|}, v_2^{|V|})$. We conclude that G has a Hamilton cycle if and only if G' has a Hamilton cycle, and the proof is complete. ∎

Our next result concerns the notorious TRAVELING SALESMAN PROBLEM —its "yes-no" version, in which each instance is supplied with a budget B, as defined in Section 6.2.

Theorem 7.3.4: *The* TRAVELING SALESMAN PROBLEM *is* $\mathcal{NP}$*-complete.*

Proof: We already know that the problem is in $\mathcal{NP}$. To show completeness, we shall reduce UNDIRECTED HAMILTON CYCLE to the TRAVELING SALESMAN PROBLEM. Given a symmetric graph G, where without loss of generality $V = \{v_1, \ldots, v_{|V|}\}$, we construct the following instance of the TRAVELING SALESMAN PROBLEM: n, the number of cities, is $|V|$, and the distance d_{ij} between any two cities i and j is

$$
d_{ij} = \begin{cases} 0 & \text{if } i = j; \\ 1 & \text{if } (v_i, v_j) \in G; \\ 2 & \text{otherwise.} \end{cases}
$$

Since G is a symmetric graph without loops, this distance function is itself symmetric; that is to say, $d_{ij} = d_{ji}$ for all cities i and j, as required. Finally, the budget is $B = n$.

Obviously, any "tour" of the cities has cost equal to the number of n plus the number of the intercity distances traversed that are *not* edges of G. Thus, a tour of cost B or less exists if and only if the number of "nonedges" used is zero, that is, if and only if the tour is a Hamilton cycle of G. ∎

Partitions and Cliques

EXACT COVER also provides a nice proof of the $\mathcal{NP}$-completeness of PARTITION. It is easiest to start from the closely related KNAPSACK problem, in which an arbitrary sum K to be achieved is given (recall its definition in Example 7.1.2):

Theorem 7.3.5: KNAPSACK *is* $\mathcal{NP}$*-complete.*

Proof: That KNAPSACK is in $\mathcal{NP}$ is clear: Given an instance of KNAPSACK $a_1, \ldots, a_n$, and K, a subset P of $\{1, \ldots, n\}$ such that $\sum_{i \in P} a_i = K$ can serve as a certificate that the answer to the given instance is "yes." It is polynomially succinct, and it can be tested in polynomial time by binary addition.

We shall now reduce EXACT COVER to KNAPSACK. We are given a universe $U = \{u_1 \ldots, u_n\}$ and a family $\mathcal{F} = \{S_1, \ldots, S_m\}$ of subsets of U. We shall construct an instance $\tau(U, \mathcal{F})$ of KNAPSACK, that is, nonnegative integers $a_1, \ldots, a_k$, and another K such that there is a subset $P \subseteq \{1, \ldots, k\}$ with $\sum_{i \in P} a_i = K$ if and only if there is a set of sets $\mathcal{C} \subseteq \mathcal{F}$ that are disjoint and collectively cover all of U.

This construction is particularly simple, because it relies on an unexpected relationship between *set union* and *integer addition*. Subsets of a set of n elements, such as those in $\mathcal{F}$, can be represented as strings over $\{0,1\}^n$ (see Figure 7-8). In turn such strings can be interpreted as integers between zero and $2^n - 1$, written in binary. Now taking the union of such sets, provided that they are disjoint, is the same as adding the corresponding integers. Since in EXACT COVER we are asking whether the disjoint union of the teams makes up the whole U, this seems to be the same as asking whether there are integers among the given ones that add up to $K = 1 + 2 + 4 + \cdots + 2^{n-1}$ —the binary number with n ones. And this is very close to an instance of KNAPSACK.

$$
\begin{array}{lll}
S_1 = \{u_3, u_4\} & S_1 = 0\,0\,1\,1 & \begin{array}{l} 0\,0\,1\,1 \;\checkmark \\ 0\,1\,1\,1 \\ +\,1\,1\,0\,0 \;\checkmark \\ \hline 1\,1\,1\,1 \end{array} \\
S_2 = \{u_2, u_3, u_4\} & S_2 = 0\,1\,1\,1 & \\
S_3 = \{u_1, u_2\} & S_3 = 1\,1\,0\,0 & \\
\end{array}
$$

(a)   (b)   (c)

Figure 7-8: From sets (a) to bit vectors (b) to integer addition in base m (c)

There is one problem with this simple reduction: The close correspondence between set union and integer addition breaks down because in integer addition we may have *carry*. Consider, for example, the sum $11 + 13 + 15 + 24 = 63$; in binary $001011 + 001101 + 001111 + 011000 = 111111$. If we translate back to subsets of $\{u_1, \ldots, u_6\}$, the sets $\{u_3, u_5, u_6\}$, $\{u_3, u_4, u_6\}$, $\{u_3, u_4, u_5, u_6\}$, and $\{u_2, u_3\}$ are neither disjoint, nor do they cover all of U. In other words, carry makes the translation between union and addition faulty.

This problem can be very easily resolved as follows: Instead of considering the strings in $\{0,1\}^n$ as integers in binary, consider them as integers *in m-ary*, where m is the number of sets in $\mathcal{F}$. That is, we have m integers $a_1, \ldots, a_m$, where $a_i = \sum_{u_j \in S_i} m^{j-1}$. We ask whether there is a subset that adds up to $K = \sum_{j=1}^{n} m^{j-1}$. This way carry is not a problem, because the addition of fewer than m digits in m-ary, with each of the digits either 0 or 1, can never result in carry. It is now clear that the resulting instance of KNAPSACK has a solution if and only if the original instance of EXACT COVER has a solution. ∎

Corollary: PARTITION *and* TWO-MACHINE SCHEDULING *are* $\mathcal{NP}$-*complete.*

Proof: There are polynomial reductions from KNAPSACK to both of these problems; recall Example 7.1.2. ∎

We next turn to three graph-theoretic problems introduced in Section 6.2: INDEPENDENT SET, CLIQUE, and NODE COVER.

Theorem 7.3.6: INDEPENDENT SET *is* $\mathcal{NP}$-*complete.*

Proof: It is clearly in $\mathcal{NP}$; and we shall reduce 3-SATISFIABILITY to it.

Suppose that we are given a Boolean formula F with clauses $C_1, \ldots, C_m$, each with at most three literals. In fact, we shall assume that all clauses of F have *exactly* three literals; if a clause has only one or two literals, then we allow a literal to be repeated to bring the total number to three. We shall construct an undirected graph G and an integer K such that there is a set of K nodes in G with no edges between them if and only if F is satisfiable.

The reduction is illustrated in Figure 7-9. For each one of the clauses $C_1, \ldots, C_m$ of F, we have three nodes in G, connected by edges so that they form a triangle —call the nodes of the triangle corresponding to clause C_i c_{i1}, c_{i2}, c_{i3}. These are all the nodes of G —a total of $3m$ nodes. The goal is $K = m$, equal to the number of clauses. For defining the remaining edges of G, node c_{ij} is identified with the jth literal of clause C_i. Finally, two nodes are joined by an edge *if and only if their literals are the negation of one another*. This completes the description of the reduction; see Figure 7-9 for an example.

Suppose that there is an independent set I in G with $K = m$ nodes. Since any two nodes from the same triangle are connected by an edge, evidently there is exactly one node in I from each triangle. Recall that nodes correspond to literals. Consider now the fact that a node is in I to mean that the corresponding literal is $\top$. Since there are no edges between nodes in I, it follows that no two such literals are the negation of one another, and therefore they can be the basis of a truth assignment T. Notice that T may not be fully defined on all variables, because the set of nodes in I may fail to involve all variables; for example, in Figure 7-9 the independent set indicated by the full circles does not determine the value of variable x_3. T may take any truth value on such "missing" variables; the resulting truth assignment T satisfies all clauses, because each clause has at

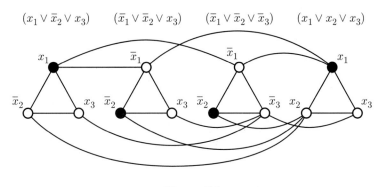

$(x_1 \vee \bar{x}_2 \vee x_3)$ $(\bar{x}_1 \vee \bar{x}_2 \vee x_3)$ $(\bar{x}_1 \vee \bar{x}_2 \vee \bar{x}_3)$ $(x_1 \vee x_2 \vee x_3)$

Figure 7-9

least one literal satisfied by T. And conversely, given any truth assignment satisfying F, we can obtain an independent set of size m by picking for each clause a node corresponding to a satisfied literal. ∎

The $\mathcal{NP}$-completeness of two other graph-theoretic problems is now immediate:

Theorem 7.3.7: CLIQUE *and* NODE COVER *are* $\mathcal{NP}$-*complete.*

Proof: They are both clearly in $\mathcal{NP}$.

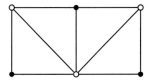 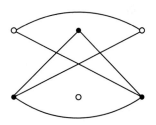

Figure 7-10

CLIQUE, requiring that *all* edges between any two nodes in the set be present, is in some sense the *exact opposite* of INDEPENDENT SET. The reduction makes this sense precise. Given an instance (G, K) of INDEPENDENT SET, where $G \subseteq V \times V$ is an undirected graph and $K \geq 2$ is the goal, we create an equivalent instance (G', K') of CLIQUE by just taking $G' = V \times V - \{(i, i) : i \in V\} - G$, and keeping the same goal, $K' = K$. This works because, as it is fairly easy to check, the maximum independent set of G is precisely the maximum clique in the *complement* of G, the graph that contains all non-loop edges that are not in G (see Figure 7-10).

Finally, NODE COVER is the exact opposite of INDEPENDENT SET in a different sense: since the nodes in a node cover $N \subseteq V$ "hit" between them all edges, the set $V - N$ must have no edges between its elements, and is thus an independent set (see Figure 7-11). Hence, $N \subseteq V$ is a node cover of G if and only if $V - N$ is an independent set of G. Thus, the maximum independent set of G has size K or more if and only if the minimum node cover of G has size $|V| - K$ or less. The reduction from INDEPENDENT SET to NODE COVER leaves the graph the same, and simply replaces K by $|V| - K$. ∎

Figure 7-11

Finite Automata

Our last $\mathcal{NP}$-completeness result concerns some of the first, and apparently simplest, mathematical objects studied in this book: nondeterministic finite automata and regular expressions.

Among all problems we introduced in the last chapter, there are only two whose membership in $\mathcal{NP}$ is not obvious: EQUIVALENCE OF REGULAR EXPRESSIONS, and the closely related problem EQUIVALENCE OF NONDETERMINISTIC FINITE AUTOMATA. Given two regular expressions, what would be a convincing certificate of their equivalence? Nothing succinct comes to mind.

If, however, we defined the *complement problem*

> INEQUIVALENCE OF REGULAR EXPRESSIONS: Given two regular expressions R_1 and R_2, is $L(R_1) \neq L(R_2)$?

then certificates seem to become possible: A certificate of the inequivalence of two regular expressions is a string belonging to the language generated by one but not the other, that is, any element of $(L(R_1) - L(R_2)) \cup (L(R_2) - L(R_1))$. Indeed, this set is nonempty if and only if the expressions are inequivalent.

But now the real difficulty reveals itself: Such certificates are legitimate in all respects except for the crucial *polynomial succinctness* property. Given two regular expressions R_1 and R_2, there is no obvious polynomial upper bound on the length of the shortest string that belongs in $(L(R_1) - L(R_2)) \cup (L(R_2) - L(R_1))$. For such a bound to qualify, it should be polynomial in the length of the two expressions, $|R_1| + |R_2|$ —that is, the number of symbols, such as $a, b, \cup, *$, and parentheses, needed to represent them. In fact, there are families of pairs of inequivalent regular expressions which differ only in strings that are exponentially long in the size of the expressions!

To obtain a problem in $\mathcal{NP}$ we must look at a restricted special case: **$*$-free regular expressions**, that is, regular expressions over union and concatenation, not containing any occurrences of Kleene star. Consider a $*$-free regular expression, such as

$$R = (0 \cup 1)00(0 \cup 1) \cup 010(0 \cup 1)0.$$

It is now easy to see that, if x is a string in the language generated by it (say, $x = 1001$ for R above), then $|x| \leq |R|$. As a result of this observation, the following problem is in $\mathcal{NP}$:

> INEQUIVALENCE OF $*$-FREE REGULAR EXPRESSIONS: Given two $*$-free regular expressions R_1 and R_2, is $L(R_1) \neq L(R_2)$?

A valid certificate is any string in $(L(R_1) - L(R_2)) \cup (L(R_2) - L(R_1))$, and all such strings are succinct, shorter than $|R_1| + |R_2|$. For an analogous problem in the domain of nondeterministic finite automata, see Problem 7.3.7.

In fact, we can prove this result:

Theorem 7.3.8: INEQUIVALENCE OF $*$-FREE REGULAR EXPRESSIONS *is $\mathcal{NP}$-complete.*

Proof: We have already argued that the problem is in $\mathcal{NP}$. We shall show that SATISFIABILITY reduces to INEQUIVALENCE OF $*$-FREE REGULAR EXPRESSIONS.

Given any Boolean formula with Boolean variables $x_1, \ldots, x_n$ and clauses $C_1, \ldots, C_m$, we shall produce two regular expressions R_1 and R_2 over the alphabet $\Sigma = \{0, 1\}$, neither of which contains an application of the Kleene star, such that $L(R_1) \neq L(R_2)$ if and only if the given Boolean formula is satisfiable.

The second regular expression, R_2, is very simple:

$$(0 \cup 1)(0 \cup 1) \cdots (0 \cup 1),$$

with the expression $(0 \cup 1)$ repeated n times. The language generated by R_2 is obviously the set of all binary strings of length n, that is to say, $L(R_2) = \{0, 1\}^n$.

Now for the construction of R_1. In contrast to R_2, R_1 depends heavily on the given Boolean formula. In particular, R_1 is the union of m regular expressions

$$R_1 = \alpha_1 \cup \alpha_2 \cup \cdots \cup \alpha_m,$$

where regular expression α_i depends on clause C_i. Each α_i is the concatenation of n regular expressions:

$$\alpha_i = \alpha_{i1}\alpha_{i2} \cdots \alpha_{in},$$

where

$$\alpha_{ij} = \begin{cases} 0, & \text{if } x_j \text{ is a literal of } C_i; \\ 1, & \text{if } \overline{x_j} \text{ is a literal of } C_i; \\ (0 \cup 1), & \text{otherwise.} \end{cases}$$

If we disregard for a moment the distinction between $0-1$ and $\top - \bot$, then strings in $\{0,1\}^n$ can be thought of as truth assignments to the Boolean variables $\{x_1, \ldots, x_n\}$. In this interpretation, $L(\alpha_i)$ is precisely the set of all truth assignments that *fail* to satisfy C_i. Thus $L(R_1)$ is the set of all truth assignments that fail to satisfy at least one of the clauses of the given Boolean formula. Thus, the given Boolean formula is satisfiable if and only if $L(R_1)$ is different from $\{0,1\}^n$ —which is precisely $L(R_2)$. The proof is complete. ∎

The equivalence problem for general regular expressions and for nondeterministic finite automata can, of course, only be harder (see the references for information about their precise complexity), and similarly for the state minimization problems for nondeterministic finite automata. None of these simply stated problems about the most primitive of computational models can be solved efficiently unless $\mathcal{P} = \mathcal{NP}$.

But how about the following less ambitious goal: Suppose that we wish, given a nondeterministic finite automaton, to find the equivalent *deterministic* one with the minimum number of states. We know that any such algorithm must be exponential in the worst case because the output may have to be exponentially long in the size of the input (recall Example 2.5.4). But is there an algorithm that runs in time polynomial in the size of the input *and the output*? Such an algorithm would spend exponential time when the output is large, but would swiftly output small automata. (The obvious algorithm which first carries out the subset construction and then minimizes the resulting deterministic automaton does not qualify, because the subset construction may yield an intermediate result that is exponentially large, even though the final output —the minimum equivalent deterministic automaton— may be polynomial.)

Unfortunately, we can show that even such an algorithm is unlikely to exist:

Corollary: *Unless $\mathcal{P} = \mathcal{NP}$, there is no algorithm which, given a regular expression or a nondeterministic finite automaton, constructs the minimum-state equivalent deterministic finite automaton in time that is polynomial in the input and the output.*

Proof: Let M_n denote the simple $n+1$-state finite automaton accepting $\{0,1\}^n$. In the reduction in the proof of the theorem, the given Boolean formula with n variables is unsatisfiable if and only if the minimum-state deterministic finite automaton equivalent to R_1 is exactly M_n.

Suppose now that an algorithm as described in the statement of the corollary exists, with a time bound of the form $p(|x|+|y|)$, where p is a polynomial, x is the input of the algorithm, and y is its output. Then we could solve SATISFIABILITY as follows.

Given any Boolean formula F with n variables, we first perform the reduction described in the proof of the theorem to obtain a regular expression R_1. Then we run, on input R_1, the purported algorithm for $p(|R_1| + |M_n|)$ steps, where $|M_n|$ is the length of the encoding of M_n. If the algorithm terminates within the allotted time, then we know how to answer the original SATISFIABILITY question: We answer "no" if the output is M_n, and we answer "yes" in the event of any other output. If, however, the algorithm does not halt after $p(|R_1| + |M_n|)$ steps, and since we know that it always halts after $p(|x| + |y|)$ steps, we can conclude that its output would be longer than $|M_n|$. Hence the algorithm's output is not M_n, and we can confidently answer "yes" to the original SATISFIABILITY question.

What we described in the previous paragraph is a polynomial-time algorithm for SATISFIABILITY —the time bound $p(|R_1| + |M|)$ is polynomial in the size of the Boolean formula F. Since SATISFIABILITY is $\mathcal{NP}$-complete, we must conclude by Theorem 7.1.1 that $\mathcal{P} = \mathcal{NP}$, completing the proof. ∎

Problems for Section 7.3

7.3.1. (a) Show that EXACT COVER remains $\mathcal{NP}$-complete even if all sets have no more than three elements, and each element appears in at most three sets. (b) What happens if either number is two?

7.3.2. Give the *full* graph (without the abbreviation of the exclusive-or gadget) that would result from the reduction from EXACT COVER to HAMILTON CYCLE if the given instance of EXACT COVER consists of the universe $\{u_1, u_2\}$ and the family of sets $\mathcal{F} = \{\{u_1\}, \{u_1, u_2\}\}$.

7.3.3. (a) Show that the HAMILTON PATH problem is $\mathcal{NP}$-complete, (1) by reducing the HAMILTON CYCLE problem to it; (2) by modifying slightly the construction in the proof of Theorem 7.3.2. (b) Repeat for the problem HAMILTON PATH BETWEEN TWO SPECIFIED NODES (the obvious definition).

7.3.4. Each of the following problems is a **generalization** of an $\mathcal{NP}$-complete problem, and is therefore $\mathcal{NP}$-complete. That is, if certain parameters of the problem are fixed in a certain way, then the problem in hand becomes a known $\mathcal{NP}$-complete problem (recall the proof of Theorem 7.2.4). One can reduce any problem to its generalization by simply introducing a new parameter, and otherwise leaving the instance as it is.

For each of the problems below, prove that it is $\mathcal{NP}$-complete by showing that it is the generalization of an $\mathcal{NP}$-complete problem. Give the appropriate parameter restriction in each case.

(a) LONGEST CYCLE: Given a graph and integer K, is there a cycle, with no repeated nodes, of length at least K? (*Hint:* What happens to this problem if K is restricted to be equal to the number of nodes of the graph?)

(b) SUBGRAPH ISOMORPHISM: Given two undirected graphs G and H, is G a subgraph of H? (That is, if G has nodes $v_1, \ldots, v_n$, can you find distinct nodes $u_1, \ldots, u_n$ in H such that $[u_i, u_j]$ is an edge in H whenever $[v_i, v_j]$ is an edge in G?)

(c) INDUCED SUBGRAPH ISOMORPHISM: Given two undirected graphs G and H, is G an induced subgraph of H? (That is, if G has nodes $v_1, \ldots, v_n$, can you find distinct nodes $u_1, \ldots, u_n$ in H such that $[u_i, u_j]$ is an edge in H *if and only if* $[v_i, v_j]$ is an edge in G?)

(d) RELIABLE GRAPH: Given an undirected graph G with nodes $v_1, \ldots, v_n$, an $n \times n$ symmetric matrix R_{ij} of natural numbers, and an integer B, is there a set S of B edges of G with the following property: Between nodes $v_i \neq v_j$ there are at least R_{ij} disjoint paths (that is, paths sharing no other node except for the endpoints) with edges in S. (*Hint:* What happens if $R_{ij} = 2$ for all i, j, and $B = n$?)

(e) INTEGER PROGRAMMING: Given m equations

$$\sum_{i=1}^{n} a_{ij} x_j = b_i, \quad i = 1, \ldots, m$$

in n variables, with integer coefficients a_{ij} and b_i, does it have a solution in which all x_j's are either zero or one? (Actually, this is a common generalization of *many* of the $\mathcal{NP}$-complete problems we have seen; how many can you find?)

(f) TAXICAB RIPOFF: Given a directed graph G with positive lengths d_{ij} on its edges, two nodes 1 and n, and an integer K, is there a path from 1 to n, not repeating any node twice, with total length K or more?

(g) HITTING SET: Given a family of sets $\{S_1, S_2, \ldots, S_n\}$, and an integer B, is there a set H with B or fewer elements such that H intersects all sets in the family?

(h) BIN PACKING: Given a set of positive integers $A = \{a_1, \ldots, a_n\}$, and two more integers B and K, can the integers in A be partitioned into B subsets ("bins") such that the numbers in each bin sum up to K or less?

(i) SET COVER: Given a family $\mathcal{F}$ of subsets of a universe U, and an integer K, are there K sets in $\mathcal{F}$ whose union equals U?

7.3.5. Show that INDEPENDENT SET remains $\mathcal{NP}$-complete even if the size K of the INDEPENDENT SET sought equals $\lceil n/2 \rceil$, where n is the number of nodes.

7.3.6. Show that the following problem is $\mathcal{NP}$-complete. DOMINATING SET: Given a directed graph G and an integer B, is there a set S of B nodes of G such that for every node $u \notin S$ of G, there is a node $v \in S$ such that (v, u) is an edge of G.

7.3.7. Call a nondeterministic finite automaton $M = (K, \Sigma, \Delta, s, F)$ *acyclic* if there is no state q and string $w \neq e$ such that $(q, w) \vdash_M^* (q, e)$. Show that the problem of telling whether two acyclic nondeterministic finite automata are inequivalent is $\mathcal{NP}$-complete.

7.4 | COPING WITH NP-COMPLETENESS

Problems do not go away when they are proved $\mathcal{NP}$-complete. But once we know that the problem we are interested in is an $\mathcal{NP}$-complete problem, we are more willing to lower our sights, to settle for solutions that are less than perfect, for algorithms that are not always polynomial, or do not work on all possible instances. In this section we review some of the most useful maneuvers of this sort.

Special Cases

Once our problem has been shown $\mathcal{NP}$-complete, the first question to ask is this: Do we *really* need to solve this problem in the full generality in which it was formulated —and proved $\mathcal{NP}$-complete? $\mathcal{NP}$-completeness reductions often produce instances of the problem that are unnaturally complex. Perhaps what we really need to solve is a more tractable *special case* of the problem.

For example, we have already seen that there is an important special case of SATISFIABILITY that can be easily solved efficiently: 2-SATISFIABILITY (recall Section 6.3). If all instances of SATISFIABILITY that we must solve have clauses of this kind, then the fact that the general problem is $\mathcal{NP}$-complete is rather irrelevant. But often a special case of interest turns out to be *itself* $\mathcal{NP}$-complete —for example, 3-SATISFIABILITY is such a case, recall Theorem 7.2.3. We next see another example.

Example 7.4.1: Most problems involving undirected graphs become easy when the graph is a **tree** —that is to say, it has no cycles, see Figure 7-12. Looking back at our collection of $\mathcal{NP}$-complete graph problems, HAMILTON CYCLE is of course trivial in trees (no tree has a cycle, Hamilton or otherwise), but so is HAMILTON PATH —a tree has a Hamilton path only if *it is* a Hamilton path. The CLIQUE problem also becomes trivial —no tree can have a clique with more than two nodes.

The INDEPENDENT SET problem is also easy when the graph is a tree. The method used for its solution takes advantage of the "hierarchical structure" of

trees. It is often useful in a tree to pick an arbitrary node and designate it as
the **root** (see Figure 7-12); once this has been done, each node u in the tree
becomes itself the root of a *subtree* $T(u)$ —the set of all nodes v such that the
(unique) path from v to the root goes through u; see Figure 7-12. Then problems
can be solved bottom up, by going from the leaves (subtrees with one node) to
larger and larger subtrees, until the whole tree (the subtree of the root) has
been dealt with. For each node u we can define the set of its *children* $C(u)$ —the
nodes in its subtree that are adjacent to it, excluding u itself— and its set of
grandchildren $G(u)$ —the children of its children. Naturally, these sets could be
empty. For example, in Figure 7-12, the root, denoted r, has two children and
five grandchildren. Nodes with no children are called *leaves*.

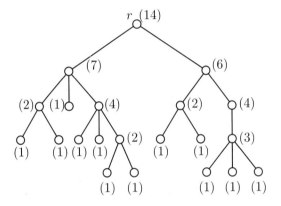

Figure 7-12

The size of the largest independent set of the tree can now be found by
computing, for each node u, the number $I(u)$, defined to be the size of the
largest independent set of $T(u)$. It is easy to see that the following equation
holds:

$$I(u) = \max\{ \sum_{v \in C(u)} I(v), \quad 1 + \sum_{v \in G(u)} I(u)\} \tag{2}$$

What this equation says is that, in designing the largest independent set of $T(u)$,
we have two choices: Either (this is the first term in the max) we do not put
u into the independent set, in which case we can put together all maximum
independent sets in the subtrees of its children, or (and this is the second term)
we put u in the independent set, in which case we must omit all its children, and
assemble the maximum independent sets of the subtrees of all its grandchildren.

It is now easy to see that a *dynamic programming* algorithm can solve the
INDEPENDENT SET problem in the special case of trees in polynomial time. The
algorithm starts at the leaves (where $I(u)$ is trivially one) and computes $I(u)$ for

larger and larger subtrees. The value of I at the root is the size of the maximum independent set of the tree. The algorithm is polynomial, because for each node u, all we have to do is compute the expression in (2), which only takes linear time. For example, in the tree of Figure 7-12, the values of $I(u)$ are shown in parentheses. The largest independent set of the tree has size 14.

Needless to say, the closely related NODER COVER problem can also be solved the same way (recall the reductions between NODE COVER and INDEPENDENT SET). So, if the graphs we are interested in happen to be trees, the fact that NODE COVER and INDEPENDENT SET are $\mathcal{NP}$-complete is irrelevant. Many other $\mathcal{NP}$-complete problems on graphs are solved by similar algorithms when specialized to trees, see for example Problem 7.4.1.◇

Approximation Algorithms

When facing an $\mathcal{NP}$-complete optimization problem, we may want to consider algorithms that do not produce optimum solutions, but solutions *guaranteed to be close to the optimum.* Suppose that we wish to obtain such solutions for an optimization problem, maximization or minimization. For each instance x of this problem, there is an optimum solution with value opt(x); let us assume that opt(x) is always a positive integer (this is the case with all optimization problems we study here; we can easily spot and solve instances in which opt is zero).

Suppose now that we have a polynomial algorithm A which, when presented with instance x of the optimization problem, returns some solution with value $A(x)$. Since the problem is $\mathcal{NP}$-complete and A is polynomial, we cannot realistically hope that $A(x)$ is always the optimum value. But suppose that we know that the following inequality always holds:

$$\frac{|\text{opt}(x) - A(x)|}{\text{opt}(x)} \leq \epsilon,$$

where ϵ is some positive real number, hopefully very small, that bounds from above the worst-case relative error of algorithm A. (The absolute value in this inequality allows us to treat both minimization and maximization problems within the same framework.) If algorithm A satisfies this inequality for all instances x of the problem, then it is called an **ϵ-approximation algorithm.**

Once an optimization problem has been shown to be $\mathcal{NP}$-complete, the following question becomes most important: Are there ϵ-approximation algorithms for this problem? And if so, how small can ϵ be? Let us observe at the outset that such questions are meaningful only if we assume that $\mathcal{P} \neq \mathcal{NP}$, because, if $\mathcal{P} = \mathcal{NP}$, then the problem can be solved exactly, with $\epsilon = 0$.

All $\mathcal{NP}$-complete optimization problems can therefore be subdivided into three large categories:

(a) Problems that are **fully approximable**, in that there is an ϵ-approximate polynomial-time algorithm for them *for all* $\epsilon > 0$, however small. Of the $\mathcal{NP}$-complete optimization problems we have seen, only TWO-MACHINE SCHEDULING (in which we wish to minimize the finishing time D) falls into this most fortunate category.

(b) Problems that are **partly approximable**, in that there are ϵ-approximate polynomial-time algorithms for them for some range of ϵ's, but —unless of course $\mathcal{P} = \mathcal{NP}$— this range does not reach all the way down to zero, as with the fully approximable problems. Of the $\mathcal{NP}$-complete optimization problems we have seen, NODE COVER and MAX SAT fall into this intermediate class.

(c) Problems that are **inapproximable**, that is, there is no ϵ-approximation algorithm for them, with however large ϵ —unless of course $\mathcal{P} = \mathcal{NP}$. Of the $\mathcal{NP}$-complete optimization problems we have seen in this chapter, unfortunately many fall into this category: the TRAVELING SALESMAN PROBLEM, CLIQUE, INDEPENDENT SET, as well as the problem of minimizing the number of states of a deterministic automaton equivalent to a given regular expression in output polynomial time (recall the corollary to Theorem 7.3.8).

Example 7.4.2: Let us describe a 1-approximation algorithm for NODE COVER —that is to say, an algorithm which, for any graph, returns a node cover that is at most *twice* the optimum size. The algorithm is very simple:

```
C := ∅
while there is an edge [u, v] left in G do
    add u and v to C, and delete them from G
```

For example, in the graph in Figure 7-13, the algorithm might start by choosing edge $[a, b]$ and inserting both endpoints in C; both nodes (and their adjacent edges, of course) are then deleted from G. Next $[e, f]$ might be chosen, and finally $[g, h]$. The resulting set C is a node cover, because each edge in G must touch one of its nodes (either because it was chosen by the algorithm, or because it was deleted by it). In the present example, $C = \{a, b, e, f, g, h\}$, has six nodes, which is at most twice the optimum value —in this case, four.

To prove the "at most twice" guarantee, consider the cover C returned by the algorithm, and let $\hat{C}$ be the optimum node cover. $|C|$ is exactly twice the number of edges chosen by the algorithm. However, these edges by the very way they were chosen, have no vertices in common, and for each of them at least one of its endpoints must be in $\hat{C}$ —because $\hat{C}$ is a node cover. It follows that the number of edges chosen by the algorithm is no larger than the optimum set cover, and hence $|C| \leq 2 \cdot |\hat{C}|$, and this is indeed a 1-approximation algorithm.

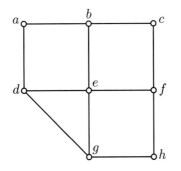

Figure 7-13

Can we do better? Depressingly, this simple approximation algorithm is the best one known for the NODE COVER problem. And only very recently have we been able to prove that, unless $\mathcal{P} = \mathcal{NP}$, there is no ϵ-approximation algorithm for NODE COVER for any $\epsilon < \frac{1}{6}$.◊

Example 7.4.3: However, for TWO-MACHINE SCHEDULING, there is no limit to how close to the optimum we can get: For any $\epsilon > 0$ there is an ϵ-approximation algorithm for this problem.

This family of algorithms is based on an idea that we have already seen: Recall that the PARTITION problem can be solved in time $\mathcal{O}(nS)$ (where n is the number of integers, and S is their sum; see Section 6.2). It is very easy to see that this algorithm can be rather trivially adapted to solve the TWO-MACHINE SCHEDULING (finding the smallest D): The $B(i)$ sets are extended to include sums up to S (not just up to $H = \frac{1}{2}S$). The smallest sum in $B(n)$ that is $\geq \frac{1}{2}S$ is the desired minimum D.

One more idea is needed to arrive at our approximation algorithm: Consider an instance of TWO-MACHINE SCHEDULING with these task lengths

$$45362, 134537, 85879, 56390, 145627, 197342, 83625, 126789, 38562, 75402,$$

with $n = 10$, and $S \approx 10^6$. Solving it by our exact $\mathcal{O}(nS)$ algorithm would cost us an unappetizing 10^7 steps. But suppose instead that we *round up* the task lengths to the next hundred. We obtain the numbers

$$45400, 134600, 85900, 56400, 145700, 197400, 83700, 126800, 38600, 75500,$$

which is really the same as

$$454, 1346, 859, 564, 1457, 1974, 837, 1268, 386, 755,$$

(normalizing by 100); thus we can now solve this instance in about 10^5 steps. By sacrificing a little in accuracy (the optimum of the new problem is clearly not very far from the original one), we have decreased the time requirements a hundredfold!

It is easy to prove that, if we round up to the next kth power of ten, the difference between the two optimal values is no more than $n10^k$. To calculate the relative error, this quantity must be divided by the optimum, which, obviously, can be no less than $\frac{S}{2}$. We have thus a $\frac{2n10^k}{S}$-approximation algorithm, whose running time is $\mathcal{O}(\frac{nS}{10^k})$. By setting $\frac{2n10^k}{S}$ equal to any desirable $\epsilon > 0$, we arrive at an algorithm whose running time is $\mathcal{O}(\frac{n^2}{\epsilon})$ —certainly a polynomial.$\Diamond$

Example 7.4.4: How does one prove that a problem is inapproximable (or not fully approximable)? For most optimization problems of interest, this question had been one of the most stubborn open problems, and required the development of novel ideas and mathematical techniques (see the references at the end of this chapter). But let us look at a case in which such a proof is relatively easy, that of the TRAVELING SALESMAN PROBLEM.

Suppose that we are given some large number ϵ, and we must prove that, unless $\mathcal{P} = \mathcal{NP}$, there is no ϵ-approximation algorithm for the TRAVELING SALESMAN PROBLEM. We know that the HAMILTON CYCLE problem is $\mathcal{NP}$-complete; we shall show that, if there is an ϵ-approximation algorithm for the TRAVELING SALESMAN PROBLEM, then there is a polynomial-time algorithm for the HAMILTON CYCLE problem. Let us start with any instance G of the HAMILTON CYCLE problem, with n nodes. We apply to it the simple reduction from HAMILTON CYCLE to TRAVELING SALESMAN PROBLEM (recall the proof of Theorem 7.3.4), but with a twist: The distances d_{ij} are now the following (compare with the proof of Theorem 7.3.4):

$$d_{ij} = \begin{cases} 0 & \text{if } i = j; \\ 1 & \text{if } (v_i, v_j) \in G; \\ 2 + n\epsilon & \text{otherwise.} \end{cases}$$

The instance constructed has the following interesting property: If G has a Hamilton cycle, then the optimum cost of a tour is n; if, however, there is no Hamilton cycle, then the optimum cost is *greater than* $n(1 + \epsilon)$ —because at least one distance $2 + n\epsilon$ must be traversed, in addition to at least $n - 1$ others of cost at least 1.

Suppose that we had a polynomial-time ϵ-approximation algorithm A for the TRAVELING SALESMAN PROBLEM. Then we would be able to tell whether G has a Hamilton cycle as follows: Run algorithm A on the given instance of the TRAVELING SALESMAN PROBLEM. Then we have these two cases:

(a) If the solution returned has cost $\geq n(1 + \epsilon) + 1$, then we know that the optimum cannot be n, because in that case the relative error of A would have been at least

$$\frac{|n(1 + \epsilon) + 1 - n|}{n} > \epsilon,$$

which contradicts our hypothesis that A is an ϵ-approximation algorithm. Since the optimum solution is larger than n, we conclude that G has no Hamilton cycle.

(b) If, however, the solution returned by A has cost $\leq n(1 + \epsilon)$, then we know that the optimum solution must be n. This is because our instance was designed so that it cannot have a tour of cost between $n + 1$ and $n(1 + \epsilon)$. Hence, in this case G has a Hamilton cycle.

It follows that, by applying the polynomial algorithm A on the instance of the TRAVELING SALESMAN PROBLEM that we constructed from G in polynomial time, we can tell whether G has a Hamilton cycle —which implies that $\mathcal{P} = \mathcal{NP}$. Since this argument can be carried out for any $\epsilon > 0$, however large, we must conclude that the TRAVELING SALESMAN PROBLEM is inapproximable.◇

Ways of coping with $\mathcal{NP}$-completeness often mix well: Once we realize that the TRAVELING SALESMAN PROBLEM is inapproximable, we may want to *approximate special cases* of the problem. Indeed, let us consider the special case in which the distances d_{ij} satisfy the *triangle inequality*

$$d_{ij} \leq d_{ik} + d_{kj} \text{ for each } i, j, k,$$

a fairly natural assumption on distance matrices, which holds in most instances of the TRAVELING SALESMAN PROBLEM arising in practice. As it turns out, this special case is partly approximable, and the best known error bound is $\frac{1}{2}$. What is more, when the cities are restricted to be points on the plane with the usual Euclidean distances —another special case of obvious appeal and relevance— then the problem becomes fully approximable! Both special cases are known to be $\mathcal{NP}$-complete (see Problem 7.4.3 for the proof for the triangle inequality case).

Backtracking and Branch-and-Bound

All $\mathcal{NP}$-complete problems are, by definition, solvable by polynomially bounded nondeterministic Turing machines; unfortunately we only know of exponential methods to simulate such machines. We examine next a class of algorithms that tries to improve on this exponential behavior with clever, problem-dependent stratagems. This approach typically produces algorithms that are exponential in the worst case, but often do much better.

A typical $\mathcal{NP}$-complete problem asks whether any member of a large set S_0 of "candidate certificates", or "candidate witnesses" (truth assignments, sets of vertices, permutations of nodes, and so onrecall Section 6.4) satisfies certain constraints specified by the instance (satisfies all clauses, is a clique of size K, is a Hamilton path). We call these candidate certificates or witnesses *solutions.* For all interesting problems, the size of the set S_0 of all possible solutions is typically exponentially large, and only depends on the given instance x (its size depends exponentially on the number of variables in the formula, on the number of nodes in the graph, and so on).

Now, a nondeterministic Turing machine "solving" an instance of this $\mathcal{NP}$-complete problem produces a tree of configurations (recall Figure 6-3). Each of these configurations corresponds to a subset of the set of potential solutions S_0, call it S, and the "task" facing this configuration is to determine whether there is a solution in S satisfying the constraints of x. Hence, S_0 is the set corresponding to the initial configuration. Telling whether S contains a solution is often a problem not very different from the original one. Thus, we can see each of the configurations in the tree as a *subproblem* of the same kind as the original (this useful "self-similarity" property of $\mathcal{NP}$-complete problems is called *self-reducibility*). Making a nondeterministic choice out of a configuration, say leading to r possible next configurations, corresponds to replacing S with r sets, $S_1, \ldots, S_r$, whose union must be S, so that no candidate solution ever falls between the cracks.

This suggests the following genre of algorithms for solving $\mathcal{NP}$-complete problems: We always maintain a set of *active subproblems,* call it $\mathcal{A}$; initially, $\mathcal{A}$ contains only the original problem S_0; that is, $\mathcal{A} = \{S_0\}$. At each point we choose a subproblem from $\mathcal{A}$ (presumably the one that seems most "promising" to us), we remove it from $\mathcal{A}$, and replace it with several smaller subproblems (whose union of candidate solutions must cover the one just removed). This is called *branching.*

Next, each newly generated subproblem is submitted to a quick *heuristic test.* This test looks at a subproblem, and comes up with one of three answers:

(a) It may come up with the answer "empty," meaning that the subproblem under consideration has no solutions satisfying the constraint of the instance, and hence it can be omitted. This event is called *backtracking.*

(b) It may come up with an actual solution of the original problem contained in the current subproblem (a satisfying truth assignment of the original formula, a Hamilton cycle of the original graph, etc.), in which case the algorithm terminates successfully.

(c) Since the problem is $\mathcal{NP}$-complete, we cannot hope to have a quick heuristic test that always comes up with one of the above answers (otherwise, we would submit the original subproblem S_0 to it). Hence, the test will often reply "?", meaning that it cannot prove that the subproblem is empty, but it cannot find a quick solution in it either; in this case, we add the subproblem in hand to the set $\mathcal{A}$ of active subproblems. The hope is that the test will come up with one of the two other answers often enough, and thus will substantially reduce the number of subproblems we will have to examine —and ultimately the running time of the algorithm.

We can now show the full **backtracking algorithm**:

$\mathcal{A} := \{S_0\}$
while $\mathcal{A}$ is not empty do
    choose a subproblem S and delete it from $\mathcal{A}$
    choose a way of branching out of S, say to subproblems $S_1, \ldots, S_r$
    for each subproblem S_i in this list do
        if test(S_i) returns "solution found" then halt
        else if test(S_i) returns "?" then add S_i to $\mathcal{A}$
return "no solution"

The backtracking algorithm terminates because, in the end, the subproblems will become so small and specialized that they will contain just one candidate solution (these are the leaves of the tree of the nondeterministic computation); in this case the test will be able to decide quickly whether or not this solution satisfies the constraints of the instance.

The effectiveness of a backtracking algorithm depends on three important "design decisions:"

(1) How does one choose the next subproblem out of which to branch?
(2) How is the chosen subproblem further split into smaller subproblems?
(3) Which test is used?

Example 7.4.5: In order to design a backtracking algorithm for SATISFIABILITY, we must make the design decisions (1) through (3) above.

In SATISFIABILITY the most natural way to split a subproblem is to choose a variable x and create two subproblems: one in which $x = \top$, and one in which $x = \bot$. As promised, each subproblem is of the same sort as the original problem: a set of clauses, but with fewer variables (plus a fixed truth assignment for each of the original variables not appearing in the current subproblem). In the $x = \top$ subproblem, the clauses in which x appears are omitted, and $\bar{x}$ is omitted from the clauses in which it appears; exactly the opposite happens in the $x = \bot$ subproblem.

The question regarding design decision (2) is, how to choose the variable x on which to branch. Let us use the following rule: *Choose a variable that appears in the smallest clause* (if there are ties, break them arbitrarily). This is a sensible strategy, because smaller clauses are "tighter" constraints, and may lead sooner to backtracking. In particular, an empty clause is the unmistakable sign of unsatisfiability.

Now for design decision (1) —how to choose the next subproblem. In line with our strategy for (2), let us choose the subproblem that contains the smallest clause (again, we break ties arbitrarily).

Finally, the test (design decision (3)) is very simple:

if there is an empty clause, return "subproblem is empty;"
if there are no clauses, return "solution found;"
otherwise return "?"

See Figure 7-14 for an application of the backtracking algorithm described above to the instance

$$(x \vee y \vee z), (\overline{x} \vee y), (\overline{y} \vee z), (\overline{z} \vee x), (\overline{x} \vee \overline{y} \vee \overline{z}),$$

which we know is unsatisfiable (recall Example 6.3.3). As it turns out, this algorithm is a variant of a well-known algorithm for SATISFIABILITY, known as the **Davis-Putnam procedure**. Significantly, when the instance has at most two literals per clause, the backtracking algorithm *becomes exactly the polynomial purge algorithm of Section 6.3.*◊

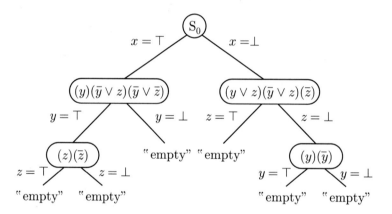

Figure 7-14

Example 7.4.6: Let us now design a backtracking algorithm for HAMILTON CYCLE. In each subproblem we already have a path with endpoints a and b, say, and going through a set of nodes $T \subseteq V - \{a, b\}$. We are looking for a Hamilton path from a to b through the remaining nodes in V, to close the Hamilton cycle. Initially $a = b$ is an arbitrary node, and $T = \emptyset$.

Branching is easy —we just choose how to extend the path by a new edge, say $[a, c]$, leading from a to a node $c \notin T$. This node c becomes the new value of a in the subproblem (node b is always fixed throughout the algorithm). We leave the choice of the subproblem from which to branch unspecified (we pick any subproblem from $\mathcal{A}$). Finally, the test is the following (remember that in a subproblem we are looking for a path from a to b in a graph $G - T$, the original graph with the nodes in T deleted).

> if $G - T - \{a, b\}$ is disconnected, or if $G - T$ has a degree-one node
>   other than a or b, return "subproblem is empty;"
> if $G - T$ is a path from a to b, return "solution found;"
> otherwise return "?"

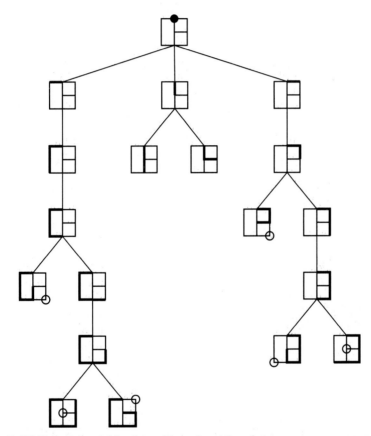

Figure 7-15: Execution of backtracking algorithm for HAMILTON CYCLE on the graph shown in the root. Initially both a and b coincide with the dotted node. In the leaf (backtracking) nodes the degree-one nodes are circled (in the middle leaves there are many choices). A total of nineteen subproblems is considered.

The application of this algorithm to a simple graph is shown in Figure

7-15. Although the number of partial solutions constructed may seem large (nineteen), it is minuscule compared to the number of solutions examined by the full-blown nondeterministic "algorithm" for the same instance (this number would be $(n-1)! = 5,040$). Needless to say, it is possible to devise more sophisticated and effective branching rules and tests than the one used here.◇

Determining the best design decisions (1) through (3) depends a lot not only on the problem, but also on the kinds of instances of interest, and usually requires *extensive experimentation*.

Backtracking algorithms are of interest when solving a "yes-no" problem. For optimization problems one often uses an interesting variant of backtracking called **branch-and-bound.** In an optimization problem we can also think that we have an exponentially large set of candidate solutions; however, this time each solution has a **cost**[†] associated with it, and we wish to find the candidate solution in S_0 with the smallest cost. The branch-and-bound algorithm is in general the one shown below (the algorithm shown only returns the optimal cost, but it can be easily modified to return the optimal solution).

$\mathcal{A} := \{S_0\}$, bestsofar:$= \infty$
while $\mathcal{A}$ is not empty do
    choose a subproblem S and delete it from $\mathcal{A}$
    choose a way of branching out of S, say to subproblems $S_1, \ldots, S_r$
    for each subproblem S_i in this list do
        if $|S_i| = 1$ (that is, S_i is a complete solution) then update bestsofar
        else if lowerbound$(S_i) <$bestsofar then add S_i to $\mathcal{A}$
    return bestsofar

The algorithm always remembers the smallest cost of any solution seen so far, initially ∞ (performance often improves a lot if bestsofar is initialized to the cost of a solution obtained by another heuristic). Every time a full solution to the original problem is found, bestsofar is updated. The key ingredient of a branch-and-bound algorithm (besides the design decisions (1) and (2) it shares with backtracking) is a method for obtaining a *lower bound* on the cost of any solution in a subproblem S. That is, the function lowerbound(S) returns a number that is guaranteed to be less than or equal to the lowest cost of any solution in S. The branch-and-bound algorithm above will always terminate with the optimal solution. This is because the only subproblems left unconsidered are those for which lowerbound$(S_i) \geq$bestsofar —that is, those subproblems of which the optimal solution is provably no better than the best solution we have seen so far.

[†] We shall assume that the optimization problem in question is a minimization problem; maximization problems can be treated in a very similar way.

Naturally, there are many ways of obtaining lower bounds (lowerbound(S) = 0 would usually do...). The point is that, if lowerbound(S) is a sophisticated algorithm returning a value that is usually very close to the optimum solution in S, then the branch-and-bound algorithm is likely to perform very well, that is, to terminate reasonably fast.

Example 7.4.7: Let us adapt the backtracking algorithm we developed for HAMILTON CYCLE to obtain a branch-and-bound algorithm for the TRAVELING SALESMAN PROBLEM. As before, a subproblem S is characterized by a path from a to b through a set T of cities. What is a reasonable lower bound? Here is one idea: For each city outside $T \cup \{a, b\}$, calculate the sum of its *two shortest distances* to another city outside T. For a and b, calculate their shortest distance to another city outside T. It is not hard to prove (see Problem 7.4.4) that the *half* sum of these numbers, plus the cost of the already fixed path from a to b through T, is a valid lower bound on the cost of any tour in the subproblem S. The branch-and-bound algorithm is now completely specified.

There are far more sophisticated lower bounds for the TRAVELING SALESMAN PROBLEM.◇

Local Improvement

Our final family of algorithms is inspired by evolution: What if we allow a solution of an optimization problem to change a little, and adopt the new solution if it has improved cost? Concretely, let S_0 be the set of candidate solutions in an instance of an optimization problem (again, we shall assume that it is a minimization problem). Define a **neighborhood relation** N on the set of solutions $N \subseteq S_0 \times S_0$ —it captures the intuitive notion of "changing a little." For $s \in S_0$, the set $\{s' : (s, s') \in N\}$ is called the **neighborhood** of s.

The algorithm is simply this (see Figure 7-16 for a suggestive depiction of the operation of local improvement algorithms):

```
s :=initialsolution
while there is a solution s' such that
    N(s, s') and cost(s') <cost(s) do: s := s'
return s
```

That is, the algorithm keeps improving s by replacing with a neighbor s' with a better cost, until there is no s' in the neighborhood of s with better cost; in the latter case we say that s *is a local optimum*. Obviously, a local optimum is not guaranteed to be an optimal solution —unless of course $N = S_0 \times S_0$. The quality of local optima obtained and the running time of the algorithm both depend critically on N: the larger the neighborhoods, the better the local optimum; on the other hand, large neighborhoods imply that the iteration of the algorithm (an execution of the while loop, and the ensuing search through the neighborhood of the current solution s) will be slower. Local improvement algorithms seek a favorable compromise in this trade-off. As usual, there are no general principles to guide us in designing a good neighborhood; the choice seems very problem-dependent, even instance-dependent, and is best made through experimentation.

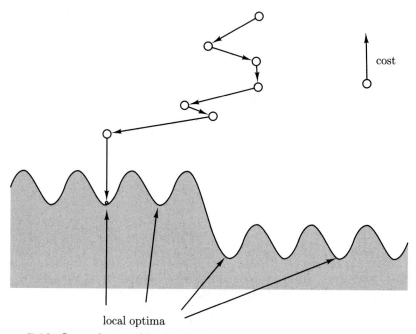

local optima

Figure 7-16: Once the neighborhood relation has been fixed, the solutions of an optimization problem can be pictured as an *energy landscape*, in which local optima are depicted as valleys. Local improvement heuristics jump from solution to solution, until a local optimum is found.

Another issue that affects the performance of a local improvement algorithm is the method used in finding s'. Do we adopt the first better solution we find in the neighborhood of s, or do we wait to find the best? Is the longer iteration justified by the speed of descent —and do we want speedy descent anyway? Finally, the performance of a local improvement algorithm also depends on the procedure initialsolution. It is not clear at all that better initial solutions will result in better performance —often a mediocre starting point is preferable, because it gives the algorithm more freedom to explore the solution space (see Figure 7-16). Incidentally, the procedure initialsolution should best be *randomized* —that is, able to generate different initial solutions when called many times. This allows us to *restart* many times the local improvement algorithm above, and obtain many local optima.

Example 7.4.8: Let us take again the TRAVELING SALESMAN PROBLEM. When should we consider two tours as neighbors? Since a tour can be considered as a set of n undirected inter-city "links," one plausible answer is, *when they share all but very few links.* Two is the minimum possible number of links in which two tours may differ, and this suggests a well-known neighborhood relation for the TRAVELING SALESMAN PROBLEM that we call **2-change** (see Figure 7-17). That is, two tours are related by N if and only if they differ in just two links. The local improvement algorithm using the 2-change neighborhood performs reasonably well in practice. However, much better results are achieved by adopting the **3-change** neighborhood; furthermore, it is reported in the literature that **4-change** does not return sufficiently better tours to justify the increase in iteration time.

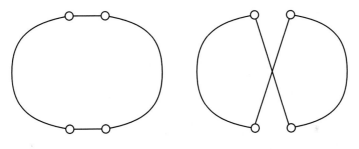

Figure 7-17

Perhaps the best heuristic algorithm currently known for the TRAVELING SALESMAN PROBLEM, the **Lin-Kernighan algorithm**, relies on λ-**change**, a neighborhood so sophisticated and complex that it does not even fit in our framework (whether two solutions are neighbors depends on the distances). As its name suggests, λ-change allows arbitrary many link changes in one step (but of course, not all possible such changes are explored, this would make the iteration exponentially slow).◊

Example 7.4.9: In order to develop a local improvement algorithm for MAX SAT (the version of SATISFIABILITY in which we wish to satisfy as many clauses as possible; recall Theorem 7.2.4), we might choose to consider two truth assignments to be related by N if they only differ in the value of a single variable. This immediately defines an interesting, and empirically successful, local improvement algorithm for MAX SAT. It is apparently advantageous in this case to adopt as s' the best neighbor of s, instead of the first one found that is better than s. Also, it has been reported that it pays to make "lateral moves" (adopt a solution even if the inequality in the third line of the algorithm is not strict).

This heuristic is considered a very effective way of obtaining good solutions to
MAX SAT, and is often used to solve SATISFIABILITY (in this use, it is hoped
that in the end the algorithm will return a truth assignment that satisfies *all*
clauses).◊

An interesting twist on local improvement algorithms is a method called
simulated annealing. As the name suggests, the inspiration comes from the
physics of cooling solids. Simulated annealing allows the algorithm to "escape"
from bad local optima (see Figure 7-18, and compare with 7-17) by performing
occasional cost-increasing changes.

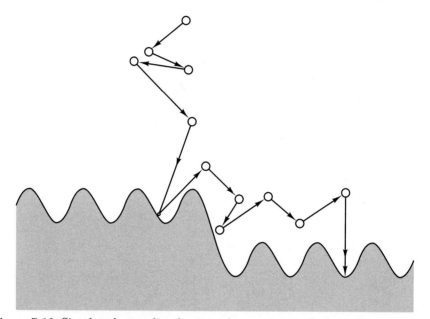

Figure 7-18: Simulated annealing has an advantage over the basic local improvement algorithm because its occasional cost-increasing moves help it avoid early
convergence in a bad local optimum. This often comes at a great loss of efficiency.

$s :=$ initialsolution, $T := T_0$
repeat
    generate a random solution s' such that $N(s, s')$,
       and let $\Delta :=$ cost$(s')-$cost(s)
    if $\Delta \leq 0$ then $s := s'$, else
      $s := s'$ with probability $e^{-\frac{\Delta}{T}}$
    update(T)
until $T = 0$

return the best solution seen

Intuitively, the probability that a cost-increasing change will be adopted is determined by the amount of the cost increase Δ, as well as by an important parameter T, the **temperature**. The higher the temperature, the more aggressively more expensive solutions are pursued. The way in which T is updated in the penultimate line of the algorithm —the *annealing schedule* of the algorithm, as it is called— is perhaps the most crucial design decision in these algorithms —besides, of course, the choice of neighborhood.

There are several other related genres of local improvement methods, many of them based, like the ones we described here, on some loose analogy with physical or biological systems (*genetic algorithms, neural networks,* etc.; see the references).

From the point of view of the formal criteria that we have developed in this book, the local improvement algorithms and their many variants are totally unattractive: They they do not in general return the optimum solution, they tend to have exponential worst-case complexity, and they are not even guaranteed to return solutions that are in any well-defined sense "close" to the optimum. Still, for many $\mathcal{NP}$-complete problems, in practice they often turn out to be the ones that perform best! Explaining and predicting the impressive empirical success of some of these algorithms is one of the most challenging frontiers of the theory of computation today.

Problems for Section 7.4

7.4.1. Give a polynomial algorithm for the DOMINATING SET problem (recall Problem 7.3.6) in the special case of trees (considered as symmetric directed graphs).

7.4.2. Suppose that all clauses in an instance of satisfiability contain *at most one positive literal;* such clauses are called **Horn clauses**. Show that, if all clauses of a Boolean formula are Horn clauses, then the satisfiability question for this formula can be settled in polynomial time. (*Hint:* When does a variable in a Horn formula *have* to be assigned $\top$?)

7.4.3. Show that the TRAVELING SALESMAN PROBLEM remains $\mathcal{NP}$-complete even if the distances are required to obey the triangle inequality. (*Hint:* Look back at our original proof that the TRAVELING SALESMAN PROBLEM is $\mathcal{NP}$-complete.)

7.4.4. Suppose that, in an instance of the traveling salesman problem with cities $1, 2, \ldots, n$ and distance matrix d_{ij}, we only consider tours that start from a, traverse by some path of length L the cities in a set $T \subseteq \{1, 2, \ldots, n\}$, end up in another city b, and then visit the remaining cities and return to a. Let us call this set of tours S.

(a) For each city $i \in \{1, 2, \ldots, n\} - T - \{a, b\}$, let m_i be the sum of the smallest and next-to-smallest distances from i to another city in $\{1, 2, \ldots, n\} - T - \{a, b\}$. Let s be the shortest distances from a to any city in $\{1, 2, \ldots, n\} - T - \{a, b\}$, plus the corresponding shortest distance from b. Show that any tour in S has cost at least

$$L + \frac{1}{2}[\sum_{i \in \{1, 2, \ldots, n\} - T - \{a, b\}} m_i + s].$$

That is, the formula above is a valid lower bound for S.

(b) The **minimum spanning tree** of the n cities is the smallest tree that has the cities as set of nodes; it can be computed very efficiently. Derive a better lower bound for S from this information.

7.4.5. How many 2-change neighbors does a tour of n cities have? How many 3-change neighbors? 4-change neighbors?

7.4.6. (a) Suppose that in the simulated annealing algorithm the temperature is kept at zero. Show that this is the basic local improvement algorithm.

(b) What is the simulated annealing algorithm with the temperature kept at infinity?

(c) Suppose now that the temperature is zero for a few iterations, then infinity for a few, then zero again, etc. How is the resulting algorithm related to the basic version of local improvement?

REFERENCES

Stephen A. Cook was the first to exhibit an NP-complete language in his paper

○ S. A. Cook   "The Complexity of Theorem-Proving Procedures," *Proceedings of the Third Annual ACM Symposium on the Theory of Computing* pp. 151–158). New York: Association for Computing Machinery, 1971.

Richard M. Karp established the scope and importance of NP-completeness in his paper

○ R. M. Karp   "Reducibility among Combinatorial Problems," in *Complexity of Computer Computations*, (pp. 85–104), ed. R. E. Miller and J. W. Thatcher. New York: Plenum Press, 1972,

where, among a host of other results, Theorems 7.3.1–7.3.7, and the results in problems 7.3.4 and 7.3.6, are proved. NP-completeness was independently discovered by Leonid Levin in

○ L. A. Levin   "Universal Sorting Problems," *Problemi Peredachi Informatsii*, 9, 3, pp. 265–266 (in Russian), 1973.

The following book contains a useful catalog of over 300 NP-complete problems from many and diverse areas; many more problems have been proved NP-complete since its appeerence.

○ M. R. Garey and D. S. Johnson   *Computers and Intractability: A Guide to the Theory of NP-completeness*, New York: Freeman, 1979.

This book is also an early source of information on complexity as it applies to concrete problems, as well as on approximation algorithms. For much more recent and extensive treatment of this latter subject see

- D. Hochbaum (ed.) *Approximation Algorithms for $\mathcal{NP}$-hard Problems,* Boston, Mass: PWS Publishers, 1996,

and for more information about other ways of coping with $\mathcal{NP}$-completeness see, for example,

- C. R. Reeves, (ed.) *Modern Heuristic Techniques for Combinatorial Problems,* New York: John Wiley, 1993, and

- C. H. Papadimitriou and K. Steiglitz *Combinatorial Optimization: Algorithms and Complexity* Englewood Cliffs, N.J.: Prentice-Hall, 1982; second edition, New York: Dover, 1997.

Index